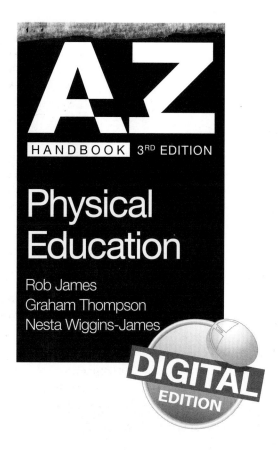

A-Z

HANDBOOK 3RD EDITION

Physical Education

Rob James
Graham Thompson
Nesta Wiggins-James

DIGITAL
EDITION

D0317669

PHILIP ALLAN
UPDATES

Philip Allan Updates, an imprint of Hodder Education, an Hachette UK company, Market Place, Deddington, Oxfordshire OX15 0SE

Orders

Bookpoint Ltd, 130 Milton Park, Abingdon, Oxfordshire OX14 4SB
tel: 01235 827720
fax: 01235 400454
e-mail: uk.orders@bookpoint.co.uk

Lines are open 9.00 a.m.–5.00 p.m., Monday to Saturday, with a 24-hour message answering service. You can also order through the Philip Allan Updates website: www.philipallan.co.uk

ISBN 978-0-340-99106-0

First published 2000
Second edition 2003
Third edition 2010

Impression number   5   4   3   2   1
Year   2015   2014   2013   2012   2011   2010

Typeset by MPS Limited, A Macmillan Company.

Printed by Antony Rowe Ltd, Chippenham, Wiltshire.

Environmental information
Hachette UK's policy is to use papers that are natural, renewable and recyclable products and made from wood grown in sustainable forests. The logging and manufacturing processes are expected to conform to the environmental regulations of the country of origin.

Contents

How to use this book

The *A–Z Physical Education Handbook* is an alphabetical glossary of terms covering all theoretical aspects of the specifications and designed for ease of use. It does not attempt to be an exhaustive list of every term within the course, but covers the major terms that should be familiar to students. The terms are drawn from the disciplines of anatomy and physiology, psychology, sociology and history, and comparative studies.

Where possible, each entry starts with a simple one-line definition and progresses to explain the term in more detail, showing how it relates to other associated areas of physical education. This is further reinforced with the use of practical examples where appropriate, as the application of knowledge is crucial to understanding the topics fully. Some entries do not allow for this structure, for example, those entries covering the various sporting organisations, and as a result these have been modified to outline their aims and current initiatives.

Utilising the cross-referencing system can increase your understanding of the subject areas. Within each entry any associated terms that can expand your knowledge appear in bold italics. The entry *flexibility*, for example, refers the reader to *cool-down*. By using this system you will gain a more complete understanding of the issues you are studying and start to develop a more synoptic approach to your study.

So while the *A–Z Handbook* is a glossary that will aid your study of physical education, it is important to recognise that it is not a textbook. This means that you will require further reading to complete your understanding of the topic. However, the more substantial entries will give you a sound introduction to the concepts and issues, in addition to providing a handy reference when you encounter concepts of which you are unsure.

During your course of study, the handbook is essentially a book to pick up to browse through and use to complement your basic understanding as well as helping to clarify new ideas. In addition, it should prove useful during revision. To help during this period, carefully selected lists are provided at the back of the handbook for the units produced by the AQA, Edexcel and OCR examination boards, subdivided for each module. Information for examinations produced by CCEA, WJEC, CIE, Scottish Higher and the IB diploma can be found on the website that accompanies this book. These lists could act as a starting point for your revision and should then be expanded using the cross-referencing system. Advice on how to achieve a grade A* can also be found on the website.

There is also a section in the appendices explaining examiners' terms. Many candidates fail to do themselves justice in examinations, not because of a lack of knowledge but through misunderstanding of question requirements or simply not following instructions. This section outlines many key examiners' terms and describes what each means. Understanding these terms can improve your examination technique considerably, allowing you to gain valuable extra marks.

Other sections in the appendices have been included specifically for the physiological aspects of the course to eliminate the need for excessive entries and to complement your studies.

A–Z Online

This new digital edition of the *A–Z Physical Education Handbook* includes free access to a supporting website and a free desktop widget to make searching for terms even quicker. Log on to **www.philipallan.co.uk/a-zonline** and create an account using the unique code provided on the inside front cover of this book.

Once you are logged on, you will be able to:
- search the entire database of terms in this handbook
- print revision lists specific to your exam board
- get expert advice from examiners on how to get an A* grade
- create a personal library of your favourite terms
- expand your vocabulary with our word of the week.

You can also add the other *A–Z Handbooks (digital editions)* that you own to your personal library on A–Z Online.

We hope that you find the *A–Z Physical Education Handbook* enjoyable to use, informative and an invaluable resource throughout your studies.

Acknowledgements

Nesta and Rob would like to thank Ffion, Ellie, Rees and Cai for being so patient during the writing of this book.

Rob James, Nesta Wiggins-James and Graham Thompson

A state: see *state anxiety*.

A trait: see *trait anxiety*.

a-vO$_2$ diff: see *arterio-venous oxygen difference (a-vO$_2$ diff)*.

abduction: a *movement pattern* involving actions away from the midline of the body or one of its body parts. It occurs in the *frontal plane,* for example at the hip joint when performing a cartwheel in gymnastics. A muscle that causes this movement is known as an *abductor*. (See appendix, page 320.)

abductor: a muscle that causes the *movement pattern* known as *abduction* at a joint. For example, the deltoid raises the arm sideways at the shoulder joint during the preparatory phase of the discus throw. In this instance, the deltoid is an abductor.

abilities are inherited, innate and generally enduring traits that an individual possesses, allowing them to complete various tasks. Certain skills require specific abilities, which can be broadly categorised into *psychomotor ability* and *gross motor ability*. The former involves the processing of information and initiation of the movement, e.g. *coordination* and *reaction time*; the latter involves actual movement, e.g. *flexibility*, *strength*, stamina, *balance* and *speed*.

aborigines: the tribe that entered *Australia* during the last Great Ice Age. Their *society* was organised and semi-nomadic, and the spiritual world was an integral feature of their philosophy. Colonisation led to disease and death through military action, and the loss of land rights only recently being recognised and compensated for in the Native Title Act 1994. This is an example of an *ethnic group* who were affected by the *White Australia policy* and their fate was similar to that of *native Americans*. They now form less than 2% of the population.

Traditional physical activities would have a functional base, for example, hunting and games as preparation for battles; they also have a strong religious and *ritual* meaning. The National Aboriginal Sport Foundation is part of the *Australian Sports Commission* and has founded the Aboriginal Sport and Recreation Programme. Aboriginal *culture* has seen a revival within a more liberal society, although aborigines still suffer severe *discrimination*.

academies of sport: training centres for the development of *elite* athletes, usually with the aim of raising the profile of sport within a country, and forming part of a national strategy in sport policy. Consequently, *national governments* are usually heavily involved in the philosophy and funding of these centres as they can help create an important *national identity*. They are based on:
- top-class *coaching*
- world-class facilities
- scientific support.

1

Academies and institutes of sport can be either **centralised** or **decentralised,** targeting specific sports, which may be traditional or new to the country. They often concentrate on national sports or on those with an **ethnic** identity, often utilising higher education or **local authority** facilities. These centres can either be isolated from the ethos of mass participation or allow mass sport to run parallel to it, forming the structure beneath the pinnacle. (See also **Australian Institute of Sport, English Institute of Sport** and **UK Sports Institute.**)

acceleration: the rate of change of **velocity**. It is a **vector quantity** possessing both magnitude and direction and is integral to many sporting situations, from sprinting to the drive in **golf**. Acceleration is calculated using the formula:

$$FORMULA: \quad Acceleration = \frac{change\ in\ velocity}{time} \quad or \quad \frac{v-u}{t}$$

where

v = final velocity

u = initial velocity

t = time.

units of acceleration = m s^{-2}

Newton's second law of motion is commonly known as the law of acceleration and states:

'The acceleration of a body is proportional to the force causing it, and the acceleration takes place in the direction in which that force acts.'

More simply, the greater the force imparted the greater the resultant acceleration. This is expressed as:

$$FORMULA: \quad F = ma$$

where

F = force

m = mass

a = acceleration.

(See also **newton** and **Newton's laws of motion.**)

accommodation (society): the process whereby different social groups live together in harmony, accepting each other's distinct identities such as language and **culture**. In sociological terms it is often used to describe the mutual tolerance of different **ethnic groups** living in the same society. This is different from **assimilation**.

acetylcholine: a transmitter substance released by the **central nervous system**, allowing muscles to contract. It is released when a nerve impulse reaches the **motor end plate** and enables the impulse to cross the synaptic cleft. If sufficient acetylcholine is released, the muscle fibre is said to have **action potential**, allowing the muscles to contract and movement to occur. In order to prevent continual stimulation, the acetylcholine is blocked by the **enzyme** cholinesterase. This allows the motor unit to prepare for new stimuli and contract again when required.

acetylcoenzyme A (acetyl coA): a compound derived from **pyruvic acid** when the **aerobic energy system** is being utilised. During the process it is oxidised to release **energy**. Before it can be totally downgraded to release energy, acetylcoenzyme A must combine with a four-carbon molecule called oxaloacetic acid to form **citric acid**. This compound can now enter the **Krebs cycle** to form carbon dioxide and water, and release energy for muscular contraction.

achievement motivation refers to an individual's interaction with the environment and their desire to succeed. Atkinson suggested an individual's level of **motivation** depends on a combination of personality and situational factors. People display either a **need to achieve** or **need to avoid failure** tendency when placed in certain situations. A situation is evaluated in terms of an individual's probability of success and the incentive value of that success, which can be expressed as:

FORMULA: $TA = (Ms - Maf) \times (Ps \times \{I - Ps\})$

where

TA = achievement motivation

Ms = motive to succeed

Maf = motive to avoid failure

Ps = probability of success

I = incentive value of success.

For example, the motivation level of a novice tennis player when faced with a match against a club player will depend on their perceived chance of success and whether or not they are prepared to face the challenge whatever the outcome, or merely not play in case they are seen to fail.

Critics of the theory argue it is too simplistic and that different performers perceive success in a variety of ways, depending on whether their tasks have an **outcome goal** or a **task-orientated goal**. (See also **Veroff's stages of achievement motivation**.)

actin: a thin protein filament found in muscle cells. It is found in the **sarcomere** and combines with **myosin** to produce movement (see **sliding filament theory**). Each actin **myofilament** is composed of two proteins:
- fibrous actin – provides active sites to which the myosin cross-bridge can bind during muscle contraction
- tropomyosin and troponin molecules – aid the attachment of the myosin cross-bridge when calcium ions are released from the sarcoplasmic reticulum during nerve stimulation.

action potential: the electrical activity that is developed in a muscle or nerve cell during activity. Occurs when sufficient **acetylcholine** has been released by the **central nervous system** and is the **stimulus** for muscle contraction.

Active Australia: a national programme run by the **Australian Sports Commission** where the focus is on participation and **Sport for All**, integrating other programmes such as **Aussie Sport** and Aussie Able into getting Australians 'up and active' at the foundation level of sport. This requires the adoption of a corporate plan by local state sport **recreation** departments. Active Australia identifies three main aims:
- to increase and enhance lifelong participation
- to realise the social, health and economic benefits of participation
- to develop a quality infrastructure with opportunities and services to support participation.

Its focus is entirely on sport for all rather than **excellence**.

active leisure takes place in *leisure* time and involves the individual personally participating in a physical activity. (See also *physical recreation*.)

Active Sports Programme: a scheme coordinated by *Sport England* based on four policy headings:

- Active schools – forms the foundation
- Active communities – looks at breaking down the barriers to participation and considers equity issues
- Active sports – links participation to *excellence* such as participation in the Millennium Youth Games
- World class – supporting the current and next generation of most talented individual athletes and teams to achieve greater success in national and international competition.

They are meant to act as building blocks and are not necessarily linear, as shown by the diagram. They also complement the Sports Council's *participation pyramid* of foundation, participation, performance and excellence. The majority of the funding will come from the *National Lottery* and there will be a strengthening of the regional set up via *local authorities*. There will be a framework around all experiences available to potential participants such as the *National Junior Sports Programme, Sportsmark* and Coaching for Teachers.

active stretching: this form of stretching activity involves the performer undertaking a stretch with no external assistance. Active stretching typically occurs when the athlete performs voluntary muscular contractions and holds the stretch for a period of 30–60 seconds. No external assistance is required. By consciously relaxing the target muscle at the limit of the range of motion, muscle elongation may occur following regular contraction.

Activemark: an award scheme for primary schools that recognises good practice within the *physical education* provision. The higher 'gold' level can also be achieved. The Activemark and Activemark Gold awards scheme recognises and rewards primary, middle and special schools that provide young children with the opportunity to receive the benefits of physical activity. It has been developed in partnership with the British Heart Foundation and has the theme 'Get active, stay active'. To achieve an award, a school needs to:

- offer a broad and balanced physical education programme
- provide an environment that encourages physical activities

- teach children the importance of staying active for life
- provide enhanced curricular provision through some additional opportunities for physical activity
- have an effective inclusion policy for disabled pupils.

Activemark Gold recognises all the above, plus:
- realistic, in-depth physical education and physical activity development plans
- a commitment to providing a range of additional, high quality opportunities for physical activity.

A team of assessors appointed by **Sport England** reviews the schools against these rigorous criteria.

actual productivity refers to a group's or team's performance of a task. Steiner (1972) suggested that this was equal to the **potential productivity** minus the losses due to **faulty processes**. A group may contain a large number of highly skilled individuals who would be expected to perform well, but fail to do so due to **motivation** problems and poor **coordination**, the result being a poor performance, possibly displaying the **Ringelmann effect** and **social loafing**. For example, a team contains several 'flair' players who may not necessarily contribute as consistently as they should during play. The coach may decide to omit one for the good of the team, replacing them with a less skilful but harder working player, thus attempting to minimise the faulty processes so that actual productivity may equal potential productivity. (See also **group productivity**.)

Adam's closed loop theory suggests the performer's movement can be modified with the use of **feedback** from the various sensory **receptors**. This is an extension of the **open loop control** theory and a closing of the circuit. The concept is based on two key factors:
- the 'memory trace', allowing selection and initiation of the movement, with no actual control
- the 'perceptual trace', allowing comparison and modification against stored motor programmes. The perceptual trace is developed through practice and any feedback, either during or after the performance, allows errors to be detected, compared to a reference of correctness and adjustments made.

For example, a gymnast completing a routine will constantly evaluate the movements being performed during the sequence and make adjustments as required to maintain **balance**, speed and control based on their knowledge of how each component should feel. The theory assumes that there is a separate memory trace for each **movement pattern**, which would not necessarily be accommodated by and recalled from the **long-term memory store**. It also suggests practice should be accurate and variance would hinder learning, which research has refuted.

Feedback detects errors

adaptive physical education sport: an umbrella term used to encompass such areas as dance, sport, fitness and rehabilitation of individuals with impairment across the lifespan. It evolved during the 1950s, from both the medical and educational perspectives, and is a popular concept in the USA, where federal *legislation* in 1975 required that teaching styles, facilities and equipment should be adapted to meet the needs of both regular and special students within the mainstream education system. There is no comparable system in the UK.

adduction: a *movement pattern* involving movement towards the midline of the body or one of its body parts. It takes place in the *frontal plane* and occurs, for example, at the hip joint, in the crossover step during the run-up phase of the javelin throw. A muscle that causes this movement is known as an *adductor*. (See appendix, page 320.)

adductor: a muscle that causes the *movement pattern* known as *adduction* at a joint. For example, the adductor brevis, longus and magnus muscles, together with the gracilis, cause adduction at the hip during the crossover steps in the run-up phase of the javelin throw.

adenosine diphosphate: see *ADP*.

adenosine triphosphate: see *ATP*.

administration: the management of the affairs of an organisation or institution such as sport as a whole or a sports club. It can be seen as developing from the community, for example a local sports club is surmounted by its regional, national and international counterparts. Organisations such as national *governing bodies* and *Sport England* are all concerned with administrative issues, such as:

- governing sport
- making decisions
- creating and distributing finances and resources.

ADP (adenosine diphosphate): a high-energy phosphate compound consisting of adenosine and two phosphate groups attached to it. During the resynthesis of *ATP*, adenosine diphosphate combines with another phosphate group to form ATP, which can subsequently be broken down to release energy for muscular contraction.

adrenaline: a hormone released by the adrenal gland at times of stress as well as before and during exercise. It is a pre-requisite for physical activity and forms the body's *fight or flight response*, which can affect the performer in a number of ways, as outlined below.

Effects on the body:
- increased heart rate
- constriction of blood vessels
- breakdown of glucose and fats
- sweat production.

Effects on performance:
- increased oxygen to the muscles – CO_2 removed
- raised *blood pressure*, increasing blood flow to muscles
- more energy released to resynthesise *ATP*
- prevents overheating, but can cause *dehydration*.

When preparing for physical activity, adrenaline can reduce activity in non-essential organs and increase activity in those organs required for the activity, namely the muscles, making it an essential ingredient during exercise.

Advanced Apprenticeship in Sporting Excellence (AASE) is an addition to the talent pathway and is part of the *Youth Sports Trust's gifted and talented* programme. When school finishes, the AASE programme takes over. There are more than 2500 talented young sportsmen and women aged between 16 and 19, in over 12 sports in England that are currently training to become world class performers. Enrolling on the AASE programme allows them to train in their chosen sport and prepare for life after sport by gaining qualifications that will set them up for the workplace or allow them to progress to university. The programme includes qualifications for work within the related fields of coaching, sport development, health and fitness, operational management of sports facilities, sports leadership and the outdoors.

After the AASE programme, there is the *Talented Athlete Scholarship Scheme*, a programme funded by the *Department for Culture, Media and Sport*, which represents a unique partnership between sport and universities. Alongside, there is *Sports Coach UK* which ensures that talented coaches are matched with talented athletes, in line with the UK Coaching Framework. It is underpinned by *UK Sport's World Class Performance Pathway*.

adventurous activities: outdoor pursuit activities which take place in the *natural environment*, often in situations which are dangerous and challenging, and which may involve the *conquest* of natural obstacles or terrain, for example rock climbing, skiing and sky diving. New activities continue to be developed, mostly as a result of technological advances, such as jet skiing and windsurfing. Many of these activities developed as a means of exploring terrain and human resources, as well as through the need to *escape* from the urban to the natural environment.

Adventurous activities are not governed by rules as such, there are no winners or losers and therefore no officials. There is usually, however, a code of *etiquette* concerning safety and *conservation* of the natural environment. Recently many adventurous activities have become sports, involving scoring systems and officials, e.g. white water slalom racing and speed climbing.

The main challenge for the participant occurs against the elements, requiring them to differentiate between real and perceived *risks* (see also *danger*). *Wilderness areas* and extreme climatic zones in the *USA* and *Australia* produce opportunities within these sports not available in the more gentle terrain and temperate climate of the UK.

advertising: paid-for communication through *mass media* such as television, newspapers or radio. Advertising and marketing have become powerful forces and sport has become a vehicle for the promotion of products and images which enable advertising companies to make profits, providing employment and income for a large number of people.

aerobic: literally meaning 'with oxygen', aerobic metabolism typically occurs during low-intensity exercises that are of long duration, such as long-distance running or *cycling*.

aerobic capacity: the ability to provide and sustain energy aerobically. It is the component of fitness that underpins all endurance-based activities such as long-distance running, cycling or swimming, as well as being a contributory factor to many other sporting situations. Key factors that determine an individual's level of *aerobic* capacity include genetics, physiology, lifestyle, sex, age, *body composition* and the quantity of training undertaken by the individual concerned. The VO_2 max of an individual is a strong indicator of aerobic capacity.

aerobic energy system: the *energy* pathway that uses oxygen to break down *glycogen* and *fat* to release energy, which can then be used to resynthesise *ATP*. Under *aerobic* conditions, the glucose molecule can be totally degraded, providing an energy yield 18 times that produced in *anaerobic* conditions. The glucose molecule is broken down in special 'powerhouses' or 'factories' known as *mitochondria*, where the *Krebs cycle* and *electron transport chain* take place. *Slow twitch muscle fibres* possess a greater number of mitochondria then *fast twitch muscle fibres* and therefore have a greater capacity to produce energy over an extended period of time. When a molecule of glucose is degraded, energy sufficient to resynthesise 38 moles of ATP is released as follows:

- 2 during anaerobic *glycolysis*
- 2 during the Krebs cycle
- 34 during the electron transport chain.

Because of the vast energy supply gained through aerobic metabolism, this system is used mainly in endurance-based activities where exercise is less intense and energy is required over a long period of time. This system is also responsible for supplying the energy required by the body at rest. Examples include running a marathon or time-outs during a basketball match.

aerobic fitness, also known as cardiovascular fitness, it is the ability of the body to perform exercise over an extended period of time in the presence of oxygen. It relies on the efficiency of the body to utilise oxygen to release energy that is stored in *glycogen* and *fats*. Sports performers who have high levels of *aerobic fitness* include marathon runners, cyclists and triathletes. In order to improve aerobic fitness, athletes should undertake a period of *continuous training* or aerobic interval training.

aesthetic: the quality of movement and an appreciation of art forms. Some sports, such as tennis and cricket, are won through technical superiority alone. However, *gymnastic activities* such as figure skating also award marks for artistic merit. These decisions are made by judges and will inevitably be determined to some extent by *subjective* opinions. The performer:

- experiences the aesthetic moment through his or her *kinaesthetic* flow patterns, making it subjective in character
- achieves the performance through knowing what to do and how to do it
- needs to be able to gain pleasure from executing a movement, as skillfulness alone does not ensure an aesthetic experience. This may be more easily achieved in *closed skill* situations such as *gymnastics* where the performer is able to focus on the inward motions with minimal *interference* from the sporting environment.

The spectators' experience, however, comes from outside the event and they need to bring understanding, interpretation and imagination, together with the ability to engage emotionally in the activity, in order to experience the aesthetic moment.

affective attitude: one of the components of the *triadic model*, this refers to the performer's emotional feelings towards an issue or *attitude object* based on past experiences or values. For example, the performer may enjoy taking part in exercise, displaying a positive attitude, but may particularly dislike swimming, showing a negative attitude.

affective learning refers to the positive *attitudes* and emotional components that may be required to prepare and compete effectively, e.g. *etiquette*, *sportsmanship*, confidence and focusing techniques. To maximise learning, this component should be combined with *effective learning* and *cognitive theories of learning*.

aggression: any form of behaviour intended to injure or harm another person either verbally or physically and, within a sporting context, outside the laws of the game. All acts of aggression are viewed as anti-social, caused by biological, sociological or environmental factors:

- Biological theories suggest individuals are born with aggressive tendencies, e.g. instinct theory argues that we have developed these traits as part of the evolutionary process of survival, and aggression is either an instinctive reaction or displayed to establish control over a particular territory. Aggressive tendencies must be released for the good of the individual (known as *catharsis*). This can be in an acceptable form, e.g. sport, or as unacceptable behaviour, e.g. violence and crime.
- Sociological theories such as the *social learning theory* propose that, through observation of others during the learning process, actions are copied and they are more likely to be repeated if they are reinforced and rewarded. The chance of repetition is increased if the model is of high status to the individual, e.g. if a top-class performer commits a foul but avoids *punishment* the observer will attempt to repeat the action given the opportunity.
- Environmental factors can lead to goals being blocked thus leading to the *frustration–aggression hypothesis*. If the performer's objective is being blocked, they may become frustrated and eventually aggressive if this continues, e.g. a performer is being well marked by the opponent and eventually commits a foul because they cannot perform as desired.

An updated version of this proposal is the *aggression cue theory*, which suggests that although frustration will cause an increase in *arousal* levels, an aggressive act will only occur if a socially learnt cue is present or the environmental situation makes committing the act acceptable (Berkowitz 1993). For example, a player may only commit an aggressive act if they receive encouragement from their coach or think the referee may not see their actions.

Actions considered aggressive in one situation may not be in another, e.g. hitting an opponent during a hockey match compared with a punch in a boxing bout. Acceptable forms of aggression are known as *assertive behaviour* or *channelled aggression*.

aggression cue theory suggests that although frustration will cause an increase in *arousal* levels, an aggressive act will only occur if a socially learnt cue is present or the environmental situation makes committing the act acceptable (Berkowitz 1993). The theory allows for some of the weaknesses of the *frustration–aggression hypothesis* as it takes into account the influence of socially learned behaviour and the situation the performer is currently experiencing. For example, a basketball player who drives for a lay-up shot is constantly blocked by an opponent causing frustration, but they may only commit a foul if the coach has encouraged and tolerated this behaviour in the past.

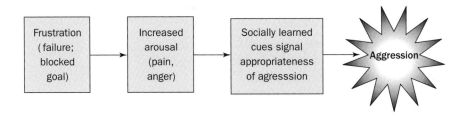

aggressive cue hypothesis: see *aggression cue theory*.

agility: a motor-based component of *fitness*, involving the ability of the performer to move and change direction and position of the body quickly and effectively while under control. For example, during a game of basketball the player has to adjust their body position while dribbling or driving for the basket when performing a lay-up shot, depending on the position of defenders. It can be measured using the *Illinois agility run test*. Unfortunately, training has little effect on an individual's agility as this is an innate characteristic and cannot be significantly improved.

agonist: also known as a prime mover, an agonist is the muscle that is directly responsible for the movement at a joint. Muscles usually work in pairs or groups to facilitate coordinated movement, with each performing a different function. For example, during a biceps curl exercise, when *flexion* occurs at the elbow joint the biceps brachii is responsible for the movement and is therefore the agonist. However, as one muscle shortens, another lengthens and is known as the *antagonist*. In this example, the antagonists are the triceps brachii. Muscles working together in this way is known as *reciprocal inhibition*. As the weight is lowered, the role of each muscle is reversed and the triceps brachii become the agonists and the biceps brachii the antagonists.

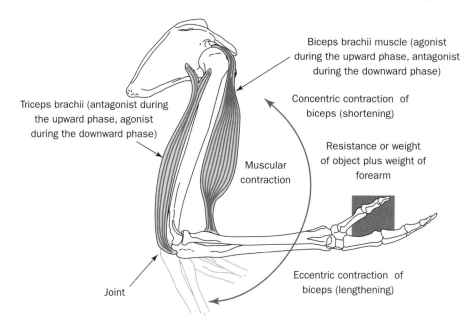

Biceps brachii muscle (agonist during the upward phase, antagonist during the downward phase)

Concentric contraction of biceps (shortening)

Triceps brachii (antagonist during the upward phase, agonist during the downward phase)

Resistance or weight of object plus weight of forearm

Muscular contraction

Joint

Eccentric contraction of biceps (lengthening)

agrarian revolution: signified a dramatic movement of the population from rural areas to the towns during the *Industrial Revolution* in nineteenth-century Britain. Farming had become less important as small farms were taken over by large landowners as a result of the enclosure system and farming practices had changed with the development of machinery, reducing the need for labour. This had a large impact on people's lives and particularly on their *rural sports*.

aims can be defined as the intended purpose of a course of action achieved via objectives. For example, some of the aims of a *physical education* curriculum may include:
- to develop a range of psychomotor skills
- to maintain and increase physical mobility and *flexibility*, stamina and strength

- to develop understanding and appreciation of a range of physical activities
- to develop positive values and **attitudes** like **sportsmanship**, competition, necessity of abiding by the rules
- to help children acquire **self-esteem** and **self-confidence** through the acquisition of skills, knowledge and values
- to develop an understanding of the importance of exercise in maintaining a healthy lifestyle.

air resistance: a force that causes a resistance to the motion of an object or body when moving through the air. The amount of air resistance created depends upon the size, weight, shape and speed of the object. Faster moving objects generate greater air resistance, which can cause deceleration of the moving body.

Performers often attempt to limit the effects of air resistance by using specialist equipment or clothing, which can include altering the shape of cyclists' helmets or wearing tight lycra clothing. (See also **Bernouilli effect** and **Magnus effect**.)

alactacid debt: also known as the fast component of **excess post-exercise oxygen consumption** (EPOC), this is the first stage of the **recovery** process or replenishment of the oxygen debt. Its function is to resynthesise **creatine phosphate** and **ATP**, and to resaturate **myoglobin** with oxygen. This is the fast stage of the **excess post-exercise oxygen consumption** and is accomplished by increasing the amount of oxygen entering the body, which explains why a performer experiences heavy breathing following exercise. This process usually takes 2 or 3 minutes and utilises up to four litres of oxygen. Once the alactacid debt has been replenished, the consumed oxygen is used to remove waste products such as **lactic acid** that may have accrued and is known as the **lactacid debt**.

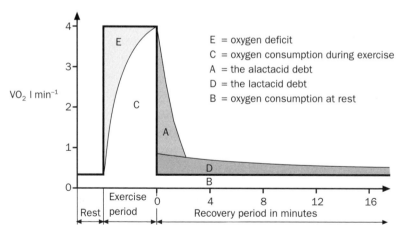

Alactacid debt

alactic energy system: also known as the ATP–PC **energy system**, this is the first energy pathway to be utilised by the body to resynthesise **ATP** without the use of oxygen. This **anaerobic** system uses stored **creatine phosphate** from the muscle cells, not for muscle contraction but purely to resynthesise ATP and maintain a constant supply of energy. A **coupled reaction** occurs very rapidly, but can only last up to 10 seconds and is therefore

11

used in activities of high intensity over a short period of time, for example high jump, shot putt and 100-metre sprint.

FORMULA:
$$ATP \rightarrow ADP + Pi + energy$$
$$CP \rightarrow C + P + energy$$
$$Energy + ADP + Pi \rightarrow ATP$$

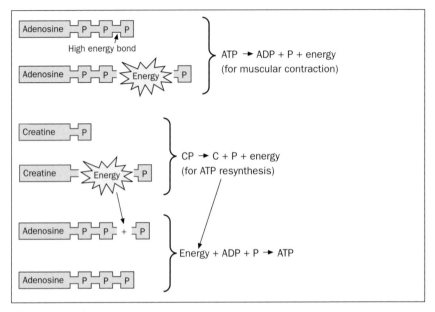

Alactic energy system

alertness is the ability to focus on specific **cues** (see **selective attention**) and refers to the concept of optimal **arousal** and the performer's level of awareness of the **stimuli**. If a high level of alertness can be maintained, the **decision-making** process can be made more effective, improving **reaction time** and performance. A defender in a game has to maintain a higher level of alertness for longer than a sprinter and may have to be alert to more stimuli.

all or none law: this principle states that when a **motor unit** receives a **stimulus** of sufficient intensity to elicit a response, all the muscle fibres within the unit will contract at the same time and to the maximum possible extent. However, if the impulse is not of a sufficient strength to cause contraction, none of the fibres within the motor unit will contract at all. In other words, single muscle fibres cannot partially contract. This does not imply that the muscle must be fully contracted or fully relaxed; the strength of contraction is determined by the number of motor units within the muscle that are contracting compared with those that are relaxing. The greater the strength required, the greater the number of motor units that contract.

Other governing factors are the availability of oxygen and other nutrients and the effects of **fatigue**. For example, more motor units will be recruited when sprinting than during a distance run, since greater strength and power are required during high intensity events.

alpinism: a development of the eighteenth- and nineteenth-century ideal of energetic outdoor pursuits in the **natural environment**. The formation of the Alpine Club in 1857 led to a trend in mountaineering among intellectuals and the higher **social classes**, which led to *exclusivity*, as they had the time and resources for such activities. It began as an extension of *tourism*, which was made more accessible by the development of the *railways*, and developed into a *competition sport*. It also had strong links with the *Romantic movement*.

altitude training: a method of training based on the principle that with an increase in altitude, the *partial pressure* of oxygen (pO_2) in the atmosphere decreases by about a half, causing the body to adapt by increasing red blood cell volume and *haemoglobin* levels. It is widely used by endurance athletes to enhance their oxygen-carrying capacity. When the athletes return to sea level, these changes remain yet the atmospheric pO_2 has increased, which means that the body can transport and utilise more oxygen, giving improved endurance performance. However, there appears to be contradictory evidence concerning the benefits of altitude training. Some athletes refrain from training at altitude as the low levels of oxygen and possibility of altitude sickness diminish the effectiveness of training, causing a de-training effect. Recent evidence suggests that living at altitude while training at sea level procures the greatest endurance performance and in doing so athletes can increase their oxygen carrying capacity of the blood by up to 150%.

alveoli: (singular alveolus) small air sacs found in the lungs where *gaseous exchange* occurs. The walls of the alveoli are extremely thin, composed of a single layer of epithelial

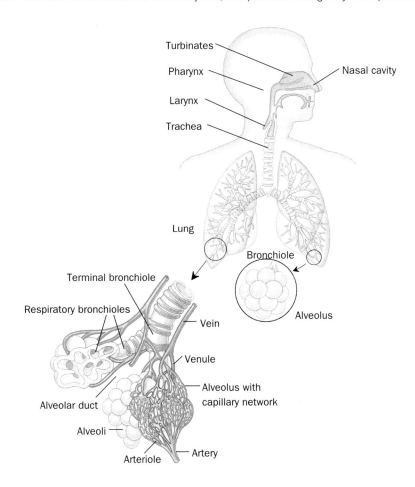

Alveoli

13

cells and surrounded by an extensive *capillary* network, which allows oxygen to enter the blood stream and carbon dioxide to be removed by the process of diffusion. The effects of exercise are inconclusive, but it is thought that endurance training might improve the functioning and *elasticity* of the alveolar walls.

amateurism: a concept that evolved in nineteenth-century England among the *upper class*, who became known as *gentleman amateurs*. It is based on the ideal that participating in sport should be for the love of it rather than for monetary gain and participation was deemed more important than winning. It encompassed the belief in *fair play* and abiding by the spirit as well as the rules of the game. It originally had a *social class* distinction as it excluded the lower classes and, within a sporting context the *corinthians* were the epitome of amateurism. However, because this definition of amateurism is socially determined, it changes over a period of time.

Sports have undergone major changes in their amateur/professional status. For example, rowing was originally open to amateurs and professionals but the gentleman amateurs disliked being beaten by their social inferiors. This resulted in a strict amateur definition instigated by the Amateur Rowing Association called the 'exclusion clause' that effectively excluded 'all mechanics, artisans and labourers'.

Terms that have evolved to describe amateur performers who receive some form of payment include:

- shamateur – describes amateurs who receive 'under the table' payments. *Trust funds* were set up to try and combat this problem
- stamateurs – describes state-sponsored amateurs. These were common in Eastern bloc countries.

Amateurs can officially receive financial aid from *sponsorship*, trust funds and organisations such as *Sports Aid* and the *National Lottery*.

American Dream is based on the idea that individuals are free to operate in a competitive economic environment, without class restrictions, in order to achieve individual wealth and status. It is also commonly referred to as *rags to riches*. It presumes a single scale of success and relies on individual qualities such as initiative, resourcefulness and a material *attitude* towards life. It is this openness that has made the American Dream attractive to many diverse cultural groups which are part of its make up. *Professional sport* in the *USA* has long been an avenue of *social mobility*, particularly useful for athletes from lower class backgrounds.

American football: a physical-contact and intimidating *invasion game*. It originated from the English game of *rugby union football* but developed along different lines in its new *culture*, taking root in the *elite* colleges such as Harvard and Yale. As a result, the game had middle-class beginnings, similar to rugby, but it was not constrained by *amateurism* as English rugby was, and the win ethic, or *Lombardian ethic*, emerged alongside professionalism. It is also referred to as 'gridiron', which emphasises its territorial features. American football is one of the dominant *American sports*.

American sports such as *American football*, baseball, *ice hockey* and *basketball* have their own unique characteristics, but they tend to share common elements that make them some of the most popular and dominant sports in the *USA*. They include:

- high scoring with no draws and fast play
- creation of entertainment through the *mass media* and *sponsorship*
- tendency to attract families rather than traditionally single-sex spectators as in the UK
- facilities that are of a high standard for both players and spectators
- operating as businesses controlled by owners, they are heavily marketed with their accompanying merchandise
- carrying of racial identity and preferences
- the *professional sport* ethos of the *Lombardian ethic* with material *rewards* for success reflects *capitalism*
- due to the size of the USA, there is not the tradition of home and away fans as in Britain, and the crowds are therefore less partisan
- well-developed children's leagues based on the adult version
- limited club structure, with development of players occurring through the inter-*collegiate* system.

American summer camps: the camping movement gained acceptance after 1900 and was initiated by teachers, Scout and Guide groups. Today there are several thousand summer *camps* throughout the *USA*, most of which are permanent camps where children reside for up to eight weeks. The camps take children from 6 to 16 years, and are responsible for their welfare. Today 'going to camp' for an extended period of time is a well-established tradition in the USA.

There has always been a tradition of sending urban children to the *natural environment* for holidays and, in a country where the summer holidays last 3 months, it is accepted for children to spend time away from their parents.

There are different types of camps:
- Private residential – these are privately owned and cater for the high-income, middle-class families. They run on a profit-making policy, provide permanent residential facilities and operate all over the country. They have a range of facilities covering various sports and crafts.
- Day camps – these can also be privately owned or run by organisations such as the *YMCA* or local towns.
- Organisational camps – these are run by Christian-based organisations such as Girl and Boy Scouts and the YMCA, although the emphasis on religion can vary.
- Camps for underprivileged children – these are operated by various social, philanthropic or religious agencies such as the Salvation Army and aim to give inner-city children a break from the urban environment. These camps are heavily subsidised, with families paying little or nothing towards the cost. The facilities are more basic and the emphasis is on the recreational experience and appreciation of the environment.
- Special needs camps – these are for people with physical or mental disabilities, diabetics and people who are overweight (often termed 'fat camps').

The routine for a typical day at a summer camp is shown overleaf.

A typical day at a summer camp

07.15	Reveille. Short optional dip or jog.
07.45	Flag raising and personal inspection.
08.00	Breakfast, followed by clean-up of the cabin or tent.
09.30	1st activity period.
10.30	2nd activity period.
11.45	Optional general swim.
12.30	Lunch.
13.30	Rest hour supervision.
14.30	1st afternoon activity period.
15.30	2nd afternoon activity period.
16.30	Free time supervision.
18.00	Dinner.
19.00	Flag lowering, followed by special evening events.
21.00	First bell – lights out for younger children.
22.00	Lights out for the seniors.

Americanisation of sports: the perceived domination of sport on a global scale by American *culture* and values as a result of the all-pervading influence of the *mass media* and intense *commercialism*.

AMI: see *athletic motivation inventory*.

amphetamines: illegal drugs taken to stimulate the *central nervous system*. In doing so they can improve *alertness* and increase *arousal*. Amphetamines can also improve blood flow to the muscles by increasing heart rate and through *vasodilation of arteries* supplying *skeletal muscles*. This, together with improved metabolism of fats gives a sense of increased energy. Despite these benefits, the ingestion of amphetamines can have serious side effects. As well as being addictive, they artificially increase heart rate and *blood pressure* and can cause the heart to beat irregularly (cardiac arrhythmia). Amphetamines are also a *diuretic* and can lead to *dehydration* and also suppress appetite, which can lead to *fatigue* during training if sufficient food has not been consumed.

Amphetamines can also cause athletes to become seriously ill after pushing themselves beyond their physiological limits.

anabolic steroids: artificially produced male hormones, such as for example stanozolol and *testosterone*, which help to repair the body after periods of stress. It is the main *doping agent* used in power, explosive and sprint events by performers to:
- build up their power by increasing muscle growth and lean body weight
- increase training time
- increase their recovery rate after training.

Aggression and *competitiveness* also increase, which is useful for gross body activities. However, the problems caused can include liver damage, heart disease and infertility. (See also *doping* and *drug testing*.)

Advantages (perceived benefits)	Disadvantages (associated health risks)
Increased muscle mass leads to increased strength	Liver damage
	Heart failure
Enables athletes to train harder at higher intensities	Increased aggression and mood swings – 'roid rage'
Increased anabolic hormones in the blood lead to faster recovery times	Development of masculine effects in females such as deepening of the voice and growth of facial hair
New 'designer' steroids are being produced by pharmaceutical companies all the time, in an attempt to remain one step ahead of the testers	Testicular atrophy, reduced sperm count, baldness and breast development in males
	In adolescents, growth can be halted through the premature maturation of the skeleton

Fortunately, there are now many tests available to detect the use of a wide range of different anabolic steroids.

anaerobic describes the performance of work without the presence of oxygen, for example sprinting, throwing, weightlifting and rebounding in various games. The energy for such activity is provided via anaerobic *glycolysis*, but the ability to resynthesise *ATP* is quickly depleted, so this form of activity can only be sustained for short periods of time, largely due to the build-up of *lactic acid*.

anaerobic capacity test measures the ability of the body to undertake exercise that is of short duration but high in intensity. It assesses the body's ability to break down *glycogen* to produce energy in the absence of oxygen. There are several procedures for measuring the anaerobic capacity of an individual, the most common being the *Wingate cycle test*.

Anaerobic capacity is important in many sporting activities that require quick, powerful movements such as the 100-metre sprint or throwing events. By testing, a coach can determine whether athletes should alter their training in order to improve their anaerobic performance.

anaerobic glycolysis: see *glycolysis*.

anaerobic threshold: see *onset of blood lactate accumulation*.

analysis of activities: the analysis of a sporting activity by breaking it down into its component parts. This can be done using a hierarchy of classifications, one of which is outlined below:

- Structural – refers to the nature of the activity such as the scoring system, the *rules*, *role (social)* of officials and *punishments* for fouls.
- Strategic – refers to the planning and decision-making aspects, with strategies devised according to the nature of the activity. For example, a trampolinist prepares a sequence of movements according to the tariff of the moves and pays attention to artistic interpretation. Strategies in a game situation can often be planned in advance, such as set plays, but they will also have to be adapted according to environmental factors, such as the opposition on the day.

- Technical aspects – refer to the skill needed to carry out the activity effectively, and in **gymnastic activities** the athlete will attempt to produce the 'perfect' movement. (See also **closed skills** and **open skills**.)
- Physical – refers to the body conditions required for a successful outcome. These can be defined in terms of **strength**, mobility, **flexibility**, **aerobic** and **anaerobic** fitness. Also, the physiques or **somatotypes** best suited to particular positions in a team can be analysed.
- Psychological – refers to the mental conditions needed for a successful outcome. This may involve a measure of **aggression** or **assertive behaviour**; concentration and ability to withstand some pain; strategic understanding and **anticipation**; ability to play as part of a team or individually.

Hierarchical structure of sport analysis

ancient cultures: societies that existed during the period of history associated with slave-based production, for example Greece and Rome. These were advanced civilisations that are considered to have laid the foundations of Western civilisation, shown through their architecture, sculpture, literature, philosophy, science and sport. The ancient Greeks strove for physical as well as intellectual **excellence,** and this was made possible through the use of slaves by the **leisured class**. Many physical activities resulted from a functional need to maintain fitness for war, appeasement of the gods and the 'man of action' concept. Several panhellenic (all-Greek) festivals provided them with the opportunity to compete peacefully in **athletics** for their cities and individual glory. The most famous were the **Olympic Games** from which our modern Olympics are derived.

angle of attack: the most favourable angle of a projectile in flight so that it achieves optimum lift due to the **Bernoulli effect**.

angling: an ancient practice that developed initially to provide food. By the fifteenth century it was practised in England as a sport and was popular with the Tudors in the sixteenth century. There was a clear distinction between the commercial and sporting aspects of fishing, but two main forms of recreational fishing emerged:
- coarse fishing – which generally took place in urban, often polluted, areas, and was popular with the industrial **working class**
- game fishing – which was a more expensive pursuit enjoyed on country estates by the **gentry**.

angular acceleration: the rate of change of *angular velocity*. Measured in rads/sec².

> *FORMULA:* Angular acceleration = $\dfrac{\text{change in angular velocity (rads/sec}^2)}{\text{time taken (secs)}}$

angular analogues of Newton's laws: Newton's laws that govern *linear motion* also underpin rotational movement. In attempting to explain *angular motion*, Newton's laws have been adapted to give angular analogues.

- Angular analogue of Newton's first law – a rotating body will continue to turn about its axis of *rotation* with constant *angular momentum* unless an external couple or *eccentric force* is exerted upon it.
- Angular analogue of Newton's second law – the rate of change of angular momentum of a body is proportional to the torque (force) causing it and the change takes place in the direction in which the torque acts.
- Angular analogue of Newton's third law – for every torque that is exerted by one body on another there is an equal and opposite torque exerted by the second body on the first.

angular displacement: a quantity of *angular motion*. Angular displacement is defined as the smallest angle between starting and finishing positions of a rotating body. Measured in degrees (°) or *radians* (rads).

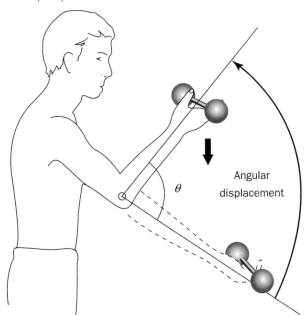

Angular displacement

angular momentum: the quantity of *angular motion* that a rotating body possesses. It is the product of *moment of inertia* and *angular velocity*.

> *FORMULA:* Angular momentum = moment of inertia × angular velocity

There is an inverse relationship between the moment of inertia of a body and its angular velocity, i.e. when moment of inertia is high, angular velocity is low and when

19

moment of inertia is low, angular velocity is high. Furthermore, this inverse relationship is proportional. Consequently, the angular momentum of a body in flight remains constant. This concept arises from Newton's first law of angular motion and is referred to as the law of conservation of angular momentum. As angular momentum cannot be changed during flight, it has important implications for sporting activities that require many rotations to be performed such as in high diving and figure skating. Currently many figure skaters attempt quadruple jumps in their routines. To ensure maximal angular momentum at take-off, the skater prepares for the jump so that at take-off the arms are out to the side and one leg extended behind them. The idea is to generate as great a torque (turning moment) as possible. The larger the force or the farther the application of force is from the axis of rotation, the larger the torque and the larger the torque the greater the angular momentum. Once in flight the skater pulls their arms and legs in as close to the longitudinal axis as possible, which decreases moment of inertia and increases angular velocity, enabling the skater to rotate quickly. On landing the skater spreads the arms out once again to increase moment of inertia and decrease angular velocity.

angular motion: the branch of *biomechanics* concerned with rotating bodies. As with *linear motion* it is possible to analyse, identify and explain the movement of rotating bodies in terms of *displacement*, velocity and *acceleration*. For example, if a trampolinist performed a tucked-back somersault, they might have rotated through 360° in 2 seconds, hence their resulting *angular velocity* will be 180° per second. However, the standard unit for angular motion is in fact *radians* per second (rads/sec), not degrees. There are approximately 57.3° in one radian, so the trampolinist's angular velocity is 3.14 rads/sec. A coach could analyse the trampolinist's angular velocity and determine whether it is necessary for them to increase or decrease the speed of *rotation* for effective performance.

angular velocity: the *angular displacement* travelled in a specified time, given in rads/sec.

FORMULA: $\text{Angular velocity} = \dfrac{\text{angular displacement (rads)}}{\text{time (secs)}}$

animal sports involve animals, whether for racing, hunting or *baiting*. Historically, these activities took place at a variety of venues:

- *horse racing* had its centre in Newmarket
- the *Shrove Tuesday* festival was the first major occasion for outdoor festivities and was popular for animal baiting
- *inns* and public houses often held dog and cock fights
- hunting became an exclusive activity (see *exclusivity*) as the Game Laws protected the rights of the larger landowners.

Animal sports are based on the notion that animals exist as a human resource and as such they often involve cruelty. This aspect began to be affected by an increase in moral standards and was a reflection of the *civilising process*, which was also being applied to other *popular recreations*. *Methodists, Puritans* and the more educated classes began the campaign to ban the more cruel sports such as cock throwing and bear baiting. This was due partly to a growing respect for animals but also to the belief that these sports were associated with *gambling* and alcohol, which encouraged the gathering of unruly sections of the community. The Society for the Prevention of Cruelty to Animals was formed in 1824 and the Cruelty to Animals Act was passed in 1835. (See also *blood sports, coursing, field sports* and *fox hunting*.)

antagonist: a muscle that has an action opposite to that of an *agonist* (prime mover) and helps in the production of a coordinated movement. For example, when the biceps contracts (shortens) to cause *flexion* at the elbow, the tricep lengthens to enable the movement to occur.

anterior: also known as ventral, this is a term of direction that refers to the front of the body or body part. For example, the tibialis anterior is a muscle that exists at the front of the tibia, while the tibialis posterior muscle is situated at the back of the tibia underneath the calf muscles. When describing the body or movements of the body, using these terms of direction is particularly useful. (See appendix, page 311.)

anticipation relies on previous experience to recognise *stimuli* and *cues* that allow the performer to process information before an event actually occurs. This often gives the performer the appearance of being highly skilled, with time to spare in their movements, e.g. an experienced batsman in cricket would watch the bowler's hand and arm action in an attempt to ascertain the type of delivery he or she could expect, thus adjusting the shot accordingly, whereas a novice batsman would watch the ball and decide which shot to play after the ball had pitched, thus having less time to react and adjust the shot if appropriate.

Anticipation can also negatively affect performance and increase *reaction time* if the initial judgement is incorrect. There are several components of anticipation:
- receptor anticipation – relies on the information gathered from the external environment, e.g. the batsman watching the actions of the bowler
- perceptual anticipation – relies on stored information in the memory, e.g. the batsman knowing what the bowler is capable of delivering
- effector anticipation – relies on knowing the feel of the movement to be performed, e.g. the timing of the shot depends on the type of delivery received.

(See also *spatial anticipation* and *temporal anticipation*.)

anticipatory rise: the pre-exercise response of the heart, resulting in an elevated resting heart rate. This occurs due to an increase in activity of the *sympathetic nervous system*, releasing the neurotransmitter substance *noradrenaline* and *adrenaline* from the adrenal glands, preparing the body for exercise is started.

Low intensity (sub-maximal) exercise, showing the anticipatory rise
(Note how heart rate has increased, even before the exercise is started.)

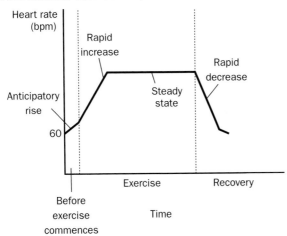

anti-doping: see *World Anti-Doping Agency*.

anxiety: negative emotional feelings caused by an increase in *arousal* levels when a performer is faced with a situation in which they feel threatened or fear failure. Individuals possess both *state anxiety* and *trait anxiety*. The former includes reactions that can be classed as *cognitive anxiety*, i.e. nervousness and poor concentration levels linked to the task, and *somatic anxiety*, i.e. body responses such as sweating, nausea, increased breathing and pulse rate. The latter is due to enduring traits that dictate how the performer will react to certain situations. Anxiety can be measured using a variety of methods including observation, self-report *questionnaires* and *biofeedback*.

anxiety management techniques: see *stress management*.

aorta: the major blood vessel that conducts oxygenated blood away from the heart and around the body.

apartheid can be defined as 'apartness' and refers to the system of racial *segregation* that operated in *South Africa* until the 1990s. In 1956 the South African government decided to make sport a formal part of its apartheid policy which excluded non-whites from many areas, for example housing and health care. A world ban on South African sport was declared in 1964, but South Africa went to great lengths to attract world-class competition. For example, in 1969 the English Rugby Union entertained a *Springbok* touring team but suffered widespread public demonstrations against its decision. The cricket and particularly rugby union *administrations* held out the longest in their support of South Africa.

appendicular skeleton: the part of the skeleton composed of the bones of the limbs, together with the hip and shoulder girdles that join on to the *axial skeleton*.

approach behaviour: the behaviour pattern of a performer who is motivated to succeed and attempt a challenging situation even if they may fail. This type of behaviour is closely linked to *achievement motivation* and should be developed. For example, the coach of a team encourages the players to attempt difficult passes or shots during the game. Even if they are not successful, the coach still offers support and the players learn from the experience. There are various strategies that can be used to develop approach behaviour, including providing positive childhood experiences and encouraging feelings of pride and satisfaction through success; gradually increasing the task difficulty but ensuring that challenging tasks are set cater for all levels of ability. It is important to raise levels of *self-efficacy*, avoid *learned helplessness* and *avoidance behaviour*.

aquatics: see *swimming* and *rowing*.

archery claims the oldest ancestry of any sport actively pursued today. It was originally practised for hunting purposes, later became important as military training and finally became a form of *recreation*. From the reigns of Henry I to Elizabeth I, archery practice was compulsory for men in order to defend the realm. Regular practice was held in church grounds and at the butts. During the *Victorian era* archery became an activity for the *leisured class* and many clubs were established. It was considered a suitable recreation for women due to the lack of strenuous exercise involved and the clubs' strict dress code could be adhered to. In 1861 the Grand National Archery Society was established as an official *governing body* for archery in the nineteenth century.

aristocracy: traditionally established as the highest *social class* whose power over society stemmed from its control of land and agricultural production. Its power was at its height in the feudal system, but became threatened by the new social group emerging as a result of the *Industrial Revolution*, namely the *middle class*. The aristocracy or *gentry* were a wealthy, *leisured class* who participated in many *recreation* pursuits such as hunting and fencing. They also acted as *patrons* to lower-class individuals and many still retain this privileged status towards certain organisations.

Arnold, Thomas: the headmaster of Rugby School from 1828 until 1842, where he directed a crusade against 'sinful' behaviour by the boys such as bullying, lying, cheating and running wild among the local community. He directed his efforts through chapel sermons and close supervision of the boys' *leisure* time. He intended that the boys remain in the school grounds to reduce the incidence of poaching and trespassing, which gave *public schools* a bad name in the early part of the nineteenth century. Arnold is known for his contribution to *muscular Christianity* but he valued games only for what they could contribute towards the *social control* of the boys rather than for their intrinsic benefits. Games could be catered for within the school grounds and rules encouraged discipline and respect.

arousal: the energised state of readiness of an individual to perform a task, motivating them to direct their behaviour in a particular manner. It can affect the performer positively or negatively, both physiologically and psychologically, depending on the individual's perception of the situation, but can be controlled to produce an effective performance. The level of arousal is controlled by the *reticular activating system,* which interprets the level of stimulation entering the body and initiates an appropriate response. The primary aim of the performer is to maintain their arousal at an optimal level suitable for the activity undertaken so that concentration and *decision-making* are not impaired. Arousal can be measured using a variety of methods including observation, self-report *questionnaires* and *biofeedback*. (See also *catastrophe theory* and *inverted U theory*.)

arterioles: small blood vessels that conduct blood from the *arteries* into the *capillary* network. They have a small diameter, which is controlled by large numbers of smooth muscle fibres. Arterioles combine with pre-capillary sphincters allowing them to *vasoconstrict* and *vasodilate*, regulating the flow of blood into the capillary bed. During exercise, some arterioles constrict to divert the blood away from non-vital areas, such as the gut and kidneys, and shunt more to the working muscles, which therefore provides them with the necessary oxygen for energy production.

arteriosclerosis: a consequence of *atherosclerosis,* this vascular disease is typified by the thickening, hardening and loss of *elasticity* of the arterial walls which can lead to *hypertension* (high *blood pressure*) and impaired blood circulation.

arterio-venous oxygen difference (a-vO$_2$ diff): the difference in oxygen content of the blood in the *arteries* and the *veins*. It is a measure of the oxygen consumed by the muscles. When at rest, approximately 25% of oxygen is utilised, but this rises to up to 85% during periods of intense exercise.

artery: a high-pressure blood vessel that carries oxygen-rich blood from the heart to the muscles and other tissues. Arteries have elastic properties helping to 'cushion out' the pulsating flow of blood from the heart. The largest artery is the *aorta*. Arteries subdivide into *arterioles*, which reduce in size the further they are from the heart. The only artery that carries blood low in oxygen is the *pulmonary artery*. Where an artery lies close to a bone, it is possible to measure the pulse rate, such as the radial, femoral and carotid sites. Arteries are essential in regulating *blood pressure*.

articular (hyaline) cartilage: see *cartilage*.

Ashbourne Royal Shrovetide football: the Royal Shrovetide Football Match occurs annually on *Shrove Tuesday* and Ash Wednesday in the town of Ashbourne in Derbyshire. It has been played since at least the twelfth century. The game is played over two days on Shrove Tuesday and Ash Wednesday, starting each day at 2.00 p.m. and lasting until 10.00 p.m. If the goal is scored (goaled) before 5.00 p.m., a new ball is released and play restarts from the town centre, otherwise play ends for the day. The two teams that play the game are known as the Up'Ards and the Down'Ards. It is a surviving *ethnic sport* reflective of *popular recreations* prior to the *Industrial Revolution*.

Ashes: a test cricket series, played between England and Australia which dates back to 1882. It is currently played biennially, alternately in England and Australia. However, since cricket is a summer game, and the venues are in opposite hemispheres, this means the break between series alternates between 18 and 30 months. A series of 'the Ashes' now comprises five test matches, two innings per match, under the regular rules for international test-match cricket. If a series is drawn then the country holding the Ashes retains them.

The series is named after a satirical obituary published in an English newspaper, *The Sporting Times*, in 1882 after the match at the Oval in which Australia beat England on an English ground for the first time. The obituary stated that English cricket had died, and 'the body will be cremated and the ashes taken to Australia'. The English media then dubbed the next English tour to Australia (1882–83) as 'the quest to regain the Ashes'.

assertive behaviour is viewed as an acceptable form of *aggression*. The actions of the performer are within the laws of the game, with no intention to harm another player, and they are goal directed. This form of behaviour is encouraged, but there is a fine line between appropriate actions that are assertive and those that become aggressive. In a sporting context, this is decided by the officials. For example, when does a sliding tackle in a football match become dangerous or when does verbal 'sledging' become unacceptable? (See also *channelled aggression* and *instrumental aggression*.)

assessment: a measure of the quality or worth of something and also how achievement is to be evaluated. Several types of assessment are used in physical education such as longitudinal student profiles that contain purely *quantitative* data (e.g. fitness tests), and generalised teacher comments which use a mixture of *subjective* and *objective* assessments. Objective assessment involves figures such as distance thrown in the javelin, whereas subjective assessment involves to some extent personal opinions of judges, as in ice skating, although objective criteria are still applied. In physical education children need to show:
- what they know
- what they can do
- what they understand.

Examinations such as GCSE and A-level are becoming an ever-more popular way in which children choose to be assessed.

Advantages of testing	Disadvantages of testing
Gives children a clear aim, a focus for their efforts	Physical education should be about enjoyment and releasing of pressure
Motivates children to learn	
Creates more teacher accountability	Time can be wasted on testing and not teaching
Recognises good teacher practice such as good organisation	Children and teachers can become demotivated if testing is inappropriate or if the testing is making unfair comparisons
Gives status to the subject and allows comparison with other subjects	Physical education should be about enjoyment and releasing of pressure

assimilation: the *integration* of immigrant communities within the prevalent *culture* by adopting its values and traditions. This has tended to be the case in Britain where *ethnic groups* traditionally have been expected to adhere to the British way of life.

association football: a type of football that originated from its *mob* form which developed at nineteenth-century *public schools* and resulted in the handling and dribbling variations of the game. The Football Association (FA) was formed in 1863 when the rules that allowed handling the ball were changed. Those who opposed this change were to form the Rugby Union in 1871.

The London football clubs dominated association football initially, but Sheffield in the north also grew in strength and formed its own association that was the forerunner of the county football associations. In 1877 these brought their own rules into line with those of the football association and the Challenge Cup, established in 1871, was to increase the popularity of association football, leading many clubs to seek membership of the Association. Initially the Cup games were played at the Oval, attracting a crowd of 45,000 in 1893, but the venue was changed to Wembley in 1895. The major changes to the game were:
- the growing dominance of the industrial *working class* as they received more free time
- the game became a *professional sport*.

This latter point was recognised with the formation of the *Football League* in 1888, which allied regular competitive fixtures with professionalism. The idea of two divisions came about when the second division emerged in the 1892–3 season and the third in 1920–1.

associationist theories of learning: also known as stimulus–response theories or conditioning theories, these imply that *learning* is based on the performer developing a relationship between *stimuli* and a response (the *stimulus–response bond*). The *environment* can be manipulated, often by the coach, to produce a certain action or behaviour which is strengthened through regular practice, e.g. a batsman may be trained to recognise a ball bowled in a certain manner (stimulus) and play the correct shot (response).

Conditioning theories are generally divided into two categories: *classical conditioning* and *operant conditioning*. (See also *drive reduction theory*.)

associative phase of learning: involves the performer physically implementing the motor programme learned during the *cognitive phase of learning*. Fitts and Posner's

25

stages of learning theory suggests this is the intermediate phase. The skill learned is refined and gross errors eliminated through repeated practice, developing an effective and consistent technique. As *kinaesthetic* awareness of the movement develops, the performer is able to provide internal *feedback* to supplement any external information. The timescale before progressing to the *autonomous phase of learning* may vary depending on the level of ability, complexity of the task, type of practice and quality of feedback.

asthma: a respiratory complication that causes constriction of the bronchial airways and inflammation of mucous membranes, which results in shortness of breath and restriction in ventilation. Asthma should not prevent participation in exercise, in fact inspiratory muscle training (IMT) or aerobic training can alleviate symptoms of the condition. For some asthmatics, however, aerobic exercise can actually trigger their asthma particularly in cold or dry conditions. This particular form of asthma is known as exercise-induced asthma (EIA). A thorough *warm-up* and *cool-down* are essential before and following exercise to help prevent EIA attacks from occurring. Bronchodilators can relieve the symptoms of asthma for all sufferers and it is essential that medication is close at hand when exercising.

atherosclerosis: a progressive disease characterised by the laying down of fatty deposits (atheroma) in the *arteries*. It is a condition associated with *cardiovascular diseases*, smoking and *obesity*.

Athlete Career and Education Programme (ACE UK): this programme is modelled on the *Australian Institute of Sport*. It provides a tailored service that encourages athletes to take control of all aspects of their lives. ACE UK enables them to identify their personal strengths and weaknesses and supports them in integratingtheir career, education and sporting demands in order to ensure all-round success in their lives. Sports performers who are part of the *World Class Performance Pathway*, *British Olympic Association* Gold Passport holders or have left these schemes during the past 12 months are eligible to benefit from the programme.

athletic activities: these include the categories of races, field *athletics* and weightlifting, and all test the explosive or sustained power of the athlete. The winner of the 100 metres is the person who reaches the tape first. All race events, whatever the form of locomotion, are decided in this way: the high jumper clears the bar, the thrower achieves the furthest distance. This relies on *quantitative* and *objective* methods of *assessment* where scientific criteria are applied. Advances in the level of technology used have allowed extremely fine units of measurement to be applied. In order to be fair the athletes adhere to strict rules and may take it in turns.

athletic motivation inventory (AMI): a *questionnaire* developed by Ogilvie and Tutko (1966) to measure *personality* traits and categorise athletes. The questionnaire was considered to be of limited use, as it was not validated and proved to be unreliable.

athleticism is defined as 'physical endeavour with moral integrity' and developed out of the English *public school* system. Its development can be considered in three stages:

Stage 1 Bullying and brutality. Before the formalisation of team games, boys would leave the school grounds and participate in rowdy behaviour. This often involved poaching, fighting, trespassing, drinking alcohol and generally bringing the school's reputation into disrepute. The abuse of the fagging system did not reflect a gentlemanly and moral lifestyle.

Stage 2 Dr Arnold and social control. Doctor **Thomas Arnold** became headmaster of Rugby School in 1828 from where he directed a crusade against personal sin, e.g. bullying, lying, swearing, cheating and running wild. Pupils were to remain on the school grounds and were forbidden to go shooting and beagling as these activities encouraged poaching. Fights were only to occur in his presence and were to be supervised by the prefects who enforced his authority.

Stage 3 Cult of athleticism. The cult of athleticism stressed the physical and social benefits of sports:

- The physical benefits were seen to counteract the effects of sedentary lifestyles, and sport was viewed as therapeutic, invigorating and cathartic. It was also seen as a break from work.
- Sport would take place within a competitive situation which would help the boys learn how to cope with winning and losing all in a dignified manner. It helped to develop leadership qualities — being captain was a high status office to hold.

athletics: sporting events that developed historically from a functional need (e.g. throwing events from hunting and war) and from rural pursuits (e.g. hurdling and pole vaulting from clearing obstacles such as ditches). Race walking or **pedestrianism** developed in Stuart and Georgian times when young men were sent ahead of the **gentry** carriage to warn the innkeeper of their imminent arrival. Wagers were placed and the gentry acted as **patrons**.

Athletics was originally professional and became a commercial activity, but it was tainted with corruption and bribery was rife to 'fix' races. This was to be its downfall, and it was later that the amateur ethos from the **public schools** took over with administrative organisations such as the Amateur Athletic Association. Athletics in the UK denotes activities such as running, jumping and throwing events. In the USA these activities are referred to as track and field and the term 'athletics' refers to other physical sporting activities.

atom: an atom is built from negatively charged electrons, positively charged protons and neutrons that have no charge. The atomic number of an atom is the number of protons it possesses. For example, hydrogen – with one proton – has the atomic number 1.

ATP (adenosine triphosphate) is a form of chemical **energy** found in all muscle cells. The high-energy phosphate molecules are broken down to release energy for all processes, including muscle contraction, nerve transmission and digestion. An adenosine triphosphate molecule is composed of three phosphate groups and an adenosine component and, when exposed to the **enzyme** ATPase, a bond is broken to release a large amount of energy, leaving **ADP**, as shown below:

FORMULA: ATP → ADP + Pi + energy

The amount of **ATP** in the muscle cells is limited and is exhausted within a few seconds. It must therefore be constantly resynthesised in order to provide a continuous supply of energy. The resynthesis of ATP requires energy to attach a phosphate group to the ADP compound, as shown below:

FORMULA: ADP + Pi + energy → ATP

The energy used to resynthesise ATP can be derived from three sources:

- *alactic energy system* – used for high intensity, power-based activities such as the 100-metre sprint
- *lactic acid energy system* – used for medium to high intensity activities such as a 400-metre run
- *aerobic energy system* – used for low intensity, endurance-based activities such as the marathon.

ATP–PC energy system: see *alactic energy system*.

atrioventricular node (AV node) is a mass of conducting cells located in the right atrial wall, forming part of the conducting system of the heart. The AV node acts as a distributor and passes the *action potential* to the atrioventricular bundle (bundle of His), which is a mass of conducting fibres that together with the branching Purkinje fibres spread the excitation throughout the ventricles. There is a delay of about 0.1 seconds from the time when the AV node receives stimulation to when it distributes the action potential throughout the ventricles. This is crucial to allow completion of atrial contraction and ensures that all the blood enters the ventricles before ventricular contraction. An electrocardiogram trace shows the relationship between electrical activity of the heart and the different stages of the *cardiac cycle*.

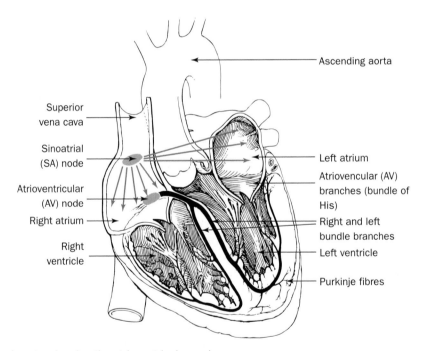

The heart – showing the atrioventricular node

atrium: (plural atria) one of the top two chambers of the heart, which receive blood returning from the organs of the body. The right atrium receives blood returning from the muscles and other organs of the body via the venae cavae, while the left atrium receives blood rich in oxygen returning from the lungs via the pulmonary vein.

attainment targets are set out in the *National Curriculum* for many subjects, including physical education. Attainment targets require children to demonstrate the knowledge, skills and understanding involved in areas of activity encompassing **athletic activities**, dance, **games**, **gymnastic activities**, outdoor and **adventurous activities** and **swimming**.

There are eight levels showing a gradation of difficulty with 'exceptional performance' criteria for the most gifted.

attention: the ability to focus on **cues** appearing in the **display (psychology)** and identify those which are relevant. Attention capabilities may vary depending on the age, experience and **arousal** level of the individual and on the nature of the task. Various forms of the concept of attention have been proposed, including **selective attention** and **attentional narrowing** linked to arousal. Capacity theories suggest that two or more tasks can be completed simultaneously, provided the total attentional capacity is not exceeded, with each task having a different attention requirement. For example, an experienced performer may be able to control the ball, look for opponents and team mates and assess numerous options at the same time, whereas a novice may devote much of their attentional capacity to control and not be able to focus on the other factors. Nideffer suggested individuals are either 'effective' or 'ineffective' attenders. The former are able to process information externally, e.g. position of players, and internally, e.g. analytical thoughts, allowing them to switch their focus of attention quickly without missing important cues. The latter experience difficulty concentrating, become confused and miss the relevant cues. As a result, certain sports or positions may be better suited to different individuals. For example, an effective attender may perform better at team sports compared with an ineffective attender, who may perform more consistently at individual activities or in a position requiring limited **decision-making**.

attentional narrowing is also known as perceptual narrowing, and links **arousal** levels directly to the individual's ability to focus on relevant **cues** and **stimuli** (see **cue utilisation theory**). If the performer reaches their optimal arousal level, they will identify the appropriate cues, but over-arousal will hinder the process. As perceptual narrowing continues, vital cues will be missed (see **attentional wastage**), leading to a decrease in performance. For example, a basketball player may not detect a team mate in an open shooting position or may fail to see a defender closing down their space as they move in to shoot.

attentional styles: Nideffer suggested that performers need to have the ability to alter their perceptual field and vary the amount and type of information that enters the body depending on the situation and the requirements of the task. For example, during a badminton doubles match the player will need to focus in a different manner when serving compared to a rally where more information needs to be assessed. Nideffer's model of attentional focus (1976) proposed that attentional style varies along two dimensions:

1 Width – refers to the number of **stimuli** requiring **attention**
  * broad – focuses on a wide range of stimuli, e.g. the badminton player needs to detect their own and opponents position on court, as well as the location, flight and speed of the shuttlecock
  * narrow – focuses on a limited range of stimuli, e.g. when serving the player focuses on the place where they wish to hit the shuttlecock
2 Direction – refers to the focus of the thought processes of the performer
  * internal – focuses on their own thoughts and feelings, e.g. the player mentally rehearsing the feelings associated with the correct **movement pattern** or **stress management** techniques to control their level of **arousal**

- external – focuses on stimuli in the environment, e.g. the location of the players and shuttlecock or the shot being played by the opponent.

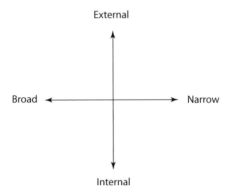

Based on the diagram, Nideffer identified four attentional styles:
- broad/external – used by players during games to detect fast-changing situations and identify the best option
- external/narrow – used by players to concentrate on specific objects or tasks, possibly with limited number of *cues*
- narrow/internal – used by players to mentally rehearse a skill or task
- internal/broad – used by coaches to analyse performance and plan future strategies and tactics.

	External	Internal
Broad	The whole arena, e.g. a playmaker reading the game	Analysing and planning, e.g. a coach working out tactics
Narrow	Focus on a single cue, e.g. a golf putt	Mental rehearsal or feel of task, e.g. focus on the grip of the racket

Attentional styles

The aim of the coach should be to identify the attentional style required in a particular situation and performers must develop the skill of switching between different styles to maximise their performance. Strategies can be developed to encourage this during phases of play. For example, during a badminton match the server may adopt a narrow/internal style to imagine how they are going to play the serve, but then immediately switch to a broad/external style when the rally begins.

attentional wastage occurs when the performer's concentration is misdirected to **cues** that are irrelevant, causing a decrease in performance. For example, during a game of netball, the player may listen to shouts from the crowd rather than focus on the position of players on court. This may be eliminated by developing the performer's **selective attention**.

attitude: a relatively stable belief or view on a specific **attitude object**. A person's attitudes are developed through past experiences, **significant others**, the **mass media** or any other interaction with the social environment. Their attitude may be positive, negative or neutral. For example, a person may swim regularly and enjoy the benefits, creating a positive attitude; a friend may have fallen into water without being able to swim, creating fear and a negative attitude; someone who has neither had the opportunity to swim nor had a bad experience may have a neutral attitude.

The **triadic model** proposes that attitudes have three components:
* cognitive – beliefs and thoughts, e.g. benefits of swimming
* affective – emotions and feelings, e.g. enjoyment of swimming
* behavioural – actions, e.g. swimming regularly.

However, an individual's attitude and behaviour may not always be predictable, e.g. they may think swimming is beneficial and fun but do not always make the time to participate. If this is the case, or a negative attitude needs to be altered by eradicating **stereotyping** and **prejudice**, the most commonly used methods are **persuasive communication** and **cognitive dissonance theory**. (See also **attitude tests**.)

attitude object: the focus of an individual's **attitude**, which may be an object, an event, an activity, a person or an idea. Such predispositions can be general or specific, e.g. a person may have a positive attitude towards sport, but a negative attitude towards swimming.

attitude tests: methods used to assess the opinions and feelings of an individual, which are used to describe their **attitude**. A variety of methods can be used, the most common of which are:
* observation of body language and behaviour
* physiological tests, e.g. heart rate and galvanic skin response
* **questionnaires** or interviews, e.g. **Likert scale**, **Thurston scale** and **semantic differential scales**.

Testing for attitude can be difficult due to the problems of **reliability** and **validity** of procedures. It may also prove difficult for an individual to express their attitude when faced with questions in a written form.

attribution: the perceived reasons for the success or failure of an event or pattern of behaviour. A team may infer they lost because of a lucky goal by the opposing team or a poor refereeing decision. The correct use of attributions are vital to ensure performers' **motivation** levels are maintained (see diagram overleaf). (See also **attribution theory**.)

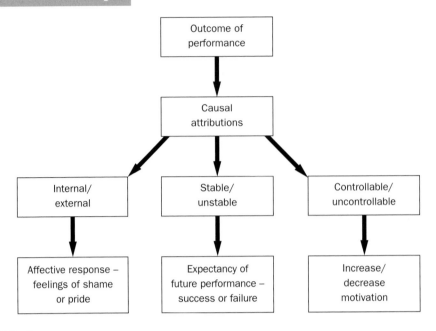

Attribution

attribution retraining involves the coach or teacher developing and changing an individual's perception of failure, allowing them to deal with it effectively and improve future performances, avoiding **learned helplessness**. For example, a talented swimmer may not believe they have the ability to succeed, but if taught a slight variation in their technique will produce considerable improvement and they will persevere with the task. **Goal setting** is vital in this process, especially the use of **outcome** or task goals rather than **performance goals**.

attribution theory suggests that the reasons perceived by an individual or team for the outcome of their actions can affect their levels of **motivation** in future performances. Attributions help to explain success and failure, ensuring motivation levels remain high. Weiner proposed four categories of **attribution** – ability, effort, task difficulty and luck – which are divided into two dimensions, as shown below.

Locus of stability	Locus of causality	
	Internal	External
Stable	Ability	Task difficulty
Unstable	Effort	Luck

However, Roberts and Pascuzzi suggested a more sport-specific adaptation of the model:

Locus of stability	Locus of causality	
	Internal	External
Stable	Ability	Coaching
Unstable	Effort	Luck
	Psychological factors	Task difficulty
	Practice	Team work
		Officials

Generally, to gain feelings of satisfaction, success is attributed to internal factors (see *self-serving bias*) and failure to external factors. To maintain *motivation* using the locus of stability, success is based on stable factors and failure on unstable factors.

audience: those people watching, who can have a positive (*social facilitation*) or negative (*social inhibition*) effect on performance. The presence of others tends to increase *arousal*, with the dominant response being the result (see *drive theory*), e.g. during a hockey match a novice will tend to make more mistakes, while the experienced player will usually display their skills effectively. Audiences cause a distraction for the performer, creating *evaluation apprehension*, which is further increased if it includes *significant others*. This can also affect experts, creating feelings of fear of failure, worry, embarrassment, etc., possibly explaining one reason why they do not always perform to their potential.

auditory system (audition): the *sensory system* concerned with gaining information from outside the body through hearing; a form of *exteroceptor*. It allows the performer to process *stimuli* from the *environment* without actually seeing them, e.g. the sound of the gun to start a race, the call from a team mate or the noise of the racket string when playing a shot.

augmented feedback: see *feedback*.

Aussie rules football dates back to 1858 when two men, Harrison and Wills, decided to design a purely Australian game. The game shows influences from cricket (oval pitch), Gaelic football (played by Irish troops) and the English game of rugby union football. It is a physical-contact *invasion game*. The size of the pitch is not set but has minimum and maximum dimensions, and is possibly one reason why the sport has not been easy to transfer to other countries.

Aussie Sport: a national sporting initiative in *Australia,* committed to the development of young people through sport. The *Australian Sports Commission* and the state departments of sport and education work closely together in order to foster positive community relationships and to ensure a coordinated approach to junior sport in their area. Aussie Sport is about:

- supporting quality teaching and coaching
- promoting and developing quality sport for young people
- making sport more accessible, easier to play and enjoyable
- fostering greater community involvement in junior sport.

Various programmes are tailored to suit different needs, including:

- Sportstart – aims at working with young children through informal play activities and playshop courses to help parents understand their children's play habits
- Sportit – designed for primary school children to learn basic motor skills used in major sports. The Modified Sport Programme is a way of reducing adult sport programmes. An example is Netta Netball
- Sport: Everyone's Game – aims to reach all groups within society and particularly those with lower active participation ratios. Examples include the Active Girl's Campaign and Willing and Able.

Aussie Sport also runs leadership programmes for secondary-school children, which can be compared with the British *Central Council of Physical Recreation* (*British Sports Trust*) Sports Leader Awards.

Australia is made up of six states, namely Victoria, New South Wales, Queensland, Tasmania, South Australia and Western Australia, and two territories, Northern Territory and the Australian Capital Territory. It is a large country with a relatively small population concentrated in urban areas, particularly in the coastal cities. There is a tropical climate in the north and a temperate climate in the south. The Pacific coasts receive the most rainfall while the interior is very dry. The problems of geography and demography make travel expensive and often limit competition opportunities in sport, so major international games are very significant to Australians.

The states retain their own parliament and governor, while legislative power is held by the federal parliament (see **federalism**) based in Canberra, and political power rests with the prime minister who heads the government. **Aborigines** were the indigenous population, but European settlers arrived in 1788 and Australia's links with Britain began. It is still a member of the Commonwealth of Nations. It became a popular country for immigration after **World War II**, resulting in a diverse **multicultural** society.

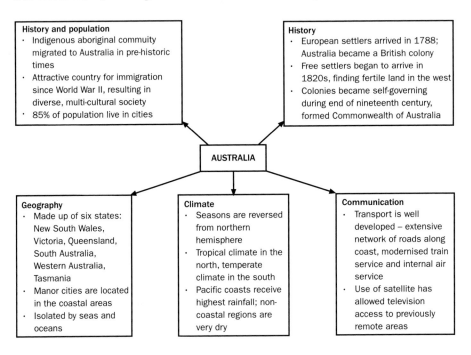

History and population
- Indigenous aboriginal commuity migrated to Australia in pre-historic times
- Attractive country for immigration since World War II, resulting in diverse, multi-cultural society
- 85% of population live in cities

History
- European settlers arrived in 1788; Australia became a British colony
- Free settlers began to arrive in 1820s, finding fertile land in the west
- Colonies became self-governing during end of nineteenth century, formed Commonwealth of Australia

AUSTRALIA

Geography
- Made up of six states: New South Wales, Victoria, Queensland, South Australia, Western Australia, Tasmania
- Manor cities are located in the coastal areas
- Isolated by seas and oceans

Climate
- Seasons are reversed from northern hemisphere
- Tropical climate in the north, temperate climate in the south
- Pacific coasts receive highest rainfall; non-coastal regions are very dry

Communication
- Transport is well developed – extensive network of roads along coast, modernised train service and internal air service
- Use of satellite has allowed television access to previously remote areas

Australian Athlete Scholarship scheme: similar to **Sports Aid** in the UK, but it receives federal money (see **federalism**) and has a larger budget. The primary aim is to give direct financial aid to **elite** athletes who will have been nominated by their national sporting bodies, which are similar to **governing bodies** in Britain.

Australian Council for Health, Physical Education and Recreation (ACPHER) deals with issues such as the amount of time devoted to physical education in schools and the training of teachers.

Australian Institute of Sport (AIS) is an organisation based in Canberra and established in 1980. It cost $100 million to construct and possesses a sophisticated sports science and **sports medicine** support service which, with the development of coaching, form its basic functions. The federal government (see *federalism*) pays approximately 95% of the money and athletes receive *scholarships* to cover expenses. Other community groups, similar to the British *centres of excellence*, can also use the facilities but they are mainly for the *elite* who reserve most of the bookings and who can afford the high fees. Out-reach centres exist in major cities as a form of decentralisation (see *decentralised*), in recognition of the size of the country, and national academies have developed as a consequence in Canberra, Brisbane, Adelaide, Melbourne and Sydney, each specialising in particular sports.

Australian Sports Commission (ASC) is based in Canberra and has two main functions:

- to increase sport participation by Australians through programmes such as *Aussie Sport*
- to increase *excellence*.

Australian sports system: located within the Department of the Environment, Sport and the Territories (DEST) under the programme of Sport and Recreation. The overall objective of the programme as stated by DEST is 'to contribute to the quality of life of all Australians by promoting and facilitating opportunities for participation in sport and recreation activities, encouraging sporting *excellence*, reducing harm associated with the use of *doping* in sport, and examining the economic and social impact of the sport and recreation industry'. This is achieved through:

- funding at the *elite* level where financial support is provided by the government
- the *Australian Institute of Sport* and the *Australian Sports Commission* supply the national sports organisations with funding and services
- state organisations fulfil a similar role at state level.

Local government is involved in supporting regional and local sports organisations by providing services and facilities in which to participate.

autocratic leader: also known as an authoritarian leader, this type of leader tells the *group* what actions to take, with very little or no input from the members of the group in terms of decision-making. They are generally not concerned with inter-personal relationships within the group and are task orientated. Research by Lewin (1935) suggested a group under this form of leadership worked hard when the leader was present, but became aggressive and independent when left alone. This is useful when the task needs to be completed quickly, is complex or is dangerous. (See also *democratic leader* and *laissez-faire leader*.)

autogenic training involves the performer imagining they are in familiar surroundings where they feel comfortable and able to relax. For example, an athlete may imagine they are lying on a beach in the sun, which initiates feelings of warmth, tranquillity and comfort. This technique is similar to that of *progressive muscular relaxation* and *self-directed relaxation*.

autonomic nervous system: also known as the involuntary nervous system, this is the part of the *central nervous system* that controls areas of the body not under conscious control, such as cardiovascular functioning (including heart rate and *blood pressure*) and respiration rate. The autonomic nervous system has two divisions: the *parasympathetic nervous system* and the *sympathetic nervous system*. The former controls bodily functions during normal resting conditions, while the latter controls the individual's reaction to situations of stress or emergency, or indeed during exercise. The effect of the sympathetic system on the heart is to increase heart rate, while the parasympathetic system returns the heart rate to its normal resting level.

autonomous phase of learning: reached when the performer demonstrates the ability to complete skilled actions with increased efficiency, accuracy and speed involving little conscious control. *Fitts and Posner's stages of learning theory* suggests this is the final stage of learning. The *information processing* time is reduced and distractions have less effect on performance. The performer has the ability to analyse their own actions, allowing external *feedback* to be used to develop finer points of technique, strategies and tactics. In order to maintain their performance at this phase, practice must continue.
(See *associative phase of learning.*)

autonomy: the freedom of individuals and organisations to act in certain circumstances. Many sports organisations are deemed to be autonomous, that is, they can act independently of the government in power. An example of this is the Sports Council (now *Sport England*) which was given a Royal Charter in 1972, leaving it free from political control.

The states in *Australia* and the *USA* also have a degree of autonomy within the wider federal system (see *federalism*). For example, they could develop different education systems and may have different laws. 'States righters' are groups that are constantly defending the rights of the states.

avoidance behaviour: the behaviour pattern of a performer who is motivated to protect their *self-esteem* and will avoid situations where they may be evaluated. Performers who develop this state of mind and act in this way often have low *self-efficacy* and possibly *learned helplessness*. This type of behaviour is closely linked to *achievement motivation*. For example, a player may be worried about missing a shot or having their pass intercepted because of negative repercussions from the coach, such as negative *feedback* or being dropped from the team for a bad performance. As a result, they tend to attempt only the easy option and avoid the difficult situation if possible. This can obviously have a negative impact on the performance of the team. The coach should attempt to develop and encourage *approach behaviour*.

axial skeleton: the structure that provides the main area of support for the body and includes the cranium, vertebral column and the rib cage. It provides sites of attachment for the limbs of the *appendicular skeleton*.

back spin: a type of spin applied to a projectile such as a tennis ball which causes a deviation of the ball upwards and its flight path to be extended, as a result of the *Magnus effect*. The boundary layer on the bottom surface of a ball struck with back spin travels in the opposite direction to the air flow. This slows the flow of air on the bottom surface and creates a zone of high pressure. The boundary layer on the top surface travels in the same direction as the oncoming air flow, causing the air to travel more quickly than that on the bottom surface and creating a zone of low pressure. The pressure differential (low pressure on top of the ball, high pressure below the ball) results in the ball moving towards the low pressure zone causing it to float and deviate upwards from the expected flight path (when the ball is struck without spin).

baggataway is the name for the earliest game of *lacrosse*, invented by *Native Americans*. The game had a religious significance and was also played as a means of training tribal warriors. Matches lasted for two or three days, with the goals marked by trees, some 460 m apart.

baiting involved a bull or bear being tied up and terriers set at it. The aim was that the dogs hang on to the bull or bear without being dislodged; the dogs would fail if they were tossed away. The activity was first recorded in the reign of Henry II and wagering took place over the individual dogs. The need for powerful jaws was important and this is how bulldogs got their name. Bear gardens were popular in the sixteenth century under the Tudors and there was one located behind the Globe Theatre. This sport was banned in 1835 with the Prevention of Cruelty to Animals Act. (See also *blood sports*.)

balance: the maintenance of the *centre of mass* over the base of support. This can occur when the body is static such as in a handstand or while the body is moving such as in the performance of a cartwheel.

balanced forces: as this name suggests, balanced forces are equal in size but opposite in direction and therefore do not cause a change in the state of motion of a body or object. As the forces are equal but in opposite directions, the two forces cancel each other out and the resultant force (*net force*) is zero. There is therefore no change in motion. Balanced forces can not only affect stationary bodies; zero net forces can also act when a body is moving at constant velocity. Some good examples of balanced forces in operation include a gymnast performing a handstand and a sprinter running at constant velocity. (See also *unbalanced forces*.)

ball and socket joint: see *synovial joint*.

ballistic stretching: an advanced form of stretching that should only be performed under the watchful eye of a coach. This is a stretching activity that usually involves bouncing in to and out of a stretched position. It is not to be recommended for all performers as it uses the momentum of the body to force the muscle beyond its normal range of movement.

Bandura's model of observational learning: see *social learning theory*.

barbarian schools: nine established *public schools,* namely Eton, Rugby, Winchester, Shrewsbury, St Paul's, Merchant Taylor, Harrow, Charterhouse and Westminster. They maintained the *gentry* tradition and remained exclusive (see *exclusivity*). The emergence of the *middle class* saw the development of the *proprietary colleges*, which were direct copies of the gentry schools.

Baron Pierre de Coubertin: see *Coubertin, Baron Pierre de*.

Baron's distraction conflict theory: a theory which proposes that athletes must focus their *attention* on the demands of the task in hand, and anything that may distract them will hinder their performance. As performers can only process a limited amount of information at a given time, the introduction of an *audience*, or the effect known as *social facilitation*, can disrupt the *information processing* system. The implication for a performer has to be that they must direct their attention to the task and attempt to ignore the distraction created by the crowd.

baroreceptors: nerve cells capable of responding to changes in *blood pressure*, which are found in the walls of the *atria* of the heart, venae cavae and aortic arch. When stimulated, the baroreceptors reduce blood pressure through *vasodilation* of blood vessels. This works in conjunction with the *parasympathetic nervous system* to reduce heart rate and therefore blood flow following exercise.

Barr sex test: this test requires a sample of cells to be scraped from the inside of a woman's cheek to determine the presence of a Barr body (sex chromatin). If the count drops below a minimum percentage, the athlete is disqualified. Some believe this to be a form of *discrimination* against women in the world of sport, as men do not have to undergo a similar test.

basal metabolic rate (BMR): the minimum amount of *energy* that the body requires to sustain life in a resting individual. It is the amount of energy the human body would expend during a 24-hour period of sleep. The main determinant of BMR is body weight and *body composition*. An individual's BMR is typically measured under standardised conditions in a laboratory after a full night's sleep where the subject is rested and relaxed and ideally having fasted for the previous 12 hours. However, this is not the most practical method so the *Harris-Benedict equation* can be used to estimate a subject's BMR.

In order to calculate an individual's approximate BMR, the following information is needed:

- sex of the subject
- weight in kilograms
- height in centimetres
- age of the subject.

Men: $BMR = 66 + (13.7 \times \text{weight in kg}) + (5 \times \text{height in cm}) - (6.8 \times \text{age in years})$
Women: $BMR = 655 + (9.6 \times \text{weight in kg}) + (1.7 \times \text{height in cm}) - (4.7 \times \text{age in years})$

baseball: an *innings game* thought to have evolved from the game of rounders. It began as a working-class sport and developed in inner cities in the USA, and as such it has similar roots to football in England. The game shares the characteristics of all the dominant *American sports*. The rules were written around 1845 and the New York Knickerbockers are generally considered to be the first organised team. It developed from a polite amateur game into a commercialised pastime, controlled by promoters and played by professionals in urban areas where there was a need for a mass of people to be entertained. Major and minor leagues developed, as did *Little League* and Babe Ruth Leagues for youngsters.

basketball: a fluid, individualistic type of *invasion game*, created by James Naismith in 1891 through his work with the American *Young Men's Christian Association*. The aim was to channel young men's energies and develop their moral character through a game based on skill rather than strength in order to give an *equal opportunity* to each player. The *YMCA* and US servicemen spread the game across the world. The International Amateur Basketball Federation was established in 1932 and it became an Olympic sport in 1936. The professional National Basketball Association in America achieved major league status in 1949. It is now accepted as one of the most popular *spectator sports* in the world and has become a symbol of black identity and black social power.

bathing machines were used at the seaside for people to change their clothing. Either a man or a horse then pulled them to the water's edge for people to modestly slip into the sea. They made their first appearance in Scarborough in 1753, reflecting the growing popularity of sea bathing, and were replaced by bathing tents or huts at the turn of the twentieth century.

behaviourist theories of learning: see *associationist theories of learning*.

Bem sex role inventory (BSRI): measures the 'masculine' and 'feminine' traits of our *personality* which are not linked simply to our biological sex. The original test consisted of 60 characteristics, completed on a 1–7 rating scale, of which 20 are typically feminine (e.g. loyal, gentle), 20 typically male (seek challenge, aggressive) and 20 neutral. These have been reduced to 30 items. The results indicate if we are masculine (low feminine, high masculine scores), feminine (high feminine, low masculine scores), androgynous (high feminine, high masculine scores) or undifferentiated (low feminine, low masculine scores). Research suggested those who succeed in sport have been found to possess higher masculine or androgynous traits.

Bergman-Österberg, Martina was appointed Lady Superintendent of Physical Education in 1881 for the London School Board. She brought with her from Sweden a belief in *Swedish gymnastics* with its focus on health and posture allied with a diet of English games such as *hockey, cricket* and *lacrosse*. She established the first teacher training college in 1885 at Broadhurst Gardens, later moving to Dartford Heath in 1895.

Bernoulli effect: a concept that uses fluid dynamics (air and water) to explain why projectiles and aeroplanes can remain in flight. An aerofoil, such as the wing of an aeroplane, is shaped so that air flowing over the top of it must travel further than that flowing underneath, and this air must therefore increase in velocity in order to reach the back of the wing at the same time as the air on the bottom. As velocity increases, pressure decreases. A pressure differential exists between the upper and lower surfaces and a **lift force** results from high to low pressure which keeps the plane in flight. This is the Bernoulli effect.

The Bernoulli effect also explains how projectiles such as the javelin and discus remain in flight. By changing the shape of a projectile and the angle of attack, the size of the lift force can be altered.

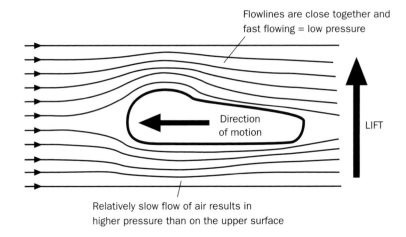

Flowlines are close together and fast flowing = low pressure

Direction of motion

LIFT

Relatively slow flow of air results in higher pressure than on the upper surface

A downward lift force can be created by manipulating the shape of the aerofoil and has been used to good effect in Formula 1 racing to allow cars to corner at speed.

Best Value: central government's agenda for modernising **local authorities** focuses on the need to make changes to the ways local authorities:
- communicate with local people
- structure and organise themselves
- seek and deliver services.

Best Value is the way local government measures, manages and improves performance. Best Value can apply to a service or a department.

Sport is one of these services. Best Value impacts on **Sport England**'s work as local authorities constitute one of its most important partnerships. The main aim of Best Value is to improve the cost and quality of local services.

The publication 'The Value of Sport' responds to the challenge and demonstrates that sport can make a difference to people's lives and to communities in which they live. It emphasises that for every pound spent on sport there are multiple returns in improved health, reduced crime, neighbourhood regeneration and improved employment opportunities.

beta blockers: **drugs** such as atenolol and oxprenolol which can be used by sport performers to steady nerves, and are useful for activities requiring **fine skills** such as shooting. They reduce the heart rate and **blood pressure** to relax nerves and stop trembling. The side effects are low blood pressure, slow heart rate and tiredness.

beta oxidation: the first step of **fatty acid** oxidation, whereby fatty acids are broken down to acetic acid before being converted to **acetylcoenzyme A** and entering the **Krebs cycle**.

Beta oxidation is used when performing low-intensity **aerobic** exercise such as jogging or cycling since more energy can be acquired from **fat** than **glycogen** and exercise can be performed for a longer period of time. However, fatty acid oxidation must occur in conjunction with **glycolysis**, because the poor solubility of fat in the blood stream makes its transportation slow.

bicarbonate ions form part of the body's **buffering** system, which helps in the removal of **lactic acid** during and following high intensity exercise. The blood is particularly efficient at buffering lactic acid due to the bicarbonate ions produced by the kidneys. These ions absorb hydrogen ions from the lactic acid to form carbonic acid, which is eventually degraded to form carbon dioxide and water, both of which are eliminated via the lungs.

FORMULA:

$$H^+ \quad + \quad HCO_3^- \quad \rightarrow \quad H_2CO_3 \rightarrow H_2O \quad + \quad CO_2$$

From lactic acid   Bicarbonate ion   Carbonic aid   Water   Carbon dioxide

Indeed, some athletes seek to improve their buffering capacity by **soda loading**, which involves drinking bicarbonate of soda an hour or so before an event. The idea here is to increase the concentration of bicarbonate ions in the blood and therefore make the removal of lactic acid more effective. Although evidence suggests that performance may be improved through this practice, side effects include vomiting and diarrhoea.

Big Four: the dominant sports in the USA: **American football**, **baseball**, **basketball** and **ice hockey**.

Big Time programmes: sport programmes for the American **collegiate** system. Huge incentives can distract athletes from academic work and are characterised by **commercialism**, poor rights for athletes and distorted views of **gender** and race. These are high profile sports with **scholarships** and entertainment values.

bilateral transfer: see *transfer of learning*.

bioelectric impedance: a test to measure **body composition**. The performer has an electrical current passed through their body and the resistance is recorded. The higher the reading, the higher the level of body **fat**, as fat does not conduct the current effectively. This test is particularly important for assessing the percentage of body fat of an athlete.

biofeedback: a measurement of the body's muscular reaction to **stress** using **objective** techniques to help control stress levels. The performer is made aware of the physiological responses occurring and employs suitable techniques to calm themselves. The effectiveness of this can be viewed immediately and accurately. Eventually, the performer can recognise the physiological changes taking place without the aid of the machinery and implement the **stress management** techniques they have learnt during competition. Commonly used methods are:

- galvanic skin response – measures the skin's electrical conductivity when sweating. If tense, more sweat is produced to remove the heat generated by the muscles
- electromyography (EMG) – measures muscle tension via a series of electrodes taped to the skin, emitting a louder sound when tension is high
- skin temperature – thermometers attached to the skin measure the temperature, which is lower during times of stress.

The disadvantages of these methods include the *interference* with performance of being 'wired-up', increased *arousal* due to being evaluated and the difficulty of using them in actual competitive situations.

biomechanics: the branch of sport science that uses mathematics and *Newton's laws of motion* to explain movement. Central to the study of biomechanics is a grounding in human anatomy and a sound understanding of Newton's laws and how to apply them to human movement. An understanding of biomechanics is essential for a coach in order to optimise an individual's performance and adjust their technique. For example, a sprinter can improve their starting technique if they understand how to exert forces in the most efficient way.

Bisham Abbey National Sports Centre: see *national sports centres*.

blocked practice involves the performer completing a set number of practices of one skill before progressing to the next skill. There is minimal *interference* from other activities to hinder learning, allowing full concentration on the specified skill. For example, a golfer will hit a set number of shots with one club during a practice session before moving on to a new club. Although this method improves performance at the time, it can have limited effect in terms of long-term learning as the golfer may not be able to reproduce the shots on the actual course. As a result, the use of random practice may be more effective.

blood doping: the removal and reinfusion of a person's blood to improve the *aerobic capacity* by increasing the numbers of red blood cells and thus increasing the blood's oxygen carrying capacity. There is a danger of increasing the viscosity of the blood (*hyperviscosity*) and 'overcrowding' the capillaries, thus blocking them, which can lead to heart failure. (See also *doping*.)

blood pressure: the force exerted by the blood against the walls of the blood vessels. It is measured using a sphygmomanometer and is usually expressed as:

$$FORMULA:\ \text{Blood pressure} = \frac{\text{systolic pressure}}{\text{diastolic pressure}}$$

and recorded as millimetres of mercury (mm Hg). Systolic pressure refers to the pressure experienced when the heart pumps blood out into the *arteries*, and diastolic pressure to the pressure in the arteries when the heart is relaxing and filling with blood. During exercise the blood pressure changes are dependent on the type and intensity of exercise being performed. During rhythmic, *aerobic* exercise the blood pressure may not alter significantly, but when periods of high intensity exercise are undertaken, such as weightlifting, the systolic and diastolic pressure rise significantly.

blood sports involve the infliction of pain or death on animals for the purpose of entertainment. They were popular in Britain up to the end of the nineteenth century and were characterised by:
- physical violence
- *gambling*
- enjoyment of the infliction of pain
- their popularity in rural and urban areas among both the *working class* and the *gentry*.

They were popular for a variety of reasons, including:
- the excitement generated, particularly as there was limited other entertainment
- the incentive of winning money was attractive

- they were cheap and accessible
- the general *culture* was violent so the concern for the welfare of animals was not of paramount importance.

Blood sports were banned in 1840 when the new era of evangelical and humanitarian concern resulted in a general *civilising process* and *urbanisation* stimulated new concepts of *recreation*. (See also *animal sports*, *coursing*, *field sports* and *fox hunting*.)

Blue: a term used at Oxford and Cambridge universities where sport performers were awarded a 'colour' for representing the team in their annual derby fixture. In the nineteenth century, 'Blues' often returned to the *public schools* as teachers to assist in the coaching of sporting activities. An old Rugbeian, Robert Collis, described the receiving of a 'Blue' as being regarded as 'a more desirable achievement than becoming a Member of Parliament. The social position it confers lasts for many years, for to be an "old Blue" is to have an assured status for life'.

BMI: see *body mass index*.

Board of Education: the government department set up to deal with the implementation of compulsory *state education* in the nineteenth century, following the Forster Education Act 1870 (see *Education Acts*). The medical division was established in 1908 in order to oversee the physical welfare of children and it was responsible for devising the *Syllabuses of Physical Training* from 1909 to 1933. The schools under their control were known as 'board schools' or 'elementary schools'.

body composition: the chemical composition of the body; typically the relative amounts of *fat* mass and fat-free mass (which includes non-fat tissues such as bone, muscle and connective tissues). It is usually measured via skin-fold tests or *bioelectric impedance*. The relative amounts of fat and fat-free mass required for different activities differ depending on the type of activity concerned. For example, activities that require strength and *muscular endurance*, such as rowing, would benefit from an increased amount of fat-free mass (muscle), while endurance athletes would not benefit from increased muscle mass as this represents a greater load to carry over longer distances.

body mass index (BMI) is used as an indicator of *obesity*. It is calculated by dividing the body mass (weight in kg) by the height of the individual squared:

$$FORMULA: \quad BMI = \frac{weight\ (kg)}{height\ (m)^2}$$

It is assumed that the higher the BMI, the greater the level of 'adiposity' or *fat*. BMI categories are:
- underweight: < 18.5
- normal weight: 18.5 to 24.9
- overweight: 25 to 29.9
- obese: 30 to 39.9
- morbidly obese (see *morbid obesity*): > 40.

Boer War: a war that took place in South Africa between 1899 and 1902. The reasons for the failure of the British army were considered to be the lack of fitness, discipline and poor general health of the *working class* and these factors were blamed for the heavy loss of life. *Swedish gymnastics* was criticised as not being effective enough in improving the fitness of the working classes sufficiently for the hardships of war. Following the Boer War in 1902, Colonel Fox of the War Office initiated the *model course*.

Bohr effect: an increase in temperature and a lowering of the blood pH level due to increased levels of CO_2 which causes oxygen to be released more readily from *haemoglobin*. This results in the oxygen–haemoglobin dissociation curve shifting to the right.

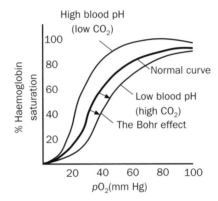

The oxygen–haemoglobin dissociation curve

Book of Sports: a declaration by King James I to his subjects in 1618 concerning lawful sports. It was aimed at protecting the people's right to **recreation**, which was under threat from the **Puritans** who were intent on prohibiting the recreational pursuits of the commoners on Sundays and other **holy days**. James I encouraged acceptable recreations following the church service, including dancing, leaping and vaulting. He also encouraged the May games, Whitsun ales and morris dances. King Charles I reaffirmed the Book of Sports in 1663.

Borg scale: a rating of perceived exertion that can be used to assess exercise intensity. Perceived exertion is used widely by the coach and athlete during training sessions to ascertain how hard the athlete is working. It is focused on the physical feelings and sensations experienced by the performer and arises from the physiological responses of the body such as muscle **fatigue**, sweating response, heart rate and respiratory responses. During the training session, the performer rates their level of exertion by considering their levels of effort, signs of distress and fatigue. The main advantage of assessing intensity in this way is that it is quick and easy to report and does not require any form of equipment. Although there are a number of different perceived exertion scales, the most widely used is the 15-point Borg scale (which ranges from 6 to 20), as shown in the table opposite.

A distance runner who is required to train for 40 minutes at a moderate level of intensity should be targeting levels 12–14 on the scale. If, however, he perceives his breathing and muscle fatigue to be very light (9 or 10 on the scale), it is obvious he needs to increase the intensity. If, on the other hand, the runner is breathing and sweating very heavily (17 or 18 on the scale), he may not be able to continue the activity for the entire 40 minutes and must therefore reduce the intensity so that it hits the 12–14 range on the scale.

Some studies undertaken to investigate the reliability of the Borg scale of perceived exertion have concluded that the correlation of the scale to the physiological responses of the body such as heart rate and percentage **maximum oxygen uptake (VO$_2$ max)** is quite high.

Rating	Perceived exertion
6	No exertion at all
7	Extremely light
8	
9	Very light (easy walking)
10	Light
11	
12	
13	Moderately hard (you feel tired but can continue)
14	
15	Hard
16	
17	Very hard (you feel very fatigued)
18	
19	Extremely hard (you cannot continue at this pace for much longer)
20	Maximal exertion (*exhaustion*)

Bosman case: a case brought about by the Belgian footballer, Jean Marc Bosman. The European Court of Justice recognised in this case that there was no reason why professional sports people should not enjoy the benefits of the single market and in particular the free movement of workers. This has resulted in national competitions being open to players throughout Europe and has revitalised major European leagues. The new *legislation* also abolished transfer fees if a player was out of contract.

bourgeoisie: one of *Karl Marx*'s two main *social classes* in society. They are the owners of the means of production and therefore the *ruling class* within a *capitalist* society. Economic power gives rise to political power.

bowls: a popular sport in the sixteenth century, encouraged by growth in the importance of *inns,* providing recreation for both the local community as well as travellers on the road. Bowling greens followed on from the alleys and were found suitable for private use in homes that had lawns. Bowling was prohibited in King James I's *Book of Sports* in the seventeenth century as it usually took place in alehouses and was accompanied by too much drinking.

boxing: an ancient sport enjoyed in Ancient Egypt, Greece and Rome. *Pugilism* (bare-knuckle fighting) was introduced to the *Olympic Games* in 686 BC and the sport was used in Roman times for gladiatorial *combat* (see *gladiator*).

Boxing was revived in England towards the end of the seventeenth century with the first organised bare-knuckle fight taking place in 1681. There were initially very few rules and even kicking was allowed. However, boxing was one of the first sports to have a code of rules, and London aristocrats, London publicans and *patrons* arranged early national championships. Two key figures helped shape the sport: James Figg, who opened an Academy of Boxing, and Jack Broughton, known as the 'father of boxing', who added respectability to the sport that led to the London Prize Ring Rules being drawn up in

1838. These rules later became known as the Marquis of Queensbury Rules. Working-class boxers often received patronage from the upper class and became folk heroes.

boycott: the refusal of a faction to participate in a sporting event in order to deliver a political message, usually the rejection of a political regime. The Soviet Union boycott of the Los Angeles *Olympic Games* in 1984 had a large impact on the event. Some countries such as the *USA* and the old Soviet Union can refuse to allow their athletes to enter a competition, whereas others such as the UK can only advise athletes as the sporting system is relatively free from political control.

Boys' Brigade: founded in Glasgow in 1883 by William Alexander Smith. The aim was to revive interest in organised religion through the provision of military-style training and uniforms. Sporting activities played an important part in countering the attraction of less socially acceptable forms of behaviour. This was part of a wider movement during the nineteenth century to promote *rational recreation* with middle class values to inner-city working-class youth. Sport in this instance was used as a vehicle of *social control* and Christian recruitment, but was popular among the working class youth who had little alternative recreation provision. Smith believed that 'by associating Christianity with all that was most noble and manly in a boy's sight, we would be going a long way to disabuse his mind of the idea that there is anything effeminate or weak about Christianity'. (See also *youth movements*.)

bradycardia literally means 'slow heart'. In exercise physiology, the term is used to denote a resting heart rate of below 60 beats per minute. It occurs largely as a result of long-term endurance training and the accompanying enlargement of the heart (*cardiac hypertrophy*). Essentially a larger heart can pump more blood around the body per beat, and therefore the heart does not need to beat as often per minute to get the equivalent amount of blood to the tissues while at rest.

bread and circuses: a theory which suggests that the mass of a population can be kept relatively content through having basic needs and entertainment provided. A cynical viewpoint may be that sporting activities can be used by governments to divert attention from social problems by channelling people's energies into a more socially acceptable form.

Brighton Declaration on Women and Sport: this occurred in May 1984 when sport policy and decision makers at both national and international level met. It was organised by the British Sports Council (now *Sport England*) and supported by the *British Olympic Association*, with 82 countries taking part. Based on discussions, the following points were developed:
- *equal opportunities* should be developed through policies and programmes
- facilities should take into account the needs of women
- physical education programmes need to take into account the needs of girls
- *elite* women should receive similar encouragement in terms of competitive opportunities, *rewards*, incentives and recognition as their male counterparts
- research and information should reflect women's involvement.

British Academy of Sport: see *UK Sports Institute*.

British Empire: a term used to describe the colonisation of many other countries by Britain. British imperialists believed they had a duty to spread their forms of government, religion and *culture,* including their sporting activities, to those nations they considered less advanced or civilised. Numerous groups of people were involved, such as soldiers, administrators, missionaries, engineers and businessmen. Occasionally, a sport was imported to Britain from a member country of the British Empire, for example British soldiers imported polo, with the first match played in England in 1871.

British Olympic Association: a National Olympic Committee (NOC). The *International Olympic Committee* requires each country to have its own Olympic committee. The British Olympic Association (BOA) is one of 205 NOCs currently recognised by the International Olympic Committee.

The BOA provides the pivot around which *Team GB* revolves prior to and during the Olympic Games. Working with the Olympic *governing bodies*, the BOA selects Team GB from the best sportsmen and women who will go on to compete in the 28 summer and 7 winter Olympic sports at the greatest sporting competition in the world.

The BOA now includes as its members the 35 national governing bodies of each Olympic sport. It is free from government control and traditionally receives no money from the government. Its aims are to:

- encourage interest in the *Olympic Games*
- foster the ideals of the Olympic movement
- organise and coordinate British participation in terms of travel and equipment of competitors and officials
- assist the governing bodies of sport in preparation of their competitions
- advise on public relations with the press
- provide a forum for consultation among governing bodies
- organise an Olympic day in the UK
- raise funds through the British Olympic appeal, mainly from private sources, business sponsors and the general public
- advise on training, nutrition and sports psychology for Olympic coaches
- provide medical and careers advice for athletes
- sponsor medical research into fitness and athletic injuries.

The BOA runs various programmes and facilities to meet the needs of Team GB athletes throughout the four-year Olympic cycle. Explore the links from the Athletes' Area of the BOA website at www.olympics.org.uk.

British Paralympic Association: the organisation responsible for selecting, preparing, entering, funding and managing British teams which compete at the *Paralympic Games* and Paralympic Winter Games. It was created following the Seoul Games in South Korea, as a more permanent structure was required. Its specific tasks are:

- to create the best possible environment for the Games
- to develop competitive standards through increased training opportunities via facilities and trained staff
- to raise sufficient funds to finance Britain's participation at international events
- to establish a clear policy framework for the ongoing tasks of the organisation and to represent Britain at international meetings and conferences.

The British Paralympic Association liaises with the National Disability Sport Organisations, the Sport Foundation, the International Paralympic Association, the *British Olympic Association, Sport England* and *Disability Sport England*. Its main focus is on *excellence* rather than *grass roots* development.

British Sports Association for the Disabled: see *Disability Sport England*.

British Sports Trust is the charitable arm of the *Central Council of Physical Recreation*. It was set up in 1989 to help in the development of sporting volunteers and leaders. This is significant as *volunteers* in the UK run most *governing bodies* and their *clubs*. The Trust trains people from all walks of life to be leaders in their community by developing the skills of leadership such as communication skills, planning and organisation and the ability to motivate others. In 1998, 43,000 people were trained, mainly between the ages of 14 and 25 via the Sports Leader Awards.

broken-time payments: payments made to compensate working-class players for loss of earnings while playing sports such as soccer and rugby union football. This tended to lead to professionalism in some sports and was looked down on by the *gentleman amateurs*.

Brundage, Avery: president of the *International Olympic Committee* from 1952 to 1972. The impact of Brundage on the Olympic movement was enormous. He had to see the *Olympic Games* through many turbulent years including the controversies over the state-sponsored amateurs of the Soviet Union; the expulsion of *South Africa* in 1972; the *International Olympic Committee*'s recognition of Taiwan as the Republic of China, isolating the People's Republic of China until 1984. He tried to steer sport clear of politics and his philosophy was:

- the Olympic Games should remain amateur
- the Olympic movement should not embrace *commercialism*
- women's role in the Olympics should be reduced
- the Olympic Games should not seek a global impact
- South Africa should not be excluded.

However, on one point he did accede – the need for television to boost the coffers by *advertising* the Olympic movement – and as a result 'rule 49' came into being. Any televised coverage of the Olympic Games exceeding 3 minutes of news briefs aired three times a day would have to be bought. He was therefore much more popular with conservatives than those with more liberal viewpoints.

BSRI: see *Bem sex role inventory*.

buffering: the process by which chemicals can maintain pH values within acceptable limits in the body and neutralise the effects of an acid such as *lactic acid*. Removal of lactic acid also relies on the buffering capacity of the body, especially the blood, which weakens and neutralises the effect of lactic acid. The blood is fairly efficient at buffering lactic acid due to the hydrogen carbonate ion produced by the kidneys. This absorbs hydrogen ions from the lactic acid and forms carbonic acid, which is eventually degraded to form carbon dioxide and water, both of which are eliminated via the lungs.

FORMULA: $H^+ + HCO_3^- \rightarrow H_2CO_3 \rightarrow H_2O + CO_2$

Indeed, some athletes seek to improve their buffering capacity by *soda loading*, which involves drinking bicarbonate of soda an hour or so before an event. The idea here is to increase the concentration of *bicarbonate ions* in the blood and therefore make the removal of lactic acid more effective. Although evidence suggests that performance may be improved through this practice, side effects include vomiting and diarrhoea.

Training with small amounts of lactic acid in the system may also improve the resistance and buffering capacity of the body. By improving blood flow to the muscle, the body becomes more efficient at moving lactic acid from the muscle into the blood, which can degrade it and prevent the associated fatiguing effects.

burnout: the progressive loss of energy and enthusiasm for an activity due to continuous high levels of *stress* created by that activity. Often the performer experiences physiological and psychological *exhaustion* as well as a reduction in their performance levels. For example, a talented young athlete may devote their spare time for several years to developing their performance. However, they either stop participating before fulfilling their potential, becoming disillusioned and fatigued with the effort of training and competing at a consistently high level, or still compete but at a significantly lower level than previously.

bursae: small sacs of *synovial fluid* located at *friction* points, usually around joints. Their function during exercise is to lubricate joints and ease joint movement, for example the prepatellar bursa of the knee joint allows *flexion* and *extension* to occur smoothly. Bursae enable people to perform all actions used in sport where stress is imposed upon the body such as running, jumping, kicking and throwing.

bush culture: the outback has an iconic status in Australian life as being uniquely Australian and was a big step forward for Australians in their steps towards self-identity. The skills of indigenous people in 'the bush', especially their tracking abilities, was seen as miraculous and became legendary in the minds of European Australians. The bush was a symbol for a national life and yet, by 1910, most Australians were urban. The idea of the bush as integral to Australian identity was reinforced in 1958 when Russel Ward published *The Australian Legend*. He argued that traits such as mateship, anti-authoritarianism, swearing and hard drinking came from the frontier experiences of real bush workers.

Butler Education Act: see *Education Acts*.

A–Z Online

Log on to A–Z Online to search the database of terms, print revision lists and much more. Go to **www.philipallan.co.uk/a-zonline** to get started.

caffeine: a mild *stimulant* that occurs naturally and is predominantly found in coffee, tea and colas. It is probably the most widely available and accessible pharmacological aid. Until 2004, caffeine was listed as a banned substance by the *World Anti-Doping Agency*, as its consumption was deemed to give performers an unfair advantage. Some studies cite that caffeine reduces the athlete's perception of muscle *fatigue* and results in an increased ability of the muscle to mobilise and utilise *fat* as a fuel. Consequently, caffeine is deemed to be of particular benefit to endurance performers such as runners and cyclists.

Advantages (perceived benefits)	Disadvantages (associated health risks)
Enhanced nervous stimulation	Caffeine is a diuretic and can therefore promote *dehydration*
Increased levels of concentration	
Increases endurance capacity by promoting the release of *adrenaline*, which increases the strength of muscular contraction and dilates respiratory structures	Possible sleep deprivation
	Muscle and abdominal cramping
Promotes *glycogen* sparing by metabolising more *fatty acids*	

camps: places where specialist groups such as the Scouts or school groups erect tents, cabins or other temporary structures for their own use. (See also *American summer camps*.)

cancellous bone is also known as spongy bone. It lies beneath and inside *compact bone* with a honeycomb or trabecular appearance. This criss-cross matrix of bony plates is developed along lines of stress on the bones and is constantly reorganised in response to the altering lines of stress. For example, the lines of stress alters when an infant starts to walk as opposed to crawl. Exercise can strengthen bones by laying down new bony plates.

capillary: a microscopic blood vessel that connects *arterioles* and venules. Capillaries are found near most cells in the body, but particularly those that require more oxygen and nutrients such as the muscles, liver and kidneys. The capillary wall consists of a single layer of endothelial cells, which permits the exchange of nutrients and waste between the blood and tissues. This is aided by the very small diameter of the vessel which squeezes the blood cell out of shape, increasing the surface area which can pick up oxygen.
  Aerobic training can cause an increase in the number of capillaries surrounding each fibre (up to 15%), allowing a greater exchange of gases, waste and nutrients between the blood and the working muscles.

capitalism: an *economic system* based on free trade and private ownership of the means of production, property and capital. The focus on maximising profits has, some would argue, led to the development of the 'good life', while others claim that the single scale of success, namely monetary values, can alienate many within a population. The *USA* is a typical example of a capitalist society. *Professional sport* in particular shares some of the characteristics of capitalism, having a heavy competitive emphasis on winning and offering *rewards* that are mostly materialistic.

carbo-loading: see *glycogen loading*.

carbohydrate: an organic compound containing carbon, hydrogen and oxygen. The hydrogen and oxygen *atoms* are usually found in a two-to-one ratio, for example glucose has the formula $C_6H_{12}O_6$. Carbohydrates (which are stored in the liver and muscles) are vital to sports performers, as they are the body's most readily available source of *energy*. They are also essential for the efficient functioning of the nervous system and the metabolism of *fat*. Ideally, an athlete's diet should consist of approximately 60% carbohydrate, which can be found in bread, pasta, rice and potatoes. Some performers seek to increase the stores within the body through *glycogen loading*.

carbon monoxide: a chief ingredient of cigarette smoke, carbon monoxide has an affinity for *haemoglobin* 250 times that of oxygen. Consequently carbon monoxide binds preferentially and monopolises haemoglobin, restricting the transport of oxygen in the body and reducing its availability to the muscles and tissues. The net effect of this is to cause the heart to work harder in an attempt to compensate for the reduced volume of oxygen reaching the muscles. Cigarette smoke can also cause an increase in the production of the blood's clotting agent fibrinogen, resulting in the increased viscosity of the blood (*hyperviscosity*) which further impedes the transportation of oxygen and can increase the incidence of the blood clotting.

cardiac cycle: the sequence of events that takes place during one complete heart beat. This includes the filling of the heart during the diastolic phase and the emptying of the heart into the arterial system during the systolic phase. Each cycle lasts approximately 0.8 seconds and occurs on average 72 times per minute. Through *cardiac hypertrophy* athletes can reduce the amount of times this occurs per minute largely due to an extended diastolic phase. There are four stages to each heart beat:
1 atrial *diastole*
2 ventricular diastole
3 atrial *systole*
4 ventricular systole.
(See diagram overleaf.)

cardiac hypertrophy: the *hypertrophy* (enlargement) of the heart due to the effects of training. Like *skeletal muscle*, cardiac tissue adapts as a result of training and cardiac hypertrophy is characterised by a larger ventricular wall and a thicker *myocardium*. Endurance athletes tend to display larger ventricular cavities, while those following high-resistance or *strength training* regimes display thicker ventricular walls. Cardiac hypertrophy is usually accompanied by a decrease in resting heart rate known as *bradycardia*.

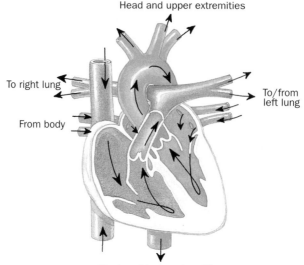

Head and upper extremities

To right lung

To/from
left lung

From body

Trunk and lower extremities

Semilunar
valves closed

Semilunar
valves open

Atrial
systole

Atrial
diastole
(atria fill
with blood)

Ventricular
diastole

Ventricular
systole
(ventricles
pump
blood into
arteries)

Atrioventricular
valves closed

Atrioventricular
valves open

The cardiac cycle

cardiac output: the volume of blood pumped from one ventricle of the heart in 1 minute.
It is equal to the product of **stroke volume** and heart rate:

  FORMULA: Cardiac output = stroke volume × heart rate

During periods of exercise, the cardiac output needs to increase to meet the demands of the
body and can rise from approximately 5 litres per minute up to 40 litres per minute. A performer
who follows a structured training programme often experiences **cardiac hypertrophy**, which is
the enlargement of the heart which in turn increases maximum cardiac output during exercise.

cardiovascular diseases: disorders of the heart and circulatory system commonly
associated with risk factors including smoking, **obesity**, hypertension (high **blood
pressure**) and lack of exercise. The diagram shows the long-term pattern of development
of atherosclerosis and arteriosclerosis. The benefits of exercise in the prevention of such

diseases are well documented. Any health-related exercise programme should involve some form of continuous or **aerobic** activity which exercises large muscle groups and is performed at low intensity (approximately 50% of **maximum heart rate**). Non-weight-bearing or partial weight-bearing activities such as swimming or cycling are ideal but brisk walking or light jogging would also be appropriate.

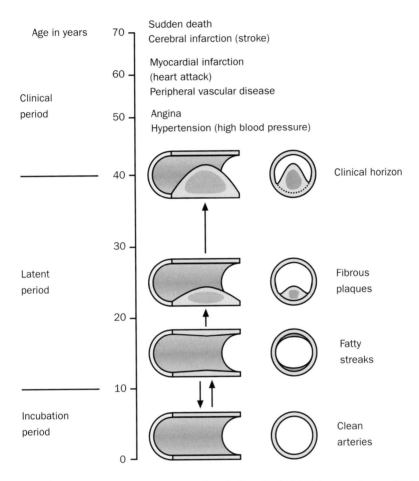

cardiovascular drift: the phenomenon whereby heart rate 'drifts' upwards over time despite the performer working at a constant rate. Cardiovascular drift typically occurs in warmer environments and is thought to link to the sweating response of the body and the associated redistribution of blood to the peripheral circulatory system (i.e. to the skin). Sweating reduces the volume of blood returning to the heart, which has the knock-on effect of reducing **stroke volume** (see **Starling's law of the heart**). The heart rate increases to compensate for the reduced stroke volume in order to maintain **cardiac output** at constant levels. **Dehydration** by 3–5% of body weight during exercise also reduces blood volume by approximately 3–5%. To reduce the effects of cardiovascular drift, whatever exercise being performed it is essential to remain hydrated in order to maintain blood volume.

cartilage: firm, resilient connective tissue, consisting of cells (chondrocytes) that exist in small spaces (lacunae) within a matrix. Cartilage is 'avascular', meaning that it does not have a blood supply and receives nutrition via diffusion from the *capillary* network outside the tissue. All bones begin as cartilage in the developing foetus and it gradually develops into solid bone. There are three basic types of cartilage:

- Hyaline/articular cartilage – found in joints at the articulation between two bones. It protects the bone tissue from wear and tear, reducing *friction* between the moving bones. Exercise can cause a thickening of hyaline cartilage.
- White fibrocartilage – a much tougher tissue found in areas of the body where high amounts of stress are imposed. For example, the semi-lunar discs of the knee joint and the intervertebral discs of the vertebral column are composed of fibrocartilage, acting as a shock absorber, particularly during exercise.
- Yellow elastic cartilage – a much more pliable tissue that offers structure to some body parts such as the ears and the nose.

cartilaginous joints: joints where the bones are linked by tough, fibrous *cartilage* and no *synovial fluid* is present. The joints are stable and possess large shock-absorbing properties, allowing only a small amount of movement. For example, the intervertebral discs between the lumber vertebrae enable *flexion*, *extension* and *lateral* flexion of the trunk.

catastrophe theory suggests that an increase in *cognitive state anxiety* will improve performance at low levels of physiological *arousal*, but will have a negative effect on performance at high levels of physiological arousal – a catastrophe. Hardy and Frazey (1987) modified the *inverted U theory*, suggesting if both cognitive and somatic anxiety are high the performance will deteriorate rapidly. For example, during training a badminton player will have low levels of arousal and complete shots successfully, but in a competition they may become over-aroused causing a dramatic reduction in performance, including loss of concentration, ineffective decisions and poor execution of shots. The player must take time to recover from this position and return to an optimum level of arousal or their performance may continue to deteriorate.

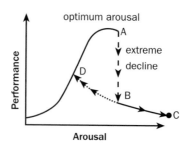

Point A – over-arousal – threshold of catastrophe

Point B – arousal level after catastrophe

Point C – continued deterioration of performance

Point D – recovery of arousal levels and gradual return to optimum arousal.

catharsis: the release of *aggression* in a positive manner, causing a reduction in levels of frustration. Instinct theory suggests this can be achieved through participation in or observation of physical activity. For example, an individual may become frustrated at work but after completing a run when they return home feel calmer. However, rather than having a cathartic effect, *social learning theory* suggests observation of some aggressive acts can lead to repetition of those actions.

Cattell's 16 personality factors questionnaire measures 16 personality *traits* of an individual, each scored on a 1–10 scale. Developed from the *Eysenck's personality inventory*, Cattell acknowledged personality was dynamic, depending on motivational, emotional and situational factors.

centering: a breathing technique used to control levels of tension before or during competition. It involves the performer relaxing the chest and shoulder muscles, then focusing on the movement of the abdominal muscles while taking slow, deep breaths. The technique is beneficial as it can redirect *attention*, can be performed anywhere and if practised can be completed quickly and privately.

Central Council of Physical Recreation: established in 1935, this organisation is the independent voice for sport in the UK.
- It promotes and protects the interests of its members – the *governing bodies* of sport.
- It represents the interests of anyone who plays sport, at any level in numerous activities.
- Most governing bodies and their clubs are run by volunteers, who are now supported by the *British Sports Trust*.

The Central Council of Physical Recreation (CCPR) liaises across a wide range of sporting activities and has divided them into six divisions:
- games and sports
- outdoor pursuits
- major *spectator sports*
- water recreation
- movement and dance
- interested organisations.

The CCPR advises the government and its agencies such as the *Department for Culture, Media and Sport* on the best possible policies for sport. It is involved in issues ranging from physical education in schools and the sale of playing fields through to *sponsorship* matters and broadcasting rights. It is financed from five main sources:
- subscriptions and donations
- industry and commerce
- sponsorship
- sales of publications and research finding
- contractual support from *Sport England*.

central nervous system: consists of the brain and spinal cord and is responsible for the *coordination* and control of the nervous system. Messages are sent to all regions of the body, including the *autonomic nervous system*, which controls the heart rate of the performer.

centralised means to draw under central control – the central government directs policy across a country. State *legislation* coordinates and supports policies, such as an education curriculum. Although the UK is not centralised, the *National Curriculum* brought in after the Education Reform Act 1988 (see *Education Acts*) was a move towards more centralisation of control over the *education* system. (See table overleaf.)

Centralisation

Advantages of centralisation	Disadvantages of centralisation
Provides uniformity of experience	Can be rigid and inflexible
Is a coordinated system	May not cater for different local needs
Funded by the government	Can be difficult to monitor the system effectively, particularly in large countries
	Can reduce the initiative of individuals

(See also **decentralised**.)

centrality: a theory highlighted by Grusky that can be seen in a game such as baseball where black people tend to occupy the outfield positions despite the fact that there used to be a very successful black baseball league. It was when white owners moved in that the status of black players began to change. They believed that the more central positions required skills such as strategic thinking, decision-making and closer social interaction and that therefore these positions were more suitable for white players. In other words, the **dominant culture** has determined the access and opportunities available, and challenging these ideological factors takes time.

centre of mass: the point at which all weight tends to be concentrated, signifying that the object or body is balanced in all directions (see **balance**). The centre of mass may be fixed, such as in a shot putt, or may move, as in humans when limbs change position. Knowledge of this can allow performers to optimise their techniques and maximise their efficiency of movement. For example, the centre of mass of a high jumper when performing the Fosbury flop technique actually passes underneath the bar, meaning it does not need to be raised as high as when performing other high jump techniques such as the Western roll. An individual will remain balanced if the centre of mass remains over the base of support, for example when performing a handstand.

centres of excellence: high-class sporting facilities that are intended primarily for developing **elite** performers but which can also be used by other sporting groups. They tend to specialise in a few areas and athletes come to them for training and support. They usually have excellent facilities, high-class coaches, financial support with sport science and medical support. A prime example would be the **National Sport Centres**.

cervical vertebrae: the top seven bones of the vertebral column, which support the weight of the head by enabling muscle attachment through the spinous process. The top two vertebrae, the atlas and axis, enable the head to move up and down and side to side respectively. (See appendix, pages 316–17.)

chaining: see **progressive part-method practice**.

Champion Coaching: see **National Junior Sports Programme**.

channelled aggression: this form of aggression involves behaviour that is within the rules of the activity and aims to successfully complete the skill but has the side-effect of inflicting harm or physical pain. For example, a rugby player will attempt to tackle an opponent legally but also as physically as possible. (See also **aggression** and **assertive behaviour**.)

character building: often referred to as a desirable outcome from participation in sporting activities. This was a widely held belief in the nineteenth century in relation to **athleticism**. Some examples of desirable character values were:

- leadership and response to leadership
- *cooperation*
- courage and bravery
- commitment to a team
- self-discipline and loyalty.

cheerleading is primarily a female role in today's **American sports** system. It is a cosmetic role which many believe perpetuates a **stereotype** of **femininity** with its emphasis on physical appearance combined with a spectator role in sport. Cheerleaders stand on the sidelines and provide entertainment for their team and their fans, provide support for the men and fill in the breaks during the games. Selection to be a cheerleader is considered a sign of popularity and acceptance.

Chelladurai's multi-dimensional model of leadership suggests the characteristics of the situation, the leader and the group members must be considered before adopting a particular leadership style. The three types of leader behaviour that affect the outcome are:

- required behaviour – depending on the situation and task
- actual behaviour – leader's action in a situation
- preferred behaviour – what the group wants depending on its skills and goals.

The effectiveness of the leader is determined by the performance of the group and its own levels of satisfaction.

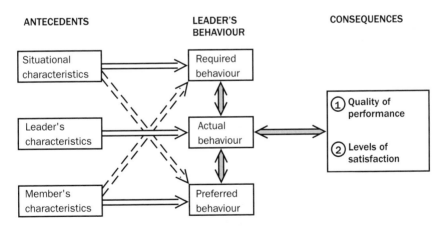

For example, a novice basketball team is about to play its first competitive game. The situational characteristics are to have fun and enjoy the game with no pressure to win. Therefore, the required behaviour is to help the players use their skills in a team situation. The members of the team are inexperienced and youthful players, so the preferred behaviour would need to provide support and encouragement to implement their skills. If the leader's actual behaviour does this, the team will enjoy the game and perform well in the match. However, as the team become older, more experienced and skilful a different approach needs to be taken if the performance is to be effective and enjoyed.

chemoreceptors: sensory cells which monitor the level of acidity of the blood. Any increase in the blood acidity (decrease in blood pH) resulting from increased carbon dioxide and *lactic acid* production will cause an increase in heart rate and ventilation rates. Chemoreceptors are sited in the aortic arch and in the carotid arteries. When exercise commences, the muscles produce carbon dioxide as a result of the breakdown of *glycogen*. Chemoreceptors detect this increase in carbon dioxide production and causes the heart to beat faster, which has two significant effects:

- increased oxygen supply to the working muscles
- disposal of carbon dioxide via the lungs.

children's sports programmes are usually copies of adult sports programmes. *Little League baseball* is an example of a well-organised sports programme for children. They are usually characterised by:

- selection
- competition
- leagues and tournaments
- modified playing areas.

Children's sports programmes are generally taken very seriously. Success is valued highly, and they are thought to be useful avenues of *socialisation*. However, several problems are associated with them, including:

- a reduction in the spontaneity and creativity of children
- they do not require the children to make their own decisions
- rule-making is externally imposed and enforced
- some of the enjoyment from sport can be lost.

choice reaction time: time taken to respond when presented with a variety of *stimuli* each with a different response. As the number of stimuli increases so does the *reaction time* (see *Hick's law*). Within a game of rugby, if a player can perform a wide range of skills, such as passing, dummying, side-stepping and kicking, their opponent will take longer to respond as they are unsure of which action will be executed. The reaction time may also be influenced by the *stimulus–response compatibility*.

chunking: a technique to increase the capacity of the *short-term memory store* by organising pieces of information together into new units or 'chunks'. For example, a free kick in a game of football will be remembered by a single number or word rather than a series of separate moves.

Church: a group of Christians who have their own beliefs and forms of worship. The clergy (Church 'employees') are distinguished from the laity (others). It has been an institutionalised form of political and *social control*.

In the early *medieval era* in England, pagan customs began to be taken over by the Church and as such were given new religious meanings. *Holy days* were put aside for feasting, which is how the word 'holiday' emerged. In many countries, towns and villages had their own special festivals and saint days, which celebrated the death of a saint. Easter is the most important feast of the Christian Church and was a time for feasting and fun. Recreations took place within a wide social pattern, and activities included *mob* football (see *mob games*), *wrestling, animal sports* and *bowls*.

After the civil war (1646) Oliver Cromwell was made Lord Protector of the Commonwealth. He allied parliamentary rule with a puritan lifestyle. Puritanism particularly objected to:

- practising sport on a Sunday
- *gambling*
- inflicting cruelty on animals
- idleness, drinking and profanity generally associates with public houses.

As many of the traditional pastimes took place after church on a Sunday they came under fierce attack from the **Puritans**.

In the eighteenth century the **Methodists** continued in the same vein as the Puritans believing the violence associated with them was against Christian principles. This was also the time when a more disciplined workforce was required to work in the large factories and mills.

The **Victorian era** brought a climate of suppressing vice and encouraging religion and virtue. However, church attendance began to decline and in an effort to restore some control over the **working class** the Church began in various ways to encourage **rational recreation** through a movement that became known as **muscular Christianity** and **youth movements** such as the **Boys' Brigade** and the Church Lads' Brigade. These movements were used to help instil religious, moral and militaristic values and to make the church a more attractive place as congregations were dwindling and hence control of the population.

circuit training: a method of training commonly used to improve strength, endurance, mobility and **aerobic** endurance. It consists of performing a series of exercises set out so that different muscle groups are worked at consecutive stations. The great benefit of circuit training is that it can allow large numbers of performers to participate, yet be easily adapted to meet the needs of individuals. Exercises can be made activity- or game-specific. Typically, circuit training is used as a general pre-season conditioning session, or to maintain fitness during the competition period.

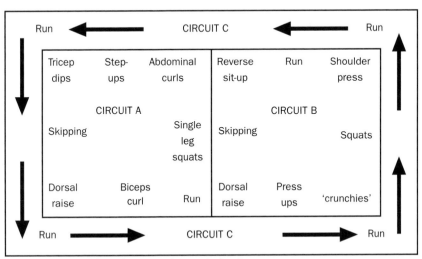

Each participant is to complete each circuit.

Circuit A = 8 exercises x 30 secs = 4 mins
Circuit B = 8 exercises x 30 secs = 4 mins
Circuit C = Run around outside = 4 mins
Repeat 2 or 3 times

Circuit training

circumduction: a *movement pattern* that is a combination of *flexion*, *extension*, *abduction* and *adduction*. It occurs at *synovial joints* where a circle can be described by the body part. True circumduction can only really occur at ball and socket joints of the shoulder and hip. For example, circumduction or at least part-circumduction occurs at the shoulder when bowling in cricket. (See appendix, page 329.)

citric acid: an intermediary product of the breakdown of glucose, produced when *acetylcoenzyme A* combines with oxaloacetic acid. In doing so the resulting citric acid molecule can be totally degraded via the *Krebs cycle* and *electron transport chain*, producing a great deal of *energy* under *aerobic* conditions (36 ATP). This method of energy production is vital to the performance of endurance-based activities and can be improved through training.

city bids: the selection of the host city is important as the success of the *Olympic Games* can often be dependent on the site chosen. Each candidate city must demonstrate to the *International Olympic Committee* that its bid to stage the world's greatest multi-disciplinary event has the support of its people and its political authorities.

Reasons why countries and cities bid for an event include:
- international recognition
- economic investment in infrastructure, tourism and attractive conference venues
- other cities in the successful country can gain through training camps
- the 'feel-good' factor for a country
- the boost to participation figures that in turn will improve the health of the population
- social *integration* and inclusion
- employment benefits
- a legacy of facilities that can be used by the community once the Games are over.

civilising process: an analysis of the evolution of human manners and the way in which changes in social structures affect an individual's *personality*, in particular how they behave towards others. Many aspects of human social behaviour, from table manners to the types of sport practised, have undergone centuries of change, increasingly requiring individuals to practise self-restraint in social situations. This process began among the *upper class* and slowly filtered down through the lower *social classes*. Codes of behaviour and *etiquette* became the *norm* and violence, which had once been a normal part of life, was controlled so that behaviour that was acceptable at one time would now be considered a form of *deviancy*.

Clarendon Commission: a government report in 1864 requiring the Commission to 'inquire into the revenues and management of certain colleges and schools and the studies pursued and the instruction given there'. The 'certain schools' referred to were the *barbarian schools*. When the report was issued, it stressed the educational importance and value of organised games for boys as agents of *character building*.

classical conditioning involves the replacement of an existing *stimulus–response bond* with a new response. Ivan Pavlov put forward his findings based on experiments with dogs and their digestive patterns in the early 1900s. He observed that dogs would salivate (unconditional response or UCR) in anticipation of the food being served (unconditional stimulus or UCS). By modifying the environment, i.e. ringing a bell (conditioned stimulus or CS) and providing food (unconditional stimulus or UCS), the dogs would still salivate (unconditional response or UCR). Over time and through repetition, the signal of the bell (conditional stimulus or CS) produced salivation (conditional response or CR) even if no food was produced.

Before conditioning	CS (bell)	→	No response
	UCS (food)	→	UCR (salivation)
During conditioning	CS + UCS	→	UCR
After conditioning	CS (bell)	→	CR (salivation)

The practical application for skill learning may include the coach giving commands at a certain time to ensure the action is completed at the correct moment, e.g. a high jumper immediately after take-off is given the instruction 'hips' to encourage them to move into the correct layout position, which will be remembered and repeated. The use of commands for *military drill* training or some aspects of *relaxation* are further examples of its use. However, the theory does not encourage the performer to understand their actions and is of limited use when teaching *complex skills*.

classification: an attempt to group sports competitors to enable fair competition. This was done by *gender* where separate competitions developed for men and women, and by weight in sports such as boxing. It is now used to include individuals with disabilities. Two types of classification have been and are used:

- Medical classification – developed in the 1940s and dominant into the 1990s. It was based on the level of spinal cord lesion. It was designed to enable individuals with similar severity of impairment to compete against one another. It was used for wheelchair and amputee athletes. Many other *disability sport* federations adopted this system resulting in a multiple classification system.
- Functional classification – an integrated classification system, which places emphasis on sport performance by disability groupings rather than by specific disability. This has enabled disability sport to move on from its original rehabilitation base to *elite*, *competition sport*. Wheelchair basketball was the first sport at the *Paralympic Games* to experiment with this system in 1992 at the Barcelona Games. This new system demands that the athletes be evaluated on what they can and cannot do in a particular sport.

Functional classification versus medical classification:

- The goal of medical classification is to enable each competitor, regardless of impairment, to compete in a fair manner with others of similar ability/disability. This causes problems of administration and logistics in dealing with numerous classes for competition.
- Functional classification provides for athletic competition based on ability, not disability. This has the tendency to eliminate the most severely affected athletes from elite competition.

classification of activities: activities can be divided into four distinct areas:

- *conditioning activities*
- competitive games and sports (see *competition sport*)
- outdoor *adventurous activities*
- *aesthetic*, movement or *gymnastic activities*.

(See also *analysis of activities*.)

classification of skills: see *skill* and *continuum*.

closed leagues have fixed numbers of teams with no relegation. This is a more stable and therefore more marketable system, common in the USA.

closed loop control: a form of *motor control* that involves the use of *feedback* to detect errors and make adjustments if required. This may occur on two levels, either sub-consciously or consciously. (See also *Adam's closed loop theory*.)

closed skills are performed in a stable, unchanging, predictable environment, which allows the performer knowledge of what is required and when. It is usually a *self-paced skill* and may be practised until the *autonomous phase of learning* is reached, e.g. gymnastic movements, athletic throwing events and weightlifting. However, some closed skills can be performed in an 'open' environment, where the position of other players may have to be considered, such as a service in a racket game or taking a penalty shot. (See also *open skills*.)

closed societies: societies in which there is little *social mobility* and individuals occupy rigid roles with virtually no opportunities to improve their social status. An example would be the Indian caste system.

clubs: groups or associations of people with common aims or interests. Sports clubs were first established in nineteenth-century England where sport was first rationalised, setting the precedent for the rest of the world. Many sports clubs are fee-paying, private institutions, usually voluntary in nature, which are affiliated to the appropriate national *governing body* for that sport. For example, a football club is affiliated to the Football Association (FA). Most sports clubs have sections for youth development, coaching, veterans and social committees. In Britain the tradition is to have single-sport clubs. In the USA there is not a strong tradition of *grass roots* development of clubs apart from the country clubs, which often operate an *exclusivity* policy.

coaching involves the instruction or training of an athlete by a qualified and experienced person. Coaches are expected to hold qualifications and have knowledge of:
- sport-specific techniques and tactics
- performance-related topics, e.g. fitness, nutrition and mental preparation
- *ethics*, philosophy and codes of practice
- management and vocational skills, e.g. planning, time and money
- teaching and coaching methodology with effective communication skills
- application to the practical coaching situation.

Coaches can be voluntary and unpaid, which is the cohort that makes up the majority of coaches in the UK, or they can coach as a full-time career. *Sports Coach UK* works with the *governing body* to raise the standards of coaching in this country. (See also *role (of the teacher/coach)*.)

coactors: individuals completing the same task as the performer, but who are not in direct competition with them. This can lead to the 'coaction effect', where the performer may be influenced by their presence, leading to *social facilitation* or *social inhibition*. For example, when training with others, a high jumper may be aware of others observing and possibly evaluating their actions, which can have a beneficial or detrimental effect on performance.

coccyx: four fused bones that form the base of the vertebral column. Its function is to act as a *process* for muscle attachment. (See appendix, page 317.)

codification: the systematic organisation of laws or rules into one recognised system or code. Codification of most sports occurred in nineteenth-century England when the foundations of modern sport were being laid. The nineteenth-century *public schools* and universities brought together the local and regional variations of traditional games and devised nationally recognised codes in order that fixtures could be played further afield to common rules.

cognition: an individual's thoughts, *attitudes* or beliefs about their behaviour and surroundings. They may be consistent, creating positive feelings (consonance) or inconsistent and in conflict with each other causing tension (*dissonance*). Cognitions are altered to change a person's attitude utilising the *cognitive dissonance theory*.

cognitive anxiety: performers' thoughts and worries concerning their perceived lack of ability to complete the task successfully caused by *stress*. The athlete often experiences feelings of nervousness, apprehension and may have difficulty concentrating before and during competition.

cognitive attitude: one of the components of the *triadic model* and refers to the performer's attitude towards an issue or *attitude object*, based on past experiences or values. For example, the performer may believe swimming is good for them and helps to keep them fit.

cognitive control: see *meditation*.

cognitive dissonance theory: a method of changing an *attitude* by creating feelings of psychological discomfort with conflicting *cognitions* within the performer. Festinger (1957) suggested the individual must experience opposing beliefs (*dissonance*) and to return to a consistent state one must become dominant. For example, an individual knows swimming is beneficial to health, but does not enjoy participating as they think it is boring, so they do not take part. To create dissonance the person may be encouraged to attend a group where the emphasis is on fun and enjoyment or linked to a new activity such as water polo. A positive attitude towards swimming may then be created. Other methods that may be employed include the use of *role models*, provision of new information and reduction in the importance of the cognitions held. (See also *persuasive communication*.)

cognitive phase of learning involves the performer gaining an understanding and creating a mental picture of the required action to form an *executive motor programme*. *Fitts and Posner's stages of learning theory* suggests this is the initial stage. Information is provided by the coach in the form of *demonstrations*, video footage, pictures, posters or verbal instruction. The performer receives extrinsic *feedback* from the coach, directing them towards specific *cues*, as they have yet to develop a full understanding of the movement requirements. The length of the phase is generally short as performers quickly retain or dismiss actions when appropriate.

cognitive re-appraisal: a method of managing *stress* by redefining the nature of the situation or the expected outcome. For example, a netball player may believe or expect to always complete the game without a single mistake and therefore worry about not achieving their aim. To overcome this *anxiety*, they could be encouraged to accept that mistakes are inevitable, be provided with performance feedback and negotiate personal short- and long-term goals.

cognitive skills: these include the performer's mental ability to solve problems, plan and make decisions, as well as their understanding of the nature of their sport. For example, tactics will be developed prior to a game, based on knowledge of the team's strength and those of the opposition. Their effectiveness will be evaluated and modified if required.

cognitive state anxiety: a performer's temporary thoughts concerning their ability to complete a specific task successfully. Recent research has shown it can be positive or negative. The athlete will often experience feelings of nervousness and apprehension, and have difficulty concentrating before and/or during competition. For example, before the start of a race or in the closing moments of a tennis match.

cognitive theories of learning: also known as insight learning or *Gestalt theory*, these theories suggest an individual learns through thinking about and understanding what is required, rather than developing a series of responses to various stimuli (see *associationist theories of learning*). The problem is solved as a whole, using previous knowledge and *perception*; no *operant conditioning* occurs. For example, a basketball player possesses the required skills to play the game but is not as effective as they could be in the game situation. The coach explains the concepts of offence and defence clearly to the player and they then understand their role within the game, and how to deploy their skills for the benefit of the team rather than just themselves. Similarly, if the player is presented with a variety of situations in training, this knowledge can be used later in the game to overcome a new problem which they may encounter.

cohesion: the dynamic process and tendency of a group of individuals to stay together and combine their efforts in order to achieve a common task, objective or goal. Cohesiveness depends on many variable factors, including the situation, member characteristics, levels of *motivation*, *leadership style* and success. It is suggested that the more cohesive a group the better the performance, but this is not always the case and can depend on two aspects of group cohesion:

- *task cohesion* – how well the group works together to complete the task, e.g. winning the match
- *social cohesion* – how well the group interacts and supports each other.

Each aspect can be independent of the other, but task cohesion is more important than social cohesion to the successful completion of the goal. For example, a football team may win most of their games but do not socialise particularly well, while a rival team get on well together but do not actually win many games. However, some conflict may produce positive results as new ideas are developed, or rivalry can motivate individuals to perform better.

Cold War: the continuing state of conflict, tension and competition that existed primarily between the *USA* and the Soviet Union and those countries' respective allies from the mid-1940s to the early 1990s. Throughout this period, the conflict was expressed through military coalitions, espionage, weapons development, invasions, *propaganda* and competitive technological development, which included the space race. The conflict included costly defense spending, a massive conventional and nuclear arms race, and numerous proxy wars.

collegiate: a term used in the USA meaning relating to college or high school.

colonialism: the policy and practice of a power in extending control over weaker peoples or areas. Examples include the 13 colonies that became the *USA* or the colonies of the *British Empire*. Many former colonial states have become or are now in the process of becoming *emergent cultures*.

combat: to be in conflict with individuals or groups. It implies a struggle and, in a sporting context, it involves one person beating an opponent. Examples of activities would be judo or wrestling where stylised moves are tested.

command teaching style: a teaching style in which the teacher adopts an authoritarian manner, making all the decisions with no input from the group. All learners experience the same actions, have little social interaction and have no decisions to make. It ensures the objectives are clear, routines are established and control is maintained. It is useful when instructing large groups of beginners or when time is limited and safety is vital. However, it does not encourage the learner to take responsibility for their learning, is of limited use for the development of *open skills* and makes it difficult for the teacher to provide individual *feedback*. (See also *Mosston and Ashworth's spectrum of teaching styles*.)

commercialism: an emphasis on the principles of commerce with a focus on profit. As *spectator sports* emerged, their entertainment value was exploited by individuals who saw the opportunity to organise regular sporting events. Promoters and agents emerged, and commercialism became an integral part of sport. Countries with a market economy (see *economic system*) were initially more open to this kind of approach as they had the environment to create profitable enterprises. (See table overleaf.)

The conditions required and characteristics for commercialism can be seen in the diagram.

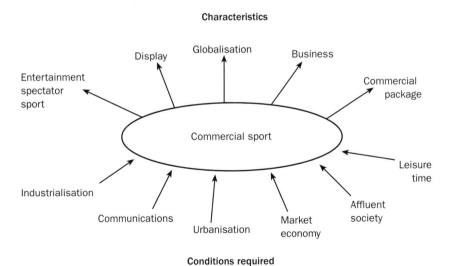

Characteristics

Display · Globalisation · Business

Entertainment spectator sport

Commercial package

Commercial sport

Leisure time

Industrialisation

Communications · Urbanisation · Market economy · Affluent society

Conditions required

Commercialism

Advantages to sport	Disadvantages to sport
Provides revenue for sports events	Uneven development across sports
Provides revenue for athletes' training	Revenue goes to already popular sports and stars
Provides income in **professional sport**	
Can help stimulate **grass roots** activity	Withdrawal of money can lead to events crashing
Can help raise standards	Political considerations can become important
Can help in the development and innovation of sport	Tensions between the sport and sponsor

commodification: the idea that sport has been turned into a commodity or asset that can be bought and sold. This includes notions of lifestyle as well as goods such as swimming pools and tennis courts. Young people are vulnerable to the hard sell of brand names with the suggestion this is not only desirable but also essential in their social acceptance.

Commonwealth Games: originally called the British Empire Games, this is the next most important multi-sport competition after the **Olympic Games**. They involve approximately 65 countries with a range of 25 sports. They maintain a strong British influence as a result of the colonisation of these countries by Britain earlier in their history. They concentrate on amateur sports and are held every four years.

communism: an **economic system** based on the abolition of private ownership and with an emphasis on state control and collective responsibility. **Social class** barriers are supposedly broken down. Athletes are subsidised by the state in order to excel and promote the superiority of communism as a political system. (See also **Marx, Karl.**)

Community Sports Leader Awards: run by the **British Sports Trust** as part of its Leadership in the Community Programme. The Community Sports Leader Award (CSLA) is a preliminary Sports Leader Award and is an effective qualification in promoting the concept of leadership roles in sport for young people over the age of 16. It enables people to assist in the voluntary activities of a club or youth organisation and to lead groups in sporting or recreational activities. This scheme operates within schools, colleges and community groups, being recognised by the **Duke of Edinburgh Award Scheme** at gold level. There is also the JSLA, Junior Sports Leader Award, and the Higher Sports Leader Award.

compact bone: also known as hard bone, this is the hard surface layer of all bones and the cylindrical shaft or **diaphysis** of **long bones**. Its function is to protect the bones from external forces or blows and allows weight-bearing to occur. The compact bone is surrounded by the **periosteum** for protection and allows attachment for **tendons**.

competition sport has as its primary aim to determine who is the best in a particular sporting activity given equal circumstances. For example, athletes are matched within categories of level of ability, such as club, county or national standard; by age, weight and often gender. They adhere to the same standardised rules and their skill level, physical and mental fitness are the main criteria of winning.

Competitive sport enables participants to compete at levels appropriate to their ability. They can compete at three levels:

- Recreational competition – a friendly and informal level of competition. The result has no significance to anyone else and although rules are adhered to no officials are likely to be present. This represents the *grass roots* end of the *continuum* and involves many people.
- Representative competition – a more formalised level of competition, administered by officials, and the participants may represent a club, district or town. The competition may be organised into leagues or tournaments where the result can affect later progression. A sense of obligation to do well is present.
- *Elite* competition – occurs at the highest level such as county, national and international. The demands on the performer are considerable, physically, mentally and emotionally, often involving the additional pressure of national pride. Very few participants actually reach these levels.

competitive state anxiety inventory (CSAI-2): form of self-report *questionnaire* measuring cognitive worry, *somatic anxiety* and *self-confidence* in a sporting situation. It is used to assess an individual's *state anxiety* and their corresponding behaviour patterns. (See also *competitive trait anxiety*.)

	HARDLY EVER	SOMETIMES	OFTEN
1 Before I compete I worry about not performing well.	a	b	c
2 When I compete I worry about making mistakes.	a	b	c
3 Before I compete I am calm.	a	b	c
4 I get nervous waiting to start a game.	a	b	c

competitive trait anxiety: the tendency of a performer to see competitive situations as threatening and to respond with feelings of apprehension or tension. An individual with a high *trait anxiety* is more likely to experience a high *state anxiety* when faced with a stressful situation, such as competition, where they feel others may be evaluating their performance (*evaluation apprehension*). For example, a gymnast who tends to worry generally will perceive the next competition as highly threatening. They may experience high levels of *cognitive state anxiety* and *somatic anxiety* which could hinder their performance. Competitors' *anxiety* levels can be measured using the *sport competition anxiety test* and *competitive state anxiety inventory (CSAI-2)* test.

competitiveness: aiming to achieve what another person is aiming to achieve at the same time. It induces an element of *conflict*. There are advantages and disadvantages to competitive sport.

Advantages of competitiveness	Disadvantages of competitiveness
Children have natural competitive instinct and, as they are more motivated to practice, enjoyment of sport increases	Continued feelings of failure can cause stress and *anxiety*
Can raise *self-esteem* and ability to cope with failure and success	The need to win can encourage unsporting behaviour

competitiveness orientation: refers to how the individual perceives success and the type of goals used to judge their performance. The targets may be *performance goals* or *outcome goals* based depending on the nature of the task and consultation with the coach. For example, a basketball player can be set the goal of improving a specific aspect of their technique, such as release of the ball or the goal may be completing a specific percentage of attempted shots relative to their ability. (See also *Vealey's model of sport confidence*.)

complex skills: *skills* that involves the performer having to think about them, consciously control them and make decisions about their execution. For example, a player preparing to make a tackle must assess the position, speed and angle of the attacker, options they may have and the position of team mates before deciding on the appropriate technique to use. Initially, when learning the skill, it may be broken down into *subroutines* for the performer to gain a fuller understanding and mastery of the task.

concentric muscle contraction involves a muscle shortening while contracting. It is a form of *isotonic muscle contraction* and occurs, for example, in the biceps during the upward phase of a biceps curl or in the triceps during the upward phase of a push-up. In this case *actin* filaments within a *sarcomere* are pulled closer together. (See also *eccentric muscle contraction*.)

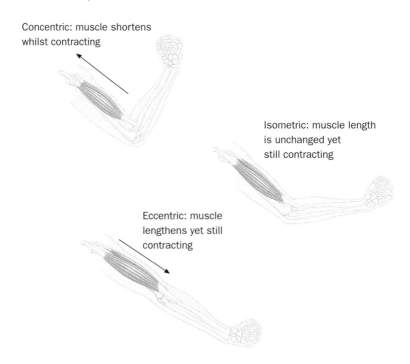

Concentric: muscle shortens whilst contracting

Isometric: muscle length is unchanged yet still contracting

Eccentric: muscle lengthens yet still contracting

concepts of physical activity: see *leisure, outdoor recreation, physical education, play, recreation* and *sport*.

Conconi test: used to measure the *onset of blood lactate accumulation* or *anaerobic threshold*. It involves monitoring the heart rate of the athlete as the intensity of exercise increases up to maximal effort. Initially, the heart rate will increase proportionally to intensity, but a point arrives at which the heart rate is no longer rising even though the intensity continues to rise. This point is known as the heart deflection point.

concurrent feedback: see *feedback*.

conditioning activities are designed primarily to improve the physical and mental condition of the performer. Examples of such activities are aerobics, *circuit training* and weight training (see *strength training*). A programme of work is set and should be followed on a regular basis if it is to have the desired effect. Some participants will use it for the general conditioning effect, while others will use it to achieve fitness for a particular sport. Some conditioning activities have developed into *competition sports* in their own right, such as weightlifting and aerobics.

conditioning theories of learning: see *associationist theories of learning*.

conflict theory: a sociological theory opposed to *functionalist theory*. This theory does not view society as a stable system. Instead, it is believed that society is made up of an ever-changing set of relationships affected by economic differences. As such society is bound by inequalities as some sections of society will have more power and control of resources than others. It is based on the ideas of *Karl Marx* and is used mainly to explain events in countries with *market economies*. It is based on the idea that workers with little control over their working lives will constantly seek entertainment and excitement. They can be coerced into their choices through consumerism and mass entertainment spectacles. Sport is a popular form of entertainment, incorporates sales and merchandising as well as ideological assumptions such as achievement-orientated behaviour, obedience and discipline. This theory tends to include a more cynical view of sport and focuses on the need for change.

conquest: a means of overcoming an obstacle such as a mountain, or a feeling such as fear, and usually involves some force, be it physical or mental. It suggests control and power over another object. In sport, it is a term used mostly in the context of outdoor and *adventurous activities*.

conservation: the protection of the *natural environment* through the planning and careful management of natural resources. Outdoor *adventurous activities* are growth sports and are providing some problems regarding conservation which need to be addressed. The areas in which they take place are often country parks, nature reserves, green belt areas, Areas of Outstanding Natural Beauty (AONB) and *National Parks*. Some of the problems caused are:

- erosion of land and rivers
- pollution caused by motor sports
- disturbance of wildlife and local residents.

Rather than simply banning these sports, organisations such as the *Countryside Commission*, the National Parks authorities and the sports *governing bodies* need to liaise in order to plan ways in which these activities can be enjoyed with minimum damage to the environment (see diagram overleaf).

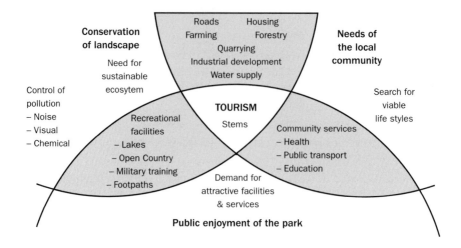

contingency theory of leadership: a leadership theory that proposes that the effectiveness of a leader is dependent on (contingent on) a combination of personality *traits* and the situation. Fiedler (1967) identified two types of *leadership styles*:

- task-centred/task-orientated leader – concentrates on completing the task, setting goals, getting the job done and performance
- relationship-centred/person-orientated leader – concentrates on developing interpersonal relationships within the group.

The effectiveness of each style depends on the 'favourableness' of the situation, which is dependent on:

- the relationship between the leader and the group
- the leader's position of power and authority
- the task structure.

The task-orientated style would be more effective in highly favourable or highly unfavourable conditions, whereas a person-orientated style would be better employed in moderately favourable conditions.

For example, the situation would be favourable if the coach of a team had an excellent relationship with the group and was respected by them, had the clear objective of winning the league and was well-resourced in terms of facilities. By comparison, another team had a poor relationship with its coach, poor facilities and no clear objectives for the group. For both of these scenarios a task-oriented style of leadership could be used. However, a third rival team has a reasonable relationship with its coach, limited facilities and a mid-table position in the league. In this instance, a person-oriented style may be the most appropriate to use.

continuous feedback: see *feedback*.

continuous skills have no clear beginning and end; the completion of one movement becomes the start of the next. This type of skill is placed on the same *continuum* as *serial skills* and *discrete skills*. Examples include swimming, cycling and running actions.

continuous training: a method of training performed for a long period of time at low intensity. Continuous training involves the performance of rhythmic exercise, using large muscle groups at a *steady state* for up to 2 hours. It is designed to improve endurance performance and is widely used in distance running, swimming and cycling. The intensity of the training should be between 60% and 70% of *maximum heart rate*, as outlined in the *Karvonen principle*. Continuous training is also recommended for health-related reasons, since the intensity of the exercise is fairly low yet benefits the cardiovascular system. It can therefore be used as part of a programme to avoid *cardiovascular diseases* and *obesity*.

continuum: an imaginary line placed between two extremes. It is used to classify items or subjects between extremities depending on how closely they match set criteria. For example, skills are often classified in this manner (see *closed skill* and *open skill*).

contract to compete: the hallmark of participation in sporting activities. It implies that each performer has entered into an unwritten contract whereby they are committed to:
- competing under the *rules* of the sport
- playing as well as they can
- allowing others the same opportunity to demonstrate their skill and effort
- voluntarily accepting and understanding the need for codes of behaviour such as *sportsmanship* and *etiquette*.

The contract can be broken when:
- these rules are broken, e.g. a foul
- *equal opportunity* is denied to others, e.g. not trying your best to win or the use of performance-enhancing drugs.

contractility: the capacity of cells to generate a force to shorten or contract for movement. Muscle fibres exhibit a high degree of contractility and in doing so enable people to perform a whole host of movements seen in the sporting arena.

cool-down: also known as a warm-down, this is a period of light, continuous activity following exercise during which time heart rate remains elevated. The purpose is to keep metabolic activity high and *capillaries* dilated, so that oxygen can be flushed through the muscle tissue, removing and oxidising any *lactic acid* that may have accumulated. This prevents pooling of blood in the veins which can cause dizziness if exercise is stopped abruptly. The final part of a cool-down period should involve a period of mobility exercises, which can also facilitate and improve *flexibility*.

cooling aids generally consist of clothing adapted to maintain the core temperature of the body. Exercising in warm environments can cause the body to overheat, leading to performance impairment. Blood flow to the exercising muscle may be reduced because there is greater blood flow to the surface of the skin in an attempt to cool the body down. Athletes have also been known to suffer from a phenomenon called *cardiovascular drift* where heart rate increases despite a constant work rate. Indeed, it is suggested that for every 1° increase in body temperature, the heart rate increases by approximately 10 beats per minute. Cooling aids include clothing usually manufactured using material designed to absorb water or with a liquid coolant integrated into it. Simple examples of cooling aids include bandanas, headbands and vests.

cooperation: working with others to achieve the same end. Some cultures are cooperative in nature, such as *primitive cultures* where the group or collective effort often means the difference between survival and death. Even within competitive team games there is an element of cooperation as the teams agree on the fixture and to abide by the rules, and the team members work together to achieve a victory.

coordination: a skill-related component of fitness involving the interaction of the motor and nervous systems. It is simply the ability to perform motor tasks accurately. Coordination is essential for most sporting tasks to be completed successfully. The performer needs to be able to combine effectively the use of various limbs to maintain *balance* and execute skills such as dribbling, passing, dodging and kicking.

core stability: the combined strength of all the muscles from your hips to your armpits, which is responsible for many things including posture. The core muscles stabilise the upper body and pelvis during dynamic movement. The *multifidus muscle*, for example, lies deep in the back and helps to stabilise the *cartilaginous joints* of the spine. The *transverse abdominis* lies under the internal obliques and helps to stabilise the lower spine and pelvis during lifting movements – it is the body's natural corset or weightlifting belt. An increase in core strength can lead to increases in virtually all other types of strength and dramatically reduces the chance of injury during *strength training*. The best method of improving core stability is with the use of a Swiss ball. Simply performing abdominal crunchies or leg raises on the Swiss ball will strengthen the abdominal and lower back muscles, the 'core' of the body's strength.

Cori cycle: a series of chemical reactions in which the *lactic acid* produced from the breakdown of muscle *glycogen* is converted to blood glucose in the liver.

corinthian: the epitome of the amateur ideal of a sportsman. Consistent with St Paul's letter to the Corinthians that 'not everyone can win but those that do should do so according to the rules and spirit of the time'. The corinthians were drawn from the elite of Victorian society and followed this code during games. For example, the Corinthian Casuals, founded in 1882, would withdraw their goalkeeper on the awarding of a penalty to the opposing side, on the principle they should accept the consequences of a foul.

Cornish hurling is a traditional game of *football* played in Cornwall. In Richard Carew's Survey of Cornwall (1603), he gives a detailed description of a game of football or hurling as it was called in Cornwall, which reveals complex *rules* and strategies (for the time) for deceiving the opposition. In the east of Cornwall, 'hurling to goales' involved teams of 15, 20, or 30 in which each player paired himself with another from the opposing team and attempted to block his advance, as in *American football* today.

'The hurlers are bound to the observation of many lawes as that they must hurle man to man, and not two set upon one man at once; the Hurler against the ball must not butt, nor handfast under the girdle; that he who hath the ball, must butt only in the other brest.' There was even an offside rule 'that he must deal no foreball, viz he may not throw it to any of his mates, standing nearer the goale than himself'.

Cotswold Games: an annual sports event that included activities for the *gentry* and the peasantry. It suffered under the *Puritan* regime but was revived by Robert Dover who, following the Restoration in the seventeenth century, wished for a return to the 'merrie England' concept where all *social classes* enjoyed recreational pursuits together. They later became known as the Dover Games.

Coubertin, Baron Pierre de: a Frenchman who revived the ancient *Olympic Games* in 1896. This resulted from him visiting England in the nineteenth century and being impressed with the English *public school* notion of *athleticism*. De Coubertin wished to draw countries together in healthy competition, free from political issues, with the aim of keeping the importance of winning in perspective. He also viewed it as a way of reviving French *nationalism*. He elected the first members of the *International Olympic Committee* hoping they would continue the spirit of the Games he had created.

Council of Europe: established in 1949, the Council of Europe focuses on cultural, sporting, educational and environmental issues; for example, the use of *drugs* in sport, the economic effects on sports investments, football *hooligans* and developing support for the *Paralympics*.

counter culture: a subsection of *society* that develops different values, behaviour, ideas and beliefs which are often in conflict with those of the *dominant culture*. Counter cultures can emerge from a common interest and from social experiences, and they are often associated with alternative *cultures*. In sport, some groups are attempting to make sport less competitive. This is a counter culture which conflicts with the dominant idea that major force in sport is competition.

The dominant concept in American sport is the *Lombardian ethic*, where winning is considered the only important thing. Therefore, 'Eco-sport' is a counter culture movement that takes a more anti-competitive viewpoint and sees the process rather than the outcome as the important thing. The New Games Foundation aims to change the way people play by creating informal situations, emphasising group effort rather than group reward.

LOMBARDIAN ETHIC	RADICAL ETHIC	COUNTER-CULTURE ETHIC
Winning is everything End justifies the means	Outcome important but so is the process	Process important Outcome unimportant Anti-competitive vie
Professionalism	'Lifetime Sport' = European Sport for all Charter, e.g. Intra Mural Sports	'Eco Sport' Healthy, Fun Enviromentally based Co-operative not Competitive

Countryside Commission: a public body with a wide range of responsibilities in England and Wales, formed under the National Parks and Access to the Countryside Act 1968. It has various functions including:
- selection and designation of National Parks, Areas of Outstanding Natural Beauty (AONB) and country parks
- establishment of long-distance footpaths and bridleways

- provision of information services about the countryside
- advice on the use of the countryside for open air recreation balanced by a concern for the *natural environment*
- carrying out research and experimental projects
- giving grants and loans to non-public bodies.

coupled reaction: a two-part chemical reaction, involving the production of *energy* in the first stage, which is used in the second stage for resynthesis of *ATP*.

FORMULA:

$$PC \rightarrow Pi + C + energy$$
$$energy + ADP + Pi \rightarrow ATP$$

coursing: a field sport where dogs or hounds are matched against one another in pairs, for the hunting of hares by sight. Hare coursing dates back to 1500 BC in the Valley of the Nile and was introduced to Britain in approximately 500 BC. Its original function was to obtain food for human survival, but the competitive element was introduced during the reign of Elizabeth I, becoming a popular social event in rural England in the nineteenth century.

Hares were flushed out of cover and the 'slipper' – the official responsible for the releasing of the dogs simultaneously – unleashed two greyhounds. The *gentry* rode on horseback and private ground was often crossed by the lower classes on foot. In the 1920s circuit tracks were built in which greyhounds trailed an artificial hare on the track to test the speed and *agility* of the dogs. *Gambling* was a popular aspect of this activity. (See also *animal sports* and *field sports*.)

courtly refers to something deemed suitable for a royal court, meaning refined in manner. *Real tennis* was developed at the French court and adopted by the British monarchy and *aristocracy*.

creatine monohydrate supplementation is a legal *ergogenic aid* used to boost levels of *creatine phosphate* in the body and therefore increase the threshold of the *alactic energy system*. Some studies have shown creatine supplementation to boost maximal strength and lean tissue mass and as such it is widely used by a variety of athletes from sprinters through to weightlifters. As with most ergogenic aids that are ingested, there appears to be a few side effects, the main ones being water retention and muscle cramps.

creatine phosphate: also known as phosphocreatine, this is a high-energy phosphate molecule found in muscle. During periods of high-intensity exercise that is short in duration, creatine phosphate is used to resynthesise *ATP* under anaerobic conditions. Sprint *interval training*, *strength training* and, more recently, creatine supplementation by athletes can increase the amount of work performed under such conditions and speed up *recovery* following exercise.

cricket: one of the oldest-established games, played from the outset by both the aristocrats and the commoners. The game reflected the feudal structure of the village and each *social class* had a particular *role (social)* assigned to them to signify their status. The game took place in the summer season when light was at a premium allowing workers time to participate. Due to its non-violent nature, the early *rules* and gentlemanliness ensured a level of respectful behaviour. The term 'gentleman versus players' distinguished the amateurs from the professionals. The Duke of Richmond drew up the first rules in 1727 and the Marylebone Cricket Club (MCC) emerged as an organisational force comparatively early in the game's development. William Clarke developed the first national touring side and The Ashes is now a traditional fixture between Britain and *Australia*.

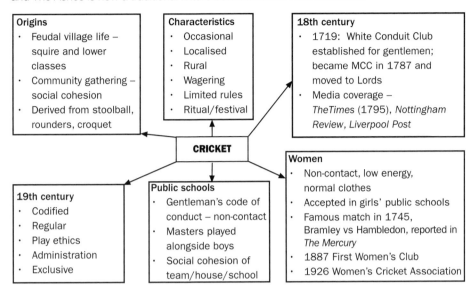

Origins	Characteristics	18th century
• Feudal village life – squire and lower classes • Community gathering – social cohesion • Derived from stoolball, rounders, croquet	• Occasional • Localised • Rural • Wagering • Limited rules • Ritual/festival	• 1719: White Conduit Club established for gentlemen; became MCC in 1787 and moved to Lords • Media coverage – *TheTimes* (1795), *Nottingham Review*, *Liverpool Post*

CRICKET

19th century	Public schools	Women
• Codified • Regular • Play ethics • Administration • Exclusive	• Gentleman's code of conduct – non-contact • Masters played alongside boys • Social cohesion of team/house/school	• Non-contact, low energy, normal clothes • Accepted in girls' public schools • Famous match in 1745, Bramley vs Hambledon, reported in *The Mercury* • 1887 First Women's Club • 1926 Women's Cricket Association

critical theory is about power in social relations and about action and political involvement in order to bring about equity, fairness and openness. In relation to sport, it recognises that people who are involved in sports use their power and resources to build up cultural practices. It recognises that conflict and harmony between different groups can coexist through negotiation, compromise and coercion. Therefore, sport will change as society changes and will at the same time exert its own considerable influence. This sociological theory attempts to help understand the complexity and diversity of societies without the limitations imposed by theories such as *functionalist theory* and *conflict theory*.

cruciate ligaments: located in the knee joint, these *ligaments* prevent anterio-posterior (front to back) movement. Together with the *lateral* and *medial* collateral ligaments, they cooperate in order to maintain the stability of the joint. Injuries to these ligaments are common in contact sports such as football and rugby but can also occur as a result of twisting in sports such as basketball (see the diagram overleaf).

CSAI-2 questionnaire: see *competitive state anxiety inventory (CSAI-2)*.

cue: a part of *stimuli* that allows the performer to discriminate between it and another stimulus, or a particular aspect of the stimulus that can guide behaviour. For example, in the *cue utilisation theory*, the coach may tell a basketball player learning how to perform a lay-up shot to focus on the square around the basket when aiming their shot.

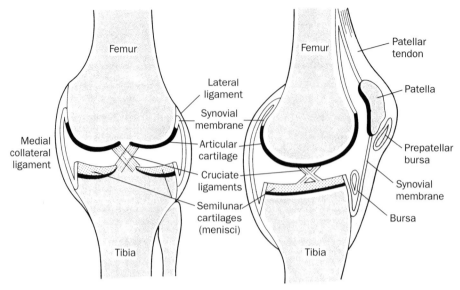

Cruciate ligaments

cue arousal theory: see *aggressive cue theory*.

cue utilisation theory involves the use of relevant *cues* to focus the performer's *attention* as *arousal* levels increase in order to complete the task successfully. This involves *attentional narrowing*. If, however, this continues as arousal increases, the performer may actually begin to miss vital cues and signals, leading to a reduction in their performance level. For example, a golfer may be playing the final holes of a close match. They usually direct their thoughts to several checks before completing the stroke, but as the pressure increases they neglect to complete their normal routine, missing key points. As a result the shot is poor, leading to a further increase in arousal levels.

culture denotes the way of life of a *society*, encompassing its language, customs, dress, the symbols and artefacts. These are passed down through the generations with whatever modifications any single generation wishes to make. Cultures can evolve gradually or occasionally change almost overnight. Individuals undergo the *socialisation* process, learning the cultural *values* of their society and institutions, and social structures are founded to achieve specific aims for that culture. Examples of different cultures are:

- *emergent cultures*
- *primitive cultures*
- *ancient cultures*
- modern (see *Western European sport* and *Eastern European sport*).

culture and sport: physical and sporting activities have different functions in different *cultures*. For example:

- *primitive cultures* – functional, where sporting activities are developed for survival, e.g. to learn how to hunt for food, defence and religious or *ritual* meanings
- *emergent cultures* – functional, survival, *integration* of peoples, *nationalism*, labour and defence

- *ancient cultures* – functional, religious and *recreation* for the *leisured class*
- modern Western *cultures* – *socialisation* for adult roles, *commercialism*, recreation and *excellence*.

cycling: an activity that reflected the technological advances and social changes in the nineteenth century. Bicycles could be mass-produced and were appealing initially to the *middle class* who required a mode of transport different from the horse. The lower classes had to await the development of the second-hand trade. The popularity of the bicycle grew because of the growing freedom of *gentry* ladies, the opportunity now available to *escape* to the countryside, the increase in clubs and various technological advances. Some of the early models were the Hobby horse (1818), the Boneshaker (1868), the Penny Farthing (1870–90), the National Royal Tricycle (1884) and the Rover Safety (1885).

Do you need revision help and advice?

Go to pages 297–330 for a range of revision appendices that include plenty of exam advice and tips.

danger: the state of being vulnerable to injury. In the sporting arena, this risk is heightened in outdoor and *adventurous activities*. *Subjective* danger is that which is under the control of the individual such as choice of safe and appropriate equipment, and choice of route; however there is no such control over *objective* danger such as an avalanche.

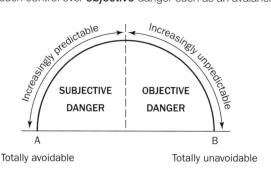

In the context of mountaineering, for example, beginners will work at the left end of the base line AB. Experienced climbers will work from the right end of the base line. (See also *risk*.)

dead space: air remaining in any area of the respiratory passages which is not involved in *gaseous exchange* between the blood and *alveoli*.

decentralised: the dispersal of power away from the centre towards outlying areas. It is a system of government or administration that is organised into smaller units with more *autonomy*. Examples include *local authorities* in Britain and the individual states in the *USA*. The government in power provides guidelines that can be interpreted according to regional needs, including the type of education system. For example, physical education in the UK traditionally had a decentralised system within which teachers devised their own syllabus. However, the advent of the *National Curriculum* brought a more centralising influence.

Advantages of a decentralised system	Disadvantages of a decentralised system
It is more flexible	Not a uniform experience nationally
It can cater for regional needs	It can be difficult to coordinate policy
Individual initiative can flourish	The quality of provision can be dependent on individual initiative

(See also *centralised*.)

decision-making: also known as the translatory mechanism, this involves the performer combining information gathered from the present environment and past experiences in order to initiate a response. *Cues* gathered from the *display (psychology)* are analysed and a *motor programme* formed. The faster the process, the quicker the *reaction time* and therefore the better the chance of success. For example, a badminton player must evaluate the position of the opponent; the speed and direction of the shuttlecock; their own skills and the chance of success. This information is then used to decide which shot it is appropriate to play.

dehydration results from the loss of body fluids. Dehydration largely occurs during athletic performance as a result of the sweating that accompanies increased body temperature. As exercise intensity increases, so does the rate at which the human body metabolises food fuels. This produces heat, which in turn leads to sweating in an attempt to cool the body and maintain body temperature. Even fluid losses of as little as 2% of body weight can cause an impairment to endurance performance by 10–20%. Fluid loss reduces blood *plasma* volume, which decreases blood flow to the muscles, increases the thickeness of the blood (*hyperviscosity*) and causes heart rate to increase.

In order to maintain optimal performance, rehydration is essential. Many endurance athletes will require drinks of a *carbohydrate* solution of 4–6% of body weight during exercise in order to boost blood glucose and stave off dehydration. A level of dehydration equal to 5% of body weight has been shown to reduce performance by 70%.

delayed onset of muscle soreness (DOMS) is characterised by tender and painful muscles often experienced in the days following heavy and unaccustomed exercise. The explanation of this soreness is quite simple and results from the damage to muscle fibres and connective tissue surrounding the fibres. The soreness is usually temporary and goes within a couple of days as the muscle fibres repair themselves. DOMS is most likely to occur following *eccentric muscle contraction* and can result from weight training (see *strength training*), *plyometrics* or even walking down steep hills.

democracy: a system of government that involves some form of election of the government by the people. Democracy is given a high value ideologically. *Capitalism* is believed to require a democratic society in order to succeed. This is the opposite of a one-party state.

democratic leader: a leader who encourages the *group* to discuss ideas and become involved in the decision-making process, but who will make the final decision themselves and oversee the completion of the task. The leader is generally more informal and relaxed within the group when compared with an *autocratic leader* but has considerably more input than a *laissez-faire leader*. Research by Lewin (1935) suggested the group led by a democratic leader continued to work and cooperate if the leader was not present. This type of leader works well with more experienced or individual performers.

demonstration: an explanation, display or illustration showing how to complete a task correctly. It is a form of visual *guidance* that is especially useful during the *cognitive phase of learning*. To be effective the demonstration must be clear, accurate and relevant. The action is more likely to be repeated if the model is of high status or respected (see *social learning theory*). For example, to teach a young gymnast how to execute a front somersault, the coach must ensure they watch a skilled performer, so they can create a mental image of the movement requirements. Often the use of verbal guidance, directing the novice to technical *cues*, can enhance the effectiveness of the demonstration.

Department for Culture, Media and Sport: the governmental 'home' of sport, providing funding for *Sport England* and *UK Sport* and various other sports councils. It is the government department responsible for government policy on sport and recreation and the *National Lottery,* as well as other cultural sectors such as broadcasting and films. It is headed by a Secretary of State, assisted by various Parliamentary Undersecretaries of State, one of which represents sport. A Sports Cabinet under the chairmanship of the Secretary of State for Culture, Media and Sport was introduced in 1999 to work alongside UK Sport and to bring together ministers with responsibility for sport in the four home countries. Major sport strategies include A Sporting Future for All (2000), *Game Plan* (2002) and the *Framework for Sport in England* (2004).

In relation to sport, this can be translated as:
- *Sport for All*, aiming to widen access to sport and recreation to the masses
- achieving *excellence* in national and international competition
- the Youth Sports Unit, which promotes the importance of physical education and sport for young
- supporting major international events, e.g. bidding for the *London Olympic Games 2012*. The Department supports the relevant organisations in terms of bidding for and staging the events
- sport as part of the overall social inclusion policy and neighbourhood regeneration work.

Recent initiatives included:
- 'Playing to Win – A New Era for Sport', which sets out the government's ambition to become a truly world leading sporting nation, capitalising on the 2012 Olympic Games and *Paralympic Games*
- *Talented Athlete Scholarship Scheme.*

detraining: see *reversibility*.

developing cultures: see *emergent cultures*.

deviancy: behaviour that goes against the society's general *norms* and *values*. This can include behaviour that goes against the law and is therefore criminally deviant, for example burglary, or against the moral values of the society but which is not criminally deviant, for example promiscuity. Deviancies can be relative according to the balance of power in society. The *dominant culture* usually decides on what is lawful and morally right and this can isolate other subsections of society who, should they form contradictory values, could be classed as *subcultures*. There are two categories of deviancy:
- negative deviancy – in sporting situations this can include violations such as deliberately fouling another player or taking performance-enhancing drugs
- positive deviancy – athletes are often encouraged to behave in ways that would be unacceptable in other spheres of life. This can be classed as overconformity or positive deviancy. Examples would be where athletes are encouraged to train obsessively; participate when injured and sacrifice other aspects of their life for the sport.

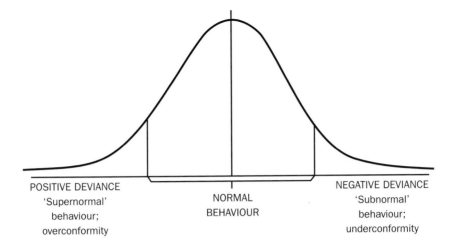

POSITIVE DEVIANCE	NORMAL	NEGATIVE DEVIANCE
'Supernormal' behaviour; overconformity	BEHAVIOUR	'Subnormal' behaviour; underconformity

Deviancy

diaphysis: the shaft of a *long bone*.

diastole: the filling of the chambers of the heart with blood when relaxing. It forms part of the *cardiac cycle*.

direct gas analysis: the most accurate measure of a performer's *aerobic capacity* or *maximum oxygen uptake (VO₂ max)*. It involves a subject either running on a treadmill or cycling on an ergometer during a test that progresses in intensity until *exhaustion* hits. The test takes place in a sports laboratory so that expired air samples can be collected and analysed throughout the test to determine how much oxygen the performers muscles have extracted and utilised.

disability sport: a term used to describe the participation in sport of disabled people. 'Disabled' in this context covers people with a physical, sensory or mental impairment. The term 'disability' is used when impairment adversely affects performance. Other terms used are handicapped sport, sports for the disabled, adaptive sport, wheelchair sport and deaf sport. Competitive sports have either been designed specifically for the disabled, such as goalball for the blind, or have been modified, such as volleyball, and wheelchair basketball and tennis. (See also *inclusiveness* and *integration*.)

Disability Sport England (formerly British Sports Association for the Disabled) promotes sport for disabled athletes. Its aims are wide-ranging and include:
- to provide opportunities for disabled people to participate in sport
- to promote the benefits of sport and physical recreation to disabled people
- to support organisations in providing sporting opportunities for disabled people
- to educate and make people aware of the sporting *abilities* of disabled people
- to enhance the image, awareness and understanding of *disability sport*
- to encourage disabled people to play an active role in the development of their sport.

With more than 50,000 members, Disability Sport England aims to make a healthy lifestyle and participation in sport a reality from the *grass roots* through to Paralympic medal winners (see *Paralympic Games*).

discovery teaching style: a style of teaching in which the teacher guides the learner to find the correct **movement pattern** by providing information, clues or asking questions when appropriate. It is an open-ended and creative approach to learning when compared with the **command teaching style**. It is useful for the creation of dance or gymnastic routines and during some outdoor activities. This method allows individuals to develop a greater understanding of the completed movements, which may be beneficial later if independent decisions have to be made. They may also have greater **motivation** and improved **self-efficacy**, as they are responsible for their own learning. Advantages of this style include a greater understanding of the task by the performer due to increased decision-making, along with a subsequent improvement in their **self-confidence** and motivation towards the task. However, this method is time consuming as well as being difficult to use with large groups, as the teacher has to adapt for individual needs, **abilities** and progress. (See also **Mosston and Ashworth's spectrum of teaching styles**.)

discrete skills have well-defined beginnings and ends, and are usually completed quickly. They are specific skills with an action that can be repeated. This type of skill is placed on the same **continuum** as **serial skills** and **continuous skills**. Examples include a dive, passing, catching, kicking and hitting.

discrimination: making a distinction or giving unfair treatment, especially because of **prejudice**. It occurs when opportunities available to one social group are not available to all and when a prejudicial attitude is acted upon. It includes:

- overt discrimination – for example, laws that form part of the structure of a society, e.g. the former system of **apartheid** or a membership clause of a private sports club. This can be officially eradicated by changing the laws
- covert discrimination – hidden or less obvious, for example people's **attitudes** and beliefs, which can be hard to dislodge.

When subordinate groups in society are discriminated against, their opportunities are limited, including opportunities of **social mobility**. Discrimination can also be affected by whether a system is 'open', as in a true **egalitarian** society, or 'closed', such as the Indian caste system. Groups that can be discriminated against include women, the disabled, lower class and **ethnic groups**.

Numerous factors can lead to discrimination in sport:

- finance – the cost of joining a sport club
- time – longer hours of employment; women with careers/family
- location – number and type of facilities available
- education – philosophy and facilities available
- information – poor **mass media** coverage of **gender** and type of sports
- cultural factors – for example, stereotyping, **social class** or religious beliefs may hinder participation
- access – transport and opportunity.

displacement: the shortest distance between the starting and finishing position in a stated direction. Displacement is therefore a vector quantity and considers how far out of place an object is from its starting position. Direction is important here, so the shortest possible route (as the crow flies) from the starting point to the finishing point is used to measure displacement. Displacement is not to be confused with distance, which is the total length of the path an object covers during its motion from a starting position to the finishing position. Distance is a scalar quantity and therefore non-directional. A 100-metre swimmer, for example, covers a distance of 100m during a swim. The displacement of the swimmer will however be zero as the swimmer ends up in exactly the same position as the starting point. Displacement is measured in metres (m).

display (psychology): the physical environment surrounding the performer. It contains various *stimuli* or *cues* which are used during *information processing*, from which the performer has to select those which are relevant at the time (see *perception*). For example, during a game of netball, the display would contain the position of team mates, opposition, umpires, spectators, location of the individual themselves on court as well as the speed and direction of the ball. (See also *environment*.)

display (socio-cultural): something exhibited or performed for others. This is a term used to denote a moment when a sporting activity has moved along the *continuum* from play to where the intention is more exhibitionist. Performing for others and providing a spectacle are central to this idea.

Play Display

dispositional theory: see *trait theory*.

dissonance occurs when a performer has two or more thoughts (*cognitions*) of conflicting views which cause feelings of psychological discomfort. When an individual experiences these feelings, the need to restore harmony or consonance is paramount, as suggested by the *cognitive dissonance theory*.

distraction conflict theory: see *Baron's distraction conflict theory*.

distributed practice: a type of practice in which the performer completes a set number of practices followed by a rest or *recovery* period, before progressing to the next set of tasks. This practice is useful with novices or less experienced performers and when the task is of a gross, complex or dangerous nature. It allows for variation and the effects of *fatigue* and can therefore raise *motivation* levels. For example, when coaching a school rugby team, the coach may develop a variety of skills within one session, allowing a recovery period after a block of strenuous skills for the players to focus their *attention* on a less physically demanding activity. An experienced performer may use the rest period for *mental practice*. The inclusion of recovery periods has proved to produce better results generally when compared with *massed practice*.

diuretics: drugs used to reduce the weight of athletes by increasing the flow of urine. Examples are hydrochlorothiazide and chlorthalidone, which are particularly beneficial in sports such as horse racing and boxing. The side effects are muscle cramps, *dehydration* and possibly kidney failure. (See also *doping* and *drug testing*.)

Doggett's Coat and Badge: the oldest sculling race in the world held on the River Thames, instituted by Thomas Doggett in 1715. Crews race for an orange livery with a silver badge, hence the title 'Doggett's Coat and Badge'.

dominant culture: the particular set of ideas, viewpoints and beliefs which are values present in a society. It will ultimately serve the interests of the *ruling class* who will have imposed them through social structures such as the **mass media**, **education** systems and the law. If these values are radically undermined, social order will deteriorate and **subcultures** can emerge, which develop different ideas and values. It is mainly the case now in the Western world that a plurality of ideas and viewpoints can coexist within one society.

dominant learnt response: see *drive theory*.

dominant response: see *drive theory*.

DOMS: see *delayed onset of muscle soreness (DOMS)*.

doping: illegal methods of enhancing performance, which have been used since athletes in ancient Greece and Rome took substances to improve their athletic **abilities**. However, drug use in modern sport has become regular and systematised. Research shows it is more than a peripheral problem and operates at both amateur and professional level, among male and female athletes and across a wide variety of sports. Factors that led to an increase in the use of drugs include advances in biology and medicine; the use of drugs in **World War II**; and the development and availability of **testosterone**, **anabolic steroids** and growth hormones in the 1950s. Drugs allow athletes to control and alter their bodies, though if used unwisely can lead to a loss of control. (See also **doping agents**.)

Why?	How do we stop doping?
• To train harder	• Random testing and out-of-season testing
• Build muscles for explosive events	• Better liaison between organisations
• Steady nerves	• Education programmes for athletes and coaches
• Weight control	• Stricter punishments and life bans
• Fear of 'not making it'	• More money into testing programme
• Rewards are worth the risk	• Unified governing body policies
• To be more exciting and entertaining	• Better technology for testing to keep up to date
• Increase aggression	• Use of role models – both positive and negative
• High expectations from peer group, coaches and media	
• Drugs easily accessible	

DOPING

Why not?	There's nothing wrong with doping
• Health risks and death	• Technologically advanced countries have an advantage
• Shame, disgrace and punishment if caught	• If it's properly monitored it's not a health risk
• Not fair competition, unnatural, cheating and immoral	• Drugs are used for medical care
• Dangerous role model for children	• People should be free to choose
• Loss of earning and sponsorship	• People don't ask to be role models

doping agents: a term used to denote any illegal drug such as cannabis or a narcotic. The *International Olympic Committee* defines doping agents as 'the administration of or use by a competing athlete of any substance foreign to the body or any physiological substance taken in abnormal quantity or taken by abnormal route of entry into the body with the sole intention of increasing in an artificial and unfair manner his/her performance in competition'. The table overleaf summarises the types of drugs used.

dorsiflexion: a *movement pattern* involving the decrease in angle at the ankle. The foot is raised upwards towards the tibia (shin bone) in the median (*saggital*) plane. For example, dorsiflexion occurs at the ankle during the 'kick' phase of the breaststroke and during the preparatory phase of a basketball jump shot as the player squats down before jumping into the air. (See appendix, page 327.)

Dover Games: see *Cotswold Games*.

draft system: the pro-draft system exists in the sports of *basketball* and *American football*. The strength of the *Big Time programmes* in the *USA* ensures a steady influx of talented players into the *professional sport* scene. The draft is ranked and basically the lowest placed professional club has the first choice.

drag: a form of fluid *friction*, this is the force that acts in the opposite direction to a moving body as it travels through a fluid (either water or air). The amount of drag experienced by performers or projectiles in sporting activity depends on a number of factors, but especially the following:

- the frontal cross-sectional area of the moving body – the larger the frontal cross-sectional area, the greater the effects of drag
- the velocity of the moving body – the faster the body or object is moving, the greater the effects of drag
- the shape and surface characteristics of the moving object or body – the less the body is streamlined and the rougher the surface of the moving body, the greater the effects of drag
- the mass of the body – the lighter the body or moving object, the greater the effects of drag

Elite swimmers will try to minimise the effects of drag by:

- minimising his frontal cross-sectional area by using appropriate technique when swimming
- minimising the surface area in contact with the water, by maintaining an ecto/mesomorphic *somatotype*
- wearing shiny swim suits, swimming hats and 'shaving down' – the practice of removing body hair to attempt to minimise turbulent flow. All of these practices allow the water to flow past the body more smoothly and limit the drag force.

drill: see *military drill*.

drive: the performer's energised state or level of *motivation* that is directed towards achieving a specific goal. The greater the need to succeed, the greater the drive. For example, an athlete with the ability to win a medal at the next *Olympic Games* may have a greater drive to train and alter their lifestyle compared with a person who jogs twice a week for reasons of personal fitness. Similarly, a novice tennis player's drive may be to learn how to serve consistently. The performers will remain motivated until they feel they have succeeded or reached their optimal level, as suggested by the *drive reduction theory*. When these objectives have been met new challenges need to be found.

Doping agents

Types of drugs used	Reasons for use	Side effects	Which sports
Anabolic steroids – artificially produced male hormones, e.g. nandrolene, **testosterone**	Promote muscle growth Increase lean body weight Ability to train harder with less *fatigue* Repair body after stress Increased **aggression**	Liver damage Heart disease Acne Excessive aggression Females: male features; irregular periods	Power and explosive events, e.g. weightlifting, athletics, swimming
Narcotic analgesics – pain killers, e.g. morphine, methadone	Reduce amount of pain Mask injury Increase pain limit	Highly addictive Increase initial injury Breathing problems Nausea and vomiting	All sports
Stimulants – stimulate the body mentally and physically, e.g. **amphetamines**, ephedrine	Reduce tiredness Increase **alertness** Increase **competitiveness** Increase aggression	Rise in **blood pressure** Rise in body temperature Increased heart beat Loss of appetite Addiction Death	*Cycling* *Boxing*
Beta blockers – can be used medically, e.g. antenolol, propanalol	Steady nerves Stop trembling	Low blood pressure Slow heart rate Tiredness	Shooting *Archery* Snooker Diving
Diuretics – remove fluid from the body, e.g. triamterene, bendrofluazide	Lose weight quickly Increase rate of passing urine	**Dehydration** Faintness Dizziness Muscle cramps	*Horse racing* Boxing
Peptide hormones – naturally occurring, e.g. **erythropoietin**/HCG, synthetic analogues, e.g. EPO	Stimulate growth of naturally occurring steroids Build muscle Mend tissue Increase oxygen transport	Muscle wasting Abnormal growth of hands and feet EPO increases red blood cells Clotting Stroke	Similar to anabolic steroids
Blood doping – injection of blood to increase number of red blood cells	Gives body more **energy** to work	Allergic reactions Hepatitis or HIV/AIDS Overload circulatory system Blood clots	Running *Cycling* Marathons Skiing

drive reduction theory suggests that learning will occur due to the performer's desire to complete the task and only by achieving the goal will their **drive** be satisfied. When the task becomes habitual or a **skill** and the **stimulus–response bond** strengthened, a new challenge needs to be set to motivate the performer to continue their development. For example, once a young tennis player learns to execute a basic forehand drive successfully, the coach will start to develop the power and accuracy of the shot before progressing to the more advanced top spin drive.

drive theory suggests that there is a linear relationship between **arousal** and performance. Later research adapted the theory, proposing that the performer's dominant learnt response would be more evident as their arousal level increased. This is often expressed as:

FORMULA: $P = f(HD)$

where

P = performance

f = function

H = habit or dominant response

D = drive.

As arousal increases, if the performer is highly skilled the performance will be of a high quality, whereas a novice will display their dominant habit: an incorrect technique. For example, a young basketball player during training has learnt the technique of a lay-up shot and is able to execute the skill reasonably well in practice. During a game situation, the pressure increases and the new skill that is not yet fully learnt is unsuccessful. However, an experienced player's lay-up would be executed properly. Critics question the theory as it does not explain the reasons why performers in the **autonomous phase of learning** often fail to complete skills in situations of high arousal. (See the diagram overleaf.)

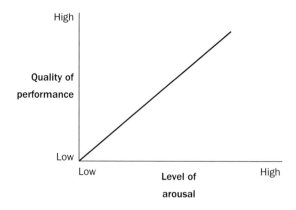

Drive theory

dropout: the issue of dropout is closely related to *burnout*. One of the problems of highly organised sport programmes is that they expose children to intensely serious sport experiences. Dropping out of sport need not always be seen as a problem but as a natural shift in children's interests. However, should a child drop out due to negative experiences then this is viewed as a problem as a negative attitude has formed. Research suggests that negative experiences are often associated with situations where competitive *abilities* and competitive outcomes are heavily emphasised.

drug abuse: see *doping*.

drug testing: a process to ascertain if an athlete has been utilising an illegal substance to enhance performance. Various factors influence the effectiveness of such tests, such as the competitive calendar, the training regime, the type of activity involved and the technological capacity of the testing equipment. Decisions about the level and timing of testing are made by *UK Sport* in consultation with the *governing body* of the sport. Testing at competitions is generally accepted as an effective method of deterring the use of *stimulants*, *beta blockers* and *diuretics*. The advantages and disadvantages of drug testing are summarised in the table opposite. The *World Anti-Doping Agency* was established to promote and coordinate the fight against *doping* in sport internationally. (See also *drug testing procedure*.)

drug testing procedure: the procedure followed for *drug testing*. Athletes can be tested for drugs at any time, either on the day of competition or during training, and either very short or no notice is given.

dual use: the use of school facilities by the local community. This policy began in the 1970s when local *education authorities* were attempting a more efficient use of sporting facilities.

Advantages	Disadvantages
Maximises use of local sporting and recreational features	Time constraints – the local community cannot use the facilities during the school day
Increases revenue	Wear and tear of facilities; maintenance problems
Facilities are local and accessible	Responsibility for the facilities is unclear
	School image may not be attractive to adults

Drug testing

Advantages of drug testing	Disadvantages of drug testing
A uniform code of testing ensures the rules would be consistent from sport to sport and country to country. No sport or athlete could gain an advantage.	Drug testing is inconsistent and false positives are prevalent. A career could be damaged by a faulty test.
Random tests are much more efficient than restricted testing periods, which give offenders an advantage in flushing drugs from their bodies and in timing their periodic cycles of use.	What is classified as 'performance-enhancing' in one sport might not provide an advantage in another. 'One-size-fits-all' testing does not take into consideration the actual effects of the substance on athletic performance.
Professional athletes who belong to a union would not face lower standards created in the give-and-take of collective bargaining. Professional leagues would not be able to bargain away higher standards in return for financial concessions.	Professional athletes have a right to bargain over every aspect of their careers.
The costs could be shared across sports and countries.	The considerable financial cost may not produce a valuable result.

Duke of Edinburgh Award Scheme: a scheme that involves young people of between 14 and 20 years making positive use of their *leisure* time by encouraging them to commit themselves to numerous, challenging activities in order to develop their personal and social skills. Established in 1956, with bronze, silver and gold awards that are recognised and valued nationally.

dynamic balance: a dimension of *balance* that entails the maintenance of a balanced position while moving. A gymnast performing a cartwheel demonstrates dynamic balance as they must maintain their *centre of mass* (hips) over their base of support (hands) throughout the duration of the movement.

dynamic flexibility: a dimension of *flexibility* that considers the speed at which body parts are moved into position about a joint. A trampolinist performing a straddle jump demonstrates dynamic flexibility.

dynamic strength: a dimension of strength where a force is exerted against a resistance resulting in a change in length of the muscle and a change in position of the limbs. This type of strength involves *isotonic muscle contractions*, *concentric muscle contractions* and *eccentric muscle contractions*. A triple jumper during the hop, step and jump phases of the skill will display dynamic strength in the muscles of the leg.

dynamic stretching involves taking the muscle through its full range of motion (the lengthening–shortening cycle) in a controlled and gradual way. Slow lunges, and controlled arm and leg swings are good examples of dynamic stretching.

dysfunction occurs when a part of the social structure does not contribute positively to the maintenance of society, resulting in disharmony and conflict. Behaviour or certain forms of organisation can upset the balance of the *social order*. This is closely related to *functionalist theory* but attempts to counter the problems associated with it, namely that everything in society is motivated by the need to allow that society to function effectively. In relation to sport, dysfunctional elements could be hooligans or when athletes are not cooperating within the sporting experience.

East German model: this became widely known as the 'East German machine' and was developed by the former German Democratic Republic in order to use sport as a vehicle for political *propaganda*. This system was similar to the old Soviet system (see *Eastern European sport*) in their early sport *talent identification* schemes and specialised *coaching* methods using scientific knowledge. Problems associated with the system are now widely known and reported, particularly institutionalised drug use. However, their more positive legacy has been the adoption by many modern *cultures* of the *academies of sport* idea.

During the 1972 *Olympic Games* quite a few medallists were scientifically selected by the East German system. The system's features included:

- a high level of organisation and structure
- a compulsory programme of PE in schools
- the early identification of sport talent
- a club system for talented individuals in separate sports
- the ruthless elimination of those who did not 'measure up'
- a scientific approach to *elite* performance training
- long-range objectives
- selected schools which had to support talent scouting competition separated into age groups
- substantial financial and material support
- 2000 training centres, 70,000 young people and 10,000 full-time coaches.

Preparations for the 2008 Beijing Games by the host country showed some of the features of this system.

Eastern European sport: from the end of *World War II* until the mid-1980s, East European sport was organised on a *centralised* approach, ideologically orientated, was state run and used as *propaganda*.

eccentric force: a force applied outside the *centre of mass* of a body that produces angular motion.

eccentric muscle contraction: involves the lengthening of the muscle under tension during movement. It is a form of *isotonic muscle contraction*. It occurs, for example, in the biceps brachii when lowering a weight during a biceps curl, or in the triceps brachii during the downward phase of a press-up. The *actin* filaments are slowly moved away from the centre of the *sarcomere*. (See also *concentric muscle contraction*.)

economic system: a term that stems from the control of material resources. Economic systems are often dependent on political *ideologies*. There are several forms, including:

- market economy or *capitalism* – which allows market forces to determine the allocation of resources. Factors of production are determined by supply and demand. This type of system allows freedom of choice and can efficiently allocate resources leading to economic growth. However, it leads to inequality of income and those with most money usually hold the most power
- socialism – a system that involves collective ownership of the means of production and a major role for the state in the provision of services. In its extreme form of *communism*, it dominated the centrally planned economies of Eastern Europe until 1989. China, North Korea and Cuba are still mainly governed in this way
- mixed economy – one that combines a market economy with some centrally planned or state-run enterprises. Governments are able to regulate the workings of the market through *legislation*. For example, the UK has a mixed economy
- transitional economy – which occurs in countries that had centrally planned economies but that are now allowing market forces to operate at least in some parts of the economy. Many East European countries are in transition.

Centrally planned economy	Mixed economy	Market economy
Production organised and run by the state	Some production state-run, e.g. large-scale, 'essential' services	Production market-driven
Labour force directed and paid by the state	State and private firms compete for factors of production and customers	Wages determined by the market
Prices of goods and services controlled		Prices determined by supply and demand

economics of sport: this area of research focuses on issues such as performers salaries and their productivity, transfer of players, structure and operation of sporting leagues, sport products, inequality of resource distribution regarding racial and sex issues. The sports industry produces vast amounts of income for governments, who also provide sport with grants. The size of the grants given to sport by different governments will often depend on their philosophy or *ideology* towards the place of sport in their society.

To some extent, the sport industry is different to other industries in that sport organisations have to collaborate with each other to produce the product, for example a football match. In other industries companies cannot collude with each other. In the *USA baseball* receives special exemption from the government's anti-monopoly *legislation*. Sporting leagues are cartels where movement in and out is strictly controlled. In the UK professional football clubs have floated on the stock exchange. They invest in new stadia and television revenues continue to expand and cause controversy over the amount of control the *mass media* should then wield.

education: the process of acquiring knowledge and skills in both a formal and informal manner. It is viewed as a life-long process but formal structures such as an education system play a major part, particularly during childhood and adolescence. In other cultures, such as *primitive cultures*, these more formal structures may not operate and education of the community takes place through their social groups. (See also *public schools* and *state education*.)

Education Acts: government *legislation* introduced with the specific aim of raising the standard of the education of children. They have been modified depending on the needs of society at the time and include.

Forster Education Act 1870 – a great milestone in social welfare as it created a system of state education whereas previously the education of the poor had been a parish responsibility. There was a developing initiative to build more schools and the Act was a result of some radical changes in social thinking by philanthropists and social reformers. The main points of the Act were as follows:

- England and Wales divided into 2500 school districts
- the churches were to decide if new schools were to be built
- school boards had to be elected to finance schools from the rates
- a small fee was required initially, to be paid by the family but the very poor could receive free education
- the school age was not less than five years but no more than 13
- in terms of physical activity, Swedish or *military drill* was permitted.

Butler Education Act 1944 – planned to reform education in Britain as it was a major social reform, aiming to ensure *equal opportunity* for all. Its main provisions were:

- there were to be 146 local education authorities rather than 300
- school-leaving age was raised to 15
- *grammar school* entry was to be free following a pass at the 11-plus examination; other children to attend a secondary modern
- secondary grammar, technical and modern schools aimed to provide the most appropriate education based on the 11-plus examination but this also proved to be a *social class* distinction
- local education authorities were to provide recreational facilities
- physical education teachers were to be given the same status as other teachers.

Education Reform Act 1988 – the Act was a far-reaching one, affecting *physical education* within the wider education system. A Conservative government seeking more control was challenging the traditionally *decentralised* system of education, which necessitated cutting the powers of *local authorities*. The following reforms were introduced:

- a *National Curriculum* for children of school age in the state school system
- statutory *attainment targets* were to provide guidelines on standards and secure some accountability
- *local management of schools*, where schools were given control of their own budgets
- some schools chose to opt out of local authority control and valued the status of being *grant-maintained schools*. They received money directly from the government. Initial funding was generous but further changes have retracted this situation.

education authorities are committees with county councils and metropolitan district councils. The Butler Education Act 1944 (see *Education Acts*) made it mandatory for them to provide recreational facilities within schools. In the 1970s and 1980s local authorities helped the education authorities by providing money and these facilities became known as *dual use* and *joint provision* facilities.

Education Reform Act: see *Education Acts*.

Edwardian period: the term given to the period from 1901–18, following the *Victorian era*. During this a time there was a heavy emphasis on improving the provision for the urban population, with increased *leisure* time for the **working class,** better transport and improved communications. The suffragettes were fighting campaigns for equal rights for women, as were the trade unions for the workers. In terms of sport, the **upper class** and *middle class* were removing themselves even further from the working class and the increase in exclusive sports clubs continued (see *exclusivity*); particular examples were *golf* and *tennis*. Social factors enabled sport to become a major entertainment market with football the most popular. The northern professionals were beginning to threaten the southern amateur hold and the minimum professional wage was set in 1904 at £4 a week. The 1908 *Olympic Games* were held in London, although public interest was not great, but other activities such as *horse racing*, *cricket* and *rugby league* were popular.

Public schools continued their sporting traditions but the state schools now followed the Forster Education Act 1870 providing the working-class children with the experiences of *military drill* and *Swedish gymnastics*. The *Syllabuses of Physical Training* were introduced by the *Board of Education* with games and recreative activities taking over from drill.

effective learning refers to the development of a performer's *motor programmes* and their execution. For example, the skills of catching, throwing, jumping and kicking. To maximise learning, effective learning should be combined with *affective learning* and the *cognitive theories of learning*.

effector mechanism: a component of the *information-processing* model, which transfers the decision that has been made to the muscular system via motor nerves. For example, after a batsman decides which shot they wish to play based on the bowler's delivery, the effector mechanism starts the movement.

effort arm: a part of a *lever* system, which represents the distance between the fulcrum and the effort force; the longer the effort arm, the less effort required to move a given resistance. The length of the effort arm can often be increased to overcome a heavy object.

egalitarian: the philosophy of the equality of mankind and the desirability of political, social and economic equality. This has led to an emphasis on equity issues in sport such as creating more fairness of accessibility to sport participation.

ejection fraction: the percentage of the blood that enters the heart which is pumped out of the left ventricle with each contraction. It is calculated by:

$$FORMULA: \quad E_f = \frac{SV}{EDV} \times 100$$

where

E_f = ejection fraction

SV = stroke volume

EDV = end diastolic volume, i.e. the volume of blood in the ventricle following the diastolic (filling) phase of the cardic cycle.

The heart of a trained athlete can contract more forcibly and can therefore eject more blood that it receives per beat. It therefore has a higher ejection faction.

elastic strength: a dimension of strength that considers the ability of a muscle or group of muscles to overcome a resistance rapidly and prepare quickly for a sequential contraction of equal force. Elastic strength is central to successful performance in those activities that are explosive in nature such as sprinting, triple jumping and gymnastic tumbling sequences.

elasticity: a property of *skeletal muscle*, which enables it to return to its original shape following contraction or *extension*. This enables repeated contractions to take place, such as when running or *cycling*.

electrolytes: trace elements such as potassium, sodium and chlorine that the help the body to maintain the optimum rate of exchange of nutrients and waste products into and out of the muscle cell and allow optimal muscle functioning.

electron transport chain: a series of oxidation and reduction reactions in the breakdown (catabolism) of glucose. It forms the final stage of the *aerobic energy system* and occurs in the cristae of the *mitochondria*. It releases *energy* which can then be used to resynthesise *ATP*. Hydrogen ions released in the *Krebs cycle* are oxidised in the electron transport chain to form water, while the electrons pass through a series of reactions and can generate large amounts of energy. The electron transport chain produces sufficient energy to resynthesise 34 moles of ATP.

eligibility rules aim to set a 'level playing field' in sport so that all competitors, in theory, have an equal chance of succeeding. Such *rules* are needed to prevent cheating; competitors are sometimes tempted to cheat because of the attractiveness of financial *rewards* in modern sport. There are eligibility rules that determine whether an athlete or sport is deemed to meet the requirements for entry to the *Olympic Games*; these rules can cover, for example, amateur status, age, *gender*, nationality and skill level.

elite: the most talented sports people or the most educationally gifted. The term suggests that only a minority can achieve the highest standards and usually determines unequal access to resources: facilities, personnel and funding. It is therefore an exclusive situation (see *exclusivity*) at the apex of the *participation pyramid* and it is suggested that the wider the base of participation the greater chance of producing elite athletes. In international competition, elite athletes are often considered to be ambassadors for their country.

emergent cultures are countries coming into being or notice. Some countries such as those in Africa, Latin America and southeast Asia can be referred to as developing countries or as less economically developed countries (LEDC). They do not necessarily come under the *communist* or *capitalist* systems, but they were in the main colonised by the wealthier countries in the West. These countries face common social and sporting problems:
- their economies were land based, yet they are experiencing a shift towards an industrial economy
- an increase in urban populations led to a less active society
- their sport infrastructure could not initially match that of the West in terms of organisation and facilities
- Western sport tends to be more specialised, requiring more resources
- *discrimination* under colonial rule usually excluded native participation in sport at a high level. Independence helped to produce the democratisation of sport where the masses can experience activities previously enjoyed by the governing class.

New independent governments face the dilemma of either providing scarce resources for the masses or funding *elite* athletes who could compete on the world stage, which would in turn provide prestige, international recognition and potential financial gain – all factors difficult for governments to ignore. Appropriate selection of activities is needed if they are to realise their aims. This will be based on the resources available and the traditions of the population.

emergent leader: a leader who gains a position of authority by emerging from within a group, with the support of the members, based on their personal expertise, skill and knowledge. For example, the members of a local football team could vote among themselves to decide who they wished to be captain. This type of leader is in contrast to a *prescribed leader*, which is chosen externally.

emotions: a state of *arousal* experienced by a performer, which can be pleasurable or unpleasurable depending on their perception of the situation. If the latter situation occurs, the body makes physiological adjustments, as suggested by the *general adaptation syndrome*, in an attempt to return to a state of equilibrium. Emotions include joy, sadness, apprehension and excitement, all of which tend to be reactions to specific situations or experiences.

endocardium: the innermost layer of the heart composed of a single layer of epithelial cells. It enables the blood to flow more easily through the heart's chambers by preventing *friction*.

endorsement: where athletes display companies' names on their equipment, clothing and vehicles. This is known as endorsing a product. The performers are contracted to declare publicly their approval of a product or service. Sports stars have emerged as personality *advertising* and are used as a 'big sell'.

endothermic reactions are those chemical reactions that occur (in the body, for example) that require *energy*. The resynthesis of *ADP* into *ATP* requires energy and is therefore endothermic. Thus:

FORMULA: ADP + Pi + energy $\rightarrow$ ATP

endowed schools: schools with a regular income, controlled by trustees.

energy: the capacity of the body to perform work. Energy is never lost. It is simply transferred from one form to another. Chemical energy in the food we eat is transferred into kinetic energy when the body moves when participating in physical activity. All energy-requiring processes of the body acquire the necessary energy from a high-energy compound that exists in all cells: adenosine triphosphate, or ATP for short.

Energy from food is stored in the bonds that make up ATP, ready to be released whenever the body requires energy. Energy is measured in joules.

Energy expenditure is mainly of concern when following a weight control programme, where we might need to analyse energy input from food and energy expenditure through exercise.

energy balance: a method of determining the fate of body weight having considered *energy* input and energy expenditure. If the number of calories consumed equals the number of calories expended, the performer should maintain their body weight. This is referred to as a neutral energy balance and is the aim for most performers. If the number of calories consumed exceeds the number of calories expended, a positive energy balance occurs, weight is gained and *fat* stores increased. A negative energy balance occurs when fewer calories are consumed than expended. Energy stored as *glycogen* and fat can be used to make up the calorie deficiency, causing a reduction in body fat resulting in weight loss.

In most cases, athletes will wish to keep their body weight stable, where energy input = energy output. Occasionally, however, they may wish to increase or decrease their weight. For example, when wishing to make a weight category in judo, a player may need to restrict their caloric intake in the days leading up to the event and so must make the necessary adjustments to their calorie intake and/or expenditure.

energy continuum: a *continuum* that reflects the relative importance and contribution each *energy system* makes to an activity. For most activities, all three energy systems are active, but there is usually one system that is dominant at any one time. It should be possible to place each activity along an energy continuum, which identifies the main energy systems in use.

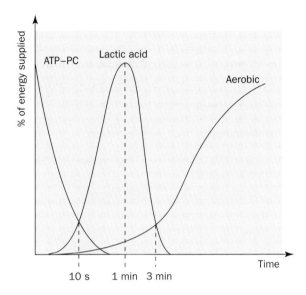

The energy continuum

energy systems: the process of *energy* production in the body for muscular contraction that occurs when chemical energy is transformed into mechanical energy. Chemical energy exists in the muscle cell in the form of *ATP*, a high energy phosphate molecule which when broken down releases the energy stored within its bonds. The energy can then be used to initiate muscle contraction and therefore movement.

The stores of ATP are limited in the body and the aim of the energy systems is to resynthesise or rebuild ATP, so that energy can be continually supplied. There are three energy systems used for the resynthesis of ATP, each operating depending on the duration and intensity of the exercise that is to be undertaken:

- *alactic energy system* or ATP–PC energy system – the first of the systems is the immediate source of energy, used in activities that are of short duration but high in intensity, such as a 100-metre sprint
- *lactic acid energy system* or *glycolysis* – the second of the systems is used in activities or periods of exercise that are of fairly high intensity, such as a 400-metre run or while running up hills in cross country
- *aerobic energy system* – the third system is the most efficient, since oxygen is available and is predominantly used in activities that are of long duration and low intensity, such as a marathon run.

97

The three energy systems

	Alactic (immediate)	Lactic acid (anaerobic glycolytic)	Aerobic (oxidative)
Substrate(s)	ATP, PC	*Glycogen* or glucose	Glycogen or glucose, *fat, protein*
Relative rate of ATP production	Very fast	Fast	Slower
Energy yield	1 ATP	2 ATP	38 ATP
Duration at maximal pace	0–10 sec	0–180 sec	> 3 min
Limiting factors	PC depletion	*Lactic acid* accumulation	Glycogen depletion
Controlling *enzyme*	Creatine kinase	PFK	PFK, lipase
Site of reaction	*Sarcoplasm*	Sarcoplasm	*Mitochondria*
Examples of activities	Power/weightlifting Short sprints Jumping, throwing	Longer sprints Middle-distance Field games	Endurance events Marathon running Field games

Essentially, all three of the energy systems are always functioning, even at rest. It is the relative contributions that each system makes in providing energy that varies. We can therefore view the energy systems as operating along a *continuum*.

English Federation of Disability Sport (EFDS) is the national body responsible for developing sport for disabled people in England. It works closely with the eight National Disability Sports Organisations (NDSOs) recognised by *Sport England* to develop sporting opportunities for the 11 million disabled people in England:

* British Amputees and Les Autres Sports Association (BALASA)
* British Blind Sport
* CP Sport
* Dwarf Athletics
* Mencap Sport
* Special Olympics
* UK Deaf Sport
* WheelPower.

English Institute of Sport (EIS) is a nationwide network of world-class support services designed to foster the talents of England's *elite* athletes. Services are offered from nine regional multi-sport hub sites and an evolving network of satellite centres.

High-performance training venues are the platform for success. The strategy and ethos of the EIS is set by its national team. The services are delivered by a coordinated network of regional teams that feature complementary skills and experience. The range of services supplied by the EIS spans sports science and *sports medicine*. Support includes applied physiology, *biomechanics*, medical consultation, medical screening, nutritional advice, performance analysis, psychology, podiatry, strength and conditioning *coaching*, sports massage and sports vision. The Performance Lifestyle programme provides supplementary career and education advice.

The quality of the delivery is assured by the close relationship the EIS is developing with national **governing bodies**, performance directors, coaches and the athletes themselves. Almost 2000 competitors are currently in the EIS system.

English Institute of Sport, Sheffield (EISS) opened in December 2003. It is Sport England Lottery funded and managed by Sheffield International Venues Ltd. EISS is one of the country's most impressive indoor sports venues and is committed to the development of UK sport at all levels. The organisation welcomes both the local sporting community and the country's **elite** athletes to benefit from its high-quality facilities.

The state-of-the-art sports development centre offers a range of highly equipped sports performance areas, including athletics, with a six-lane 200-metre indoor track and indoor throws area, badminton, basketball, boxing; handball, judo, netball and volleyball. (See also **national sports centres**.)

environment: see **display (psychology)**.

enzyme: a biological catalyst that is a protein found in the body used to speed up chemical reactions, especially in the processes of **energy** release. Endurance training can improve the activity of oxidative (**aerobic**) enzymes, which work on breaking down our food fuel to release the energy stored within. In doing so the body's ability to utilise **glycogen** and **fat** as a fuel is increased which promotes a greater amount of available energy and an improved performance. Under **anaerobic** conditions the enzymes responsible for the breaking down of **creatine phosphate** and our glycolytic enzymes respond positively to anaerobic training, such as sprint **interval training** and **strength training**.

EPI: see **Eysenck's personality inventory**.

epicardium: see **pericardium**.

equal opportunity: the principle and practice of providing all people with the same chance to succeed irrespective of their sex, age, **gender**, physical ability or religious group. In the descriptive sense human beings patently do not possess the same amount of physical, mental or moral qualities. In the prescriptive sense, however, people ought to treat each other with equal respect, dignity and consideration. During the twentieth century there has been a growing democratisation of education, the workplace and sport in order to reduce the amount of **discrimination** felt by some sections of the population.

ergogenic aid: a substance or object that is used to enhance athletic performance. These can range from simple nasal strips (designed to improve oxygen intake) through to performance enhancing drugs (such as **human growth hormone**). Ergogenic aids generally fall into one of four categories:
- pharmacological, e.g. **amphetamines**/**caffeine**
- hormonal, e.g. **anabolic steroids**/human growth hormone
- physiological, e.g. **blood doping**/recombinant **erythropoietin**
- nutritional, e.g. creatine supplementation/**glycogen loading**.

Performers turn to these ergogenic aids in the hope of gaining a winning edge. Although many ergogenic aids are legal, others are illegal and instead of enhancing performance can actually impair it, sometimes with fatal consequences.

erythropoietin (EPO) is a naturally occurring hormone produced by the kidneys which stimulates red cell production. Increases of erythropoietin are very beneficial to the athlete as they increase the blood's oxygen-carrying capacity. This can occur naturally through **altitude training** but since the introduction of a synthetic version (recombinant erythropoietin, or Rh EPO) it has become the endurance cheater's choice of drug.

Although it has proven benefits such as increases in **haemoglobin** content, **fatigue** index and **maximum oxygen uptake (VO$_2$ max)**, EPO has a fatal side. In the early 1990s several Dutch cyclists died as a result of injecting EPO. It is not known how many red blood cells the drug produces when injected and it is thought that increased viscosity of the blood (**hyperviscosity**) can lead to clotting and heart failure. The production of the body's natural EPO will also be compromised.

escape: to get away from or break free. With **industrialisation** in the eighteenth and nineteenth centuries, the movement of people from rural areas to the towns, poor working and living conditions led to the need for those people to get away and experience the **natural environment**. Numerous activities have been associated with the idea of escape, such as cycling and rambling.

esteem: to have great respect or high regard for. Talented athletes who reach the pinnacle of their sport are awarded honour and prestige that raises their social status. Such athletes may also become **role models** to younger people and their own **self-esteem** is also raised by a sense of achievement.

ethics: derived from the Greek word 'ethike', meaning science of morals or character. Ethics can be the moral principles or set of moral values held by an individual or group. It raises issues that have a moral dimension, such as debates over **doping** in sport and **gamesmanship** versus **sportsmanship**.

Ideal			Real
		Motives	
	good	bad	
Excellent play			Win at all costs
		Intentions	
	good	bad	
Sportsmanship – good game strategy			Gamesmanship – deceitful strategy
		Actions	
	right	wrong	
Purpose – establish dominance through **excellence**			Purpose – take out of game, do physical, emotional, mental harm

ethnic groups have racial, religious, linguistic and/or certain other traits in common. The social group usually sees itself as a distinct unit and attempts to preserve its identity through maintaining traditions and customs. Where a group forms a minority in the population this need can be heightened. In the 2001 census 7.9% of the UK population described themselves as belonging to an ethnic group.

ethnic sports: see *Ashbourne Royal Shrovetide football*, *Cornish hurling*, *Highland Games, Lakeland sports* and *wrestling*.

etiquette: the customs or rules governing behaviour regarded as correct or acceptable in social or official life. Often a conventional but unwritten code of behaviour is followed by members of a social group. An example in sport may be shaking hands before a match (see *sportsmanship*).

European Charter on Sport for All: *legislation* requiring governments to promote sport as an important factor in human development. They should encourage and enable every individual to participate in sport, notably all young people, who should receive *physical education* and acquire basic sports skills. Participation should also take place in a safe and healthy environment. In cooperation with the appropriate sporting organisations, governments should:

- ensure that everyone with ability and interest should be able to reach their own levels of personal achievement or publicly recognised levels of *excellence*
- protect and develop the ethical and moral basis of sport, protecting sports and sports people from exploitation for political, commercial and financial gain, including *doping*.

European model of sport: in 1998 the European Commission identified sport as performing five functions within society:

- educational
- social
- cultural
- recreational
- public health.

The Commission's main role is to consult with sports organisations across Europe to plan for sport development and identify potential problems. Europe can be seen as having two distinct identities: *Eastern Europe* and *Western Europe*. However, the structure tends to include the elements outlined below:

- there is a *grass roots* approach, which is different from the approach in the USA, which has a more professional base, linked to business
- *national identity* is important – the Amsterdam Declaration states 'sport represents and strengthens national or regional identity by giving people a sense of belonging to a group, uniting players and spectators'. International competition remains an important element in countries demonstrating their *culture* and nationhood. This is again different from the USA where there is less need for inter-state competitions
- traditionally modern sport has its roots in Europe where the birth of *industrialisation* occurred and it has a set place within our societies
- European Union regulations can be applied to sporting matters.

In 2006, the Independent European Sport Review identified two important features in the European sports model: (1) the rapid and irreversible trend towards commercialisation of sport, and (2) the development of the European Union into a wider political, economic and legal structure now extending to 27 member states.

eustress: a form of positive *stress* that performers actively seek to test their *abilities* to the limit. It can enhance performance by focusing *attention* and heightening the *emotions* felt. If the individual successfully completes the task in situations involving *danger* or high *expectation*, it can lead to high levels of *intrinsic motivation* and self-satisfaction. For example, many *adventurous activities* can initiate this response, as do performances in front of *significant others*.

evaluation apprehension: a form of *anxiety* caused when an individual perceives their performance is being judged by an *audience*. Cottrell (1968) suggested *social facilitation* occurs in the presence of others, but higher and detrimental *arousal* was caused if the performer felt others were assessing their actions. For example, an athlete may execute techniques in training correctly, but in competition may worry about what the spectators think of their performance. The result may be a deterioration in performance.

evangelism: the practice of spreading the Christian gospel. It emphasises personal conversion and faith for salvation. In the nineteenth century the evangelists restricted the recreations of the *working class* believing their *popular recreations* to be sinful and associated with *gambling* and alcohol.

eversion: a *movement pattern* that takes place at the ankle characterised by the *lateral* turning the sole of the foot outwards. For example, during the breaststroke 'kick' action in swimming, the foot is everted to increase the contact of the foot with the water. (See appendix, page 330.)

excellence: a special ability beyond the norm, to which many aspire but few go on to achieve. For our purposes we mean the superior, *elite* athletes at both amateur and professional level who reach the pinnacle of performance in their chosen sport. Excellence usually suggests a specialism in one or a few activities and is judged against national and international standards. For example, the developers of excellence in sport are usually **Sport England**, the national **governing bodies**, **Sports Coach UK**, the **British Olympic Association** and **local authorities**. The pursuit of excellence in sport is encouraged for a variety of reasons, including:
- sport can bring about change in people's lifestyles which have become increasingly sedentary and controlled
- curiosity about individual and human potential often means sport is called 'the last frontier'
- sport can provide alternative employment with the added attraction of high social status if high-level success is achieved
- it can give individuals a high sense of *self-esteem*, a feeling of quality or worth in their lives
- sporting success can boost national pride and morale and accrue economic benefits
- mass populations can be entertained in socially accepted activities
- the base of the *participation pyramid* can be increased by others wishing to participate in sport.

However, the problems with attempting to develop excellence include:
- it is elitist – it only serves the interests of a few
- costly resources are required for a minority of sport participants

- over-specialisation and obsession with a physical activity can occur, which may have damaging physiological and psychological effects
- the moral value of sport can be lost due to the 'win at all costs' attitude that is likely to be exacerbated when the stakes are higher.

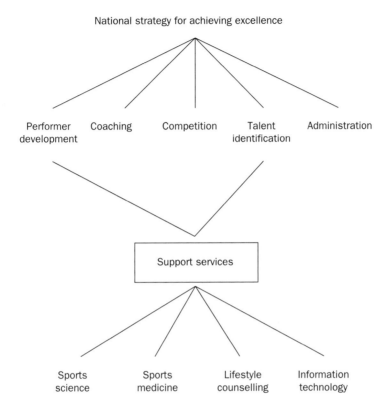

National strategy for achieving excellence

Performer development · Coaching · Competition · Talent identification · Administration

Support services

Sports science · Sports medicine · Lifestyle counselling · Information technology

Excellence

excess post-exercise oxygen consumption (EPOC) is sometimes referred to as oxygen debt. It is the amount of oxygen consumed during *recovery* above that which normally would have been consumed at rest in the same period of time. An oxygen debt will accrue whenever the body has undertaken some form of *anaerobic* exercise. This will occur at quite intense levels of exercise, lasting up to 3 minutes or when the anaerobic threshold has been exceeded (see diagram overleaf). Typically, an oxygen debt consists of two stages:

1. A fast stage or *alactacid debt* – the oxygen is used during recovery to resynthesise fuels used in the *alactic energy system*, i.e. *ATP* and *creatine phosphate*. This happens very quickly and lasts for about 2 or 3 minutes and explains why a 100-metre sprinter can perform repeated bouts of very high intensity with very little rest. Some of the oxygen during this stage is also used to re-saturate myoglobin.
2. A slow stage or *lactacid debt* – the oxygen is used to clear the body of *lactic acid* that will have accrued during the exercise period and provides the oxygen that supplies the cardiac and respiratory muscles with the energy to remain elevated during the recovery period. This is a much longer process and the heart rate and respiratory rate can remain elevated for up to 1 hour.

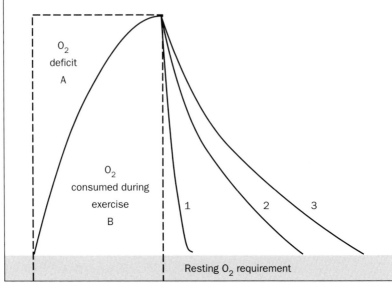

A+B = Total oxygen demand during period of exercise in excess of that required at rest.

1 = Fast component or alactic EPOC
2 = Lactic acid EPOC
3 = Non-oxygen deficit EPOC
2+3 = Slow component
1+2+3 = EPOC or 'oxygen debt'

Excess post-exercise oxygen consumption (EPOC)

exclusion: a shorthand label for what can happen when individuals or areas suffer a combination of linked problems such as unemployment, poor skills, low incomes, poor housing, high crime environments, bad health and family breakdowns.

In the most intensive study of exclusion Europe-wide, it is seen that unemployment and low income lead to exclusion from a fair share of social 'goods' and capital in the form of recognition, income and work. Combinations of aspects of exclusion can be said to lead to double deprivation, for example, being elderly and from an ethnic minority. If exclusion is prolonged in youth it can have lasting effects in terms of playing recreationally, socialising and competing to achieve. The opportunity to realise sporting potential is significantly influenced by an individual's social background.

Governments now regard sport and recreation as having wider benefits to society, particularly in helping people feel included and important in their own communities. (See also *inclusiveness*.)

exclusivity: belonging to or serving a privileged minority. An example is a private school or private sports club. Access is denied to others who may not meet the criteria and this can involve *discrimination*.

executive motor programme: this organises a series of *subroutines* into the correct sequence to perform a movement, adapting it to changes in the environment. Motor programmes are based on a hierarchical structure, involving movements that are autonomous at the lower level with more complex subroutines at the peak. As the performer becomes more skilled, the existing executive motor programme is relegated and superseded by a new programme. For example, a tennis player will initially develop the skill of hitting the ball by learning the stance, grip, swing and follow-through. When the *autonomous phase of learning* is reached, these form part of the new programme, which may include drive, smash, volley and lob. These in turn may become forehand shots, and so on. These well-learnt programmes are often considered to be under *open loop control* theory, while the actions that need some sort of evaluation are under *closed loop control*. However, some of the limitations of these theories were answered by the *schema theory*.

exhaustion: the final stage of the *general adaptation syndrome*, when the body begins to fail to cope with the effects of *stress*. The performer starts to develop various physiological disorders, which can include heart disease, high *blood pressure* and the inability to fight infection.

exothermic reactions are those chemical reactions that give off *energy*. For example, the breakdown of *ATP* releases energy for muscular contraction.

FORMULA: ATP → ADP + Pi + energy

expectations: generally accepted codes of behaviour and roles within a group or society that are actively promoted. They are used as part of the *socialisation* process. Positive expectations from a coach or teacher can motivate the performer to fulfil those expectations. For example, a coach may encourage *assertive behaviour* during the game situation of all players, rather than acts of *aggression*, which may lead to fouls and penalties. Expectations can also be negative when they are informed by *stereotypes* and *prejudice*.

experiential learning involves the performer learning by doing. Gallway (1977) suggests the individual should be allowed to discover *movement patterns*, experience the consequences and subsequently modify the action to cope with the situation. Learning is based on the use of *internal feedback*, making the performer responsible for the understanding of the action and developing *kinaesthesis*. For example, a football player is given the task of shooting from different positions. During the practice session they develop a 'feel' for how hard to kick the ball for the shot to be effective.

expiration: breathing out or the process by which air is forced out of the lungs into the atmosphere. At rest, this is usually a passive process involving a relaxation of the inspiratory muscles (external intercostal muscles and the diaphragm) and elastic recoil of lung tissue. During exercise, expiration becomes a more active process, which involves the internal intercostal muscles speeding up the process by pulling rib cage down. In addition *skeletal muscles* such as the latissimus dorsi and the abdominal muscles assist the action.

expiratory reserve volume (ERV) is the maximum volume of air that can be expelled from the lungs after a normal *expiration*, which for an average adult male is approximately 1500 cm^3. During exercise the expiratory reserve volume decreases to enable an increase in the performer's *tidal volume*. (See appendix, page 330.)

explosive strength: a dimension of *strength* that considers the rate at which strength is applied. A performer with high levels of explosive strength such as a shot putter will be able to overcome a resistance with a high speed of contraction.

extension: a *movement pattern* involving an increase in angle of articulating bones. For example, in performing a press-up, the angle between the humerus and ulna increases causing extension at the elbow. A muscle that causes extension is known as an *extensor*, which in the case of a push-up is the triceps brachii. Extreme extension, usually at an angle of greater than 180°, is known as hyperextension. (See appendix, page 326.)

extensor: a muscle that causes *extension*. For example, the quadriceps femoris causes extension of the lower leg at the knee joint when kicking a football.

external feedback: see *feedback*.

externally paced skills involve the performer reacting to the changing environmental conditions. They have little control over when the movement has to be executed. These types of skill are placed on the same *continuum* as *self-paced skills* and are often examples of *open skills*. Examples include receiving a pass during a game of hockey, white water rafting or batting in a game of cricket.

exteroceptors gather information from outside the body. They allow the performer to detect *stimuli* from the *display (psychology)* by means of vision, touch, hearing, smell and taste. Other components of the *sensory system* include proprioceptors and introceptors.

extra-curricular sport takes place outside the normal school timetable. The main focus is on improving performance standards rather than the educational process that is the main emphasis in the *physical education* lesson. It is viewed as an opportunity for children to extend their interest or ability in physical activities. The changes in society and education in the last 20 years have affected such opportunities with a reduction in emphasis on the sporting *elite*. Factors affecting extra-curricular activities have been:

- the teachers' strikes in the early 1980s, which diminished teacher goodwill
- financial cuts felt in terms of transport
- the *local management of schools* enabled schools to boost their funds by selling off playing fields
- the increasing amount of *leisure* and employment opportunities available to teenagers meant competing for the school team seemed less attractive
- the anti-competitive lobby became more vocal espousing the idea that competition was harmful to children.

The focus of the 1995 government publication *Sport: Raising the Game* is mainly on reinstating the status of school sport within school life, also evident in the *PESSCLS* policy (Physical Education and School Sports Club Links Strategy).

extra-mural sports: inter-school competitions in the *USA*, which can be informal or highly organised and serious. The students go through a more selective process than the *intra-mural sports*. The activities are widely reported by the press and the local community takes considerable interest.

extrinsic motivation: *motivation* for success based on the external *rewards* given to the performer which can influence behaviour. They are used for *reinforcement*, to shape behaviour in an attempt to encourage repetition of the action. Reinforcers can be tangible, such as cups, medals, certificates or money, or intangible, such as praise, a round of applause, social status, recognition or the glory of winning. Care must be taken not to overuse extrinsic rewards as the performer may become over-reliant on them and if withdrawn the performer may lose the motivation to continue participating. Their use should be combined with a performer's *intrinsic motivation*.

extrovert: a person who is sociable, active, outgoing, optimistic and impulsive. These *traits* are said to be due to the relative insensitivity of their *reticular activating system* to incoming sensory information, leading to low levels of *arousal*. As a result they need to increase stimulation levels to avoid boredom and prefer situations that involve other people or challenges. It has been suggested extroverts cope better with competitive, pressurised, stressful situations and occupy positions of responsibility. In comparison, *introverts* possess the opposite traits and are placed at the other end of the *continuum*. These characteristics can be measured using *Eysenck's personality inventory* or *Cattell's 16 personality factors questionnaire*.

Eysenck's personality inventory (EPI) measures the personality traits of an individual along two dimensions – introversion–extroversion and stable–neuroticism – using a *questionnaire* requiring a series of 'yes' or 'no' responses. A personal profile is then constructed with a score for each dimension. Usually most people do not fall into the extremes of each category. Within the test is a lie scale, which invalidates the results if exceeded. (See also *trait theory*.)

Aiming for a grade A*?

Don't forget to log on to **www.philipallan.co.uk/a-zonline** for advice.

fag: a young public schoolboy who performs menial chores for an older boy or prefect. *Thomas Arnold* discouraged this system, believing it to be open to abuse and leading to bullying. In relation to sporting activities, the younger boys would 'fag at *fives*' meaning they would collect the balls while the older boys played the game.

fair: travelling entertainment with side-shows. It was at the fair that the **working class** had some fun, saw new faces and experienced fresh amusements. The fair, especially in the *medieval era*, was granted by the king and could last up to three days. Both fairs and markets would bring in merchants and traders. They were usually granted to the **Church** and often landed on *holy days* or feast days in honour of a saint. Entertainment was a key feature with jugglers, minstrels, freak shows, bear *baiting*, cock fighting, dicing, wagering and dancing.

fair play is defined by the ***European Charter on Sport for All*** as much more than playing within the *rules*. It incorporates the concepts of friendship, respect for others and always playing in the right spirit. It is defined as a way of thinking not just of behaving. It concerns issues such as the elimination of cheating, ***gamesmanship, doping***, violence, exploitation, unequal opportunities, excessive ***commercialisation*** and corruption. Fair play is a positive concept. If practised fairly, sport is a culturally enriching experience and an individual is given the opportunity for self-expression and personal achievement. Sport promotes responsibility to others and for the environment. According to the European Charter on Sport for All, providers of sporting activities should make fair play a central concept.

far transfer: see *transfer of learning*.

Fartlek training: a form of endurance conditioning where the ***aerobic energy system*** is stressed due to the continuous nature of the exercise. The key to this type of training is that the speed or intensity of the exercise is varied so that both the ***aerobic energy system*** and the ***anaerobic energy system*** can be stressed. Fartlek sessions are usually performed for a minimum of 45 minutes, with the intensity of the session varying from low-intensity walking to high-intensity sprinting. Traditionally, this form of training has taken place in the countryside over varied terrain, but this alternating pace method could be practised anywhere in your local environment for, example:

- a 15-minute jog at 60% *maximum heart rate*
- a sprint for one lamp post/easy jog for three lamp posts
- repeat ten times
- walk for 90 seconds
- a 5-minute jog at 75% maximum heart rate, and so on.

The benefits of this training are that it can be adapted to the individual, is easy to administer and can also be fun, offering variety to what some regard as the monotony of continuous jogging. Since both aerobic and anaerobic systems are stressed through this method of training, a wealth of sportspeople can benefit and it is particularly suited to those activities that involve a mixture of aerobic and *anaerobic* work, for example, games such as rugby, netball, soccer or hockey.

fast twitch muscle fibre: a type of muscle fibre suited to high intensity, power activities involving anaerobic work. These fibres have a low oxidative capacity and a high glycolytic capacity. The physiological characteristics of fast twitch fibres differ greatly from *slow twitch muscle fibres*, which include:

- possession of greater amounts of ATPase – the *enzyme* responsible for splitting *ATP*
- a more highly developed sarcoplasmic reticulum, which means greater amounts of calcium can arrive at the muscle cell initiating quicker contractile speeds. Indeed, slow twitch fibres take approximately 110 milliseconds to reach maximal tension while fast twitch can reach it in a mere 50 milliseconds
- the ability to generate greater force than slow twitch motor units since there are more fast twitch fibres per motor unit than in slow twitch motor units.

Fast twitch fibres are also known as type 2 fibres and are commonly subdivided into:

- type 2a or fast oxidative glycolytic (FOG) fibres, which pick up certain slow twitch characteristics as a result of endurance training. They therefore tend to have a greater resistance to *fatigue* and are used during an 800 m run.
- type 2b or fast twitch glycolytic (FTG), which fibres can generate much greater forces and are used during a 100 m sprint.
- type 2c, which have recently been recognised and are recruited for extremely explosive activities such as the power lift.

fat: an organic lipid compound formed from glycerol and *fatty acids*. It exists in the body in many forms, including adipose tissue, triglycerides and *free fatty acids*. Fat is our major *energy* source with up to 70% of our energy derived from it at rest. When sufficient oxygen is available to the muscle cell, fatty acids constitute the favoured fuel for energy production and during low-intensity exercise fat is a major source as the body tries to spare the limited stores of *glycogen* for higher intensity bouts of exercise. Due to the hydrophobic (low water solubility) quality of fat, energy production is slow so the body cannot use fat as its sole fuel source and energy production is therefore usually fuelled by a combination of fat and glycogen. One explanation of an athlete 'hitting the wall' is that all their glycogen stores have been depleted and the athlete is trying to metabolise fat as a sole fuel source. Endurance training can encourage the body to utilise fat as a fuel, thus depleting glycogen less. However, the risks of excessive fat consumption are well documented, so it is recommended that an athlete's diet should not consist of more than 30% fat of total calories consumed.

fatigue occurs when the body is unable to resynthesise *ATP* for *energy*. This is caused by three main factors:

- lack of oxygen – leading to a build-up of *lactic acid* and lowering of the levels of blood acidity
- lack of *creatine phosphate*
- lack of *glycogen* and glucose.

The onset of fatigue can be delayed by utilising appropriate training methods to delay the *onset of blood lactate accumulation* and improve the *aerobic energy system*.

fatty acids: during digestion, the body breaks down *fats* into fatty acids, which can then be absorbed into the blood. Fatty acid molecules are usually joined together in groups of three, forming molecules called triglycerides which are then stored in the muscle cell. *Free fatty acids* are the components of fat that can be used by the body to produce *aerobic* energy.

faulty processes: the causes of a group not reaching its potential or fulfilling its goal. The *actual productivity* of the group does not match its *potential productivity*. The causes usually fall into the two categories of coordination problems and motivational losses. The former may include lack of teamwork, poor execution of tactics and poor concentration, while the latter is due to a lack of universal commitment to the same goals. Some group members perhaps feel less valued, illustrating the *Ringelmann effect* and elements of *social loafing*. (See also *group productivity*.)

federalism: where the powers of government are divided between the national and the state or provincial governments. For example, when the *USA* sought to free itself from Britain, it created a system where the powers of the new national government were restricted but it could act on matters of national interest such as defence.

feedback: information received by the individual or group either during or after completion of the performance. It can be used for a variety of purposes including the detection and correction of errors, for providing *motivation* during the learning process and *reinforcement* of actions. The nature of the feedback given will alter depending on the performer's *stage of learning*, but it is vital that all information is accurate, limited to key points and relevant to the individual or group. Various forms of feedback are outlined below:

- Intrinsic or internal feedback – received from within the performer via proprioceptors (see *sensory system*) developing a *kinaesthetic* awareness. As the performer becomes more skilled, they are able to detect and correct their own faults. For example, a more experienced gymnast completing a vault will be able to feel if they opened from the tuck position at the correct time.
- Extrinsic or external feedback (augmented feedback) – received from outside the performer usually via sound or vision, through their *exteroceptors*, from the coach, teacher, team mates or even spectators. This form of information is used extensively during the *cognitive phase of learning* and *associative phase of learning*. For example, a less experienced gymnast completing a vault will rely on *guidance* from the coach concerning their performance, as they have not yet developed their kinaesthetic awareness fully. (See also *knowledge of performance* and *knowledge of results*.)
- Continuous/concurrent feedback – a form of feedback received during the activity via proprioceptors or kinaesthesis. For example, a badminton player knows if he or she is hitting the shuttlecock properly because of the 'feel' and sound experienced during the rally. Information may also be received from an external source, e.g. a coach.
- Terminal feedback – received after the activity. For example, it may be given immediately by the coach or some time later, such as when analysing a video of the performance.

- Positive feedback – used as a form of reinforcement if the performance was successful, encouraging a repetition of the action. For example, the coach of a netball team would praise a good shot or attempt at the ring.
- Negative feedback – received if the performance was incorrect, to discourage a repetition of the action. For example, the coach of the same netball team would highlight faults in a poor attempt.

female education lagged behind that of boys for many years. This was based on the assumption that women required social accomplishments rather than intellectual development. The idea was challenged in the *Victorian era* when pioneers such as Frances Buss and Dorothea Beale founded the North London Collegiate School and Camden School for Girls and the Cheltenham Ladies' College. These were to become serious educational establishments for the *upper class* and *middle class*.

The Schools Inquiry Commission 1868 encouraged the girls' foundation schools. In 1881 universities recognised that girls fulfilled the degree requirements of boys. By 1898, following the Endowed Schools Act, there were 80 *endowed* girls' schools. The 1918 Act gave girls the same educational advantages as boys. *Martina Bergman-Österberg* was to have a long-lasting effect in her role following her appointment in 1881 as Lady Superintendent of Physical Education for the London School Board.

femininity: the characteristics associated with being a woman. The *stereotype* of femininity has tended to restrict the feminine role, constraining women to act out defenceless and helpless roles and effectively keeping them out of many forms of sport. This stereotype was a powerful force during the *Victorian era* with its emphasis on the 'medical vulnerability', emotional nature and social limitations of women. Women's sport struck a balance between the beginnings of physical liberation and what was considered socially respectable. Women are constantly trying to redefine their roles and therefore femininity is a changing concept.

fencing: the dextrous use of a sword for attack or defence. It has its roots in the traditions of knightly chivalry and today it is a sport practised throughout the world with three weapons: the foil (origin – sporting purposes), the epee (origin – infantry fighting) and the sabre (origin – cavalry weapon). By the sixteenth century the broadsword was made obsolete as its military function was no longer required but professional swordsmen still used it for staging exciting sporting contests. New fencing weapons and styles were imported from Europe and the rapier in the sixteenth century became popular, as were fencing lessons which formed part of a gentleman's education. Duels were commonly used as a means of settling disputes. Fencing developed popularity in the *public schools* and universities during the nineteenth century. In 1861 it was included in the curriculum of the army school of *physical training*.

Festinger's attitude theory: see *cognitive dissonance theory*.

Fiedler's contingency model of leadership: see *contingency theory of leadership*.

field sports: an umbrella term to cover activities such as *fox hunting*, hare *coursing*, *angling*, shooting and deer stalking.

fifty plus: a campaign in 1983 by the Sports Council to raise participation in physical and sporting activities for this age group. This age group is increasingly affluent as personal pensions have improved during the twentieth century and people have more disposable income. They are also generally more active and healthier than ever before and an increase in activity can help prevent the onset of ageing. The social benefits are also stressed as this can be a time of dramatic change for many people: some may be widowed, some may retire or be made redundant and family obligations may change. Active lifestyles can help people overcome great social change. This group of people comprises a potentially rich market for sport.

fight or flight response: the reaction of someone when faced with a situation of perceived *danger* or threat that occurs during the 'alarm' stage of the *general adaptation syndrome*. The secretion of hormones by the nervous system increases the *arousal* level causing physiological changes such as increased heart rate and breathing. The performer either deals with the situation or avoids it. For example, a footballer facing a penalty shoot-out will either take their turn or decline, leaving the task to others.

fighting game: a contest of the most direct kind between two individuals. Examples are *boxing*, judo, *fencing*, *wrestling* and *martial arts*. The modern versions have rule structures to contain potential physical harm to opponents. They use systems of points for hitting targets or the 'hold' as a form of domination and take place within a confined area and a set period of time.

fine skills involve the performer executing accurate and precise actions using small muscle groups. These types of skill are placed on the same *continuum* as *gross skills*. Examples include a snooker shot or throwing a dart. Some skills combine both fine and gross skills, such as the use of the fingers during spin bowling combined with the overall run-up and delivery.

Finland: the Finnish Sport Federation (FSF) runs sport in Finland with little government intervention. Individual sports organisations are responsible for their own sport, similar to the national *governing bodies* in the UK. The Finnish Olympic committee oversees Olympic matters only. Much government funding is directed at local level sport, so *grass roots* participation has a high status. Skiing is a popular traditional sporting activity.

In Finland, sporting life is largely based on volunteer activities. *Local authorities* provide sports facilities. The Ministry of Education's role is to create favourable conditions for sports and physical activity. The Ministry leads, develops and coordinates sports policy and finances sports in order to promote health-enhancing, competitive and performance sports and related civic activities with a view to advancing wellbeing and health and supporting children's and young people's growth through sports. The government co-finances sports provision, supporting the activities of 130 federations with some 30 million euros annually. The Department for Cultural, Sport and Youth Policy and its Sports Division direct, develop and coordinate sport policy, assisted by the National Sports Council.

There are 7800 sports clubs in Finland. Annually, 350,000 children and young people and 500,000 adults use the services of sports clubs and federations. The most popular sports among adults are walking, including Nordic walking, and cycling. Children's and young people's favourite sport is football.

One in ten Finns takes part in organised competitive sports but only few of them aim at the world top. There are between 2000 and 4000 athletes competing at the national level, of whom only 500 to 800 become world-class athletes.

Fishbein's attitude theory suggests a person's behaviour can best be predicted based on their 'behavioural intention'. If they have a positive *attitude* and intend to participate they are more likely to do so. The influence of *significant others* is also relevant and can affect a performer's intent, as they wish to conform to social *norms*, i.e. it is socially desirable. For example, an individual has a positive attitude toward watersports, but this does not mean they take part regularly in all watersports due to a lack of time, facilities or injuries.

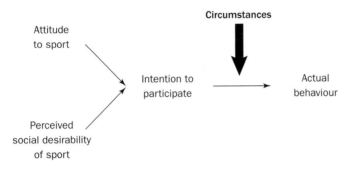

fitness: the ability to meet the demands of your environment or lifestyle. Each individual has different requirements depending on the nature of their job, circumstances and *leisure* activities. Fitness is generally subdivided into:

- *health-related fitness*, which includes *strength*, *speed*, stamina, *muscular endurance*, *flexibility* and *body composition*
- *skill-related fitness*, which includes *agility*, *balance*, *coordination*, *reaction time* and *power*.

Components of fitness for different activities can be identified and developed according to the requirements and ability of the individual. (See also *measurement of fitness*.)

fitness testing: see *measurement of fitness*.

FITT regime: the *principles of training* of frequency, intensity, time and type.

Fitts and Posner's stages of learning theory proposes that a performer will experience three progressive phases of development when learning a new skill. They are:
1 the *cognitive phase of learning*
2 the *associative phase of learning*
3 the *autonomous phase of learning*.

fives: a ball game similar to squash but played with bats or hands. It was played at *inns* and other public places, becoming popular in the nineteenth century *public schools*, but as it was an individual game it did not gain favour with the masters. Therefore, it was mainly played in recreational time by the boys and consequently did not establish well-known formal *rules*. Individual schools had their own variations of the game.

fixator: a muscle that allows the *agonist* to work effectively by stabilising the bone to which the origin of the muscle attaches. Fixators stabilise the bone on which the *origin* of the agonist attaches, so that it can pull against the bone to achieve an effective contraction. For example, during the biceps curl, the trapezius acts as the fixator, stabilising the scapula (the origin of the biceps) so that the biceps can pull against it to raise the lower arm.

fixed joint: also known as fibrous joints, these are bones connected by fibrous tissue and that have no joint cavity. There is no observable movement and they include the sutures of the cranium.

flat bone provides suitable sites for muscle attachment, with the *origins* of the muscles often attaching to them. Examples include the sternum, the bones of the cranium, the bones of the pelvis and, on close inspection, it can be seen that the bones of the ribs are also flat, offering protection to the internal organs of the body. The pelvis, sternum and cranium also produce blood cells.

Fleishman's taxonomy of motor abilities: a method of classifying a performer's *abilities*, which are subdivided into 11 perceptual and 9 physical motor abilities. The perceptual motor abilities include *coordination*, precision, aiming, *reaction time*, manual dexterity and *speed*; the physical motor abilities are more linked to gross movement and components of fitness such as *strength*, *flexibility*, *balance* and stamina.

flexibility: the range of movement possible at a joint. Flexibility is determined by the *elasticity* of *ligaments*, *tendons*, the strength of the surrounding muscles and the shape of articulating bones. Often the degree of movement is determined by the type of joint, since joints are either designed for stability or mobility. Flexibility is lost very quickly through inactivity and must therefore be constantly developed by the athlete. Mobility training should be carried out at the end of a training session when muscles are usually warm, as part of a *cool-down*. Flexibility can be measured by the *sit-and-reach test*, providing an indication of the flexibility of the lower back and hamstrings.

flexion: a *movement pattern* or joint action characterised by the decrease in angle between the two articulating bones. For example, in the performance of a biceps curl, where the lower arm moves towards the shoulder, the angle between the humerus and radius decreases, causing flexion at the elbow. A muscle that causes flexion is known as a *flexor*. In the case of a biceps curl, the biceps brachii is the flexor. (See appendix, page 326.)

flexor: a muscle that causes *flexion*. For example, the biceps femoris cause flexion of the lower leg at the knee joint.

fluid intake: see *water*.

folk sports: activities originating from or traditional to the common people of a country. They often originated from rustic festivals or *rituals*, for example, *mob games*, running events and *wrestling*.

football: any of various games played with a round or oval ball and usually based on two teams competing to kick, butt, carry or otherwise propel the ball into the opposing team's goal or territory. Variations include *Aussie rules football*, *American football* and *association football*. The game originated as a *mob game* and as such there were many local variations.

Football League: an organisation that exists for the benefit of its membership, the professional clubs. Its strength is the week-by-week programme of League matches, but its role has always been different to the Football Association (FA) who formed the Cup competition. They are two separate bodies with similar but some competing interests. (See also *association football*.)

forced expiratory volume (FEV1) is the percentage of *vital capacity* that can be expired in 1 second. This is usually about 85% and gives an indication of the overall efficiency of the airways.

Forster Education Act: see *Education Acts*.

Foundation for Sport and the Arts: an organisation set up by the pools promoters in 1991 to channel funds into sport and the arts. The pools provide approximately £60 million annually that can be used for the benefit of sport. The Foundation works closely with the sports councils and administers grants while its main aims are to:
- support the improvement of existing facilities
- assist the construction of new sport venues
- help with appropriate sports projects (schools, disabled, Olympic and Paralympic teams).

fox hunting: the pursuit of a wild fox with a pack of hounds. Each hunt has its own designated area called the hunt country. The hunt meets at a predetermined place and moves off to a draw – particular woodland or other habitat where foxes are likely to be found. The hounds work as a pack and are bred for intelligence, stamina and speed.

By the turn of the eighteenth century, fox hunting had become one of England's premier sports with a fashionable following. It represented the power structure of the countryside. By the late *Victorian era* and early *Edwardian period*, subscription packs developed where members of the hunt would contribute significantly to the master's expenses. Women and children were also included and the hunt was very much a social occasion. The *railways* enabled wealthy urbanites to join the event. Fox hunting is controversial in the UK, where a ban was introduced in 2004. (See also *blood sports*.)

Framework for Sport in England: this strategy, introduced in 2004 by *Sport England*, sets out a vision for sport in England – to be the most active and the most successful sporting nation in the world by 2020. Sport England will be working with sport's *governing bodies* to develop a coordinated approach to national planning for sport. As recommended in *Game Plan*, 20 priority sports have been identified, on which 20 *Whole Sport Plans* are based. In addition, nine Regional Plans will be developed by regional sports boards.

franchise: authorisation given to an individual or group by a company to sell its goods in a particular way. *Professional sport* leagues in the USA are 'closed corporations' limited to a fixed number of teams and known as franchises. Private investors back the schemes and profits are paramount. It is a *mass media* and commercially controlled system – television *audiences* are seen as potential markets. Some concerns exist about the control of sport from the *governing bodies* of the sport to these franchises. Twenty20 cricket is an example.

Frank-Starling mechanism: see *Starling's law of the heart*.

free body diagrams are used to show the relative magnitude and direction of all the forces that are acting on an object or body in a given situation. The length of the arrow in a free-body diagram reflects the magnitude of the force and the position of the arrow head reveals the direction in which the force is acting.

Key points to remember when constructing free-body diagrams:
- Always draw your direction of motion arrow first.
- Make sure your weight arrow originates from the *centre of mass* of the body.

- Make sure your **reaction force** originates from the point of contact between two surfaces. Remember that there may be more than one reaction force acting.
- If there is uniform vertical motion and there is more than one reaction force acting, the combined length of the reaction force arrows will be equal to the length of the weight arrow.
- For upward **acceleration**, the reaction arrow will be longer than the weight arrow.
- For downward acceleration, the reaction arrow will be shorter than the weight arrow.
- For forward acceleration, the **friction** arrow (or thrust) will be longer than the **air resistance** arrow.
- For deceleration, the friction arrow will be shorter than the air resistance arrow.

Where the friction arrow is equal to the air resistance arrow, we can assume that there is a zero **net force** and that the body is moving at constant **velocity**.

free fatty acids: the primary source of energy, which is derived from **fat**, that is used by the muscles. Once freed from the triglyceride molecule (the stored form of fat), free fatty acids (FFA) enter the blood stream and can be transported around the body. Once inside the muscle cell, the FFAs undergo **beta oxidation**, a catabolic process that takes place in the **mitochondria**. Beta oxidation produces **acetylcoenzyme A** which can then enter the **Krebs cycle** and follow the same path of metabolism as **glycogen**. Fat metabolism can generate much more energy since the fat molecule contains more carbon, which produces more acetylcoenzyme A and therefore more electrons can enter the **electron transport chain**. One free fatty acid molecule can yield up to 131 **ATP** molecules when completely oxidised compared to 38 molecules of ATP yielded from glucose. (See also **fatty acids**.)

friction: a force that opposes the relative motion of two bodies in contact with one another. Friction is a force which acts on the interface of surfaces that are in contact, and acts in the opposite direction to the direction of motion. The magnitude or size of the frictional force determines the relative ease or difficulty of movement for the objects in contact. Factors affecting friction include:

- the roughness of the surfaces in contact – the rougher the surfaces, the greater the friction. For example, football studs or spikes worn by athletes are designed to increase friction. Hard courts with a rough surface will also increase friction
- the greater the downforce or mass of an object, the greater the friction. A mountain biker will sit back over the driving wheel when riding up a muddy slope in order to gain a better grip of the tyre on the surface
- warmth of surfaces – dependent on the surface, this will either increase or decrease friction. Consider the metal blade of an ice skate moving over the ice, for example. This will heat up and create a thin film of water, which decreases the friction between the two surfaces.

frontal axis: also known as the anterior–posterior axis, this is an imaginary pole that runs through the body from front to back. Movements such as **abduction** and **adduction** that take place in the **frontal plane** occur about the frontal axis. A gymnast performing a cartwheel does so about the frontal axis.

frontal plane: also known as the coronal plane, this is an imaginary line that divides the body down the anterio-posterior plane, i.e. into front and back halves. Joint actions that work parallel to this plane are said to operate in the frontal plane. Such **movement patterns**

include ***abduction***, ***adduction***, ***lateral flexion*** of the neck and trunk, scapulae elevation and depression and scapulae protraction and retraction. A knowledge of the planes of movement is essential when analysing movement. (See appendix, page 314.)

frontier: the limit of knowledge of a particular field. Sport is often called 'the last frontier' as we still do not know the limitations of human achievement in sport. It is an emotive term for Americans as it also links to the history of the settlement of their country as each frontier was moved from east to west. Qualities required to push back any frontier, be it geographical or of a sporting nature, are bravery, courage, strength and determination.

frustration–aggression hypothesis: this suggests that when the goal of a performer is blocked, they become frustrated and this always leads to ***aggression***. If released through an aggressive act, ***catharsis*** occurs and the performer is able to return to a stable emotional state. However, if they are unable to release their frustration via an aggressive act, this merely causes more frustration and the cycle starts again. For example, a basketball player who drives for a lay-up shot is constantly blocked by an opponent, causing frustration and the subsequent aggressive act may involve breaking the rules and fouling the defender. This results in a reduction in frustration allowing the player to refocus on the game.

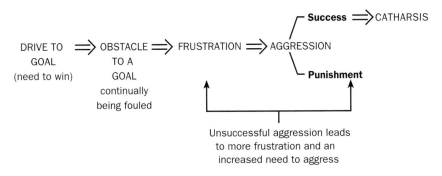

However, the theory does not account for acts of aggression that are premeditated, learnt from others (see ***social learning theory***) or purely instinctive. Also, not all frustration experienced during performance will lead to an aggressive act as often performers employ various ***stress management*** techniques to control increasing levels of arousal. Some studies have been developed based on the theory incorporating environmental factors and the effects of social learning (see ***aggressive cue theory***).

functional classification: see ***classification***.

functionalist theory: an approach in ***sociology*** that seeks to explain the existence of social structures by the role they perform for society as a whole. It is a structural theory beginning its analysis at the level of society rather than the individual. It focuses on the interdependence of parts and how the functioning of parts is essential for the wellbeing of the whole. For example, how do the family unit, the economy of a country, the education system and the system of sport work together to contribute to the smooth running of the society as a whole? It proposes that social systems naturally seek to find a balance through an emphasis on consensus, common values and coordinated organisation. In relation to sport, supporters of functionalism would ask questions such as:

- do sports provide *socialisation* experiences through which people learn the values of their society and can sport help relieve tensions that could cause conflict?
- do sports create unity and help integrate peoples?
- do sports tend to help people achieve and help social progress?
- do sports help people understand survival skills should their society face external change?

Criticisms of the theory suggest that it:

- is a conservative approach, stressing order at the expense of conflict
- ignores individuals in focusing only on the structural elements
- focuses on the present without any sense of the past.

(See also *dysfunction*.)

functions of sport: see *culture and sport*.

funding for sport: a sum of money set aside for the purpose of sport, which can be obtained from a variety of sources, including individuals, commercial interests and national governments. Funding is available to individuals as well as groups and organisations. (See also *Department for Culture, Media and Sport*, *National Lottery*, *sponsorship* and *Sports Aid*.)

fusiform muscle shape: muscles characterised by bundles of muscle fibres (fasciculi) that lie parallel to each other and have a *tendon* at either end of the muscle belly. Fusiform muscle shapes, such as the biceps brachii and triceps brachii, are designed for speed rather than strength since their fibres may shorten by up to 50% of their resting length enabling a wider range of movement. (See also *pennate*.)

A–Z Online

Log on to A–Z Online to search the database of terms, print revision lists and much more. Go to **www.philipallan.co.uk/a-zonline** to get started.

galvanic skin response: see *biofeedback*.

gambling: risking or betting something, usually money, on the outcome of an event or sport. The upper and lower classes enjoyed this pastime in almost all sports, but it was something to which the *middle class* with their reforming morality objected. First, they attacked the *blood sports* of *baiting* and cock fighting and then gambling. In *horse racing*, off-course betting and pub betting were made illegal, effectively discriminating against those who could not afford to attend weekday race meets. As a consequence, illegal street betting became the *norm* and the result was the publication of the Street Betting Act in 1906. The improved communications of the *railway*, the telegraph and the press combined to cause an enormous interest in betting, permitting a whole industry to arise that would encourage and profit from regular gambling. This was epitomised by horse racing and, later, greyhound racing.

game: a contest with *rules*, the result being determined by skill, strength or chance. This category includes *fighting games, invasion games, net games, innings games* and *target games*. Games require territorial domination either through runs, goals or hits on target. The success of individuals or teams can be measured either quantitatively through number of goals scored or more subjectively by judges and their interpretations, such as in *boxing*. They are different to *athletic activities* and *gymnastic activities* because they are inherently interactive, apart from certain games like golf. This interactive nature requires *decision-making* by the players in response to their opponents' actions, for example, a scrum half deciding what to do following the scrummage.

Game Plan: published in December 2002, this document was produced jointly by the UK government's Strategy Unit and the *Department for Culture, Media and Sport*. With sections that include comparative participation and sports performance data, research statistics and theories underpinning the value of sport, it details the government's vision and strategy for sport from both a mass participation and performance perspective up until 2020.

Game Plan attempted to provide both a rationale and an action plan for the development of sport itself and the reduction of social *exclusion* through providing opportunities in sport participation based largely on the claims made for sport in the Report of the Social Exclusion Units' Policy Action Team 10. Game Plan made suggestions toward sport being a potential instrument in achieving the government's wider sociopolitical agenda of combating social exclusion.

gamesmanship: the art of winning games or defeating opponents by clever or cunning means without actually cheating. It involves bending the *rules* without actually breaking them, going against the ideal of *sportsmanship*. An example is a tennis player faking an injury prior to the opposing player serving, in order to make them lose the flow of their *movement pattern*.

GAS: see *general adaptation syndrome*.

gaseous exchange: the movement of gases into and out of the blood stream, taking place at two sites in the body: the lungs and the muscle or tissue cell. This occurs through the process of diffusion, which explains the movement of gases and other dissolved substances from areas of high concentrations to areas of lower concentration. The blood in the pulmonary capillaries surrounding the *alveoli* is low in oxygen content but high in carbon dioxide, while the air inside the alveoli is of high oxygen concentration and of low carbon dioxide concentration. Therefore, oxygen diffuses into the blood stream at the lungs, attaching itself to *haemoglobin*, and travels around to the muscles. Carbon dioxide, on the other hand, diffuses into the alveoli, where it is breathed out. The opposite happens at the *capillaries* surrounding the muscle fibres. The muscle fibres have a relatively low concentration of oxygen, since they have used it up to produce *energy*, yet they have a high concentration of carbon dioxide, a by-product of that process to produce energy. Consequently, oxygen diffuses into the muscle while carbon dioxide diffuses from the muscle into the blood stream, where it is transported around to the lungs to be expelled. During exercise, gaseous exchange occurs much more rapidly since there are greater differences between oxygen concentrations inside and outside the muscle. Training can also promote capillarisation, which improves the efficiency of the whole gaseous exchange process.

gender: used by sociologists to describe the cultural and social attributes of men and women, which are manifested in masculinity and *femininity*.

gene doping: an *ergogenic aid* that involves the illegal use of gene therapy to enhance performance. Gene doping is considered to be the next big thing to challenge the integrity of sport. While gene therapy is typically used in medicine to alter a person's DNA so that they can combat disease more effectively, the concern is that it may be hijacked by unscrupulous sports doctors and coaches to enhance the performance of athletes. With physiological outcomes such as increased red blood cell production and increased muscle growth, it is clear why some performers may be tempted by gene doping. Although there is no hard evidence of performers doing gene doping, the threat is there. (See also *doping*.)

Advantages (perceived benefits)	Disadvantages (associated health risks)
Engineering of hormones that increase muscle mass	This practice is still in an experimental stage and there could be significant health risks attached
Engineering of hormones to increase the production of red blood cells	There is a moral issue relating to altering the very fabric of a person
Testing may be unable to distinguish between naturally produced red blood cells or *testosterone* and that which the body has been genetically engineered to produce	

general adaptation syndrome: Seyle proposed that the performer experiences three stages of physiological reaction when faced with a situation that induces *stress*. The three stages of the general adaptation syndrome (GAS) are:
1 alarm reaction stage – initiated when the perceived stressful situation occurs, causing increases in heart rate, blood sugar level, *adrenaline* and *blood pressure*. This may prompt the *fight or flight response*

2 resistance stage – the body systems attempt to cope with the **stressors** if they are not removed, by reverting to normal functioning levels if possible, or a state of **homeostasis**

3 exhaustion stage – the continued presence of the stressors will prove too much for the body to cope with, causing heart disease, stomach ulcers and high blood pressure. The body fails to deal with the continued demands placed on it and is unable to fight infection.

general motion is a combination of linear and angular motions. It is the most common type of motion we see in sport today. Running and swimming are great examples of **linear motion** as the trunk often moves linearly due to the angular movements of our arm and legs.

gentleman amateur: a **social class** distinction of the amateur code. The gentleman amateur was drawn only from the **upper class** and was regarded as having qualities of refinement associated with a good family, i.e. being courteous, cultured and well-educated. Although they may have participated in some activities with their lower-class professional counterparts, there was no shame should they lose, as they were not being paid, nor were they involved in serious training.

gentry: persons of high birth or social standing, usually denoting persons just below nobility in social rank.

Gestalt theory: developed by a group of German scientists who proposed learning occurred through the performer understanding the relationship of the whole action rather than individual parts. (See also **cognitive theories of learning**.)

gifted and talented: part of the UK government's wider strategy to improve gifted and talented education. In sport, it aims to improve the range and quality of teaching, **coaching** and learning for talented sportspeople in order to raise their aspirations and improve their performance, **motivation** and **self-esteem**. It also aims to encourage young talent to join sports clubs and strengthen the relationship between schools and national **governing bodies**. Up to 10% of pupils in primary and secondary schools will be supported. It includes the introduction of talent development **camps** for pupils in Years 6 and 7. Nationally, the programme includes:

- a web-based resource for teachers, coaches and parents
- a national support network for talented young athletes with disabilities
- national governing body-organised national performance camps for **elite** young athletes
- a national faculty of gifted and talented trainers to provide continuing professional development
- extra curriculum provision for academically able 11–16 year olds in physical education and sports studies
- a school-based profiling and tracking system.

girls' public schools: in the late 1800s the education of girls was poor. It was pretentious and costly, with an emphasis on accomplishments for society, such as dancing, rather than for the intellectual development of the girls. 'Medical' reasons to limit women's sports participation were legitimised. Any degree of **competitiveness** was not conducive to the social image of how women should behave.

In the **Victorian era**, constructive education for women was regarded as a threat to the **norms** for behaviour for that society. As the struggle for women's rights developed, their increased wealth in the nineteenth century enabled women even greater **leisure** time.

The pioneers of **female education** had to overcome mountains of **prejudice**. Two of these pioneers were Frances Buss and Dorothea Beale. Frances Buss founded the North London Collegiate School and Camden School for Girls, while Dorothea Beale transformed the derelict Cheltenham Ladies' College and turned it into a serious educational establishment for the **upper class** and **middle class**.

gladiator: a man trained to fight in arenas to provide entertainment. The gladiator began life in ancient Greece or Rome as someone who fought with weapons against another gladiator or with wild animals, but the term is now used in high-profile **professional sport**. The similarities between a modern and ancient gladiator would be that both athletes:
- are involved in a physical contact sport relying on physical strength and speed
- have a strong likelihood of injury resulting in an early end to a career
- are treated as expendable
- might be bought and sold through transfer deals and treated as commodities
- are paid by results
- have little control as they are 'owned' by a coach or manager
- have high **mass media** status and are treated as heroes.

gliding joint: see **synovial joint**.

globalisation: the process of the increasing interdependency of societies on a worldwide scale. This can be particularly evident in economic and cultural terms. In the latter the **mass media** images drawn from a worldwide arena are transmitted into people's homes through satellite or cable television and as a result the most influential are those media companies that are spread throughout the world. There is a danger of different **cultures** losing their identities and pastimes as the values of Western sport become increasingly dominant across the world. Examples of globalisation in sport are:
- the influx of foreign players into home teams
- sport organisations like other businesses are expanding their markets into as many countries as possible
- the **International Olympic Committee** has gradually incorporated National Olympic Committees from nearly 200 nations, turning the event into the most successful and lucrative media sports event in history
- the use of well-known athletes to endorse company products.

Gloucestershire cheese rolling: the annual Gloucestershire cheese rolling and wake has been taking place for hundreds of years. Documentary evidence shows that cheese rolling on Cooper's Hill was already an old **popular recreation** in the early 1800s. It could have evolved from early fertility rites and hopes of a successful harvest or to safeguard the commoners' rights of the inhabitants of the hill. It is now a well-established tourist attraction, although health and safety issues could threaten its survival in the twenty-first century. During the cheese rolling, fit, mostly young, men and women throw themselves down a very steep hill in pursuit of a rolling cheese. The winner keeps the cheese.

glycaemic index (GI) is a measure of the effect different foods have on blood glucose levels. Foods with a high GI provide a rapid surge in blood glucose levels, whereas those with a low GI release their **energy** more slowly. The glycaemic index therefore is an indication of the absorption rates of different foodstuffs. Foods with a high glycaemic index can be absorbed and used rapidly by the body and can cause blood glucose levels to fall very quickly. Consuming an energy bar or fizzy drink just prior to exercise may give you an immediate energy buzz but this will be short lived. Foods with a low glycaemic index, on the other hand, are absorbed at a much slower rate and break down to release energy more steadily, so that blood glucose levels are maintained for longer giving more sustained energy to the performer.

glycogen: the stored form of *carbohydrate* in the body. It is composed by linking large numbers of glucose molecules together, which are stored in the liver and muscles. Typically, the liver can store approximately 80 g of glycogen, while the muscles store approximately 15 g of glycogen per kilogram of muscle tissue and it forms the preferred fuel in activities of fairly high intensity such as an 800-metre run. However, the body's stores of glycogen could provide sufficient *energy* to fuel a 15 km run if used as a sole source of energy – or even further if used in combination with *fatty acids* – and a marathon runner will use a mixture of both glycogen and fatty acids through the duration of the event. Pace is a vital factor in the success of a marathon, since the faster the athlete runs the more heavily they rely on stores of glycogen. However, it is essential that stores of glycogen are not completely used up as the body cannot rely on the use of *fat* as a sole source of energy and the athlete may well 'hit the wall'.

glycogen loading: also known as carbo-loading, this is the manipulation of the dietary intake of *carbohydrate* prior to a competition in which athletes try to maximise stores of *glycogen*. This process involves depleting the glycogen levels seven days prior to the event through endurance-based training, followed by starving the body of carbohydrate for the next three days. On the remaining days leading up to the competition, the athlete consumes high carbohydrate meals while reducing training intensity. Some research suggests that the performer who follows this method can boost stores to almost double of that which can normally be stored by the muscle. Other research, however, does not fully support the benefits of glycogen loading.

A recommended carbohydrate loading regimen is as follows (Source: Williams, 1989):
- Day 1 moderately long exercise bout (should not be exhaustive)
- Day 2 mixed diet; moderate carbohydrate intake; *tapering* exercise
- Day 3 mixed diet; moderate carbohydrate intake; tapering exercise
- Day 4 mixed diet; moderate carbohydrate intake; tapering exercise
- Day 5 high-carbohydrate diet; tapering exercise
- Day 6 high-carbohydrate diet; tapering exercise or rest
- Day 7 high-carbohydrate diet; tapering exercise or rest
- Day 8 completion

Note that the moderate carbohydrate intake should approximate 200 to 300 g of carbohydrate per day; the high carbohydrate intake should approximate 500 to 600 g of carbohydrate per day.

glycolysis: literally meaning 'the breakdown of sugar', this term refers to the series of chemical reactions that degrades glucose to form *pyruvic acid*. This process takes place in the *sarcoplasm* of the cell in the absence of oxygen, which is more commonly known as anaerobic respiration, causing the release of *energy* to resynthesise a net gain of two *ATP* molecules. Since glycolysis does not require oxygen, some energy can be released from glucose fairly rapidly and is therefore used as a form of energy production in those activities that are of fairly high intensity and last for up to 3 minutes in duration. The 400-metres hurdles event is an excellent example of where glycolysis will form the predominant energy pathway. If there remains insufficient oxygen in the body, pyruvic acid is converted to **lactic acid** by the **enzyme lactate** dehydrogenase (LDH). Lactic acid causes muscle **fatigue** if it accumulates. **Interval training** can improve the body's glycolytic capacity.

goal setting: a method of enhancing the performance of an individual by increasing **motivation**, focusing **attention** and reducing **anxiety** levels. An achievable but challenging goal or target is set that is specific to the individual, usually by agreement between the performer and coach, which must be evaluated within a certain deadline. This can be simplified using the synonym SMARTER, where:

- S – specific
- M – measurable
- A – achievable
- R – realistic
- T – time related
- E – exciting
- R – recorded

For example, a young javelin thrower needs to develop his or her technique and certain aspects of fitness, including strength and speed. The weaknesses are measured, recorded for comparison in the future and used as a basis for the goals to be set. The goals should be a mixture of short- and long-term targets to facilitate motivation and progression, which may be reviewed over a period of weeks or months. In comparison, an Olympic thrower may set goals over a period of months and years, planning their development towards major championships. If used correctly, the disheartening effect of **plateaus** in performance can be avoided or minimised. Different types of goal can be set, including **outcome goals**, **performance goals** and **process-orientated goals**.

golden triangle: the symbiotic relationship between sport, the **mass media** and **sponsorship**. For example, with television rights comes large sponsorship deals, which allows further development and profile of a sport.

golf: a **target game**, the origins of which are thought to derive from ancient activities played by Patagonian Indians, and from games called 'jeu de mal' in France and 'het kolven' in Holland. However, the Scots claim they were responsible for developing the game into its present form. The game was originally accessible to ordinary people but they were soon driven out of the game with the development of expensive equipment and private courses. The **clubs** were governed by the higher **social classes** and women were admitted on the understanding that a level of **segregation** was accepted. By 1898 there were 220 ladies clubs but the Victorian belief in the physical inferiority of women led to them playing on miniature versions of courses. Even today, women are discriminated against at club level, particularly in playing times, voting and shareholding.

Golgi tendon organ: proprioceptors (see **sensory system**) found at the attachment of muscle and **tendon** fibres that are sensitive to changes in muscle tension and force of contraction. When tension is too great, these receptors inhibit the contracting muscle (**agonist**) and excite the **antagonist**. In this way, damage to muscle and tendon can be prevented. It is thought that regular **strength training** reduces the sensitivity of Golgi tendon organs which enables the agonist to produce more forceful contractions.

goniometer: a piece of equipment used to measure the range of motion at a joint. The 'head' of the goniometer is placed at the axis of **rotation** of a joint while the arms are aligned longitudinally with the bone. A measurement in degrees can be taken, which gives an **objective** reading that can be used to assess improvement. One small disadvantage of this piece of equipment is that it is not always easy to identify the axis of rotation of a joint.

governing bodies: organisations responsible for their individual sport. Governing bodies were set up when **rules** for the sports needed to be agreed so that all **clubs** and individuals could compete on equal terms. Examples of governing bodies are the Football Association (FA) and the Amateur Swimming Association (ASA). Their main functions are to:

- establish rules and regulations, in accordance with the international sport federations
- organise competitions
- develop **coaching** awards and leadership schemes
- select national teams at international events
- liaise with relevant organisations.

In the UK governing bodies are autonomous, which means they are free from political control with the **Central Council of Physical Recreation** representing their views to **Sport England**. Governing bodies had to cope with many changes in the latter half of the twentieth century, including:

- the growth of new sports, setting a challenge to the older traditional sports
- the decline in **extra-curricular sport** and a dependence on governing bodies to fill this gap
- the blurring in definition between amateur sport and **professional sport**
- the need to compete internationally with countries who have developed systematic forms of training. This has meant that British governing bodies have had to devote more money to the training of their **elite** athletes just to be able to compete.

Funding is drawn from member clubs, associations and individual members or via grant aid from Sport England. Governing bodies also need to seek **sponsorship** in order to finance their responsibilities. The diagram overleaf outlines the possible structure of a governing body.

An example of the structure of a governing body

grammar schools are selective schools with entrance via an 11-plus examination. They were intended to cater for the most able children, effectively a small percentage of the population. It was hoped that they would provide quality educational opportunities for working-class children, but in reality a large percentage of entrants are still from middle-class backgrounds.

grant-maintained schools: schools that under the Education Reform Act 1988 (see *Education Acts*) have been allowed to opt out of *local authority* control, receiving funding directly from central government. Initially funding was generous, but this has fallen off considerably. The scheme was introduced by the UK government who wanted schools to have more independence in how they managed their budgets.

grass roots: the lowest level of the *participation pyramid*. This is where the masses are encouraged to take part in active pursuits and occurs within the school physical education programme, recreational spheres and lower club levels.

Great Man theory: a theory proposed during the last century, stating that leaders are usually men born with innate traits or characteristics, such as intelligence, *self-confidence*, assertion, looks and a dominating personality. The theory has little credence today as many other factors influence the emergence and dominance of leaders, such as the situation and the nature of the group being led. (See also *emergent leader* and *prescribed leader*.)

gross motor ability: innate characteristics that allow movement to occur, such as *speed*, *strength*, stamina, *flexibility* and *coordination*. An individual during movement combines them, along with their *psychomotor abilities*, to produce an effective performance. Different *skills* require different *abilities*, for example a gymnast and a tennis player both need speed, strength and flexibility but to differing degrees. (See also **Fleishman's taxonomy of motor abilities**.)

gross skills involve the performer executing actions involving large muscle groups and movement. These types of skill are placed on the same **continuum** as **fine skills**. Examples include running, throwing, jumping and swimming.

group: two or more people who interact with each other and influence behaviour, usually to achieve a common goal. It has been suggested that they have a collective identity, shared objectives with structured interaction and modes of communication, which distinguishes them from a crowd, as shown below.

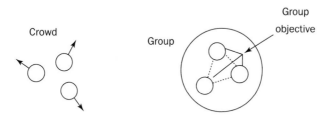

(See also **group dynamics**.)

group dynamics: a group is constantly developing and changing when interaction takes place. Tuckman suggests four key stages of development:
1 forming – development of relationships
2 storming – conflict between group members establishing roles
3 norming – group gains stability and **cohesion**
4 performing – individuals work together towards collective goal.

For example, a cricket team at the start of a season has a new coach, captain and several new players. During practice and warm-up matches, discussions may take place as new members of the team establish themselves, but soon their roles are formed and each player knows what they are expected to contribute in order to achieve the team's **potential productivity**. (See also **group productivity**.)

group environment questionnaire (GEQ) is a questionnaire which measures the cohesiveness of a **group** in sport-specific situations, based on the factors of **task cohesion** and **social cohesion**. Carron, Widmeyer and Brawley (1985) based their **questionnaire** on the interaction, unification and **motivation** of individuals to remain in the group.

group productivity: the effectiveness of a **group** can be assessed using the formula:

FORMULA: Actual productivity = potential productivity – faulty process

where potential productivity is the quantity and quality of the group's resources relevant to the task.

Steiner proposed that an effective group needs to be more than simply a collection of talented individuals; they must be able to work collectively together. For example, it is common for a manager to omit a player who appears to be the most skilful in favour of a less talented player, as they will contribute more to the overall team performance.

growth plate disorders: injuries that can occur in young athletes. From birth, bone starts out as a shaft with **cartilage** at each end. The cartilage at the heads of bone gradually transforms into bone. However, a thin section of cartilage always remains to allow new growth to take place and make bones longer, until full maturity is reached. This is the growth plate and is the weakest part of the bone and hence more susceptible to injury. When a growth plate is injured, the injury causes it to close over, prematurely causing the bone to stop growing. Avoidance of explosive repetitive actions, impact activities and weight training (see **strength training**) should ensure that growth plate disorders are prevented and bones reach full maturation.

guidance: information that is provided for the performer by the coach or teacher to aid the learning of skills more effectively. The form of guidance used depends on the situation, the nature of the task as well as the ability and **personality** of the performer. The four main types of guidance are:

- visual – involves the performer attempting to create a mental picture of the action, by looking at a **demonstration**, video, OHT, slides, posters or pictures. Often the display can be modified by using cones, chalk marks, hoops or target areas. Useful in the cognitive and associative phases of learning
- verbal – usually provided by the coach to complement the visual guidance, highlighting relevant **cues** or providing feedback. This method can be utilised during all stages of learning, but can be more effective with experienced performers, who can translate the information into mental images more easily
- manual – involves the performer being physically placed, forced or supported into the correct positions. This is useful in situations that may be dangerous or require the performer to develop confidence, such as learning a gymnastic vault. It is used to develop the **kinaesthetic** awareness of a movement, for example the hands and arms of a novice batsman are held by the coach and guided through the shot to develop timing and **coordination**
- mechanical – provides support, similar to manual support, but involves some sort of device, for example, a swimming float or belt harness.

guided discovery teaching style: see *discovery teaching style*.

gymnastic activities rely on repetitive *movement patterns*. Examples are gymnastics, trampolining, ice skating and diving. Technical expertise and artistic interpretation are the two main factors that are assessed. The body is used as an art form, with appearance and individuality forming an important element. Judges usually assess the outcome and therefore *assessments* are *subjective* and *qualitative* in nature.

gymnastics: practice or training in exercises that develop physical *strength*, posture and *agility*. The origin of the sport can be traced back to the ancient civilisations of China, Persia and Greece. The term derives from the word 'gymnos' meaning 'naked', which is the state in which Greek youths practised for military training. This took place in a gymnasium (meaning 'public place'). Modern gymnastics developed along two fronts:

- the club system – following Jahn's system based on strength, via his inventions of the parallel bars and rings
- the education system – via Ling's **Swedish gymnastics**, which was to form the bedrock of early state school physical exercise in British schools. However, gymnastics could not rival team games in popularity in the nineteenth-century **public schools** due to its foreign origin and lack of team-building qualities.

The English system was based on Archibald Maclaren's gymnasium, which combined a mixture of activities such as fencing, climbing ropes, wrestling and vaulting. This was considered suitable for the training of officers in that it developed physical skills and character-building qualities. The army formed the Army Gymnastic staff, which was to become the Army Physical Training Corps following the realisation of the lack of fitness of soldiers in the Crimean War. Leading clubs formed a national ***governing body***, the British Amateur Gymnastics Association, in 1890.

Do you need revision help and advice?

Go to pages 297–330 for a range of revision appendices that include plenty of exam advice and tips.

haematocrit: the volume of red cells expressed as a fraction of the total volume of blood. It is therefore also a measure of the state of hydration of the blood, as it concerns the proportion of blood cells to *plasma*. Normal haematocrit for males occurs in the region of 42–45%. If it is too high, there may be too many red blood cells in the blood relative to plasma, resulting in an increase in the thickness of the blood (*hyperviscosity*), which slows down the flow and hinders oxygen transport to the muscles. This high value can also reflect that *dehydration* has occurred, which can cause serious problems in endurance events. Drinking plenty of fluids is essential to prevent performance from deteriorating and to keep the body in an adequate state of hydration.

haematology: the study of blood and its component parts.

haemoglobin: a substance in red blood cells (erythrocytes) consisting of the protein 'globin' and the iron-based red pigment 'heme'. The main function of haemoglobin is to transport oxygen and carbon dioxide to and from the muscle cell. The recommended normal value for males is between 14 and 18 g per decilitre of blood and low haemoglobin levels can lead to premature *fatigue* as there is a limit to the oxygen-carrying capabilities of the body. However, low levels can be easily rectified by increasing the amount of iron consumed in the diet. Endurance athletes often attempt to increase their levels of haemoglobin prior to competition through *altitude training*, although its benefits are still under debate.

Harris-Benedict equation: a method of calculating the *basal metabolic rate (BMR)* of a performer.

FORMULA:

Men: BMR = 66 + (13.7 × weight in kg) + (5 × height in cm) − (6.8 × age in years)
Women: BMR = 655 + (9.6 × weight in kg) + (1.7 × height in cm) − (4.7 × age in years)

Haxey Hood: a kind of rugby game where a leather tube is slowly walked by a large unorganised rugby scrum to one of four pubs, where it remains until the following year's game. The official story is that in the fourteenth century Lady de Mowbray was out riding towards Westwoodside on the hill that separates it from Haxey. As she went over the hill, her silk riding hood was blown away by the wind. Thirteen farm workers chased the hood all over the field. So amused was she by this act of chivalry and the resulting chase that she donated 13 acres of land on condition that the chase for the hood would be re-enacted each year. This re-enactment over the centuries has become known as the 'Haxey Hood'. Today, at twelve noon work in the parish comes to a standstill and people start to make their way to Haxey village to gather and take part in the traditional *ritual*. At around 12.30 p.m. the officials start a tour of the ale houses involved and drink free drinks at each pub, provided by the landlord, as a token of good luck to try and bring the Hood its way. It is a surviving **ethnic sport** reflective of pre-industrial **popular recreations**.

health: the state of physical, social and mental wellbeing where we are free from disease. Health has at its core physical, mental and emotional dimensions that allow a person to lead an active and contented lifestyle. When considering the terms 'fitness' and 'health', it is possible to explain how an athlete may well be physically fit but may be classed as unhealthy if they are suffering from a mental illness such as depression.

health-related fitness considers the role that exercise has in the pursuit of healthier lifestyles. It has long been known that exercise can help in the prevention of medical problems such as **cardiovascular diseases** and **obesity**. It focuses on prescribing exercise regimes for the general population as opposed to the **elite** athlete.

Henley Regatta: see **regatta** and **rowing**.

herbal remedies: natural dietary supplements taken by sports performers for a range of largely unsubstantiated claims, from those claiming to increase muscle-building hormones to those that claim to burn fat. Examples of herbal remedies and supplements include ginseng and echinacea.

heuristic: comes from the Greek word 'eurisko' meaning 'serves to discover or reaches understanding of'. Through heuristic play, children are satisfying their natural need to explore, and are discovering for themselves the properties and behaviour of different objects and materials. The play eliminates any sense of failure as is has open-ended possibilities rather than pre-determined goals set by adults. This type of learning began to be incorporated in **Moving and Growing** and **Planning the Programme** using a guidance style of teaching.

Hick's law states that **reaction time** will increase in a linear fashion as the amount of information to be processed increases. Therefore, the greater the number of options a performer is faced with, the slower the reaction time: in other words, their **choice reaction time** will be slower. For example, a badminton player who is able to execute a variety of shots will have an advantage over their opponent, as they do not know which to expect. In contrast, a player who has a limited range will be easier to play against, as they can only play the shuttle to certain areas of the court, thus making reaction time quicker. (See also **simple reaction time** and **stimulus–response compatibility**.)

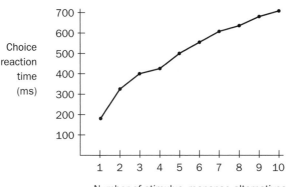

Number of stimulus–response alternatives

hierarchy of needs: see *Maslow's hierarchy of needs*.

high culture: a term describing the arts, such as the opera and ballet, usually patronised by the elite in society. The arts usually reflect the privileges of wealth, education and free time. Activities pursued by this group of people are not made easily accessible to the lower *social classes* and there is a sense of cultural separatism. These activities are often considered to operate on a more intellectual and refined manner to those of *low culture*.

high-organisation skills involve *subroutines* that are difficult to separate and practise in isolation. The development of the subroutines has to occur as part of the whole movement. Examples include *discrete skills* such as the sprint start or golf swing. The skills are the opposite of *low-organisation skills*.

high quality physical education and sport is linked to pupils:
- who show a strong commitment to making physical education and sport an important and valuable part of their lives
- know and understand what they are trying to achieve
- understand how physical education nand sport contribute to a healthy lifestyle
- have the confidence to get involved
- develop the necessary skills and are in control of their movements
- respond effectively to a range of different competitive, creative and challenging type activities, as individuals and in groups
- think clearly and make appropriate decisions
- show a desire to improve and achieve
- have the stamina, suppleness and strength to keep going
- enjoy physical education and school and community sport.

Higher Sports Leader Awards (HSLA) are a progression from the *Community Sports Leader Awards* providing candidates of 18 years or over with the skills and experience to lead sport activities for a variety of community groups. The award is recognised as a stepping stone into employment in the sports and *leisure industry* and into higher education. It includes national *governing body coaching*, officiating and leadership awards. It is recognised by the *Duke of Edinburgh Award Scheme* at gold level.

Highland Games: traditional festivals emerged from the struggles and developments peculiar to Scottish society. The activities were originally functional to the survival of society. Types of activities were hill racing, throwing of the strength stones/tossing the caber and recreational pastimes of labourers and woodmen. Well-known venues are Braemar, Lonach, Aboyne and Glenisland.

Images often linked to such games include:
- kilted athletes
- émigrés from all over the world
- *subcultures* of the 'heavies'
- bagpipes
- *sponsorship* by Scottish whisky industry
- clan chiefs.

The Highland Games have been a symbol of *nationalism* following the destruction of Scottish *culture* by the British *administration*. As an athletic festival, they also provide employment for a band of semi-professional athletes who tour the basic circuit that developed in the north and the borders.

hinge joint: see *synovial joint*.

hockey: a field game played by 11 players each trying to score in the other team's goal with the aid of curved sticks. This is an example of an *invasion game*, with its origins in many ancient variations of stick and ball games. The word 'hockey' appears to have come into use in the nineteenth century when it became more organised. Blackheath is accepted as being the first hockey club, while the Teddington club used the game as winter exercise for their cricket players. The Hockey Association was formed in 1886, the Fédération Internationale de Hockey in 1924 and the Women's Hockey Association in 1895. Women adopted this game in the second half of the nineteenth century following the 'no-contact' rule in the men's game.

holism: the idea that the whole is greater than the sum of its parts. In sociological terms the entire social structure should be studied rather than focusing on small parts. In terms of the human being, this translates to the idea that the mind, spirit and body need to be developed to produce the 'whole man'.

Hollander's model: see *personality*.

Holme Pierrepont National Water Sports Centre: see *national sport centres*.

holy day: a day on which a religious festival is observed. Examples of such days were Shrovetide and Sundays, the weekly holy day. As well as national holy days of Easter, Christmas and Whitsuntide, many parishes had their own local festivals often numbering about 30. They mostly came between spring and autumn, giving opportunities for football, wrestling, boxing, animal sports, morris dancing and primitive forms of bowls. These occasions, particularly those with pagan associations, were criticised by the *Puritans* in the sixteenth century. Even Sunday was considered too sacred for play. In the nineteenth century the holy days were significant for the *working class*, as they were some of the few occasions they had free for recreational activities.

home advantage: in sport, the presence of others can be beneficial or detrimental to performance depending on the task, nature of the crowd and their proximity to play. The effects of *social facilitation* can be experienced by performers on home ground, which can help by increasing *motivation* and often lead to more victories, especially during the early rounds of a competition. However, performers might experience more pressure at home grounds if they are defending champions, due to higher *expectations*, which can negatively affect the result.

homeostasis: the process by which the body maintains its constant internal physiological state. For example, the body responds when experiencing stress by attempting to return to its stable state, e.g. slowing heart and breathing rates, or the body shivers if cold to raise the body temperature. (See also *general adaptation syndrome*.)

hook: a form of side spin applied to a projectile or ball such as a golf ball, which causes a deviation of the ball left of its expected flight path according to the *Magnus effect*. The boundary layer on the right-hand surface of the ball travels in the opposite direction to the air flow. This slows the flow of air on the right-hand surface and creates a zone of high pressure. The boundary layer on the left-hand surface travels in the same direction as the oncoming air flow, causing the air to travel more quickly than that on the right-hand surface and creates a zone of low pressure. The pressure differential (high pressure on the right-hand side of the ball, low-pressure on the left hand side of the ball) results in the ball moving towards the low pressure zone, causing it to swerve and deviate to the left of its expected flight path when struck without spin.

hooligans: disorderly, noisy and violent people, often part of a gang. The term is mostly used in relation to the game of football, which has had a long and fluctuating history of crowd disorders dating back to the seventeenth and eighteenth centuries. Hooligans tend to go to matches with the intention of engaging in aggressive and violent behaviour.

The diagram below outlines some of the factors and issues that underlie football hooliganism; it shows how these might impact on a football match, and the measures that the authorities might take to prevent and control hooliganism.

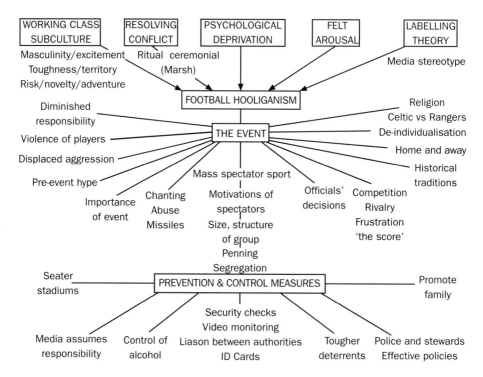

horizontal extension: also known as horizontal *abduction*, this is a *movement pattern* that occurs at the shoulder joint. This movement can be demonstrated by raising your arm out in front of you, so that your arm is parallel to the ground; this is *flexion* of the shoulder. From here, move your arm outwards towards the sides of your body – you have just performed horizontal extension of the shoulder. Perhaps the best example of horizontal extension is during the preparation phase of all throwing events such as the javelin throw.

horizontal flexion: also known as horizontal *adduction*, this is a *movement pattern* that occurs at the shoulder joint. This movement can be demonstrated by raising your arm out in front of you, so that your arm is parallel to the ground; this is *flexion* of the shoulder. From here, move your arm towards the midline of your body – you have just performed horizontal flexion of the shoulder. Perhaps the best example of horizontal flexion is during the execution phase of a discus throw.

horse racing: an equestrian activity derived from warfare, chariot racing and hunting. Two main types of racing emerged:
- across the flats – point to point
- over the sticks – steeplechasing under National Hunt rules.

By the 1750s the *Jockey Club* was in existence, making it one of the first sports to develop a national *administration*, giving it a commercial and bureaucratic control over the activity. Racing became confined to thoroughbreds descended from Arabian, Turkish or Barbary steeds imported into England and it was initially an upper-class activity but became adopted by the lower class as they could undertake *gambling* without actually attending the meetings. The Derby held at Epsom downs is a fine example of the mix of the *social classes* at a sporting event.

Hull's drive reduction theory: see *drive reduction theory*.

human growth hormone (HGH) is an artificial substance used illegally to stimulate protein synthesis and ultimately increase muscle mass. An increase in muscle mass is directly linked to increases in muscle strength and is therefore of benefit to a wide range of sporting activities from weightlifting to rugby. Other benefits include increased bone density and decreases in body fat that results from the increased metabolic activity that accompanies increases in muscle mass. However, the risks of taking human growth hormone by far outweigh the advantages. These risks include abnormal development of bone and muscle tissue (particularly the broadening of facial features, hands and feet). Abnormal enlargement of internal organs, particularly the heart, can lead to heart disease and ultimately failure. Human growth hormone has also been linked to an increased risk of high *blood pressure* and diabetes.

Advantages (perceived benefits)	Disadvantages (associated health risks)
Increased muscle mass leads to increased strength	Abnormal development of bone and muscle tissue
Enables athletes to train harder at higher intensities	Excessive enlargement of vital organs such as the heart can lead to heart failure
Facilitates the recovery from training	Broadening of the hands, face and feet can occur
Decreases percentage of body fat by increases in metabolic activity	Increased risk of some cancers
Increases bone density	
As HGH occurs naturally in the body, it can be difficult to test for	

hunting: the pursuit and killing or capture of game and wild animals. Hunting is a controversial issue: some people strongly oppose it, while others defend the activity. (See also *fox hunting*.)

hurling: see *Cornish hurling*.

hydrostatic weighing: a method of *assessment* of *body composition*. Hydrostatic weighing considers the displacement of water when the body is submerged in a tank.

By dividing the body mass of the subject by the volume of water displaced when immersed, body density can be calculated:

$$FORMULA: \quad Body\ density = \frac{body\ mass}{volume\ of\ water\ displaced}$$

Body density can then be used to predict the percentage of body fat of the individual. The body weighs less in water than out of water because fat floats. A large fat mass will make the body lighter in water. The greater the difference between weight in the water and weight out of the water, the higher the percentage of body fat.

Advantages	Disadvantages
Validity and reliability are both high, giving accurate predictions of body fat percentage	Requires a large hydrostatic weighing tank
	Some subjects may suffer *anxiety* from being immersed in the water
	The subject's *residual volume* is needed for the calculation

hyperbaric chambers: specialised chambers that are used to treat sporting injury by delivering air to the injured performer with an oxygen concentration of 100% (the air we breathe normally has a concentration of approximately 21%). The oxygen is delivered to the patient under high pressure, which not only saturates the *haemoglobin* but also forces the oxygen into the blood *plasma*. Therefore, the total volume of oxygen transported to the injured tissue is increased by 10–12 times. The highly oxygenated blood facilitates the turnover of tissue cells, reduces swelling and speeds up the healing process, allowing performers to recover in half the time of conventional treatments.

hypertrophy: the increase in size or mass of a body organ or muscle, often associated with exercise. It is an adaptive response to training. For example, endurance training may well enlarge the heart (*cardiac hypertrophy*), whereas *strength training* can cause an increase in mass and cross-sectional area of *skeletal muscle*.

hyperviscosity: an excessive resistance to the flow of blood due to its increased thickness that may result from a performer using illegal *ergogenic aids* such as *recombinant erythropoietin* (Rh EPO).

hypnosis: a method of *relaxation* used to reduce *anxiety* levels by placing the performer in a sleep-like state by altering their level of consciousness. At the present time it is not used extensively by sportspeople as the full effects are not fully understood.

hypoglycaemia: low blood-glucose level. Blood-glucose levels can become depleted during low-intensity, long duration exercise such as cycling or marathon running. An athlete may maintain their level of performance by keeping blood glucose levels to near normal levels by *carbohydrate* feeding during the exercise. It is not advisable, however, for athletes to ingest any carbohydrates between 15 and 45 minutes before the exercise period, since this can have an adverse effect, causing hypoglycaemia. It can cause a significant rise in insulin production, causing a very high and inefficient usage of glucose by the muscles, which leads to premature *fatigue*.

hypokinetic disorders occur when the neural pathways from the *central nervous system* do not function properly, causing limited control and uncoordinated movements. Such conditions include Parkinson's disease and Huntington's disease. The term hypokinetic disorders is also used to define those medical conditions which arise directly as a result of an inactive lifestyle. They largely affect the musculo-skeletal and cardio-respiratory systems. Examples of such conditions include *obesity*, diabetes, arthritis and coronary heart disease.

hypoxic tent: see *oxygen tent*.

Are you studying other subjects?

The *A–Z Handbooks (digital editions)* are available in 14 different subjects. Browse the range and order other handbooks at **www.philipallan.co.uk/a-zonline**.

ice baths: the immersion of a performer's body (usually legs) in ice cold water, which is believed to relieve muscle soreness that accompanies hard training or competition. Ice baths can treat both injury and the tissue swelling and soreness that occurs following hard exercise and is believed to speed up the *recovery* process. Immersion in cold water allows even and controlled constriction of blood vessels surrounding all the muscles, effectively squeezing and draining blood and waste products away from the leg muscles. On leaving the ice bath (after about 6 minutes or so) the muscles are flushed with a rush of fresh oxygenated blood, which carries the nutrients and components necessary to revitalise the damaged and sore tissue. Ice baths speed up recovery so performers can push themselves harder in subsequent training sessions.

ice hockey: hockey played on ice. It is an *invasion game* and one of the dominant *American sports*. It is one of the most violent team games – fighting is part of the action and is expected. The physical speed of the game and the implement used has made this game fast and brutal with the players dressed for protection. In contrast to basketball, ice hockey is predominantly played by white people and this is probably due to its origins in sub-Arctic Canada.

iceberg profile: see *profile of mood states*.

ideologies: a systematic set of beliefs that serve the interests of a social group in society. Developed by *Marxist* sociologists, ideologies are associated with power and the ability of the *ruling class* to promote its own values.

Illinois agility run test: a test designed to measure *speed* and *agility*. A ten-metre square is marked out with four cones at each of the corners in a sports hall. Four cones are placed 3.3 metres apart, bisecting the square. The subject lies prone (face down) at one corner and on the command 'go' runs the course as fast as possible, weaving in and out of the cones. The time taken is recorded and compared to standard tables.

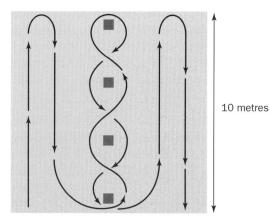

10 metres

Illinois competition questionnaire: see *sport competition anxiety test*.

imagery: also known as visualisation or mental rehearsal, imagery is a *relaxation* technique involving the formation of mental pictures to help reduce *stress* levels, increase confidence and concentration. It can be used in a variety of ways to either create the expected experience of a new situation or recall the feelings of a past situation. The performer can use the technique to develop a variety of sensations, as outlined below:

- pictures of escape to a calming place away from the pressure of competition
- recreation of the *kinaesthetic* feeling of a successful movement; for example, what was the execution of a converted penalty like?
- creation of images of what may happen and how to deal with them. This can reduce *anxiety* levels and *reaction times* as the performer feels they have been in the situation before
- creation of emotional feelings that may be experienced when placed in a stressful situation, such as success, victory and control
- creation of sounds in the situation, e.g. either the ball on the bat or external sources that may be distracting, such as the crowd during the execution of a penalty kick.

Imagery can be either internal or external. Internal imagery involves a sportsperson seeing themselves from within completing the action or in the situation, experiencing the kinaesthetic feelings. External imagery, however, involves the sportsperson seeing themselves as if they were spectators or on film.

To be effective, the technique must be:

- practised regularly, both during training and competitive situations
- have realistic goals or targets
- used frequently in short periods of time with vivid pictures created
- successful in outcome.

(See also *mental practice*.)

impulse: the product of force and time, impulse is the length of time that a force is applied to an object. It therefore follows that if there is any increase in the force applied or the time over which the force is applied, the outgoing momentum of the object will increase. Impulse can therefore be used in sporting activity to:

- add speed to a body or object
- slow down moving bodies slowly on impact.

For example, the O'Brien technique whereby a shotputter performs a 1¾ turn before release does so to maximise the time over which a force is applied to the shot, increasing the outgoing *acceleration* of the shot. Similarly, a follow through is used in racket and stick sports to increase the time the racket or stick is in contact with the ball, which will also increase the outgoing momentum of the ball (as well as giving direction).

A fielder in cricket will cradle a fast-moving cricket ball by meeting the ball early and withdrawing the hands in the direction of the ball's motion. This increases the time over that their hands are in contact with the ball, cushioning the impact and preventing the ball from bouncing off uncontrollably.

inclusion: see *inclusiveness*.

inclusiveness: all people should be able to have their needs, *abilities* and aspirations recognised, understood and met within a supportive environment. These needs can range from learning and physical disabilities as well as needs arising for those who are disadvantaged or disaffected because of social or economic circumstances. All these people are at risk of social *exclusion*. The government has a policy to promote social inclusion in the context of the National Strategy of Neighbourhood Renewal.

An inclusive approach is being developed by a number of organisations. An inclusive organisation would:

- put the individual at the centre of its policies
- recognise and support diversity by striving to meet the widest possible range of needs
- seek to achieve the best 'match' between provision and needs of the individual
- provide staff training and development
- liaise with other relevant organisations and foster *joined-up thinking*.

Inclusiveness recognises diversity of needs but in practical terms for disabled individuals it does not necessarily mean *segregation* or an integrated environment. For some, an integrated approach that allows them to work alongside their peers, with additional support if required, may be the right option. However, the fundamental principle remains always that the provision must be appropriate to meet the assessed needs of the individual.

individualism: constitutes one-half of the central dichotomy of sociology, that is, the relationship between the individual and society. Sociologists are interested in the way in which individuality is affected by social forces and, in some respects, socially constructed.

Industrial Revolution: a period in England in the middle of the 1700s which developed over 100 years. It resulted in a dramatic movement of people from rural areas to the towns, transforming societies from their agricultural base to a factory system. During this time *rational recreation* developed on a large scale. (See also *industrialisation*.)

industrialisation: the process whereby a society moves from a predominantly agricultural base to one where the economy is dominated by manufacturing. Urbanisation is a consequence of industrialisation as a vast body of people moved to towns to seek employment and consequently live in smaller, cramped spaces. Transport and communications also develop with canals, roads and *railways*. Industrialisation caused many changes to many *popular recreations*. *Mob games* declined due to lack of space and the *civilising process* of society.

inequality: see *social inequality*.

inertia: the reluctance of a body to move or change its state of motion. This suggests that a body or an object has a tendency to resist any change in its state of motion – if a body is travelling in a straight line at constant velocity, it will continue to do so unless acted upon by a force. Likewise, if an object is at rest, it will not move until a force large enough to overcome its inertia acts upon it. The bigger the mass of an object, the harder it is to move or change its motion and therefore the larger the quantity of inertia it has. A sumo wrestler has a large amount of inertia and is therefore difficult to move. Moving objects or bodies that have high inertia will need a large force to change the state of motion. Consider two runners sprinting at the same speed. The larger, heavier sprinter will have greater inertia and will therefore be more difficult to stop than the smaller, lighter sprinter.

inferior: any structure below or closer to the foot than another. For example, the inferior vena cava lies below the superior vena cava within the heart. (See appendix, page 311.)

information processing involves the performer gathering data, processing the relevant stimuli to form a decision, which is then executed by the muscular system. The process consists of three basic stages:

- Stimulus identification (***input***) – where information is collected from the display, via the sensory system. The process of ***selective attention*** eliminates any information that is deemed irrelevant. For example, during a middle-distance race, the athlete may take note of his and other runners' positions, the ***speed***, the distance to the finish and the crowd shouting at them. The ***noise*** from the crowd is irrelevant and will not form part of the second stage of the process.
- Response selection (***decision-making***) – the relevant information is assessed, a decision made based on previous experience is stored in the memory and an ***executive motor programme*** is formed. For example, a runner may decide to 'kick' for the finish 300 m from the end of the race knowing his own and others' strengths and weaknesses.
- Response programming (***output***) – the motor programme is carried out via the ***effector mechanism*** and the muscular system. In this case the runner increases their pace in an attempt to win the race.

In order to assess the effectiveness of the decision and completed action, ***feedback*** is obtained from a variety of sources, either internally or externally. This allows the performer to develop a ***kinaesthetic*** awareness and make adjustments if required for the future if a similar situation arises. For example, the runner may have won the race and knows the tactics were correct and could be utilised again. However, if the race had been lost the decision to increase the speed at that distance from the finish could be evaluated and taken into account in similar circumstances again.

innings game: a game where there is an 'in' team and an 'out' team, with each having an innings providing them with the opportunity to score. The playing area is defined as infield and outfield. The infield gives the opportunity for striking the ball in order to score runs, while the outfield is used to field or defend the ball and cut down the opportunities for the opposing side to score runs. The aim is to get the other team out. Examples of such games are ***cricket***, rounders, ***baseball*** and softball.

inns: pubs or small hotels providing food or accommodation. The inn had always been the social meeting place in rural areas and was used by the ***gentry*** in the nineteenth century as a stopping place on long journeys. A tradition of games developed, encouraged by the innkeepers to increase their business; examples include ***fives***, ***rackets***, ***boxing***, ***coursing***

and *quoits*. Many of the new developing sports clubs met in such places and they formed mutually beneficial partnerships. For example, the village cricket team perhaps used the field next to the inn; bowling greens and boxing rings were built on the premises.

input: the first stage of *information processing*, where data from the surrounding area enters the body via the *sensory system*. For example, during a game of rugby, the player receives details of his or her own position on the pitch as well as those of their team mates and the opposition; the location, the speed and direction of the ball; the decisions of the referee; instructions from the coach; the reactions from spectators as well as a variety of *kinaesthetic* information. These *cues* are then transferred and filtered via the *selective attention* mechanism to the *decision-making* mechanism.

insertion: a point of attachment for *skeletal muscle*. The insertion is the muscle attachment (*tendon*) on the bone that the muscle puts into action. For example, the insertion of the biceps brachii is on the radius and when the biceps brachii contracts the force is transmitted to the radius via the insertion, and *flexion* of the elbow occurs.

insight learning: see *cognitive theories of learning*.

inspiration: the process of drawing air into the lungs by the contraction of the diaphragm and external intercostal muscles. Contraction of the inspiratory muscles causes an enlargement of the thoracic cavity and therefore an expansion of the lungs. When the lungs have expanded, the air molecules within them have further to travel before striking a surface. Consequently the pressure within the lungs falls below that outside the body (atmospheric pressure) and creates a pressure differential. Since air always moves from areas of high pressure to areas of lower pressure, air rushes into the lungs. During exercise, to ensure maximal inspiration, other muscles help the respiratory muscles, including the sternocleidomastoid, scaleni and the pectoralis minor. (See also *partial pressure*.)

inspiratory capacity: the total inspiratory ability of the lungs, the sum of *tidal volume* and *inspiratory reserve volume*. (See appendix, page 330.)

inspiratory reserve volume: the volume of air that can be breathed in following resting *inspiration*. This is an important aspect of our *inspiratory capacity*, since it enables greater expansion of our lungs during exercise, a time when more oxygen needs to be inspired. During exercise, the inspiratory reserve volume decreases to enable the increase in *tidal volume*. (See appendix, page 330.)

instinct theory: see *aggression*.

Institute of Leisure and Amenity Management (ILAM) is the professional body for *leisure* professionals. The institute represents every aspect of leisure, *culture* and recreation management and is committed to the improvement of management standards. The institute plays a key role in the development of leisure management through education, research, information, debate and discussion with government and national agencies. Members are from the public, private, commercial and voluntary sectors.

Institute of Sport Sponsorship: one of the main organisations concerned with sport *sponsorship* in the UK. It was set up in association with the *Central Council of Physical Recreation* Sports Sponsorship Advisory Service and acts as a grouping of commercial companies and public bodies with an interest in sport. It works in conjunction with *Sport England* to coordinate the *Sportsmatch* scheme.

institution: an organisation or establishment founded for a specific purpose such as a hospital, church, school or sports *club*. Institutions are founded on certain principles and rules, which are embodied in codes of behaviour. They can perpetuate outdated sets of values and can retain and reinforce *discrimination*. Such organisations differ from random groups in various ways:

- individual members can come and go while the organisation will survive this movement
- goals guide the individuals as to how they are expected to behave
- decision-making and enforcement procedures operate in order to control members
- members have roles assigned to them.

instrumental aggression: see *channelled aggression*.

instrumental values: those linked directly with physical performance, such as skilfulness and health development. These are some of the values with which we justify the benefits of participation in physical education and sport.

intangible reinforcers: see *reinforcement*.

integration is the act of incorporating individuals into mainstream society. This can include religious and racial groups, disabled and socially disadvantaged groups.

In terms of disabled people, it relates to the able bodied and disabled taking part together in the same activity at the same time; in contrast, *segregation* means disabled people participating among themselves. There are advantages and disadvantages with each approach. With integration the disabled participant may not be able to participate fully and the able bodied may find it unchallenging and obviously safety issues would have to be resolved. However, it can help the disabled participant feel more included in society and can help raise their *self-esteem* when they achieve success. Segregation on the other hand reinforces the notion of being different from the rest of society and there is a prerequisite of facilities being available for use by such groups and yet disabled participants may achieve more success in this environment. Integration can also help with *inclusiveness*.

interactionism: an analysis of society, which begins from the perspective of the individual to give meaning and intention to sociological theory. It focuses on the day-to-day activities of the millions of individuals who make up society, rather than seeing individuals as at the mercy of society (which is the perspective of *structural functionalism*). It recognises the constraints put on individuals but allows for creative action. Research is based on the small-scale interactions of everyday life, such as those at a sports club. This would be seen as a product of the interaction of the various people involved and would not just focus on the power held by the administrators.

interactionist theory proposes that the personality of an individual is formed due to a combination of their innate traits and their interaction with the environment. This is often represented as:

$$FORMULA: \quad B = f\,(PE)$$

where

B = behaviour   P = personality trait

f = function   E = environment.

This helps to explain some of the weaknesses in the *trait theory* and *social learning theory*. For example, an experienced rugby player may appear extroverted and forceful on the field of play because of the nature of the game and their own skill level. However, when playing other sports in which they are less skilled, such as golf, they may be more introverted and calm because the situational requirements are different. The coach can use this knowledge to identify particular behaviour patterns within specific situations and attempt to modify the actions of the performer if appropriate. For example, the coach may have to develop *stress management* techniques if the rugby player suffers from overwhelming *anxiety* every time they are faced with a kick to win the game.

inter-collegiate sport: many colleges in the *USA* compete with each other in a wide range of sports. Inter-collegiate sport has the following characteristics:
- there is competition for cash or non-cash prizes
- students compete against professionals
- spectators pay to watch matches and competitions
- athletes are subsidised
- athletes are recruited and paid and professional coaches employed.

Some complaints are aimed at the lack of importance placed on the academic programmes and this is especially the case in the *Big Time programmes*.

interference occurs when additional information is presented to the performer that may hinder the *information processing* time of the initial *stimulus*. This often takes place within the memory phase. As a result the coach should ensure instructions are short, precise and with sufficient time allowed for the performer to understand and take in the details. (See also *single-channel hypothesis*.)

internalisation: the process whereby values and ideas are taken in by individuals as their own. The *socialisation* process is said to be the internalisation of values.

international diplomacy: countries using sport in order to achieve political ends. As sport has a worldwide appeal, it can be used by governments. An example was the ping pong diplomacy used by China. The US table tennis team was in Japan in 1971 when it received an invitation to visit China. From the early years of the People's Republic, sports had played an important role in diplomacy, often incorporating the slogan Friendship First, Competition Second. The team and accompanying journalists became the first *American sports* delegation to set foot in the Chinese capital since 1949.

International Olympic Committee (IOC) is the organisation that generates almost all international sporting activity. It was established in 1894 by *Baron Pierre de Coubertin* and is based in Lausanne in Switzerland. It is responsible for the control and development of the *Olympic Games* and the Olympic movement. There are two organisations:
- the Session – which takes decisions on issues such as *doping*, political *boycotts*, television contracts and the world sport development
- the Executive Board – which is responsible for the organisation of those policies. Attempts are made to make representation as balanced as possible, from poor to wealthy countries.

The IOC is a powerful organisation with huge financial reserves. If it gives a sport eligibility status, it can boost the profile of that sport considerably. The organisation is under considerable pressure from national Olympic committees, *international sport federations* and national governments. However, the nature of the IOC has allowed considerable corruption to take place, for example, the bribery of members for their vote by bidding host cities.

International Olympic Committee president: in July 2001 Jacques Rogge became the eighth *International Olympic Committee* president after representing Belgium's National Olympic Committee.

international sport federations: the organisations responsible for their individual sports. Their main responsibilities are to:
● formulate rules that will be adhered to by the national *governing bodies*
● organise events
● arrange *sponsorship* and television contracts.

An example is FIFA.

interval training: a method of training that involves alternating periods of exercise and rest (relief). This is probably the most popular type of training used in sport for training the *elite* athlete, as it is versatile and can be used in almost any activity, although it is most widely used in *swimming*, *athletics* and *cycling*. Interval training can improve both *anaerobic* and *aerobic capacity*, enabling the athlete to exercise at the specific intensity necessary to train the relevant *energy system* for that activity.

To train the *aerobic energy system*, the work interval should be much longer, perhaps up to 7 or 8 minutes in duration. The intensity should be moderate (and certainly faster than any pace undertaken during *continuous training*) and measured as a percentage of personal best times for the distance or using target heart rates. The longer exercise periods mean that fewer repetitions are needed, maybe only three or four in one session, which can be performed in one set. In order to put extra stress on the aerobic system, the *recovery* time is usually much shorter in comparison to the work period. A work : relief ratio of 1 : 0.5 may be used, where the athlete rests for half the time it takes to complete the work period.

The requirements of an interval training session can be expressed as the interval training prescription. For example, a swimmer may have the following session prescribed:

> 2 sets × 4 repetitions × 200 m training distance
> work : relief ratio = 1 : 0.5

For aerobic development:

> 6 repetitions × 5 minute duration
> work : relief ratio = 1 : 1

inter-war years: the period from 1919 to 1939, in the years between the ending of *World War I* and the beginning of *World War II*. There were two dominant moods following World War I:
● to build a new country with values learned from the conflict
● to regain some sense of fun and frivolity.

The initial burst of lavish living by the *upper class* was not to last. In the UK the general strike of 1926 culminated in economic depression, high unemployment and similar trends in Germany led to the rise of Hitler in the 1930s. Social deprivation and delinquency led to the need to occupy young men in physical recreation. This was to lead to the beginnings of formal government policies for recreation provision. In 1937 the forerunner of the *Central Council of Physical Recreation* was established. The **working class** participated mainly on Saturday afternoons. Football saw enormous crowds; dog racing was first held on a track in 1926; bowls and darts were still popular **pub games**. It was still the exception to go on holiday, apart from during the **wakes** week when the mills and factories closed down. Only the wealthy went abroad at this stage. International sport was continuing to develop, with the **Olympic Games**, the cricket Test Series and **mass media** coverage beginning to make sport stars into national heroes (television coverage started in 1938).

intra-mural sports: highly structured competitive sports and games in American schools. They are played to a high level as well as involving participation of a recreational nature, where the emphasis is on the social experience. They occur outside regular school classes or hours with teams organised on the basis of grade, class and house.

intrinsic feedback: see *feedback*.

intrinsic motivation: *motivation* based on the internal satisfaction received by the performer, which can influence behaviour. It is used for **reinforcement**, to shape behaviour in an attempt to encourage repetition of the action. The desire of an individual to participate for the sake of the activity rather than the glory and prizes of winning is a powerful factor, and determines whether or not an individual may continue with and display commitment to an activity. For example, a rower may have the desire to train to develop personal fitness, to better their own performance, for the challenge the sport offers them and the enjoyment they receive from participating. Knowledge of an individual's intrinsic motivational factors could be combined with various forms of **extrinsic motivation** to maximise the performer's **drive**.

introceptors: see *sensory system*.

introvert: a person who is quiet, unsociable, passive, careful and reserved. They display *traits* said to be the result of a highly sensitive **reticular activating system**, which causes a constantly higher natural level of **arousal**. This means that introverts do not need to seek additional stimulation to function at an optimal level. As a result they are said to avoid situations that cause over-arousal, choosing instead individual activities that require precision rather than force, e.g. shooting and archery. In comparison, **extroverts** possess the opposite traits and are placed at the other end of the **continuum**. These characteristics can be measured using **Eysenck's personality inventory** or **Cattell's 16 personality factors questionnaire**.

invasion game: a game where teams are able to invade their opponents' territory. Examples are **hockey**, netball and **basketball**. Scoring is usually in the form of goals or points and the winner is the team who scores the most goals or points within the allocated time period. Invasion games are essentially about maintaining possession of the ball or object by passing effectively within the team, or creating possession by tackling or interception. Some allow contact while others forbid it. **Open skills** are mostly used as the environment is constantly changing and strategies are usually based on attacking and defending.

inverse stretch reflex occurs when the *muscle spindle apparatus* detects the muscles stretching and triggers an opposing contraction for protection and prevention of injury. The faster the stretch, the stronger the reflex. Therefore, there is a need to stretch gradually during a **warm-up** period before activities to increase the range of **flexibility**.

146

inversion: a *movement pattern* or joint action taking place at the ankle, characterised by the *medial* turning of the sole of the foot inwards. For example, this occurs when a football player turns their foot inwards before executing a pass with the outside of the boot. (See appendix, page 330.)

inverted U theory proposes that as *arousal* levels increase, so does the level of performance, but only up to an optimum point, which is usually reached at moderate levels of arousal. After this point further increases will cause the performance to deteriorate, as shown in the diagram below.

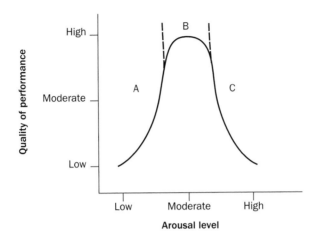

A – under-aroused (lack of concentration and **attention**)

B – optimal level

C – over-aroused (lose focus, miss **cues** and may become anxious).

However, several factors need to be considered to determine the optimum level of arousal or *zone of optimal functioning*, including:

- the nature of the task – skills that are complex or require fine muscle movement, such as snooker, golf putting and archery, need a lower level than those of a gross or simple nature, for example, running, weightlifting or rugby tackle
- the skill level of the performer – those who are experienced may be able to cope with higher levels of arousal as their movements are autonomous, compared with novice performers who need to focus more carefully on relevant cues. For example, a novice netball player will need to concentrate on the basic shooting action and become over-aroused when confronted with a defender, whereas an expert will be able to execute the skill under such pressure
- the personality of the performer – those who are more **extrovert** in nature can cope with higher levels of arousal and excitement compared with **introverts**.

The diagram overleaf shows three different zones of optimal functioning, depending on these factors.

(See also **catastrophe theory** and **drive theory**.)

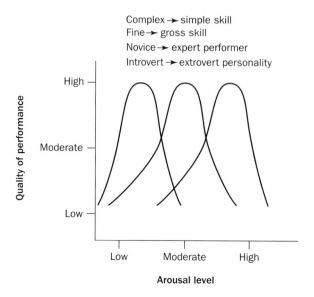

Complex → simple skill
Fine → gross skill
Novice → expert performer
Introvert → extrovert personality

Inverted U theory – zones of optimal functioning

irregular bone: a type of bone so named due to its complex, individual shapes and the difficulty in classifying it. They have a variety of functions including protection and muscle attachment. For example, the vertebrae offer both protection of the spinal cord and attachment for muscles of the back and neck.

isokinetic muscle contraction: an action that occurs when the speed of shortening of the muscle remains constant over the entire range of movement. Maximum force can also be exerted at all joint angles of the movement. This type of training relies on specialist equipment, either electronic or hydraulic where the speed of contraction can be preset. (See also *isometric muscle contraction* and *isotonic muscle contraction.*)

isometric muscle contraction occurs when there is no active shortening or lengthening of the muscle during contraction, with the muscle length remaining static. Isometric contractions occur when the force of the muscle equals the weight or load of the object lifted. For example, the biceps brachii contracts isometrically when holding a weight steady and the elbow joint remains at 90°, or holding a static *balance*. Alternatively, isometric contractions can occur when the weight of the object is too great for the force generated within the muscle, for example when pushing against a wall. Isometric training can produce significant gains in strength and remain an important form of training for the rehabilitating athlete. (See also *isokinetic muscle contraction* and *isotonic muscle contraction.*)

isotonic muscle contraction occurs when the tension remains constant and where the muscle shortens or lengthens by pulling on another structure such as the *origin*; for example, the legs during the running action. Isotonic contractions such as those experienced when using weight training equipment can greatly increase gains in muscular strength and endurance. Both concentric and eccentric contractions are forms of isotonic muscle contraction. (See also *concentric muscle contraction*, *eccentric muscle contraction* and *strength training*.)

Jacobsen's progressive relaxation: see *progressive muscular relaxation*.

Jockey Club: the *governing body* that controls and regulates *horse racing* both on the flats and over the jumps. It was one of the earliest governing bodies to be established in the mid-eighteenth century.

joined-up thinking: a term used to describe changes in government thinking and policy when attempting to counteract huge social problems. It is an attempt to integrate policies by various organisations liasing with each other. In the past, schemes were often set up in isolation, such as those to combat crime or increase sport participation. Nowadays, it is understood that such schemes can impact on other social needs. The *Best Value* policy is an example where government sees that sport can make a valuable contribution to delivering the four key outcomes of employment, crime reduction, health and better qualifications. In terms of funding, there has also been a shift towards *local authorities* sharing costs for *leisure provision* as in *joint provision*.

joint provision: money made available from the education authorities for enhancing, enlarging and making additions to the facilities provided by the education authority. There is usually a centre manager and sound management has made these facilities available to the public in the evenings and weekends. It is different to *dual use* policies.

jousting: *combat* between two mounted knights tilting against each other with lances. It was popular in the *medieval era* and took place in tournaments providing popular social occasions for the wealthy sections of society and military training for young knights. Jousting declined in popularity in the *Tudor period* as the ethos of society and warfare changed, becoming a relic of chivalry and *courtly* love.

Junior Sports Leader Awards (JSLA) are intended for young people over the age of 14 working within a youth organisation or the school environment. The training and practical work is intended to give participants an appreciation of the skills required to lead sporting activities. Participants can graduate to the *Community Sports Leader Awards* and Higher Sports Leader Award.

Karl Marx: see *Marx, Karl*.

Karvonen principle: a method used to determine the correct intensity of training, through calculation of the training zone. Karvonen developed a formula to identify correct training intensities as a percentage of the sum of the maximum heart rate reserve and resting heart rate. The maximum heart rate reserve of a performer can be calculated by subtracting their resting heart rate [HR(rest)] from their ***maximum heart rate*** [HR(max)]:

FORMULA: Maximum heart rate reserve = HR (max) − HR (rest)

where an individual's maximum heart rate can be calculated by subtracting their age from 220, i.e.

FORMULA: HR (max) = 220 − age

Karvonen suggests that a training intensity of between 60% and 75% of maximal heart rate reserve should be used for the average athlete, although this can obviously be adapted to account for individual differences. An example of the calculation is shown below:

FORMULA: Training heart rate 60% = 0.6 (max HR reserve) + HR (rest)

The benefit of this principle is that it gives the athlete and coach some precise figures to use to ensure that they are training at the correct intensity. This principle also satisfies the principle of individual differences as the maximum heart rate reserve is dependent upon the resting heart rate of an individual.

Kenya: a republic in East Africa that became a British protectorate in 1895 and a colony in 1920. It gained independence in 1963 and is a member of the Commonwealth. The Kenya Amateur Athletic Association (KAAA) arranged to finance the Kenyan athletes as early as the 1950s by providing them with international competition and training, recognising they could be of world-class standard if they were given support. The community development officers organised meetings at local, divisional and district level. Standards rose and Kenyan athletes began to collect medals in the ***Commonwealth Games***. The National Secondary School Championships were initiated and became a productive nursery of international talent. The first Olympic medal was won in the 1964 Tokyo Games, followed by eight more in the 1968 Mexico City Games. In Seoul, Kenya won the gold medal in each running event from 800 m to 5000 m. The country now has two world-class stadiums: the Moi International Sports Centre and the Nyayo National Stadium.

The government has posted sports officers to all provinces and districts to develop sports programmes with the result that new talent emerges from rural areas. At the national level, the Kenya National Sports Council is supervising more than 30 individual sporting associations with world-class potential in hockey, boxing, volleyball, karate and soccer. Basketball is the fastest growing sport in Kenya (boasting a national league), the women's team featured in the World Championships in Australia and the men's is currently ranked fourth out of all African countries. Kenyan players have become a hot commodity within the highly competitive US market, with players on **scholarships** at the American institutions. (See also **emergent cultures**.)

key stages: four subsections within the **National Curriculum** for different age groups.
- key stage 1 – ages 5–7. Activities include games, **gymnastics** and dance. The emphasis is developing **simple skills**
- key stage 2 – ages 7–11. Activities include those mentioned above and also **athletic activities**, outdoor and **adventurous activities** and **swimming**. The emphasis is on developing more **complex skills** and beginning to plan and evaluate performance
- key stage 3 – ages 11–14. Options are given as to which activities can be followed and students refine their motor skills and develop strategic understanding
- key stage 4 – ages 14–16. Students follow selected areas of activity as well as undertaking different roles such as coach and official.

Kick It Out: the brand name of the campaign Let's Kick Racism Out of Football, which was established in 1993. Kick It Out was established as a body in 1997. It works throughout the football, educational and community sectors to challenge **discrimination,** encourage **inclusiveness** and work for positive change. The campaign is supported and funded by the game's **governing bodies**, including the founding body the Professional Footballers' Association (PFA), the Premier League, the Football Foundation and the Football Association (FA).

kinaesthetic describes sensations that are felt by the performer concerning movement of the body, weight distribution and muscle tension. This information is received via the proprioceptors (see **sensory system**) and allows learning and evaluation of **movement patterns** to take place. For example, during a race a hurdler can alter particular aspects of the technique if they do not feel correct kinaesthetically.

kinaesthetic differentiation: a component of **coordination**, kinaesthetic differentiation is the ability to correctly adjust muscle tension to achieve the desired outcome; for example, knowing how hard to strike a snooker ball. (See also **kinaesthetic**.)

kinesiology: the study of the movement of body parts. It considers the action of the musculo-skeletal system as well as the mechanics of movement. When studying kinesiology, it is helpful to consider the following:
- the names of the muscles contracting
- the function of the muscles contracting
- the role of the muscle; for example, is it an **agonist**, **antagonist** or **fixator**?
- the type of muscle contraction: **isotonic muscle contractions**, **concentric muscle contractions**, **eccentric muscle contractions**, **isokinetic muscle contractions** or **isometric muscle contractions**
- the **movement patterns** occurring at the joints as result of the contraction
- the plane in which the movement takes place: **saggital plane, frontal plane** or **horizontal plane**.

See appendix, pages 320–25.

Kingsley, Charles: one of the most influential exponents of the **muscular Christianity** movement. He helped to combine the Christian and chivalric ideal of manliness, returning to the Platonic concept of the 'whole man'. Kingsley believed healthy bodies were needed alongside healthy minds. He also led the hygienic movement that was to have a powerful effect on the working conditions of the poor in the nineteenth century.

kitemarks: these will reward delivery of the national *Physical Education, School Sports and Club Links strategy*, so they will therefore be open only to schools that are in a Schools Sport Partnership. Kitemarks will be awarded annually, automatically though the national school sport survey, so there will be no need to complete a separate application form.

knowledge of performance: information received by a performer about their execution of their technique or motor programme. This form of *feedback* is usually received from an external source, such as a coach, but can also be internal or *kinaesthetic*, if the performer is experienced or in the *autonomous phase of learning*. The technological development of visual *guidance* has improved the quality of the knowledge of performance that can be provided. For example, the coach of a sprinter may analyse his or her technique from the starting blocks with the use of video, identify weaknesses and adjust the training programme accordingly. If used effectively, not only does performance improve but so too does the athlete's *motivation*. (See also *knowledge of results*.)

knowledge of results: information received by a performer about the outcome of an action. The results may be obtained in a variety of forms, including the number of goals scored, recorded times or distances, number of rally wins or accuracy of the pass. This form of *feedback* is gained externally, either visually or through a coach, and is essential to the development of skills during the *cognitive phase of learning* and *associative phase of learning*. When this information is combined with effective *knowledge of performance*, a player or athlete can modify their actions in the future.

Krebs cycle: the second stage of the *aerobic energy system*, where *glucose* is broken down, allowing resynthesis of *ATP*. The process reduces *acetylcoenzyme A* to carbon dioxide and hydrogen *atoms*, which are in turn passed on to the *electron transport chain*. Three reactions occur:
1 *citric acid* is oxidised and hydrogen is removed
2 carbon dioxide is formed and expelled via the lungs
3 energy is produced, sufficient for the resynthesis of two moles of ATP.

lacrosse: a ball game invented by *native Americans*, now played by two teams who try to propel a ball into each other's goals by means of long handled rackets or crosses (French Canadian for hooked stick). It is thought to have survived the arrival of white settlers as it was a fast, exciting game that matched those of the developing *American sports*. English *girls' public schools* adopted the game in the nineteenth century and it has retained its public school ethos. (See also *baggataway*.)

lactacid debt: the slow component of *excess post-exercise oxygen consumption*. It is the volume of oxygen consumed following exercise which is used to break down any *lactic acid* that may have accrued. The oxygen consumed during this phase may also be used to supply the respiratory muscles and the heart with *energy* to remain slightly elevated during the *recovery* period. Depending on the intensity of the prior exercise, the lactacid debt may take up to an hour or two to complete. A large lactacid debt will occur when running 400 m or swimming 200 m in a personal best time.

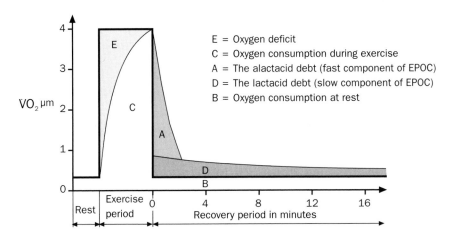

E = Oxygen deficit
C = Oxygen consumption during exercise
A = The alactacid debt (fast component of EPOC)
D = The lactacid debt (slow component of EPOC)
B = Oxygen consumption at rest

lactate: a salt of *lactic acid* usually found in the blood. Lactic acid and lactate are not the same compound. When lactic acid is oxidised, hydrogen (H^+) is removed and the remaining compound when combined with sodium (Na^+) or potassium (K^+) forms a salt – a lactate. Often the terms lactate and lactic acid are used interchangeably, since large quantities of blood lactate assume that large amounts of lactic acid has formed in the muscle cell.

FORMULA: $CH_3CHOHCOOH \rightarrow CH_3CHOHCOO^- + H^+$
              lactic acid   lactate ion   hydrogen ion

lactate tests: the measurement of blood *lactate* used to determine the intensity at which an athlete is working. Many types of lactate tests can be used. For example, the performer could be required to run at speeds of 12, 14, 16 and finally 18 kph, and at the end of each stage blood samples are taken by a small prick on the finger and analysed for blood lactate. The point at which blood lactate rises significantly indicates the point of **onset of blood lactate accumulation**, and the running speed which corresponds to this is recorded. Improvements in endurance ability can be observed, when lower lactate levels are recorded for the same intensity of exercise; this shows that the body has adapted to cope better with this intensity of exercise through **buffering** lactic acid.

lactic acid is formed when the body is exercising under **anaerobic** conditions and at high intensity. It is a by-product of **glycolysis**, formed when **pyruvic acid** is acted upon by the **enzyme** lactate dehydrogenase (LDH). As lactic acid is derived from **glycogen** (it is simply glycogen that has not been completely degraded), it is not – as many people mistakenly believe – a waste product but can be a source of **energy**. It is only once lactic acid has started to accumulate in the muscle that the **fatigue** associated with it takes its toll. As the body does not like working anaerobically, lactic acid can be viewed as the body's in-built braking system. It essentially stops the body from working when there is insufficient oxygen available. Lactic acid accumulation is associated with activities of high intensity such as a 400-metre run or 200-metre swim.

lactic acid energy system: the means of **energy** provision, which breaks down **glycogen** in the absence of oxygen (see **glycolysis**). Glycolytic **enzymes** work on breaking down the glucose molecule into **pyruvic acid**, which is converted to lactic acid when there is not sufficient oxygen available. In breaking down glucose to pyruvic acid, sufficient energy to resynthesise two moles of **ATP** molecules is released. However, this represents only 5% of the energy stored within the glucose molecule, since in the absence of oxygen the lactic acid produced inhibits the further breakdown of the glucose molecule. This system does, however, release energy relatively quickly and is therefore responsible for supplying ATP in high intensity, short-term exercise such as a 400-metre run or 200-metre swim. Although the lactic acid system is used in those activities that last between 10 seconds and 3 minutes, it will also operate in more endurance-based activities when the **anaerobic** threshold is exceeded due to the lack of oxygen available to the working muscles. (See the diagram under **glycolysis**, page 124.)

laissez-faire leader: a type of leader who allows the **group** to make their own decisions, offering them little help with the decision-making process. A laissez-faire leader generally adopts a passive role and as a result the task is less likely to be completed. Often if the group is left alone, members become aggressive towards each other, do little work and give up easily. (See also **autocratic leader** and **democratic leader**.)

Lakeland sports: a traditional sporting festival based in the Lake District of northwest England.

'Upon Stone Carr there have been held, time out of mind, races and other sports, such as wrestling, leaping [high jump] tracing with dogs [hound trailing].' (1787)

In the English Lake District, one can draw a parallel between a sheep-based economy and many of the sporting occasions tending to have social significance during the early nineteenth century. Shepherds travel to buy and sell sheep. In this way a show would be born; families treat the occasion as a 'day out'. Following the showing and selling of sheep there would be sports and dances. Such events were based on a seasonal economy.

laminar flow: the smooth flow of air around a moving object. Most implements used in sport travel relatively quickly and are not uniformly shaped. This prevents the smooth flow of air around the object, causing *drag*. Through *streamlining,* athletes have attempted to minimise drag and promote laminar flow. For example, cycle helmets have been shaped like a tear drop, the best shape to encourage laminar flow, and cyclists adopt more streamlined positions with their bodies.

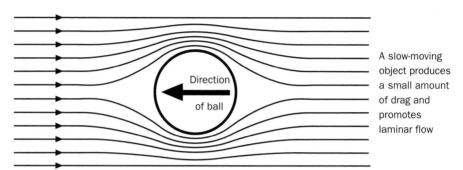

A slow-moving object produces a small amount of drag and promotes laminar flow

'land of the fair go': as the *USA* became the land of opportunity epitomising the slogan *rags to riches*, so *Australia* is seen as the 'land of the fair go'. This means everyone has a chance to succeed in an *egalitarian* society.

lateral: a term of direction that means towards the outside of the body. Lateral *rotation*, for example, takes place at the shoulder during the *recovery* phase of the breaststroke arm pull, since the humerus rotates at the shoulder joint towards the outside of the body. (See appendix, page 311.)

lawn tennis: tennis played on a grass court. It was developed in the nineteenth century from the aristocratic pastime of *real tennis*, played on a sophisticated indoor court. Major Wingfield took most of the credit for the game's popularity. His invention, which he called 'Spharistike', had an hour-glass court. He provided a commercial product that could be bought in kit form, consisting of a net, posts, rackets and balls, making it attractive to the *middle class* eager to develop their own forms of recreation and who also had large suburban gardens. They were to go on to form the *clubs* and develop the *administration*.

The Marylebone Cricket Club took the game one stage further, calling it lawn tennis and adopting an oblong-shaped court. It ousted croquet from the lawns of the middle class. It was also considered suitable for ladies to play, since they could play privately and it was not too energetic. In this way, lawn tennis reflected and encouraged the growing liberation of women in these *social classes*. It was adopted in the *girls' public schools* as it was deemed respectable and accepted by the family. The game was popular in this increasingly leisured society but working-class participation was delayed until the provision of public facilities and its introduction into state schools, which only happened well into the twentieth century. Lawn tennis was to change from an elitist amateur game to a highly professional one with all the trappings of *commercialisation*.

leadership: the behavioural process of influencing another individual or group towards achieving their goal. Early psychologists proposed the *Great Man theory* suggesting people were born with leadership characteristics, whereas more recent studies refute this claim arguing that *social learning theory* is more relevant. Individuals who naturally evolve into leaders from within the group are known as *emergent leaders*, while those nominated by others outside the group are *prescribed leaders*. To be successful, both types should be flexible in their approaches varying their *leadership styles* depending on:
- personal characteristics – experience, ability, age and personality
- group characteristics – size, age, experience
- situational demands – task complexity, goals and available resources.

(See also *Chelladurai's multi-dimensional model of leadership* and *contingency theory of leadership*.)

leadership styles: the method adopted by an individual to lead a group. There are a variety of styles available depending on the nature of the group and the situation, including:
- *autocratic leader*
- *democratic leader*
- *laissez-faire leader*.

(See also *leadership*.)

learned helplessness: feelings experienced by an individual when they believe that failure is inevitable because of negative past experiences. For example, a young gymnast who has been unable to master a headstand *balance* will not attempt the skill in the future because they feel their failure is due to a lack of ability, rather than due to lack of effort or task difficulty (see *attribution theory*). The phenomenon can be either specific, as in the case of the gymnast's attitude towards balances, or general, in which they may feel negative towards all sport. It is important to develop the *self-confidence* of the performer and set them realistic, achievable goals so they develop *need to achieve* characteristics. (See also *achievement motivation*.)

learning: any relatively permanent change in behaviour that occurs as a direct result of experience. An individual who trains and practises will know if learning has taken place, as their uncontrolled actions alter to become recognised *skills*. This occurs in phases, as suggested by *Fitts and Posner's stages of learning theory*.

LEDCs: less economically developed countries (see *emergent cultures*).

legislation: the act or process of making laws. There has traditionally been little sport legislation in the UK as a result of trying to keep sport and politics separate. However, there has been an increase recently as players are becoming more accountable for their actions on the field of play and supporters are now bound by legislation following the growth of *hooliganism* in the 1970s. There has also been educational legislation, e.g. the Education Reform Act 1988 (see *Education Acts*) that affects physical education through the *National Curriculum*. Increases in levels of legislation often reflect governments seeking more control in a given area. The money made through sport makes it of economic interest also.

leisure: time when there is an element of freedom for the individual to choose what to do. The time which provides this element of freedom is called 'surplus time'; that is, time left over from domestic responsibilities, work and satisfying essential bodily needs like eating and sleeping. This time is not evenly distributed across the population, for example, retired people have a lot of leisure time while a working mother probably has the least. This does not necessarily mean the retired group uses leisure facilities the most, as these people probably also have the least income and limited mobility. Leisure therefore is culturally determined and concepts such as **high culture** and **low culture** emerge. How people decide to use their leisure time will depend on many factors such as their income and what activities are commonly practised among their peer group.

There are numerous uses of leisure time and these would be classed as recreational pursuits. Leisure should benefit the individual and have meaning in terms of personal development for **relaxation**, entertainment, self-fulfilment and self-realisation, while allowing people to develop skills. As such it has instrumental value.

Leisure can have either a high or a low status in **society**, depending on the values of that society. For example, in Western societies leisure has traditionally been seen to have a lower status than work. This stemmed from the **Protestant work ethic**, whereas under **communism** the term **purposeful leisure** is used. In recent time, the nature of leisure has changed and grown dramatically. The reasons for this include:

- working hours have been reduced by the application of technology
- labour-saving gadgets enable people to spend less time on domestic chores
- increase in life expectancy
- increase in disposable incomes
- decline in the role of traditional structures like the **Church** and family
- education for everyone
- mobility of a large section of the population
- public provision of leisure facilities
- early retirement
- unemployment.

Benefits to the individual	Benefit to society
Gives relief from stress/**catharsis**/relaxation	Keeps mass of population occupied/ **social control**
Promotes physical and mental wellbeing	
Provides a challenge	Recreates energies for work
Active leisure = health/fitness	Maintains cultural traditions
	Provides economic profit
Entertains	

leisure industry: collectively, those organisations where individuals pay for access to **leisure** facilities. The development of the leisure industry followed **industrialisation** and leisure is now seen as part of a **capitalist** system with global interests.

leisure provision: various organisations are responsible for providing local communities with **leisure** and recreational facilities. They can be classed as private, voluntary and public, as shown in the table overleaf.

Leisure provision

Private sector	Public sector	Voluntary sector
Privately owned, registered companies	Business operations run by *local authority* departments	Business operations owned by members
Trading on normal profit/loss or self-financed	Trading on set prices/charges, etc. according to pre-set budget	Possibly on trust/charity basis; trading on normal profit/loss/ breakeven
Managed by owners and their employees	Managed by local authority employees	Managed by members committee; may employ staff
Must operate and survive in open market/make a profit/ compete	May involve subsidies as a matter of policy/council tax or equivalent	Financed by members fees/ fund raising/*sponsorship*

leisured class: this term began to be used in the late nineteenth century. It referred to the new emerging *ruling class*. A division of labour in society tended to place higher values on certain activities, for example business would be rated above farming even though more menial jobs may make a more effective contribution to *society*. In terms of *leisure*, different groups identified themselves with different cultural pursuits. The leisured class would want to disassociate itself from the more common pursuits of the lower classes. Thus, activities which required more money, education and time would be more favoured by the leisured class. The role of women could be narrowed as a wife who did not need to work and could act as a symbol of a man's status and wealth.

levers produce turning movements about a fixed point called a fulcrum. In the human body bones act as levers, a joint as the fulcrum and muscles provide the effort or force to move the lever about the fulcrum. Levers are central to all movement that occurs in the body. There are three classes of lever in the body and each is determined by the relative positions of the fulcrum (F), resistance (R) and effort (E):

- First-class lever – one where the fulcrum lies between the effort and the resistance, for example, the elbow joint when throwing the javelin. This class of lever can be put into action quickly and apply speed to an object or projectile.

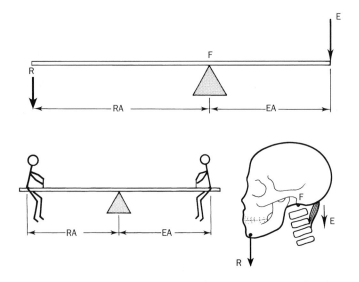

- Second-class lever – one where the resistance lies between the fulcrum and the effort, for example when raising up on to tiptoe. This lever system is efficient and can overcome great forces. It is best illustrated by a high jumper rocking on to the ball of their foot during take-off

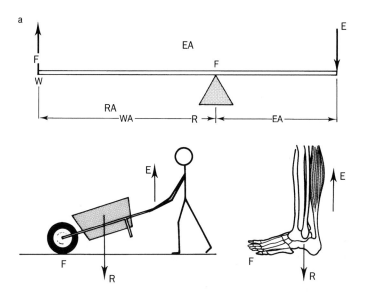

- Third-class lever – occurs when the effort lies between the resistance and the fulcrum. This is the most common type of lever in the body and can easily be seen at the elbow when performing a biceps curl.

To determine the class of lever operating, think of the component in the middle of the system, i.e. 'For F R E think 1 2 3.'

Lifelong Learning: a government policy that aims to enable people to be occupied in activities that will enrich their lives, as well as that of the community, for a very long time. Activities such as *golf*, *bowls* and *swimming* are sporting activities that people can continue with for the rest of their lives. Traditionally, the British physical education programme has consisted of a diet of team games and yet research suggests these activities are not successful in retaining people's interest at a participation level as they get older. Since the 1970s, schools began to offer other activities, sometimes using community facilities in an attempt to foster in young people the opportunities available in their wider community.

lifetime sports: a range of activities that can be carried on throughout life, such as badminton and rambling. All generations are encouraged to become involved and some believe the *National Curriculum* in schools should reflect this trend with a move away from purely traditional activities. The emphasis is on lower energy output and participating for fun, attempting to dispel the myth that sport is the prerogative of the young. Veteran sections in *clubs* are also beginning to take this aspect into account.

lift force: a force created wherever there is a pressure differential between the air flowing along opposite surfaces of a projectile or object. Lift forces are created due to the *Bernoulli effect* and the *Magnus effect*. An upwards lift force can cause the extension in flight of projectiles such as the discus and javelin. It is important to note that a lift force can also be downwards, an example of which includes the use of spoilers or diffusers in Formula 1 motor racing.

ligaments: tough, fibrous connective tissue that attaches one bone to another. Typically, ligaments occur at joints and are responsible for stabilising them to enable effective movement to take place. For example, the knee joint is composed of an intricate network of ligaments, including the *lateral* and *medial* collateral ligaments that prevent any sideways movement, while the *cruciate ligaments* prevent anterio-posterior (forwards and backwards) movement of the tibia. This therefore limits the movement at the knee joint to *flexion* and *extension* and enables us to run and kick. The shoulder joint, on the other hand, allows a much wider range of movement since there is a less intricate network of ligaments.

Likert scale: a *questionnaire* evaluating the attitude of an individual. It is composed of a series of statements, with which the individual has to indicate how much they agree or disagree. The scale usually has five gradings, ranging from 'strongly agree' to 'strongly disagree'. This allows the individual to express a wider opinion towards the *attitude object* than a *Thurstone scale*. (See also *attitude tests*.)

Lilleshall National Sports Centre: see *national sport centres*.

line of gravity: an imaginary line that extends from the *centre of mass* directly down to the ground. The line of gravity is important when considering the stability of a body or object. The closer the line of gravity is to the centre of the base of support, the more stable the body. A gymnast performing a handstand, for example, will ensure that their line of gravity falls directly between their hands supporting them.

linear motion: the movement of an object or body occurring in a straight line when a force acts upon it. For example, a sprinter who runs down the track in an upright position, with no turning or *rotation*, experiences linear motion. In comparison, however, a gymnast performing a somersault would experience *angular motion* during the rotation phase. (See also *Newton's laws of motion*.)

linear performance curve: see *performance curves*.

lipoprotein: a protein containing a lipid produced by the liver. It can combine with cholesterol and triglycerides to make them water-soluble, allowing them to be easily transported by the cardiovascular system and used by the body. *Aerobic* exercise can increase high-density lipoproteins (HDLs) which have been proven to lower the risk of *cardiovascular diseases*.

Little League: a well-established children's sport programme in the *USA*. A good example is Little League *baseball*, which is now a big business employing full-time professional employees and volunteers. Parents initially set up such programmes, catering for different age groups with different divisions. Children are selected by competitive trials and winning is highly valued. Following local and regional playoffs, an annual world series is held. It is valued for its *competitiveness*.

local authorities: the political bodies that control towns, cities and rural areas which are distinct from national governments. They are administrative areas of government that look after local issues such as education and recreation. There are two tiers: county councils and district councils. Local authorities have a heavy burden in providing for *leisure* and this is mainly the responsibility of one specialist department. However, as *legislation* is permissive – that is, local authorities are not required by law to provide facilities – it is not surprising that wide variations in provision and expenditure can occur. Reasons why local authorities will provide for leisure are:

- it is in popular demand from local residents
- it is increasingly valued for its own benefits and not just to reduce other social problems like vandalism
- it is seen to be of economic benefit to a local area, particularly in its ability to attract tourism.

local management of schools (LMS) is a system that has allowed individual schools freedom to run their own budgets and make their own choices away from the local education authority.

Lombardian ethic: a dominant concept in American sport, said to be based on the saying of the coach Vince Lombardi: 'Winning isn't the most important thing, it's the only thing.' This emphasises the competitive, achievement-orientated, reward-based type of sport behaviour.

London Olympic Games 2012: on 6 July 2005 the *International Olympic Committee* announced that London was to host the 2012 *Olympic Games* and *Paralympic Games*. The Games will bring more than 28 days of sporting activities in the summer of 2012 and they will provide a lasting legacy for future generations. It is hoped that the Games will help London's long-term plans for economic growth and social regeneration.

Creation of the Olympic Park involves restoring large tracts of land in east London, with new green spaces and revived wetlands. The Olympic Village will become a desirable and socially diverse new residential area, providing 3600 new homes in a community transformed by the Games.

The Games will create opportunities for businesses, bringing thousands of new jobs in sectors ranging from construction, hospitality, *mass media* and environmental services.

161

Great sporting facilities, including swimming pools, a velodrome and hockey facilities, will allow community use following the event. The Games will inspire a new generation to greater sporting activity and achievement and help to foster a healthy and active nation. Although the Games will be held in London, the regions are also hoping to benefit.

long bones: cylindrical-shaped bones found in the limbs of the body. Their primary function is to act as *levers* to facilitate movement. For example, in the action of running, the upper leg muscles (quadriceps) contract to raise the thigh (femur) and pull the foot off the floor; in a second contraction they pull on the shin bone (tibia) to cause *extension* at the knee and the foot is placed back on to the floor. This forms one single stride; when this occurs repeatedly, a running action takes place. A second vital function of long bones is the production of blood cells, which occurs deep inside the bone (see the diagram below). Examples of long bones include femur, tibia, humerus and phalanges (although the latter are not great in length, they are cylindrical and so also fall into this category).

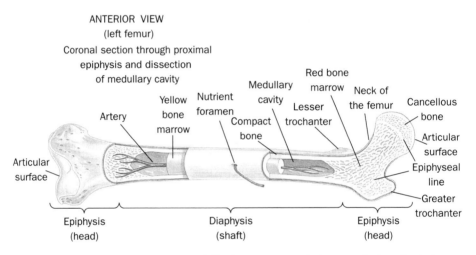

ANTERIOR VIEW
(left femur)
Coronal section through proximal
epiphysis and dissection
of medullary cavity

Epiphysis (head) — Diaphysis (shaft) — Epiphysis (head)

Long-Term Athlete Development (LTAD) is an approach that was designed to help prepare players to reach *elite* levels, but is equally valid for a healthy lifelong participation in sport. The ten-year rule, which refers to the ten years of practice required to become an expert or proficient performer, seems frightening, but does not just refer to ten years of sport-related activity. Some athletes move into an elite sport at a late stage, having played other sports. The LTAD approach suggests that playing other sports is part of the ten-year development programme. In contrast, many coaches lose talented players because they no longer enjoy themselves, so coaches and sporting bodies are beginning to re-examine how youngsters are prepared for sport. There are usually six phases in the LTAD model, shown in the table opposite.

long-term memory store: a component of the *memory* process, which has the capacity to store vast amounts of information for an unlimited period of time. When a performer is faced with a new situation, the relevant stimuli are processed via the *short-term memory store* and a comparison is made with any similar past experiences. If any recognition occurs, the similarities are recalled and returned to the short-term memory store or working memory, so a decision can be made and a motor programme (see *executive motor programme*) constructed. Any relevant stored data can make the *decision-making* process quicker and

Phases in the LTAD model

Phase	Approximate age range (years)	Objective
1 FUNdamentals	6–8 (girls) 6–9 (boys)	To build overall movement skills
2 Learning to train	8–11 (girls) 9–12 (boys)	To learn fundamental sports skills
3 Training to train	11–15 (girls) 12–16 (boys)	To build fitness and specific sports skills
4 Training to compete	16+	To refine skills for a specific event or position
5 Training to win	16+	To maximise performance in competition
6 Retainment		To keep players/athletes involved in physical activity

therefore enhance the execution of the skill. For example, a rugby player who is faced with a situation involving a complicated set pattern of play will have the capability to complete the sequence if it has been practised sufficiently to be retained in the long-term memory. Similarly, if confronted with an overlap situation, the player will know which option is the most suitable and **reaction time** can be reduced if a comparable scenario has been experienced in the past. The long-term memory can be improved through practice and 'overlearning' motor programmes, so that the performer progresses towards the **autonomous phase of learning**.

Lottery fund: launched in 1994, the **Sport England** National Lottery fund had a broad policy strategy:
- to introduce the Priority Areas Initiative for some of England's most deprived communities
- to set and achieve a target of funding 1000 community projects in the first year
- to fund a new national stadium and a **UK Sports Institute**
- to fund some of the UK's talented young sport stars.

The Lottery Act (1998) and the revised directions from the Secretary of State for the **Department for Culture, Media and Sport** allowed for a more pro-active approach.

The two-fund approach:
- Community Projects Fund – will contain three parts: the small projects award up to £5000; capital awards (over £5000) concentrating on community provision, and revenue awards (over £5000) which will concentrate on combatting the social **exclusion** of young people who could progress given adequate support.
- World Class Fund – includes the UK Sports Institute; capital support for specialist national facilities other than the UK site; revenue support through the world-class programmes and world-class events to support bringing international competitions to this country.

(See also **National Lottery**.)

low culture: this traditionally refers to the cultural pursuits of the mass of the population. Individuals choose their own **leisure** pursuits within the context of their own **culture**, values and identity. Low or popular culture does not usually require sophisticated levels of appreciation or understanding. It is accessible and therefore to some extent is defined by what is made available by the leisure market forces. It is usually exciting and dramatic, for example football and boxing.

low-organisation skills can be easily broken down into *subroutines*, allowing each to be practised in isolation. Examples include swimming stokes which can be subdivided into arm action, leg action and breathing technique. These skills are the opposite of *high-organisation skills*.

lower class: see *working class*.

lumbar vertebrae: the third section of the vertebral column, consisting of five lumbar vertebrae which are the largest of all the individual vertebrae. Their large centrum or body offer a great deal of weight-bearing capacity, while their large *processes* secure the attachment of the muscles. This muscle attachment, together with the intervertebral discs of *cartilage*, form *cartilaginous joints*, which enable *flexion* and *extension* (forward and backward movement) and *lateral* flexion (side to side movement) of the trunk. For example, when performing a pike jump in trampolining, it is the cartilaginous joints between the lumbar vertebrae that enable the performer to touch their toes. (See appendix, page 316.)

lymphatic system: a network of vessels that carry excess fluid away from tissues, preventing saturation and swelling of the tissues and muscles. Following exercise, excess fluid can cause swelling and pain in the associated muscles and tissues and a *cool-down* can help remove this excess fluid by draining it away via the lymphatic system. Training can improve the efficiency at which the lymphatic system drains away the excess fluid and thereby prevents muscle pain.

Aiming for a grade A*?

Don't forget to log on to **www.philipallan.co.uk/a-zonline** for advice.

macro cycle: part of the *periodisation* process, the development of a macro cycle is central to effective training planning. A macro cycle is based around long-term *performance goals* and can last between 1 and 4 years, such as training for the *Olympic Games*. A performer training for the Olympics may follow a 4-year macro cycle.

macronutrients: dietary elements that provide *energy*. *Fats*, *carbohydrates* and *proteins* are the chief macronutrients and are so called because we need more than just a few grams of these daily.

Magnus effect: the *Bernouilli effect* applied to spinning objects is known as the Magnus effect. It is concerned with the flow of air or water past a moving object and the creation of differences in pressure between opposite sides of the object. When a spinning object travels through the air, the air molecules in contact with the object spin with it creating what is known as a 'boundary layer'. This boundary layer will eventually collide head on with the main air flow on one side of the object (see the diagram overleaf). This slows the flow of air down on this one side of the object, which causes pressure to increase and a pressure differential to occur. The pressure differential causes a Magnus force, directed from high pressure to low pressure. For example, playing a top spin shot in tennis causes a pressure differential between high pressure at the top of the ball and low pressure at the bottom of the tennis ball. As objects will always move from areas of high pressure to areas of low pressure, the ball is pulled downwards. Furthermore, the Magnus force is heightened with new balls in tennis since the nap or fuzz of the ball traps a much larger boundary layer and causes a greater pressure differential.

manual labour clause: the formal exclusion of manual workers by the Amateur Rowing Association in 1882. It excluded anyone who was by trade 'a mechanic, artisan or labourer' but was abolished in 1890. It was a device to retain a social distinction in sport as the *gentlemen amateurs* did not wish to be beaten by lower-class professionals nor could they socialise with them after the sporting event.

Maori culture: the indigenous inhabitants of *New Zealand*, who before colonisation by Britain had an integrated, cooperative political system. A fixed rank in society from birth negated the need for competition. This is an example of a 'closed' social system similar to the Indian caste system. The individual identified with the tribe and the means of production were collectively owned. *Recreation* was an important element in Maori life, with many of the games derived from tribal myths, and it served to conserve the ancient folklore. In Maori culture, games to serve various functions include:

- training for war
- acquiring grace and skill
- contributing to economic efficiency

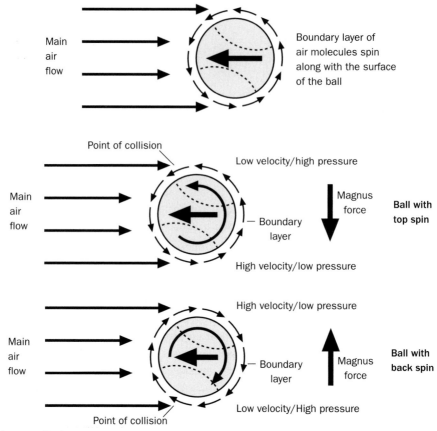

Magnus effect

- recreation
- promoting tribal loyalty
- an outlet for healthy competition in an otherwise cooperative social system.

manual guidance: see *guidance*.

market segments: Sport England has developed 19 sporting market segments to help clarify the nation's attitudes and motivations – why people play sport and why they do not. The segments analyse the English adult population according to sports participation, motivations and barriers to doing more sport. The market segmentation data will assist Sport England in delivering an increase of 2 million additional adults taking part by 2012. The 19 segments are:

- 'Ben': competitive male urbanites
- 'Jamie': sports team drinkers
- 'Chloë': fitness class friends
- 'Leanne': supportive singles
- 'Helena': career focused females
- 'Tim': settling down males

- 'Alison': stay at home mums
- 'Jackie': Middle England mums
- 'Kev': pub league team mates
- 'Paula': stretched single mums
- 'Philip': comfortable mid-life males
- 'Elaine': empty nest career ladies
- 'Roger and Joy': early retirement couples
- 'Brenda': older working women
- 'Terry': local 'old boys'
- 'Norma': later life ladies
- 'Ralph and Phyllis': comfortable retired couples
- 'Frank': twilight years gents
- 'Elsie and Arnold': retirement home singles.

martial arts: activities that relate to, or are a characteristic of, war. Examples are judo, karate, tai kwando. They are *combat* activities and mainly derive from Eastern *cultures*, often being founded on certain philosophies or religions.

Marx, Karl: a German sociologist who has been credited as the founder of *communism*. This is a sociological perspective that stressed that economics is the base of social life and progress is made through the struggle or conflict between the different *social classes* (e.g. *bourgeoisie*, *proletariat*). Critics argue that it is a determinist theory allowing for little freedom to individuals and that too much emphasis on conflict denies the *social order* that characterises most societies.

Marxism: a political and economic perspective that developed from the work of *Karl Marx*. He stressed the role of conflict between the *social classes* in society rather than *social order*. This conflict is based on economic dimensions. The *ruling classes* (*bourgeoisie*) own the means of production and control the resources, so they have economic and political control over the *proletariat* or lower classes.

This theory, however, does not recognise:
- the freedom of individuals to exercise their free will
- social order as it exists in most societies.

Maslow's hierarchy of needs proposes that individuals have various levels of motivational needs, both physiological and psychological, that must be fulfilled in a specific order. People continue to strive to satisfy those needs lower down the hierarchy before progressing to the next level. For example, the basic needs of thirst, hunger and warmth must be satisfied before progressing to the higher needs of *esteem* and self-fulfilment. The diagram overleaf shows the hierarchy. In terms of sporting activity, a performer may reach the highest level by achieving success, receiving acclaim or mastering a skill. However, this cannot be achieved until he or she feels safe and comfortable, allowing them to experience the *motivation* to explore new challenges.

mass culture: see *low culture*.

mass media: forms of mass communication to the general public, comprising newspaper, radio and television broadcasting. The initial developments occurred in the eighteenth

M

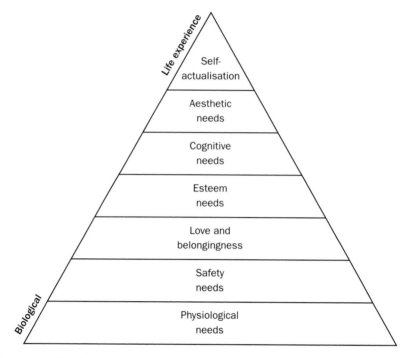

Maslow's hierarchy of needs

century, and towards the end of the twentieth century new technologies increased the influence of the media even more through satellites, computers and the internet.

Advantages to sport	Disadvantages to sport
Boosts participation figures	Rule changes to be more media-friendly
Boosts funds for the sport	Perpetuates *discrimination*, e.g. less female sport shown
Higher profile can be given to *minority groups*	
Can help with detailed analysis of an event	Commercial interest may come first, not the interest of the sport
Reaches global *audiences* immediately	Reduces *funding for sport* with less television coverage
Helps referees	Lack of coverage can reduce participation
	Dictation of players' commitments and timing of events

mass participation: see *Sport for All*.

massed practice involves the repeated *practice* of skills over a period of time, with little or no *recovery* periods. This form of practice is useful with well-motivated, experienced performers, who possess good levels of fitness and with tasks that are simple and discrete in nature, e.g. shooting at goal or racket strokes, such as the tennis serve or badminton smashes. Care should be taken when using this method to avoid boredom, fatigue and *overtraining*.

matrix: an area of the *mitochondria* where the **Krebs cycle** takes place.

maximum heart rate: an individual can calculate an estimate of their maximum heart rate by subtracting their age from 220. For example, an 18-year-old student will have a maximum heart rate of 220 − 18 = 202 beats per minute (bpm). By exercising at a percentage of our maximum heart rate, we have an **objective** method of calculating and monitoring training intensities. It is advised that the trained athlete works at between 70% and 85% of their maximum heart rate, whereas the person exercising for health-related reasons should work at between 60% and 75%. Therefore, if we took a trained 18-year-old student:

FORMULA: 70% = 0.7 × 202 = 141 bpm
85% = 0.85 × 202 = 172 bpm

We now have two figures which represent the athlete's training heart rate or **training zone**. As long as their heart rate lies between 141 and 172 bpm, benefits of training will occur. This has particular use for monitoring intensities in endurance-based activities such as long-distance running, swimming or cycling. The maximum heart rate can be personalised by following the Karvonen formulae.

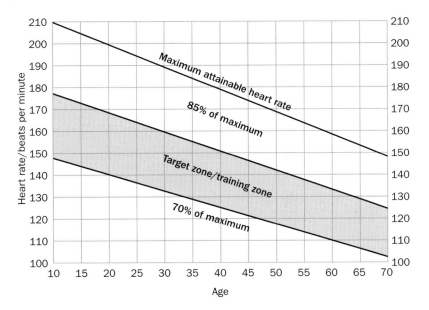

maximum oxygen uptake (VO$_2$ max): also known as maximal oxygen consumption, this is the maximum volume of oxygen that can be taken in, transported to and consumed by the working muscles per minute. Maximum oxygen uptake is the best way of determining endurance performance. A marathon runner who undertakes long periods of exercise using the **aerobic energy system** and whose muscles are extremely efficient at utilising oxygen would be expected to have a high maximum oxygen uptake. It can only truly be measured under laboratory conditions through direct gas analysis, whereby athletes undertake a task, such as running on a treadmill, that becomes progressively more difficult, and a computer analyses the relative concentrations of oxygen and carbon dioxide that are inspired and expired per minute. The test continues until a point is reached when the body's oxygen consumption does not increase with increasing workloads. At this point, the athlete is working at their *aerobic* limit, i.e. their maximum oxygen uptake, and it can be recorded in absolute terms: 'l/min' for non-weight bearing activities, or relative to body weight in 'ml/kg/min'. The higher the value, the more efficient the body is at exercising under aerobic conditions.

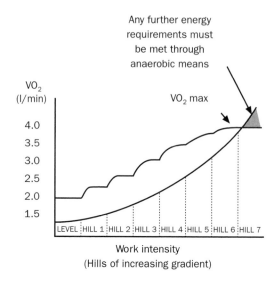

Maximum oxygen uptake is largely genetically determined and can only normally be improved by 10–20% through training. The graph below shows the expected norms for different groups of athletes.

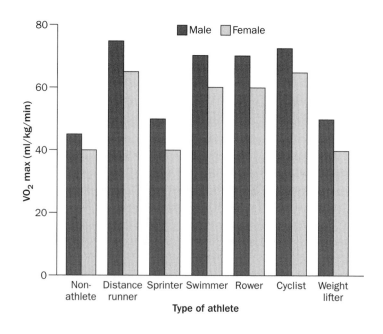

May Day: the first day of May, traditionally a celebration of the coming of spring. It stems from Roman times and hence was heathen in origin. The May games consisted of activities such as dancing round the maypole, archery, war-like shows, stage plays and bonfires. Some countries still recognise it as a day of holiday for workers.

measurement of fitness: a range of tests used to assess an individual's level of fitness. These tests can identify strengths and weaknesses in performance, physiological potential, success of training programmes and can be used to compare against norms within their group. The table below outlines some common fitness tests.

Fitness component	Recognised test	Evaluation of test
Aerobic fitness	*Multi-stage fitness test*	Compared to standard Sports Coach
	Direct gas analysis PNC 170 test	UK tables
Anaerobic fitness	*Wingate cycle test*	Objective data from computer
	OBLA	printouts
Strength	Handgrip dynamometer	Scores compared to standard tables
Muscular endurance	NCF abdominal conditioning test	Scores compared to standard Sports Coach UK tables
Flexibility	*Sit-and-reach test*	Scores compared to standard tables
Body composition	*Bioelectric impedance*	Objective values that can be
	Skinfold measurements	compared to standard tables and
	Hydrostatic weighing	norms
Speed	30-metre sprint	Times compared to standard tables

mechanical advantage: a measure of the relative efficiency of *lever* systems. Mechanical advantage occurs in lever systems where the *effort arm* is longer than the *resistance arm*. This means that the lever system is very effective at overcoming and moving heavy loads. The second-class lever system at the ankle/ball of the foot is a great example of a lever system in mechanical advantage as the body weight is shifted relatively easily with minimal outlay of effort when rocking up on to tip toes.

mechanical disadvantage: a measure of the relative efficiency of *lever* systems. Mechanical disadvantage occurs in lever systems where the *resistance arm* is longer than the *effort arm*. This means that the lever can be put into action very quickly but is not as effective at moving heavy loads or overcoming resistance. The first-class lever system at the elbow when throwing is a great example of a lever system in mechanical disadvantage, since projectiles such as a javelin can be launched at great speed.

mechanical guidance: see *guidance*.

mechanoreceptors: a group of sensory cells in the muscles that detect the amount of movement taking place. Mechanoreceptors form part of the cardiac, respiratory and vasomotor regulatory control centres, providing information relating to the extent of muscle contraction taking place.

media: see *mass media*.

media-constructed athletes: athletes become household names and the public's perception of them is generated by the *mass media*. The media has the power to 'make or break' an athlete's career. Their media persona can lead to lucrative *sponsorship* deals, which can lead to intrusion into private lives.

medial: a term of direction meaning towards the midline of the body. Medial *rotation*, for example, takes place at the shoulder during the 'pull' phase of the breaststroke arm action, since the humerus rotates at the shoulder joint towards the midline of the body. (See appendix, page 311.)

medical classification: see *classification*.

medieval era: also known as the middle ages, the years between 1066 and 1485 are generally known as the medieval era. The bulk of the population was rural, but towns were emerging and with them came the development of the professions, e.g. medicine and law, from which the *middle class* were to grow. Festivals and feasts played a large part in recreational pastimes, but military activities still played a major role in times when defence was of paramount importance. Popular activities were *mob* football (see *mob games*), wrestling, animal *baiting*, skittles and *bowls*.

meditation: the use of controlled breathing to help clear the mind to focus on specific *cues* or thoughts. Specific words, sounds or chants, known as 'mantras', are learnt and practised allowing the performer to reduce levels of *anxiety* and relax. This should be carried out ideally in a quiet place, to induce feelings of calm.

melting pot: a term used to describe the influence of the universities, particularly Oxford and Cambridge, in pooling the experiences and developments that occurred in the gentry *public schools*. The different versions of games became codified at the universities, giving a national interpretation of rules that were to become adopted worldwide.

memory: a system within the brain that allows information to be organised, retained and retrieved at a later date (see the diagram opposite). It is a central component of *information processing* allowing *decision-making* to occur. The faster a performer can retrieve information from the memory about past experiences, the better the chances of a successful outcome. For example, a basketball player in the attacking half of the court detects certain *stimuli*, which are compared with similar situations previously experienced. If similarities are recognised, the decision-making process is faster, allowing the player to execute the appropriate skill more quickly than a player who has not been in that position before.

Memory is subdivided into several phases:
- *short-term sensory store* – information retained for up to 1 second
- *short-term memory store* – limited information retained for up to 30 seconds
- *long-term memory store* – permanent store with vast capacity.

There are numerous methods that can be utilised to improve the efficiency of a performer's memory, including practice, chaining (see *progressive part-method practice*), *chunking*, *mental practice* and *imagery*.

meniscus (plural menisci) is a crescent-shaped pad of *cartilage* found between the articulating surfaces of the knee joint. Its function is to aid the articular cartilage in preventing wear between the tibia and femur as well as to increase the shock absorption properties of

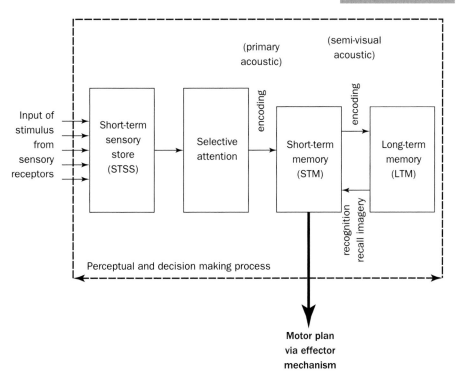

Memory phases

the knee joint which enable us to run and jump. The menisci may be torn by a violent blow such as a tackle in football or by a sudden twisting movement, sometimes causing loose bits of cartilage to float in the joint capsule and interfere with the joint action. The introduction of keyhole surgery has meant that such problems can be easily remedied with little long-term effect on joint mobility.

mens sana in corpore sano translates as 'a healthy mind in a healthy body' – a famous Latin quotation. Its general usage expresses the concept of a healthy balance in one's mode of life. Similar to the Platonic concept of the 'whole man' and **athleticism** of the **public schools** and **muscular Christianity**. The physical benefits were seen to run parallel to the moral and spiritual benefits.

mental practice involves the mental or cognitive rehearsal of a skill without physical movement. An individual visualises the situation that has to be completed, which can reduce learning time for novices and prepare experienced performers for competition, reducing *reaction time* and improving *anticipation*. It is a useful technique to employ during the *recovery* periods of training to focus an athlete's mind and control their levels of *arousal*. The figure overleaf shows the comparison of effects of mental practice and physical practice on performance over a period of days.

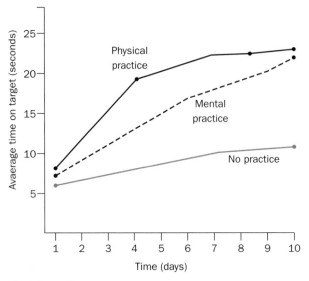

Mental practice

mental rehearsal: see *imagery*.

mental relaxation: see *meditation*.

meritocracy: a social system where rewards and occupational positions are allocated based on merit rather than on hereditary or *social class* factors. Modern industrialised countries and their education systems are seen to be more meritocratic than in the past. However, privileged lifestyles still ascribe advantages such as private education and access to higher status occupations.

meso cycle: part of the *periodisation* process, the development of a meso cycle is central to effective training planning. A meso cycle comprises a number of *micro cycles* and lasts between 1 and 3 months. An example of a meso cycle could be the development of strength endurance in the pre-season phase of training.

metabolic equivalent values (MET values) are the ratio of the work metabolic rate to the resting metabolic rate. The use of MET values is a method of measuring an individual's energy expenditure when considering their body weight. The body typically burns 1 kcal per kilogram of body weight per hour (expressed as 1 kcal/kg/hr) at rest, which represents 1 MET. Sitting quietly at rest, therefore, has a MET value of 1. A game of squash, however, has a MET value of 12, meaning the body burns 12 kcal/kg/hr.

Methodists: followers of a system of faith developed by John Wesley and which is a non-conformist denomination. In the nineteenth century Methodists believed *popular recreations* to be sinful, being associated with drinking and *gambling*. The Methodists were among the strongest opponents of *animal sports* in the eighteenth and nineteenth centuries and were to have a detrimental effect on *recreation* pastimes for the lower classes. They tried to provide alternative religious activities combining recreation with a spiritual cause.

micro cycle: part of the *periodisation* process, the development of a micro cycle is central to effective training planning. Essentially a micro cycle is a group of training sessions or units, usually organised over the period of a week, but can last up to 3 weeks. They usually focus on one particular component of performance and can be either fitness or skill-related.

micronutrients: dietary elements that provide a number of metabolic functions within cells, such as vitamins and minerals. They are called micronutrients because we only need them in relatively small quantities.

middle ages: see *medieval era*.

middle class: the traditional *social class* grouping that stands between the *upper class* and the *working class* and is usually associated with non-manual work such as clerical or professional work such as teaching. The middle class emerged through the *Industrial Revolution* and they were part of the civilising process on nineteenth-century society and were a strong religious and moral force, restricting blood sports and rationalising many sports, i.e. they developed rules, structured competitions and *governing bodies*.

military drill: training in procedures or movements and use of weapons. Strict and often repetitious training or exercises used as a method of teaching in the nineteenth-century state schools. (See also *model course*.)

Minister for Sport: a British government minister whose main responsibility is to oversee and coordinate sport at a national level. S/he works in the *Department for Culture, Media and Sport*.

minority groups: groups in society that occupy a smaller percentage within a population. In many cases, this can mean less access to positions of power and influence. (See also *ethnic groups*.)

minute ventilation: the total volume of air taken to the lungs per minute. It is the product of *tidal volume* (the volume of air taken to the lungs per breath) and frequency (the number of breaths taken per minute), and at rest this volume should lie between 6000 and 7000 ml per minute. Since both frequency of breathing and tidal volume increase during exercise, there is a significant rise in minute ventilation. However, changes in minute ventilation following submaximal training are fairly insignificant.

mitochondria (singular mitochondrion) are the powerhouses of the muscle cell which plays a central role in the production of *ATP* under *aerobic* conditions. Endurance athletes such as tour cyclists would be expected to possess larger and more efficient mitochondria in the muscles of their legs in order to optimise ATP and therefore energy production. Both the size and number of mitochondria can be increased through a programme of endurance training.

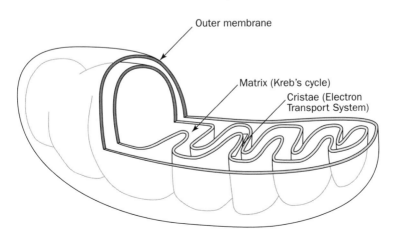

Mitochondria

mixed economy: see *economic system*.

mob: an unorganised, unruly mass of people who are engaged in some form of disorder. The mob was symbolic in the nineteenth century of everything that the *upper class* feared. Following the French Revolution, the mob came to represent a threat to their privileged lifestyle from the lower orders. (See also *mob games*.)

mob football: see *mob games*.

mob games: games played by an unorganised, unruly mass of people such as *mob* football and mob hockey. These games were a form of *popular recreation*, characterised by:
- occasional play
- few, simple rules
- limited structure and organisation
- participation-based rather than spectator-based
- needing physical force rather than skill
- lower-class development
- being local rather than regional or national
- limited equipment and facilities.

model course: a policy of *military drill* used in state schools, which was initiated in 1902 by Colonel Fox of the War Office. The lack of fitness, discipline and poor general health of the *working class* had been noted in the *Boer War* and blamed for the heavy loss of life suffered. The aim was to improve:
- the fitness of the working class for military preparation
- their familiarity with *combat* and weapons
- discipline and obedience among the working class.

It was characterised by:
- the use of commands issued by the teacher or non-commissioned officers (NCO)
- children standing in military-style rows and obeying commands
- large numbers being catered for in a small space
- movements that were free-standing requiring no apparatus, and therefore cheap.

However, the problems of the course were that:
- adult exercises were performed by children
- it did not take into account children's physical, mental or emotional needs
- there was no educational content
- *individualism* was submerged within a group response
- the use of NCOs lowered the status of the subject.

moment arm: the distance between the point of application of force and the fulcrum of a *lever* system. The moment arm relates to either the *effort arm* or *resistance arm* of the lever.

moment of force: also known as torque, this is the rotational effect of an applied force. It is dependent on the distance of the point of application of the force from the fulcrum and the magnitude of the force. It is measured in newton metres (NM). The longer the moment of force the greater the turning effect.

moment of inertia: a measure of the resistance of an object to **angular motion**. It is the body's reluctance to initiate **rotation** or, if already undergoing angular motion, its resistance to change its state of rotation; this can be compared to its linear counterpart. The moment of inertia of a body is determined by two key factors:

- its mass
- the distribution of its mass around the axis of rotation.

The larger the mass of an object, the greater its moment of inertia and vice versa. Consequently, it is more difficult to apply **back spin** to a shot putt than to a basketball as the shot putt has a much larger mass and therefore a higher moment of inertia.

The further the mass of a body is away from the axis of rotation, the greater its moment of inertia and the larger the force required to make it rotate (or stop it spinning if rotation is already occurring). If the body's mass is concentrated about the axis, the moment of inertia will be lower and the rate of rotation faster.

The moment of inertia can be calculated as follows:

FORMULA: $= \Sigma \, (m \times r^2)$

where

MI = moment of inertia

Σ = sum of

m = mass of body part

r = distance from the axis of rotation.

The clearest example of the impact of the moment of inertia in a sporting context is seen in trampolining when comparing the rate of spin of a layout somersault and a tucked somersault. In a layout somersault, the mass is distributed further away from the axis of rotation, the trampolinist has a large moment of inertia and a comparatively low rate of rotation. In the tucked position, the trampolinist's mass is concentrated closer to the axis of rotation, the moment of inertia is lower and the rate of spin higher. It is possible, of course, to change the moment of inertia once in flight. The trampolinist, for example, performing a tucked back somersault increases their moment of inertia by kicking out of the somersault and extending their body. This slows the rate of rotation and allows the trampolinist to spot their landing.

momentum: the amount of motion a moving object or individual possesses and is the product of its mass and **velocity**:

FORMULA: Mo = mv

where

Mo = moment of inertia

m = mass

v = velocity.

A prop forward in rugby with a mass of 90 kg and a velocity of I0 m/s has a momentum of 900 kg m/s. As the mass of an object or person tends to remain constant in sporting situations, any change in momentum must be as a result of change in velocity. A long jumper, for example, will change their run-up so that they are travelling at their highest velocity at take-off, in an attempt to optimise their momentum.

mood states: see *profile of mood states*.

morbid obesity: severe *obesity* in which a person's *body mass index* is over 40. This condition is associated with having a body weight high enough to pose a severe risk to health.

Mosston and Ashworth's spectrum of teaching styles: a *continuum* of teaching styles based on who makes the decision about the learning environment. The type of teaching style is chosen by the teacher based on a number of factors, including the nature of the task, the situation, the ability of the performer as well as the personality and experience of the teacher. The coach or teacher should take note of these variables and be flexible in their use of the styles in order to maximise the learning environment. There are numerous styles, as indicated in the diagram below, with the most common being:

- A: *command teaching style* – all decisions made by the teacher, with no pupil input
- C/D: *reciprocal teaching style* – decisions made predominantly by the teacher with some input from the performer
- F: *discovery teaching style* – decisions made by the performers, with some guidance and input from the teacher
- I/J: *problem-solving teaching style* – all decisions made by the performer, with no teacher input.

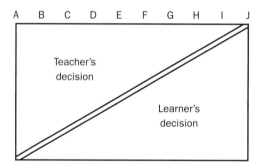

motherland: the cultural legacy of England in *Australia*.

motivation: the internal mechanisms and external *stimuli*, which arouse and direct behaviour. It is generally suggested that we have two basic motives that require fulfilment: our physiological and psychological needs (see *Maslow's hierarchy of needs*). Each performer has differing needs that motivate them to participate, which fall into two broad categories:

- *intrinsic motivation* – involves gaining self-satisfaction or pride from achievements; the desire to challenge oneself; or simply the enjoyment of taking part. For example, an individual may decide to learn how to play squash as a form of recreation in order to develop their fitness levels and to see if they can master the game
- *extrinsic motivation* – involves receiving either tangible or intangible *rewards*. The former includes medals, cups, certificates or money, while the latter may involve praise from a coach, family, peer group or the *mass media*, as well as glory, social approval or achievement records.

Many examples of extrinsic motivation can be used to reinforce learning but should be used with care, as the overuse of extrinsic rewards can undermine the intrinsic values needed for long-term participation. For example, a novice swimmer may be encouraged to learn to swim for numerous reasons including the safety, enjoyment, social and health benefits received. To maintain their interest, awards and badges may be used, but care must be taken to ensure the swimmer does not simply continue because of the next reward – otherwise what happens after the final badge? Ideally, a performer should be motivated by a combination of intrinsic and extrinsic rewards in order to optimise learning. (See also *achievement motivation*, *arousal* and *attribution theory*.)

motor ability: see *gross motor ability*.

motor control: the regulation and adaption of bodily movements. It is suggested that individuals achieve this on three levels, depending on the extent to which the *central nervous system* is involved:

- level 1 – *open loop control*, automatic, requiring no conscious control; for example, catching a ball or running
- level 2 – *closed loop control*, some *feedback* received via *kinaesthetic* awareness and any adjustments are made subconsciously with little conscious attention from the performer; for example, holding a balance
- level 3 – closed loop control, feedback received and conscious decisions are made to adjust the movement, requiring attention from the performer, for example, a beginner learning to dribble has to continually evaluate and adapt their actions.

The majority of situations may require each performer to alternate between all three levels and will vary depending on the level of experience. For example, the novice will have to concentrate while dribbling more than an expert, who can perform the skill without apparently thinking about its execution.

motor end plate: the functional junction between the nerve and the muscle cell. It is the point at which the motor nerve stimulates the muscle fibre and causes contraction.

motor neurone: a nerve cell that conducts nerve impulses from the brain and spinal cord to muscles and to initiate contraction. Neurones have three distinct parts:

- a cell body that contains a well-defined nucleus
- dendrites that receive impulses and conduct them towards the cell body
- an axon – a single, long, thin extension that sends the impulse towards the muscle.

The ends of the axon terminals contain bulb-like structures known as synaptic end bulbs, which form part of the *neuromuscular junction*. Without the complex structure of motor neurones, it would not be possible to perform the coordinated movements required for sporting activities. (See the diagram overleaf.)

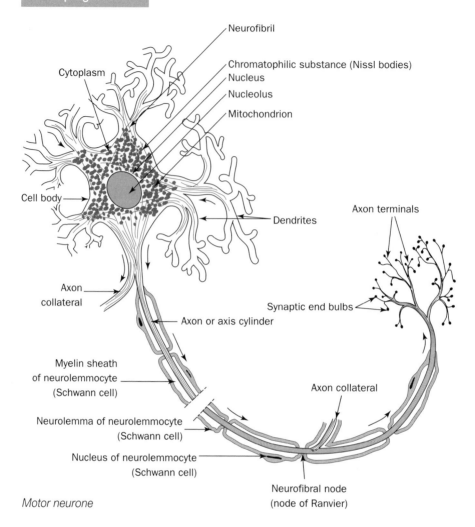

Neurofibril

Chromatophilic substance (Nissl bodies)
Nucleus
Nucleolus
Mitochondrion

Cytoplasm

Cell body

Axon terminals

Dendrites

Axon
collateral

Synaptic end bulbs

Axon or axis cylinder

Axon collateral

Myelin sheath
of neurolemmocyte
(Schwann cell)

Neurolemma of neurolemmocyte
(Schwann cell)

Nucleus of neurolemmocyte
(Schwann cell)

Neurofibral node
(node of Ranvier)

Motor neurone

motor programme: see *executive motor programme*.

motor skill: the physical execution of a movement by combining various abilities. Each skill requires different abilities to be effective and usually combines with **cognitive skills** and **perceptual skills**. Motor skills include a tennis serve, hurdling, running and rock climbing.

motor unit: consists of the *motor neurone* plus all the fibres which that neurone innervates. Muscle fibres within a muscle are under the control of different motor neurones, just like pupils within a school are assigned to different forms or tutor groups. The number of motor units that are recruited for a specific contraction is determined by the strength needed for a given action. For example, when performing a biceps curl to a maximum, all the motor units within the biceps brachii are recruited to enable the highest possible force to be generated. However, if a lighter weight is lifted, then only the number of motor units required to lift the weight will be recruited. A motor unit follows the **all or none law**, so that if a motor unit is recruited then all the fibres within the unit will contract to their maximum possible extent. Furthermore, the number of fibres assigned to a particular motor unit varies depending on the precision of movement required. For example, a motor unit of the eye may only have as few as ten fibres under its influence, since such movements require great control, while the gastrocnemius which is designed for strength may have up to 2000 fibres per motor unit. In this way, efficient yet effective muscle contraction can occur in all movements undertaken within the sporting arena.

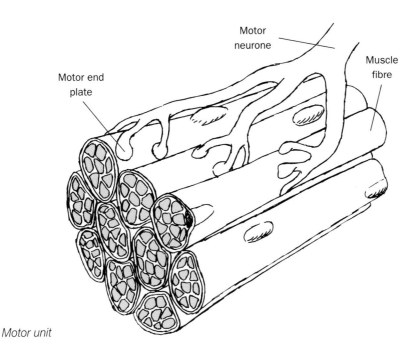

Motor neurone

Muscle fibre

Motor end plate

Motor unit

movement analysis: see *kinesiology*.

movement approach: freedom, self-discovery and self-expression were encouraged in *physical education* lessons following *World War II*. Much of this was based on the philosophy of Dewey who proposed that activities could be educationally valid because of the intrinsic value of movement for its own sake. Emphasis was placed on individual discovery of solutions to physical problems and personal interpretation replaced the group response. The movement approach was readily adopted in primary schools, whereas in secondary schools educational gymnastics and dance were distinguished from the more traditional work of Olympic gymnastics and games.

movement pattern: also referred to as joint actions, a visual description of the movements possible at a joint. It is central to analysing movement. (See appendix, pages 326–30.)

movement time: the time taken between the start of a movement and its completion. When the performer has made their decision based on the various *stimuli* from the environment and the message has been sent to the muscular system (see *reaction time*), the time taken to complete that *executive motor programme* is recorded. For example, it would be the time a water polo player takes from the start of the shooting action to the finish of the action. (See also *response time*.)

Moving and Growing: also referred to as joint actions, a Ministry of Education publication in 1952 that, together with *Planning the Programme,* replaced the old

181

Syllabuses of Physical Training and were developed for use in primary schools. They combined the two influences of obstacle training from the army and movement training from the centres of dance. These publications developed as a result of changes in educational thinking which was to make learning more child-centred. The activities focused on included agility, playground and more major game skills, dance and movement to music, national dances and swimming. The key characteristics that distinguish them from earlier forms of physical activity in state schools are that it was exploratory, creative, individual and fun.

Much Wenlock Olympian Games: a festival of sporting activities established in 1850 at Much Wenlock by Dr Penny Brookes who formed a National Olympic Association. It had all the trappings of a rustic festival, with the events including football, cricket, *quoits*, a blindfold wheelbarrow race, and chasing a pig through the town. By the 1870s the events included track and field *athletics*, such as the pentathlon and tilting at the ring (a version of the *jousting* tournament). It was based on the spirit of *amateurism* placing the ideals of *fair play* and team spirit high above any material objectives. *Baron Pierre de Coubertin* visited these games in the years preceding the foundation of the modern *Olympic Games*.

multicultural: a society that incorporates the *cultures* of other groups, particularly other *ethnic groups*. The food, customs and religious beliefs of these groups can have an effect on the *dominant culture*. Different views exist about whether ethnic groups should be assimilated into the main culture or can coexist alongside it. Education policies have had to adjust to cater for the requirements of these groups. Traditional sporting activities in the West are not always appropriate for different cultures. (See also *accommodation* and *assimilation*.)

multifidus muscle: a major contributory muscle to *core stability*, the multifidus provides stability of the adjacent vertebrae of the spine. In doing so, it stabilises the lower back and pelvis *before* movement of the arms and/or legs occurs. Good core stability allows the muscles that put the limbs of the body into action to generate greater forces by pulling against a more stable base, in this case the trunk.

multi-stage fitness test: a test used to predict *maximum oxygen uptake (VO$_2$ max)*. Devised by the National Coaching Foundation (now *Sports Coach UK*), it is a progressive shuttle run test that starts off easily and becomes progressively more difficult. Subjects are required to run as many shuttles of 20 m as possible, keeping in time to the bleeps emitted from a pre-recorded tape. This becomes more difficult, however, since the difficulty increases with each level attained and the speed and intensity of running must be increased accordingly. Subjects continue to run as long as possible until such a time when they can no longer keep up with the bleeps. Once the subject withdraws from the test the level, the shuttle number attained can be recorded and compared to standard tables which translate the score into a predicted VO$_2$ max value.

Municipal Reform Act 1835: this Act provided local councils that were elected by local authorities the *legislation* allowing them to raise money to provide the means for improving the moral, mental and physical state of the masses. Recreational facilities began to appear in the 1850s whereas, prior to this, only the *upper class* had access to such facilities. Provision included libraries, museums and parks. The parks were popular and constructed to:
- encourage rational sport that was rule-based with underlying moral qualities
- provide socially acceptable alternatives to the public house and *gambling* and thereby gain *social control* of the masses

- encourage a fitter, healthier workforce
- acknowledge an increase in social justice and reform
- appease the growing pressure from the lower classes for more facilities
- raise the profile of local areas for urban prestige.

muscle pump: aids the blood's return to the heart via the veins and is an essential part of the *venous return mechanism*. The contraction of *skeletal muscle* compresses on localised veins which squeezes blood towards the heart. Pocket valves in the veins prevent any backflow and therefore ensures the smooth return of blood. During exercise the venous return increases dramatically, since there are more frequent and stronger muscular contractions ensuring that blood returns to the heart quickly, ready to be pumped around the body once again. If exercise is stopped suddenly without performing a *cool-down,* the venous return mechanism slows due to the cessation of the muscle pump and this may cause blood to pool in the veins and hinder the removal of *lactic acid* that may have accumulated during the exercise period.

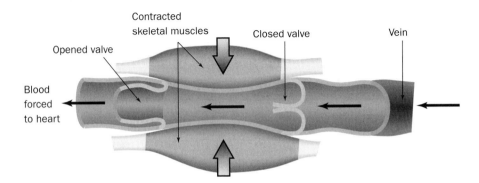

Muscle pump

muscle spindle apparatus: receptors that lie between the muscle fibres detecting the degree of stretch within the muscle. They transmit information to the spinal cord and brain concerning the muscle's length and the rate of lengthening. In order to perform specific movements, the brain must know the current state of the muscle so that it can be adjusted appropriately, essentially preventing the muscle from overstretching and causing injury. When performing *plyometrics*, for example, on jumping down from a box the quadriceps muscle group is stretched, the muscle spindles detect the degree of stretch, and to prevent the muscle from stretching too far cause an instant *concentric contraction* which shortens the muscle and causes an explosive jump upwards. (See the diagram overleaf.)

muscle tone: sustained partial contraction of portions of *skeletal muscle*. A muscle may be in a state of partial contraction at any given time, since some fibres may be contracted while others relax. This tightens the muscle but contraction is not sufficient to initiate movement. Muscle tone is essential for maintaining posture, for example, the multifidus and transverse abdominis contract continually to create good core stability, while the neck muscles will contract to support the weight of the head but do not contract enough to pull the head all the way back. When performing a handstand in *gymnastics*, muscle tone in the arms and shoulders is essential to maintain *balance*.

α (alpha) motor neurones

γ (gamma) motor neurones

Sensory muscle spindle neurone

Sensory nerve endings

Non-contractile part of muscle spindle

Contractile part of muscle spindle

Capsule

3 muscle fibres of muscle spindle (intra-fusal)

Ordinary muscle fibres (extra-fusal)

There may be up to 60 muscle spindles
in a skeletal muscle

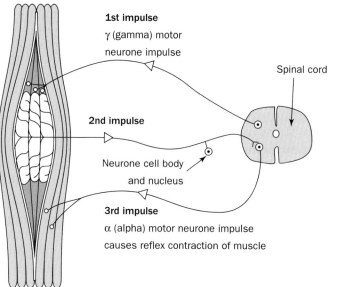

1st impulse
γ (gamma) motor
neurone impulse

Spinal cord

2nd impulse

Neurone cell body
and nucleus

3rd impulse
α (alpha) motor neurone impulse
causes reflex contraction of muscle

Muscle spindle apparatus

muscle twitch: the response of a muscle fibre to a single *stimulus*.

muscular Christianity: an evangelical movement combining the Christian and chivalric
ideal of manliness. It was the return of the Platonic concept of the 'whole man'. It aimed to
improve one's ability to be courteous, gentle, brave and enterprising, reverent and truthful,
selfless and devoted. It included the belief that healthy bodies were needed alongside
healthy minds and moreover that moral understanding could be developed through *athletic*

activities. However, it was not just any type of activity: muscular Christianity encouraged *rational recreation* and pursuits that took place in the *natural environment* such as cycling and rambling.

muscular endurance: the ability of a muscle to undergo repeated contractions and avoid *fatigue*. Muscular endurance is a major component of fitness required in activities where one or more muscle groups work at medium to high intensity for periods of time lasting up to 5 or 6 minutes. A good example is competitive rowing, where muscles of both the upper and lower body work continually throughout the race. This aspect of fitness is largely based on the efficiency of the *lactic acid energy system* and the *buffering* capacity of the body, but can be improved through training. Any training for muscular endurance should work at improving these systems, for example, by undertaking *interval training* with a work : relief ratio of 1 : 1. Various tests can be performed to measure muscular endurance, including the National Coaching Foundation abdominal conditioning test.

myo-: a prefix meaning 'pertaining to muscle'.

myocardial infarction: also known as a heart attack, this is the death of cardiac tissue, which results from an insufficient blood supply reaching the *myocardium*.

myocardium: the thickest portion of cardiac tissue (lying between the *pericardium* and the *endocardium*), which is responsible for pumping blood around the body. The heart of a trained athlete is larger than that of a non-athlete and is characterised by a thicker myocardium allowing the heart muscle to contract with a much greater force and pump more blood out of the heart per beat (*stroke volume*). At rest, this means that the heart does not need to pump as many times per minute to get the same volume of blood flowing to the muscles. However, during exercise, the increased thickness of the myocardium together with an increased heart rate means that the volume of blood flowing to the muscles (*cardiac output*) increases substantially.

myofibril: a thread-like structure, many of which combine to make up a muscle fibre, forming the contractile unit of *skeletal muscle*. They run longitudinally through the muscle fibre and are composed of two *myofilaments*: one thick protein named *myosin* and a thinner protein called *actin*. The interaction of actin and myosin occurs via the *sliding filament theory*, which explains the process of muscle contraction at molecular level.

myofilament: extremely fine molecular proteins that make up a *myofibril*. The action of the myofilaments is responsible for the contraction of the myofibrils and therefore the muscle as a whole. There are two types of myofilaments: a thick *myosin* filament and a thin *actin* filament. It is the interaction between these two myofilaments via the *sliding filament theory* that can explain muscle contraction and which is therefore central to our understanding of movement.

myogenic: the capacity of the heart to generate spontaneous *action potentials* (impulses) that cause the heart to contract. Essentially, the heart does not need to wait for an action potential to arrive from the brain, but can emit its own from the pacemaker (see *sinoatrial node*). This means that during exercise the heart can respond quickly to ensure adequate supply of blood, hormones and nutrients to the muscle cells.

myoglobin: a form of *haemoglobin* that occurs within the muscle cell that transports oxygen to the *mitochondria*, in order to produce energy via the *aerobic* energy pathway. The *slow twitch muscle fibres* used for endurance-based activities contain more myoglobin than *fast twitch muscle fibres* due to their need for oxygen. It is also myoglobin, an iron-based protein, that gives slow twitch fibres their characteristic red colour. Endurance training has shown to increase muscle myoglobin content by up to 80%.

myosin: the contractile protein that makes up the thick *myofilaments* of muscle fibres and enables the muscle to contract according to the *sliding filament theory*.

A–Z Online

Log on to A–Z Online to search the database of terms, print revision lists and much more. Go to **www.philipallan.co.uk/a-zonline** to get started.

nAch: see *need to achieve*.

nAf: see *need to avoid failure*.

narcotic analgesics: any of a group of drugs such as opium and morphine that produce numbness and stupor. They are taken to reduce or mask pain, as well as for the pleasant feelings they induce. Side effects associated with them are respiratory problems, depression, dependence and addiction. (See also *doping*.)

National Collegiate Athletic Association (NCAA) is responsible for the inter-scholastic athletic programmes in the larger American colleges. The organisation was established in 1906 to control and create order in American college athletics. There are four major membership divisions according to the size and quality of the sport programmes. The NCAA acts as a monopoly in its control and, in the 1980s – when women's sport began to attract revenue of its own – the NCAA took over from the Association for Intercollegiate Athletics for Women (AIAW). The NCAA is able to make considerable sums of money from selling broadcasting rights for revenue-producing sports. The courts restricted its monopoly in the 1980s but it remains a powerful organisation in amateur sports.

National Curriculum: introduced by the Education Reform Act 1988 (see *Education Acts*), which laid down what should be taught to children between the ages of 5 and 6 in state schools. It was an attempt to raise standards in education and make schools more accountable for what they teach. League tables are published so comparisons can be made between schools. *Attainment targets* and programmes of study have been laid down within *key stages*. This was a move towards the *centralisation* of education.

national governing bodies: see *governing bodies*.

national governments: various governments, individuals and administrators have sometimes used sport and physical activity to serve certain political ends. (See the diagram overleaf.)

national identity: a state or country possessing unique identifying characteristics; something by which a state is recognised. Sport represents and reinforces images of regional and national identity. Powerful symbols are used, such as national anthems, team colours, flags and ceremonies. For example, the Scottish rugby ground at Murrayfield evokes vivid messages and images of Scottish identity and nationhood, and the Tour de France epito-mises French national identity. Some newly developing countries use success in sport to help create a national identity, such as *Kenya* and running. *Globalisation*, however, has served to confuse cultural identity as communities become fragmented and genetic mixing of *ethnic groups* occurs.

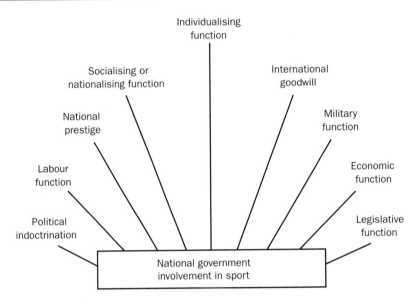

National governments

National Institute of Sport: a national organisation founded to promote *elite* sport. Each country has its own system to develop talented performers, who often progress to use specialist facilities, with top-quality coaches and scientific support. Examples of such centres include the **UK Sports Institute**, the **Australian Institute of Sport** and the French centre in Paris, INSEP. (See also **academies of sport**.)

National Junior Sports Programme was launched in 1996 by the English Sports Council (now **Sport England**) in conjunction with the **Youth Sports Trust**. Its aim is to encourage young children from the age of 4 to become involved in sport. It provides kit, coaching and places to play, as well as identifying the more talented performers from a wider base. Many teachers have received training with the aid of funding from the **National Lottery**, Sport England, the Youth Sports Trust and business **sponsorship**. There are five main elements:

- Top Play – aimed at children aged 4–9 years, this is a general introduction to core games and skills
- Top Sport – aimed at children aged 7–11 years, whereby sport-specific skills are developed
- Top Club – aimed at helping sports clubs to establish quality improved provision for young people aged 11–18 years
- Champion Coaching – concentrates on the delivery of quality after-school coaching for young people aged 11–14 who are reaching or have reached performance level.
- Top Link — 14–16 year olds in school based volunteering.

National Lottery: a game of chance set up on a national scale in which tickets are sold, one or more of which may later qualify the holder for a prize. In Britain this was established in 1994 and is run by the Camelot Group who are granted a licence by the National Lottery Commission. For every pound spent on the lottery, a percentage goes to the **Lottery fund** to support 'good causes'. So far over 317,000 projects, large and small, have benefited from Lottery funding.

Fourteen organisations are in charge of giving Lottery funding to good causes. These organisations act independently of government and cover arts, heritage, sport, community and voluntary groups as well as supporting projects concerned with health, education and the environment. In sport, for example, Lottery funding lottery has contributed £65,544 towards the **World Class Performance Pathway** budget from 2005–2009 (approximately two-thirds of its budget). Lottery funding will also be available for the 2012 **Olympic Games** and **Paralympic Games** in London.

There are advantages and disadvantages of Lottery funding for sport, as outlined in the table below.

Advantages of Lottery funding	Disadvantages of Lottery funding
Allows more sportsmen and women to be supported while training	Taxpayers' money could be spent on more vital causes such as health
Gives sportsmen and women greater access to specialist coaching and better facilities	Can provide a 'get out' for the government in funding sport which does benefit society in terms of health
Allows amateur sport to continue despite increasing commercial pressure and the growth of professional sport	Sportsmen and women may not work hard enough to justify their grants

National Parks: areas of land controlled by the state in order to preserve its natural beauty and wildlife. There are 14 National Parks in Britain including, for example, those in the Brecon Beacons, Dartmoor, the Lake District and Snowdonia. These areas are governed by the National Park Authorities, which are local government bodies consisting of local councillors, together with members appointed by the Secretary of State for the Environment, Food and Rural Affairs. National Parks can cater for a wide range of interests: they provide walkers with pleasant open countryside for enjoyment, accommodation for tourists and a livelihood for farmers and foresters, quarrymen and gamekeepers. They were established for two reasons: to ensure landscape **conservation** and to allow access to mountains and moorlands.

national sports centres are run by **Sport England** to provide appropriate training facilities for the **elite** performer as well as being open to the public. They are used extensively by the **governing bodies** of sport and there are currently five in Britain:

- **English Institute of Sport, Sheffield** – this state-of-the-art sports development centre offers a range of highly equipped sports performance areas including boxing, judo, badminton, netball, basketball, volleyball, handball and athletics, including a six-lane 200 m indoor tracks and indoor throws area.
- Lilleshall, Shropshire – major facilities include indoor and outdoor tennis courts, specialist gymnastic areas, several sports halls, squash courts and associated conditioning rooms.
- Plas y Brenin National Mountain Centre, Snowdonia – major facilities include climbing walls, indoor canoe training pool, ski slope, fitness room and easy access to Snowdonia National Park.
- Bisham Abbey, Buckinghamshire – major facilities include tennis courts (indoor and outdoor courts with various playing surfaces), two artificial turf pitches, grass pitches, weight-lifting platforms and associated conditioning rooms.

- Holme Pierrepont National Water Sports Centre, Nottingham – major facilities include a *regatta* lake, white water slalom course, water ski lagoon, sports hall and associated conditioning rooms.

nationalism: a sentiment based on common cultural characteristics that binds a population. It often produces a policy of national independence or separatism. Sport can develop the feelings of patriotism and loyalty to one's country that are characteristic of nationalism. For example, during a major championship the progress of the team is followed and nationalism can intensify as the later stages are reached.

native Americans: the original inhabitants of North America – the American Indians. There are nearly 2 million native Americans in the *USA* made up from over 200 cultural groups, though Anglos (British settlers) have tended to *stereotype* them into one group and may refer to them as 'Indians'. Sport among these groups has traditionally been associated with *ritual* and ceremony, although little research has been carried out because Indian culture has undergone many changes following the colonisation of the USA. In modern sport, only when success and achievement have been notable in *American football* and *baseball* has any *mass media* attention been focused on them. Native American participation in sport has generally been limited due to:

- poverty and poor health
- lack of equipment and programmes
- *prejudice*
- cultural isolation.

In 1983 the Iroquois national *lacrosse* team was established reflecting the origins of the game. The term 'Hispanic' is a generic term used to describe people whose origins can be traced to Spanish-speaking countries (approximately 22 million) and whose cultures are related by language, colonial history or Catholicism. Examples are Chicanos and Puerto Ricans.

There are approximately 6.7 million 'Asian Americans' in the USA, but very little sociological research has been done on any of these groups in relation to sport participation. Generally they are discriminated against in terms of racial stereotypes which make belonging to sports groups difficult and also their traditions may not always coincide with the true *American sports*.

natural environment: a term usually associated with the natural world, including land, air and sea. The latter half of the twentieth century saw an increase in concern for its survival. Pollution, loss of the green belt and increasing inroads into more isolated areas of the countryside are some of the issues that environmental groups are raising at a political level. In terms of *recreation*, the natural environment was valued in the eighteenth and nineteenth centuries as an *escape* from the polluted towns. The trend for outdoor activities began with rambling, climbing and cycling, firstly with the *upper class* and *middle class,* and then with the *working class* as they gained more free time and transport enabled them to access the countryside.

Country parks, nature reserves, green belt areas and areas of outstanding natural beauty as well as *National Parks* are all seeing an increase in use. Conflicts can emerge between landowners and recreation users and *conservation* is a key issue.

nature versus nurture: this debate concerns the relative importance of an individual's innate qualities ('nature') versus personal experiences ('nurture') in determining or causing individual differences in physical and behavioural traits. The view that humans acquire all or almost all their behavioral traits from nurture is known as *tabula rasa* ('blank slate').

Although nurture has historically been referred to as the care given to children by the parents, with the mother playing a role of particular importance, this term is now regarded by some as any environmental (i.e. not genetic) factor in the contemporary nature versus nurture debate. Therefore, the definition of nurture has been expanded in order to include the influences on development arising from prenatal, parental, extended family and peer experiences, extending to influences such as **mass media**, marketing, and socioeconomic status.

near transfer: see *transfer of learning*.

need to achieve (nAch) refers to the personality characteristics possessed by individuals, which are used to explain their levels of motivation towards a task. The **achievement motivation** theory suggests such performers gain pride and satisfaction from participation; display perseverance while completing the task quickly and efficiently; are prepared to take risks and challenges and they like **feedback** and personal responsibility. For example, a club-standard tennis player will be happy to play someone of a similar or better ability if offered the opportunity without worrying about the outcome. They would rise to the challenge and use the experience they may gain in the future. (See also **need to avoid failure**.)

need to avoid failure (nAf) refers to the personality characteristics possessed by individuals, which are used to explain their levels of motivation towards a task. The **achievement motivation** theory suggests such performers will attempt to avoid shame and humiliation when participating: they will avoid situations of risk, i.e. those with a 50 : 50 chance of success and hence choose tasks that are either very easy or very difficult in nature. They also dislike personal **feedback** or positions of responsibility and tend to attribute reasons for their actions to external factors, such as the opposition, luck or other circumstances beyond their control. For example, a club tennis player high in need to avoid failure will tend to choose opponents who are better or worse than themselves because they are not expected to win or should do so easily. As a result, the outcome will not be a reflection of their ability and they are therefore motivated to avoid failure. (See also **need to achieve**.)

negative performance curve: see *performance curves*.

negative reinforcement: see *reinforcement*.

negative transfer: see *transfer of learning*.

net force: also known as the resultant force, this is the final (or overall) force acting on a body once all the other forces acting have been considered.

net game: games that involves opponents being separated by a net, such as tennis and volleyball. They can be individual and team games, the winner being decided by who wins the most games, sets or rubbers. Mainly **open skills** are utilised except when the game is started by a serve. Domination is achieved by playing shots which the opponent is unable to return.

neuromuscular junction: the area of contact between the **motor neurone** and the muscle fibre. It is the point at which muscle fibre innervation occurs providing that there is sufficient **acetylcholine** available to diffuse across the synaptic cleft and produce an **action potential**.

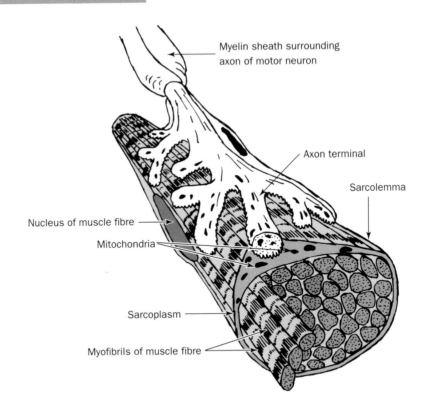

Myelin sheath surrounding
axon of motor neuron

Axon terminal

Sarcolemma

Nucleus of muscle fibre

Mitochondria

Sarcoplasm

Myofibrils of muscle fibre

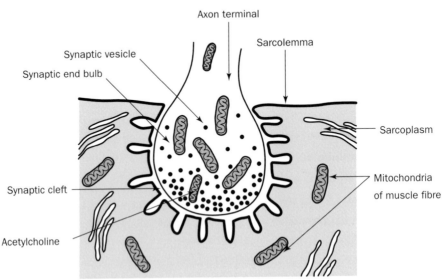

Axon terminal

Sarcolemma

Synaptic vesicle

Synaptic end bulb

Sarcoplasm

Synaptic cleft

Mitochondria
of muscle fibre

Acetylcholine

Neuromuscular junction

neurotic personality: a person who is touchy, restless, aggressive, moody and anxious. They display traits linked to their *autonomic nervous system*, which responds quickly and powerfully to stressful situations, causing such emotional reactions. In comparison to those with a *stable personality*, they possess the opposite *traits* and are placed at the other end of the *continuum*. These characteristics can be measured using *Eysenck's personality inventory* or *Cattell's 16 personality factors questionnaire*.

New Zealand: an independent dominion within the Commonwealth, comprised of two main islands (North Island and South Island) plus Stewart Island, the Chatham Islands and a number of minor islands in the southeast Pacific. The original Maori inhabitants surrendered sovereignty in 1840 and were finally subdued by 1870. The game of *rugby union football* has been used to develop a *national identity*, with the All Blacks a clear symbol of the country they represent. (See also *Maori culture*.)

newton (N) is the standard unit of force. One newton represents the force required to give a 1 kg mass an *acceleration* of 1 m/s^2. This stems from Newton's second law of motion, which states that:

FORMULA: $F = ma$

where

F = force

m = mass

a = acceleration.

If we know the mass of a sprinter and their acceleration over 3 seconds, it is possible to determine the amount of force that was necessary to produce that acceleration.

Newton's laws of motion: motion can be described by Newton's three laws of motion.

The first law of motion (N1)

This is the law of inertia, and states:

'Every body at rest, or moving with constant velocity in a straight line, will continue in that state unless compelled to change by an external force exerted upon it.'

So, in order to change the motion of an object or performer, a force must be applied. For example, to move a golf ball off a tee, a force must be applied to it from the club head. Likewise, for a sprinter to move out of the blocks, the sprinter must exert a force from their muscles. Furthermore once the golf ball is in flight it will continue to move at constant velocity until acted upon by a force, in this instance *air resistance* acts as the force to slow the ball down, as does gravity which causes the ball to land on the fairway.

The second law of motion (N2)

This is the law of acceleration, and states:

'The acceleration of a body is proportional to the force causing it, and the acceleration takes place in the direction in which that force acts'.

This is often expressed as:

FORMULA: $F = ma$

where

F = force

m = mass

a = acceleration.

This suggests that the greater the mass of an object, the greater the force required to give the same acceleration. If mass remains constant, then the greater the force applied, the greater the acceleration. For example, more force is applied to the shuttlecock in an overhead clear to create a greater acceleration than when performing a drop shot.

The third law of motion (N3)

This is the law of reaction, and states:

'When one action exerts a force on a second object, there is a force equal in magnitude but opposite in direction exerted by the second object on the first.'

or, more simply:

'To every action there is an equal and opposite reaction.'

When a swimmer, for example, exerts a force on the starting blocks, the blocks exert an equal and opposite **reaction force** on the swimmer, propelling them forward into the water. Once in the water, the swimmer must exert a backward force on the water in order to move forward.

noise: information that is gathered from the environment that is irrelevant to the performance. This can cause the performer to take longer to detect relevant **cues** and slow the **information processing** system. During a game, a player may have to ignore shouts from the crowd, effects of the weather or any tactics employed by their opponents to distract them.

noradrenaline: also known as norepinephrine, this is a hormone released from the adrenal medulla via the **sympathetic nervous system**. Noradrenaline has many functions in the body but specifically prepares the body for its **fight or flight response**. It is the action of noradrenaline that increases heart rate and causes the force of contraction of the cardiac muscle fibres to increase during exercise. This, together with its function of increasing blood glucose levels, enables the athlete's muscles to receive the necessary nutrients required for optimal performance.

norms: established standards of behaviour shared by members of a social group and to which each member is expected to conform. They include expected patterns of behaviour such as **etiquette** and can also have moral dimensions. They are learned through the process of **socialisation**.

nutrition pyramid: a guide as to how much of each food group or nutrient a performer should be eating. The food groups towards the base of the pyramid represent the nutrients that should make up the majority of the performer's diet (i.e. fresh fruit and vegetables and carbohydrate-rich foods), whereas those towards the top of the pyramid represent those nutrients that should be consumed in smaller quantities. The diagram opposite identifies the types of food that fall into each group and gives an indication as to the amount that should be consumed in an athlete's diet.

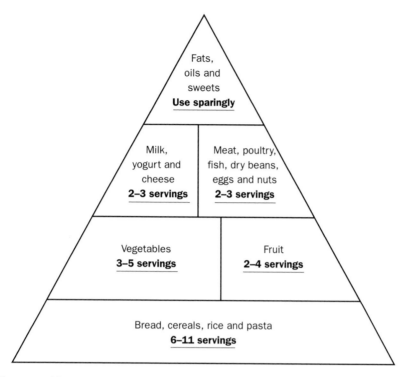

Fats,
oils and
sweets
Use sparingly

Milk,
yogurt and
cheese
2–3 servings

Meat, poultry,
fish, dry beans,
eggs and nuts
2–3 servings

Vegetables
3–5 servings

Fruit
2–4 servings

Bread, cereals, rice and pasta
6–11 servings

Nutrition pyramid

Do you need revision help and advice?

Go to pages 297–330 for a range of revision appendices that include plenty of exam advice and tips.

obesity: a condition that accompanies a sedentary or inactive lifestyle, caused by an imbalance between energy intake and expenditure which results in an excessive increase in the body's total quantity of fat. Typically, men with more than 25% body fat and women with more than 35% are clinically defined as obese. Obesity can lead to increased incidence of *cardiovascular diseases* such as *atherosclerosis*, hypertension, heart disease and strokes as well as other complications including gall bladder disease and diabetes.

Since obesity is the result of an imbalance between energy intake and expenditure, it follows that by increasing energy expenditure through exercise, obesity can be prevented. Exercise also suppresses appetite and increases the *basal metabolic rate*. However, care should be taken when prescribing an exercise programme for the obese and account taken of their limited exercise capacity. Activities should be of low intensity, low impact and *aerobic* in nature, such as walking, swimming or cycling, and the intensity should only be increased very gradually. Obesity can be determined by the *body mass index*, where a BMI of 30 and over defines obesity, and one of 40 or more defines *morbid obesity*.

objective: undistorted by personal interpretation or bias. Where possible testing should be objective, allowing for comparison of results that are meaningful. For example, various physiological and psychological tests, including the *multi-stage fitness test* and the *sport competitive anxiety test*, produce results that cannot be open to individual interpretation or *subjective* analysis.

OBLA: see *onset of blood lactate accumulation*.

observational learning: see *social learning theory*.

Ogive performance curve: see *performance curve*.

old boy: a male ex-pupil of a *public school*. The old boys in the nineteenth centuries would financially support their schools, would often go back into teaching and sport fixtures would be held against current students. (See also *old boy network*.)

old boy network: the appointment to power of former pupils of the same small group of well-established *public schools* or universities. It has served to perpetuate traditional elite values in society and can repress *social mobility* of the lower classes. (See also *old boy*.)

Olympic bids: the way in which national governments, sport organisations and cities bid, in competition with others, to win the approval of the *International Olympic Committee* to host the *Olympic Games*. They do this for a variety of reasons:
- civic and national pride
- political gain
- economic benefits.

The selection of the host city is vitally important, as the success of the Games can often be dependent on the chosen site. Each candidate city must demonstrate to the IOC that its bid to stage the greatest multi-disciplinary event in the world has the support of its people and its political authorities. A manual containing evaluation criteria is available and the Evaluation Commission evaluates each **city bid**. Following allegations of misconduct during the Salt Lake City bid for the 2002 winter Olympics, changes were made. A selection college was put in place for Turin 2006. This selection college selects two cities from among six finalists. The selection of the host city takes place immediately after on the same day. The **International Olympic Committee president** was unable to vote on this occasion.

Olympic Games: the greatest panhellenic (all-Greek) festival, held every four years in honour of Zeus at ancient Olympia, which lasted over 1000 years. The modern revival consists of international athletic and sporting contests held every four years in a selected country, since their inception by **Baron Pierre de Coubertin** in Athens in 1896. Contestants were inspired by his vision of countries drawn together in healthy competition, where the taking part was important, not necessarily the winning. Baron de Coubertin established the **International Olympic Committee** to oversee the running of the Games and each member country now has a National Olympic Committee. The Olympic flag shows five interconnecting rings, in different colours displayed on a white background, representing the five continents: Europe, Asia, Africa, Oceania and the Americas.

The Olympic motto is 'Citius, Altius, Fortius' which means 'swifter, higher, stronger' and the six goals of the Olympic movement are to develop:

- personal excellence
- sport as education
- cultural exchange
- mass participation
- fair play
- international understanding.

The Games have been affected by political situations as they are given prominent **mass media** coverage and thus can be used to promote political messages. For example, the Soviet **boycott** of the Los Angeles Games in 1984 was one of the most dramatic occasions following the 1980 American boycott of the Moscow Games. The Games were founded on an amateur basis, as de Coubertin was disappointed with the growing **commercialisation** of nineteenth-century sport. Today, some countries could not host the Games as commercial considerations are high due to the enormous cost involved. Nevertheless, there is fierce competition to host the Games and put in an **Olympic bid**. This has also led to incidents of corruption at the highest levels, within both the **administration** and performer levels.

Olympic Oath: in the early **Olympic Games**, all competitors were required to take an oath. Today, one athlete is chosen to take the oath on behalf of all competitors. 'In the name of all the competitors I promise that we shall take part in these Olympic Games, respecting and abiding by the rules which govern them in the true spirit of sportsmanship.' Officials also take an oath to officiate fairly.

Olympism: a philosophy of life, exalting and combining in a balanced whole the qualities of body, will and mind. Blending sport with culture and education, Olympism seeks to create a way of life based on the joy found in effort, the educational value of good example and respect for universal fundamental ethical principles.

onset of blood lactate accumulation (OBLA) is the point at which *lactic acid* starts to accumulate in the blood, usually taken when blood lactate levels reach 4 mmol per litre of blood. It typically occurs when the body converts to *anaerobic* means of energy production. Below this point the body can work aerobically and therefore sustained low-intensity exercise can take place, since no lactic acid has accumulated. However, exercise above the point of OBLA can usually only last for approximately 1 minute. For example, imagine how your legs feel at the end of running a flat-out 400-metre run.

OBLA always occurs below the performer's *maximum oxygen uptake (VO$_2$ max)*. The higher the percentage of VO$_2$ max at which OBLA occurs, the better that individual is at endurance-based activity. Typically, OBLA in the untrained performer occurs at approximately 50% of VO$_2$ max, while in trained endurance athletes, it may be delayed until 80% of VO$_2$ max has been attained. Following a training programme that includes bouts of both *aerobic* and anaerobic work, the point of OBLA can be delayed and improvements in performance take place.

VOBLA = 4.10 m s^{-1}
% VO$_2$ max = 86.2

Running speed (m s^{-1})

	3.58	4.02	4.47	4.92
HLa (mmol/L)	2.9	3.7	5.7	9.1
HR (bpm)	166	179	187	197

The test shows that this squash player is using a large percentage of his VO$_2$ max, resulting in a more successful endurance performance

open loop control suggests that some movements are performed without conscious control because they are so well learned and appear automatic. The *executive motor programmes*, which are stored in the *long-term memory store*, can be retrieved very quickly when required and are performed without the need for *feedback* and adjustment during the execution of the task.

Input ➡ Executive mechanism ➡ Effector mechanism ➡ Output

This process usually occurs during the completion in a *closed skill* (for example, skipping or running), but can also take place in an *open skill* such as catching a ball. However, most sportsmen and women experience both open loop and *closed loop control* throughout their performance, alternating between each depending on the task difficulty and level of skill performance.

open skills are performed in an unstable, changing, unpredictable environment to which the performer must continually react, adjusting their position and actions as required. It is usually an **externally paced skill** requiring the performer to evaluate the situation quickly, and select and adapt an appropriate response. Such skills, for example, include all games involving passing and receiving a ball or racket sports where the position of an opponent on court will determine the selection of the stroke to be played. (See also **closed skills**.)

open societies: those societies where there is a great deal of **social mobility** in the class structure. They are more common in the Western democracies where **capitalism** is prevalent. Based on meritocracy, social mobility is usually achieved through qualifications gained via the education system. Sport can also be used for this purpose; for example, performers who excel in their chosen sport can often reap financial rewards and improve their lifestyle.

operant conditioning: also known as trial and error learning, this is a theory which states that learning is more effective if the performer is concerned with the action and its consequences, as it increases or decreases the probability of it reoccurring. It is one of the **associationist theories of learning** but differs from **classical conditioning** because the action of the performer is shaped through manipulating the environment and reinforced, either strengthening or weakening the **stimulus–response bond** depending on the outcome. For example, to develop accuracy, a games player has to hit a target and receives reinforcement by observing his of her success or failure. The coach may provide three forms of reinforcement:

- positive **reinforcement** – increases the likelihood of the action being repeated
- negative reinforcement – decreases the chance of repetition
- **punishment** – could be used to strengthen or weaken the stimulus–response bond.

Some **complex skills** may need to be broken down into **subroutines** and learned in stages, reinforced and developed progressively. For example, a high jumper may practice the run-up, take-off, layout and landing in isolation, receiving reinforcement, such as praise, to ensure the correct technique is repeated when the complete action is performed. However, care should be taken not to provide too much positive reinforcement, so that the performer constantly seeks praise and becomes over-reliant on it, causing a reduction in performance levels if withdrawn. **Thorndike's laws of learning** were based on trial and error learning, which when utilised help to strengthen the stimulus–response bond and support these theories.

opiate of the masses: the metaphor 'opiate' has been interpreted in several ways. The word 'morphine', the principal and most widely known and widely produced opiate, means 'dream-inducer'. In this sense, opium is what you give someone when you want them to experience a fantasy instead of a reality. In the case of sport, it is the suggestion that sport can be used by the controllers of society to keep the masses content, unquestioning of any social injustices.

organisations: see **institutions**.

origin: the point of attachment of a muscle (**tendon**) on to a stationary bone against which the muscle can pull. It occurs at the opposite end of the muscle **insertion** and usually occurs on the nearest **flat bone**. Major muscle origins and insertions are highlighted in the table overleaf.

Origin of major muscles and insertions

Muscle	Function	Insertion	Origin
Pectoralis major	Flexes upper arm Adducts upper arm	Humerus	Sternum Clavicle Rib cartilage
Latissimus dorsi	Extends and adducts upper arm	Humerus	Vertebrae (T5–L5) Iliac crest
Deltoid	Abducts, flexes and extends upper arm	Humerus	Clavicle Scapula Acromion
Biceps brachii	Flexes lower arm	Radius	Scapula
Triceps	Extends lower arm	Olecranon process	Humerus Scapula
Iliopsoas (iliacus/psoas major)	Flexes trunk Flexes thigh	Ilium Vertebrae Femur	Ilium Vertebrae Femur
Gluteus maximus	Extends thigh	Femur	Ilium
Gluteus medius Gluteus minimus	Abducts thigh	Femur	Ilium
Hamstring group Biceps femoris Semimembranosus Semitendinosus	Flexes lower leg Extends thigh	Tibia Fibula	Ischium Femur
Quadricep group Rectus femoris Vastus medialis Vastus lateralis Vastus intermedius	Extends lower leg Flexes thigh	Tibia (via patella tendon)	Ilium Femur
Sartorius	Flexes hip and knee	Anterior superior Iliac spine	Tibia
Adductors Longus Magnus Brevis	Adducts thigh	Femur (linea aspera)	Pubic bone
Gastrocnemius	Plantar flexion Flexes knee	Calcaneus	Femur
Soleus	Plantar flexion	Calcaneus	Fibula Tibia

As a rule of thumb, the **origin** of a muscle is the nearest *flat bone*; the *insertion* is the bone that the muscle puts into action.

Osgood's semantic differential scale: see *semantic differential scales*.

ossification: the process of bone formation. Some bones are formed directly in membranes, known as direct or intramembranous ossification. Examples include the *flat bones* of the skull and the patella. Other bones gradually replace hyaline cartilage from the foetal stage through to full maturation in our late teenage years. This is known as indirect or endochondral ossification and examples include the *short bones* and *long bones* of our limbs.

osteoarthritis is a disease characterised by pain and impaired function at joints largely due to the deterioration of the joint cartilage. Osteoarthritis can arise from a poorly designed exercise programme and overuse. However, regular *aerobic* exercise that is non or partial weight-bearing (such as swimming or cycling) should be encouraged to help control the pain associated with osteoarthritis. General mobility training will also help promote effective joint functioning. It is thought that increased activity can help promote the growth of new cartilage and nourish existing cartilage. If done incorrectly, however, an exercise programme can cause long-term injury and damage to the joints.

osteocyte: a mature bone cell. Throughout life, bone is constantly remodelled so that it becomes stronger along the lines of stress. Unwanted cells are reabsorbed by 'bone-breaking cells' (osteoclasts) and then replaced by 'bone-making cells' (osteoblasts) along lines of stress. For example, when running greater stress is imposed on the bones of the leg; osteocytes are therefore laid down along these lines of stress to increase the strength of the bone.

osteoporosis: a bone condition that leads to weak or porous bones that can that can lead to bone fractures or breaks. Bones are living tissue and are constantly being rebuilt. In osteoporosis the rate of bone loss is greater than the rate of bone growth, leading to a reduction in overall bone mass. Osteoporosis is particularly prevalent in post-menopausal women since the female hormone oestrogen is important in maintaining bone. When oestrogen levels drop following the menopause, bone loss accelerates.

The risk of osteoporosis is lower for people who are active, particularly those who undertake weight-bearing activities (such as jogging) three times per week. These activities promote bone growth, leading to denser and stronger bones.

outcome goal: a goal that is set to judge the performance of the individual against others and the end result. For example, a sprinter may be set the goal of either winning the race or finishing in the top three places to qualify for the next round. The efficiency and manner of their performance is not relevant, only the final result. If the *goal setting* is realistic and within the performer's capability, when they achieve the aim, their motivation is increased. However, it can be demotivating if the performer is unsuccessful, especially after repeated attempts. If this is the case, it may be more appropriate to use *performance goals* or *process-orientated goals*.

outdoor education: participation in outdoor pursuit activities in the *natural environment* in order to develop educational values. For example, a school may offer orienteering within the school grounds or arrange a visit to a *National Park* or other area where *adventurous activities* may be undertaken.

outdoor pursuits: see *adventurous activities*.

outdoor recreation: participation in outdoor pursuit activities within the *natural environment* in an individual's free time.

output: the third stage of *information processing*, involving the completion of the selected action or movement. This occurs as a result of the *effector mechanism*, or system of nerves and muscles, implementing the *executive motor programmes* which have been formulated during the *decision-making* process. For example, a rugby player during open play may pass the ball to a player in close support having made a decision based on the available information from the *display (psychology)*. Various mechanisms have been suggested as to how such movements are controlled and executed including those discussed in the *open loop theory*, the *closed loop theory* and *schema theory*.

Outward Bound Trust: a worldwide organisation that began to pioneer outdoor activities in the 1940s. It works in partnership with the *Duke of Edinburgh Award Scheme*, aiming to promote personal development training for young people by placing them in challenging situations such as expeditions and skills courses.

overtraining: caused by an imbalance between training and *recovery*, which usually occurs when insufficient time has been left for the body to regenerate and adapt before embarking on the next training session. In the search for the best possible performance in competition, *elite* athletes are often tempted and prone to increase training loads and frequency of training above optimal levels, which can lead to symptoms of overtraining. These symptoms include enduring *fatigue*, loss of appetite, muscle tenderness, sleep disturbances and head colds. The coach can identify overtraining syndrome by physiological testing, which may show the athlete having an increased oxygen consumption, heart rate and blood *lactate* levels at fixed workloads. In order to combat overtraining, the coach should advise prolonged rest, and a reduction in training workloads for a period of weeks or even months. This should restore both performance and competitive desire.

Oxbridge: a word used to refer to the most prestigious universities in Britain: Oxford and Cambridge. Despite some democratisation of student recruitment, the large majority of students are still the products of the *public school* system who go on to occupy positions of power in many of the UK's social structures such as politics and business. Several annual sporting occasions between the two capture the attention of the public and *mass media*, for example the Varsity rugby match and the Boat Race.

oxygen debt: see *excess post-exercise oxygen consumption*.

oxygen deficit: the volume of additional oxygen (to that used during exercise) required to complete the entire activity aerobically. At the very beginning of exercise (even at low intensities) or when exercise is of high intensity, it is likely that the body will need to work anaerobically for a period of time as there may be insufficient oxygen available to use the *aerobic energy system* exclusively to provide the energy for muscular work. Therefore, there becomes a deficit in oxygen supply. The oxygen deficit represents the amount of extra oxygen required to enable the entire activity to be completed using the aerobic energy system. Since it takes a while for the aerobic system to activate and provide the muscles with energy at the beginning of activity, a deficit will always occur.

oxygen tent: a specialised chamber that regulates the amount of oxygen available to an injured performer while they sleep. Oxygen tents replicate the low oxygen conditions of altitude and seek to enhance the production of red blood cells in the body. Oxygen tents are not used as a direct treatment of an injury sustained by a performer, but rather to minimise losses in fitness incurred during the *recovery* period. The injured performer can sit or more usually sleep in specially designed hypoxic chambers, which simulate the low oxygen concentrations and conditions of altitude. As a result, the physiological load placed on the performer is increased while the body responds by stimulating the production of red blood cells, allowing improved oxygen transport and minimising losses in *aerobic fitness*.

oxyhaemoglobin (HbO2) is *haemoglobin* that is saturated with oxygen. In order to be transported in the blood, oxygen must combine with haemoglobin to form oxyhaemoglobin. The oxygen is then released at the tissue or muscle site to enable metabolism to take place. Males generally have higher levels of haemoglobin than females, which explains their greater potential for *aerobic* activity.

Are you studying other subjects?

The *A–Z Handbooks (digital editions)* are available in 14 different subjects. Browse the range and order other handbooks at **www.philipallan.co.uk/a-zonline.**

parallelogram of forces: a method of determining the size and direction of the resultant or *net force* when two forces are acting on an object or body. The resultant force R can be determined by constructing a parallelogram using the vectors F1 and F2. The resultant force acts along the diagonal of the parallelogram. For a right-angled parallelogram, the resultant force can be calculated using Pythagoras' theorem.

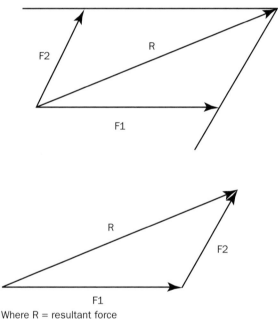

Where R = resultant force

Paralympic Games: originated as an annual sports meeting for semi-paralysed competitors. It is properly called the International Stoke Mandeville Games after the founding hospital in Buckinghamshire, England and was originally known as the Paraplegic Games. The idea of such *athletic activity* was conceived during *World War II* as recommended treatment for patients whose lower limbs and trunk were paralysed, and developed into regular competition. The international aspect to the Games was strengthened in 1960 when they were held in the Olympic city of Rome and they have expanded considerably, with the Sydney 2000 Games attracting over 4000 athletes, 2000 coaches and many other supporting officials. 'Paralympic' means parallel to the Olympic Games – not paraplegic Olympics – and the Games are concerned with ability, athletic endeavour and elite performance. The current symbol of the Games was launched in 2003. It is a symbol of motion, with three agitos (from the Latin for 'I move') encircling a centre point. The three colours (red, blue and green) are the colours that are the most widely represented in national flags around the word. The Paralympic motto is 'Spirit in Motion'.

parameter: information stored within a *schema*, which helps to initiate a response using the appropriate speed and force required. A performer who develops a wide range of parameters will have a better chance of successfully completing the skill, as they will be more familiar with the requirements when confronted with them in a game situation. For example, a netball player who executes their shots from a variety of positions on the court will need to use a slightly different action for each in terms of direction, force and speed. If during training they have practised from varied locations, they can modify their action more effectively than a player can who has only developed their shooting action from one or two places.

parasympathetic nervous system: primarily responsible for conserving the body's energy and its effects tend to oppose those of the **sympathetic nervous system**. It is one of the two subdivisions of the **autonomic nervous system**. Following exercise, the parasympathetic nervous system restores the heart rate and respiratory rate to normal resting levels.

part-method practice: a performer attempts to develop specific **subroutines** of a skill in isolation before putting them into the correct sequence. This **practice** method lends itself to long sequences (gymnastic routines), **complex skills** (hurdling), low-level organisation skills (swimming) or dangerous tasks (gymnastic vaulting). It is useful for those performers who are beginners, have limited motivation or attention span, and for those who need to rectify particular faults in technique.

partial pressure: the pressure exerted by an individual gas when it exists within a mixture of gases. Partial pressure of a single gas is denoted by p and to calculate the total pressure of a gas we simply add together all the partial pressures of the individual gases. For example, atmospheric pressure is composed of three main gases, nitrogen, oxygen and carbon dioxide:

$$\text{Atmospheric pressure} \left(760 \text{ mm Hg}\right) = pN_2 + pO_2 + pCO_2$$

If the fractional concentration of the gas is known, it is possible to calculate the partial pressure that each gas exerts. For example, approximately 21% of atmospheric pressure is made up of oxygen. The pressure that oxygen therefore exerts in the whole gas can be calculated as follows:

$$\text{Atmospheric } pO_2 = 760 \text{ mm Hg} \times pN_2 + pO_2 + pCO_2$$
$$= 160 \text{ mm Hg}$$

However, the reason why partial pressure is so important to us is that it determines how much oxygen we can get into the body and how much carbon dioxide can be expelled, since a gas will always move from areas of a higher partial pressure to areas of a lower partial pressure. Quite simply, because the concentration of oxygen is greater outside the body than inside, a 'pressure gradient' is formed and oxygen moves into the body's blood stream. The greater the pressure gradient across the respiratory membrane, the more rapidly oxygen diffuses across it. When exercising, more oxygen is used up in the muscles and causes a greater pressure gradient enabling a quicker uptake of oxygen. Partial pressures (mm Hg) of respiratory gases and nitrogen in atmospheric air, alveolar air, blood and tissue cells are given in the table.

	Atmospheric air (sea level)	Alveolar air	Deoxygen-ated blood	Oxygenated blood	Tissue cells
pO_2	160.0	105	40	105	40
pCO_2	0.3	40	45	40	45
pN_2	597.0	569	569	569	569

participation pyramid: a sport development *continuum* intended to enable people to learn the basic sports skills with the possibility of reaching a standard of sporting *excellence*.

- Foundation – learning basic movement skills, knowledge and understanding; developing a positive attitude to physical activity. The physical education programme in schools can represent this stage.
- Participation – exercising one's *leisure* option for a variety of reasons, including health, fitness and social. This stage is represented by *extra-curricular sport* at school, club level and during recreational time.
- Performance – improving standards through *coaching*, competition and training. The higher club and regional levels of performance would represent this level.
- Excellence – reaching national and publicly recognised standards of performance. National and international competition would represent this level.

Participation pyramid

passive stretching: a stretching technique that relates to the range of movement which can occur with the aid of external force. This is generally performed with the help of a partner who can offer some resistance, although body weight and a piece of equipment such as a dyna-band or towel can also be used. One method of *flexibility* training that has emerged from passive stretching is *proprioceptive neuromuscular facilitation*. This seeks to decrease the reflex shortening of the muscle being stretched (called the stretch reflex) that occurs when a muscle is lengthened to its limit.

patron: a person who sponsors any kind of athlete or artist from their own private funds. Patronage tends to occur among a privileged class within a hierarchical society. In the nineteenth century, wealthy aristocrats who wanted to be associated with new styles and trends would sometimes spend large amounts of money on sporting events and particular athletes, especially those involved with *boxing* and *pedestrianism*. A group of patrons would join together to form an association which would then organise the sport. When patrons withdrew their funds, the effect was similar to a modern day sponsor pulling out of an event, usually leading to a decline in the activity or athlete.

peak flow experience: the state that performers sometimes experience when the timing of movements and actions appears perfect. Performers suggest when this happens they are experiencing the ultimate intrinsic experience. Csikszentmihalyi (1975) identified some common characteristics during the 'flow experience', including the total ability to complete the challenge successfully and complete absorption in the activity. Other factors were clear goals, being totally focused on the task, an apparent loss of consciousness and an almost subconscious feeling of self-control.

It is also suggested that there is a link between somatic *arousal* (physiological response) and cognitive arousal (thought processes). When the performer has reached the correct level of somatic arousal and the cognitive arousal is low, peak flow is more likely to occur.

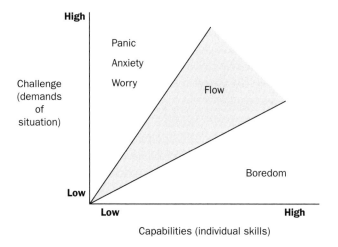

Peak flow experience

pedestrianism: an early form of race walking. In the eighteenth and nineteenth centuries, with only *horse racing* and *boxing* as rivals, pedestrianism was very popular with much *gambling* involving men against time, distance and other walkers. Captain Barclay was a famous walker who in 1809 walked 1000 miles in 1000 consecutive hours. A pedestrian was also a lower-class individual who earned part of his money by competing in sporting activities for money, particularly *rowing*, footraces and *cricket*. It was the forerunner to the term 'professional'.

pennate: a muscle shape designed for strength. The pennate (featherlike) muscles are characterised by an arrangement of muscle fibres around a central **tendon** and exist in the body where strength is required. For example, the tibialis posterior (unipennate) and soleus (bipennate) occur at the back of the lower leg and are responsible for lifting the whole body's weight off the floor when performing the high jump. Other examples of pennate muscles include the pectoralis major (multi pennate) and the orbicularis muscles of the eyes and mouth (circum pennate).

perception: the interpretation and analysis of information gathered from the environment by the sensory system. The various stimuli enter the **short-term sensory store**, where the relevant information is extracted by the process of **selective attention** before being transferred on to the **decision-making** phase. For example, when a tennis player receives details of their opponent's location on court, together with the speed and direction of the ball, they will use that information to analyse what options are available before deciding which shot to play next in the rally.

perceptual motor ability: see *psychomotor ability*.

perceptual narrowing: see *attentional narrowing*.

perceptual skills involve the accurate interpretation of information received via the **sensory system**, which allows the appropriate movement to be executed. For example, a good batsman will usually analyse the delivery of the bowler accurately before deciding which stroke to play. (See also **perception**.)

performance refers to a temporary occurrence that may not necessarily be repeated. For example, on a particular day a tennis player may beat an opponent who has a much higher ranking, but is unable to repeat their success in the future. On that day they executed their *skills* effectively and achieved the correct level of **arousal** but may not be able to replicate their victory. The aim of each performer should be to reach the **autonomous phase of learning** so that their performance is as consistent as possible.

performance curves: curves plotted on a graph to provide a visual representation of the performance of an individual over a period of time, allowing analysis and evaluation. Often they are comprised of several types of curve, which need to be interpreted in order to assess the development or regression of the performer. The four types of curve are illustrated opposite:
1   negatively accelerated curve – indicates a large improvement initially with little development in the later stages
2   positively accelerated curve – indicates minor improvements initially with large developments in later attempts
3   linear curve – indicates gradual improvements in relation to the number of attempts or time taken
4   ogive or S-shaped – any combination of curves 1, 2 and 3.

An individual may reach a **plateau** in performance, showing a period of no improvement.

Performance curves

performance goals are used to judge the performance of the individual against their own standards, rather than in comparison with their competitors. For example, a sprinter may set a number of goals for a race, including a good reaction to the starter's gun, effective arm action and how close they ran to their personal best time, rather than the finishing position. If the *goal setting* of the coach is realistic, the performer can evaluate their own actions and not worry about comparison with others. This helps to reduce *anxiety*, allowing the runner to remain motivated wherever they finish. The performance goals may influence the *outcome goals* that are set.

performance pyramid: see *participation pyramid*.

pericardium: also known as the epicardium, this is the outermost layer of the heart. It has many functions, but its primary role is to protect the *myocardium*. However, it also prevents over-distension of the heart, particularly when it beats maximally during exercise and serves to anchor the heart in position. Pericardial fluid prevents *friction* between the membranes and tissues of the heart as it beats.

periodisation: the organisation of training throughout a season into blocks or chunks so that an optimal physiological and psychological peak can be reached. Periodisation is an essential ingredient to any training programme which should contain several phases.

- First, a solid training base is needed, which will include both general strength and endurance training. For a runner this might involve hill running, long *interval training* or *circuit training* with weights.
- After this foundation has been laid, the runner can develop more specific skills and training sessions will become more intense, focusing on a pace more closely related to that required in competition.
- In order to prepare for competition, the runner will need to taper their training. Here, the quantity of training may be reduced to enable the body to recoup maximum energy stores prior to competition, and more race-specific training, such as sprint starts for a sprinter, will be the norm. Also, the athlete will prepare psychologically through techniques such as *mental practice*. This should enable the athlete to peak for their most important race of the season and this would normally last for between 1 and 3 weeks.
- The final phase is arguably the most important – the transition period. This is essentially a period of active rest, where the athlete can escape the stresses and strains of training and competition and prepare themselves for the following season.

(See the table overleaf.)

Period	Phase	Activities
Preparation	Phase 1	Development of endurance base, general conditioning
	Phase 2	Higher intensity training, anaerobic work, skills and technique, competition-specific training
Competition	Phase 3	Maintenance of fitness, fine tuning, tactical development
	Phase 4	*Tapering*
	Phase 5	Season's peak performance
Transition	Phase 6	*Recovery*/active rest

periosteum: the thin membrane covering the surface of all bones. It is an important feature of the *skeletal system* as the periosteum enables *tendons* to attach to the bones (via *Sharpey's fibres*), which allows movement. It is also responsible for bone growth, since the periosteum contains the bone-building cells known as osteoblasts. Therefore, the periosteum is responsible for strengthening the bones as a result of an exercise programme.

person-orientated leader: see *contingency theory of leadership*.

personality refers to the more or less stable, enduring, unique pattern of *traits* which determine our behaviour. Researchers have attempted to link personality with sporting performance, but with few conclusive results. Various theories suggest how our personality is formed:

- *trait theory* – personality is innate and stable over time
- social learning theory – personality is formed due to the effect of the environment and learnt experiences, which can alter over time
- *interactionist theory* – personality is formed due to a combination of traits and the environment.

For success in sport, the coach must view and treat each individual differently according to their own personalities. Also, each performer must evaluate their personality and understand how their traits can affect performance, and so learn to control their moods and *arousal* levels depending on the situation.

Hollander (1967) suggests personality is constructed of three layers (see the diagram opposite), each separate but inter-related layer causing some aspects of behaviour to alter depending on the environment.

- Psychological core – basic attitudes, values, motives and self-worth which remain fairly constant.
- Typical responses – the middle layer represents the usual behaviour in a given situation based on the psychological core, for example, displaying acts of *sportsmanship*.
- *Role-related behaviour* – the outer layer depends on the specific situation and may cause personality and behaviour to alter considerably. The pressure or demands of the

situation may require different behaviour, for example an experienced performer may appear quiet and thoughtful when being coached within their own team but when the roles are changed and they are *coaching* a junior team appear loud and assertive.

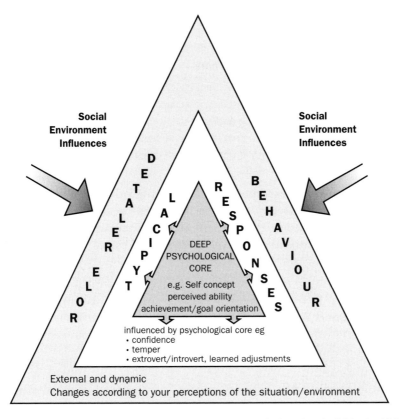

personality tests: methods used to assess the characteristics of an individual, which are used to formulate their unique *personality*. A variety of methods can be used, the most common of which are:

- *questionnaires* – the most commonly used methods, involving a series of questions. For example, *Eysenck's personality inventory*, *Cattell's 16 personality factors questionnaire* and the *sport competition anxiety test*.
- observation – the behaviour of the individual is watched and recorded. This is very *subjective* and there are problems with validity.
- interviews – one-to-one discussion, sometimes involving projective tests, such as the *Rorschach inkblot test*.

Testing for personality is difficult due to the problems of *reliability* and *validity* of procedures.

persuasive communication: a technique to alter the *attitude* of an individual. The person is exposed to new information or experiences in an attempt to change their mind. The effectiveness of employing this method depends on the status of the person delivering the message, the quality of that message, the nature of the *audience* and the situation at the time. For example, within a young football team several players display a negative attitude towards training and only want to play matches. The coach may arrange for a well-known player to visit a **coaching** session to outline the type of training they follow, explain the reasons why they practise skills and the benefits they have received as a result. (See also **cognitive dissonance theory**.)

philistine schools: the middle-class copies of the established **public schools** for the **gentry**. Examples are Cheltenham College, Marlborough and Clifton.

phosphocreatine: see **creatine phosphate**.

physical activity: an umbrella term encompassing any activity that requires an individual to exert a certain amount of energy, resulting in an increase in their heart rate. Physical activities range from walking, skipping and athletics, to games and outdoor and adventerous activities. Individuals can participate on a recreational basis or perform within a more competitive and organised sporting structure, including adhering to externally enforced rules.

physical activity readiness questionnaire (PAR-Q) is a **questionnaire** designed to assist individuals in determining whether they should see their doctor before undertaking a physical exercise programme. Typically, this questionnaire asks up to 12 'yes/no' health-related questions. If participants answer 'yes' to any of the questions, they are advised to discuss the exercise programme with their doctor before becoming physically active. Such a questionnaire is essential for all participants commencing a programme for health-related reasons, and anyone over the age of 60 should always consult their doctor first.

Physical and Sport Education (PASE) is a professional development programme in Australia for teachers delivering physical activity as part of the education system. The range of professional development activities can be categorised as follows:

- school-based/initiated activities – activities in this category can include teachers participating in seminars or workshops that are initiated and conducted by and for teachers at that school
- school-based curriculum project programs – this category includes activities that involve teachers in a project that originates from outside a school but is conducted at the school level
- professional development at schools and resource **centres of excellence** – included in this category are activities that are initiated and conducted by schools that have been developed/chosen as sites of **excellence**
- programs initiated by an employing authority – typical of this category are courses that are developed and implemented by education systems. These are often run on a large scale and may lead to a formal qualification
- teacher professional association programs – the education community is supported by a large number of teacher professional associations, which are typically curriculum-based
- professional development resources – this category includes resources that have been developed for use by teachers, teacher educators and trainers as the basis of a professional development program.

physical culture: an umbrella term for thinking sociologically about sport, exercise and leisure as being highly organised, institutionalised forms of physical activity. It is linked to the **social construction of the body,** the view we have of ourselves and those around us.

Sport is a social process and our views are also shaped by **mass media** images and by the **commodification** of sport.

Within education physical education and school sport have been used to instil cultural **norms** and **values** such as **fair play**, commitment and self-discipline. This process began in the **public schools** with the cult of **athleticism** and **muscular Christianity**.

physical education: the instilling of knowledge, skills and values through the medium of physical activity in an educational setting. It is an academic discipline that has, as its primary focus, the study of human movement with the aims of enhancing total human development and performance. It aims to do this through the experience of a range of physical activities, such as team, individual, competitive and non-competitive sports. Total development means acquiring activity-specific skills and knowledge, as well as fostering positive **attitudes** and **values** that will be useful in later life. Physical education can help us achieve a quality of life and vitality that can be lacking in sedentary lives. The key words that characterise physical education are:

- range of physical activities
- movement
- activity-specific skills
- knowledge
- values
- educational setting.

(See also **National Curriculum**.)

Physical Education, School Sport and Club Links (PESSCL) strategy: a national policy that aims to enhance the take-up of sporting opportunities by 5- to 16-year-olds. Part of the government's national school sport strategy, it demonstrates the increasing trend towards developing strong links between schools and local clubs. The strategy has nine key strands listed below, each designed to maximise opportunities for young people to access high-quality physical education and school sport.

- Sports Colleges
- School Sport Partnerships
- Professional Development
- **Step into Sport**
- Club Links
- Gifted and Talented
- Sporting Playgrounds
- Swimming
- The QCA's PE and School Sport Investigation.

physical recreation: physical participation opportunities for all members of the community in their **leisure** time. The participant is still involved in skilful, competitive and strategic activities but at a less sophisticated level than the performance end of the **participation pyramid**. For example, individuals may play badminton for a club or simply book a court at a local leisure centre in their free time.

physical training: exercise that is wholly to do with training the body for fitness, commonly termed PT. This concept was strong in the nineteenth- and early twentieth-century state schools where the **Syllabuses of Physical Training** were taken from the army field books.

There is no element here of the cognitive, social or moral development associated with the later term *physical education*.

Pierre de Coubertin Awards: named after the founder of the modern *Olympic Games*, these take place on an annual basis to recognise Australian senior secondary students who demonstrate attributes consistent with *Olympism* through participation and commendable behaviour in sporting activities.

All Australian secondary government and non-government schools are invited to nominate one recipient from years 10, 11 or 12 for the Pierre de Coubertin award each year. Each nominee must participate actively in the school's physical education program with a consistently positive attitude and must have represented the school in a sport.

ping-pong diplomacy: a term developed following the visit of the American table tennis players and later swimmers to China as part of an attempt by the USA to restore diplomatic relations with China, which refuses to recognise Taiwan as an independent nation. Even now the pressures are evident.

pivot joint: see *synovial joint*.

Planning the Programme: a primary school publication issued by the Ministry of Education in 1953, which was to replace the existing *Syllabuses of Physical Training* and ran parallel to the *Moving and Growing* initiative.

plantar flexion: a *movement pattern* characterised by the increase in angle at the ankle, when pointing the toes. This form of extension occurs in the median (*saggital*) plane and occurs at the ankle when performing a handstand or swimming freestyle. (See appendix, page 327.)

Plas y Brenin National Mountain Centre: see *national sport centres*.

plasma: a pale yellow fluid that forms the liquid component of the blood. Its components are water (90%), *proteins* (8%) and salts (2%) and plasma makes up to 55% of blood volume. Plasma is an important constituent of the blood since it helps transport hormones as well as assisting in the transport of fats and fat-soluble vitamins – important ingredients for successful exercise performance. However, for trained athletes, endurance training brings about a significant increase in plasma volume (haemodilution) which, in turn, causes an increase *stroke volume* due to its decreased viscosity. This improves the ability to transport oxygen to working muscles, thus facilitating energy production within the *mitochondria*. Plasma also transports approximately 3% of the oxygen inspired.

plateau: a period of time in which no improvement occurs in an individual's performance or level of attainment. This may be indicated in a *performance curve*. It may occur for a number of reasons, including:

- the complexity of the task
- the need to consolidate the skill level while progressing between the stages of learning
- lack of motivation
- boredom or lack of variety in practice
- *fatigue*, injuries or *overtraining*
- the performer's natural ability level
- limited *coaching* knowledge
- unrealistic targets or goals.

A plateau should be avoided if possible in order to prevent demotivation. When required, the coach should evaluate in conjunction with the athlete why this has occurred and discuss appropriate methods to overcome the situation, including developing an understanding of the concept of a plateau.

play: 'a voluntary activity or occupation exercised within certain fixed rules of time and place, according to rules freely accepted but absolutely binding, having its aim in itself and accompanied by a feeling of tension, joy and the consciousness that this is different from ordinary life' (Huizinga).

The characteristics and values of play are:

Play

is spontaneous
↓
is voluntary
↓
is fun
↓
has a non-serious end product
↓
has intrinsic value
↓
brings satisfaction
↓
heightens arousal
↓
is creative
↓
is uninhibitive

plural societies: the existence in society of different *ethnic groups* having distinctive ethnic origins, cultural forms, religions, etc. This is usually as a result of a policy of *accommodation*. Examples of such countries would be Western democratic *cultures* such as France, the UK and USA.

pluralism: a state of society in which several groups have *autonomy* but are interdependent and have equal power. This theory does not accept that only an *elite* makes decisions but that the state considers the opinions of many different interest groups and then acts in the best interests of everyone.

plyometrics: a type of training designed to improve both power and elastic strength. It commonly takes the form of 'bounding' and 'depth jumping' in which an athlete drops down from a box, lands and immediately rebounds on to a second box top. The theory behind it is that when the athlete drops down and lands on the floor, the quadricep muscle group undergoes an *eccentric muscle contraction*, i.e. it lengthens and pre-stretches the muscle. This pre-stretch enables the muscle to exert great forces when it eventually shortens, and the greater the pre-stretch, the greater the elastic energy stored and the more force is exerted by the quadriceps when they shorten. Furthermore, when the muscle is lengthening it actuates the stretch reflex, which prevents the muscle from overstretching and causes a rapid, forceful *concentric muscle contraction*. Plyometrics is often performed by sprint athletes, hurdlers and jumpers, as well as being part of a general conditioning programme for most activities.

Eccentric   Concentric

PNF: see *proprioceptive neuromuscular facilitation*.

politics: the science and art of government; dealing with the form, organisation and *administration* of a state or part of one, and of the regulation of its relations with other states. 'Political' means belonging to or pertaining to the state, its local and national government and policy. Politics is very much about power and the groups that wield it. (See also *national governments*.)

POMS: see *profile of mood states*.

popular recreations: recreation pursuits popular before the onset of the *Industrial Revolution*. These activities were characterised by:

- being occasional, due to little free time
- having few, simple and unwritten rules
- the activity being participation-based rather than spectator-based
- physical force rather than skill
- lower-class involvement
- local rather than regional or national events
- limited structure, equipment and facilities.

(See also *mob games*.)

positive feedback: see *feedback*.

positive performance curve: see *performance curves*.

positive reinforcement: see *reinforcement*.

positive thinking: a method of *stress management* that encourages the performer to evaluate the situation and logically plan their course of action. This allows *anxiety* to be reduced. This may involve the individual adjusting their *attentional style* and concentrating on the narrow (internal) dimension. The aim should be to provide objective evidence to dispel negative thoughts such as training times achieved, previous success and quality of training undertaken in preparation for the event. This in turn should improve **self-efficacy** and help to control **arousal** levels.

Attribution retraining can also be helpful in these situations by encouraging the performer to attribute control internally. Being in control of the situation will help develop both general confidence and self-efficacy. By persuading a performer to take responsibility for themselves and cope with the situation, a teacher or coach can help the performer to deal with any problems they may have to face. The performer can be helped to take responsibility by getting them involved in setting their own goals. Realistic short-term and long-term **performance goals** should be negotiated.

positive transfer: see *transfer of learning*.

post-competition meals: meals consumed following exercise to promote **recovery**. The replenishment of muscle **glycogen** stores can take up to 48 hours following endurance activities such as triathlons or marathons, but most activities will not require anywhere near this length of time. The synthesis of glycogen is at its most efficient within the first 2 hours of the end of the exercise period, so an athlete should be encouraged to consume a carbohydrate-rich meal within the first 45 minutes to an hour of finishing a competition. This period of time after exercise when the muscles are most receptive to refuelling with glycogen is known as the 'carbohydrate window'. The main problem with hitting the carbohydrate window, however, is that exercise is in fact an appetite suppressant and performers rarely feel like eating so soon after the competition.

post-school gap: the **dropout** rate in sport participation on leaving full-time education. Following the Wolfenden Report on Sport and the Community in 1960, the Sports Council (now **Sport England**) made this group (13–24 years) one of its target groups. Reasons for the decline are due to:
- the cost of participation
- the unfamiliarity with local facilities
- the facilities being less accessible
- a widening of other interests.

posterior: also known as dorsal, this is a term of direction that refers to the rear of the body. For example, the tibialis posterior is a muscle that exists at the back of the tibia, while the tibialis **anterior** muscle is situated at the front of the tibia along the shin. When describing the body or movements of the body, it can be particularly useful to use these terms of direction. (See appendix, page 311.)

potential productivity refers to the best possible performance of the members of a group, taking into account their ability, skill level, opponents, task difficulty and expected outcome. However, rarely does each individual within the group perform to their maximum potential and it is usually the role of the coach to eliminate any **faulty processes**. For example, the US Olympic **basketball** team composed of the top players from the National Basketball Assocation (NBA) would be expected to have higher potential productivity than most other national teams. However, simply having the best players does not guarantee success, as they may not work effectively as a team. (See also **group productivity**.)

power: the work done per unit of time, which when considering human movement is the product of strength and speed. Power is obviously of benefit in activities in which the highest intensity of work is required, such as in weightlifting or during a 100-metre sprint. If a performer can increase their power, this can improve their performance as:

- the same amount of work (strength) can be performed in a shorter period of time (speed)
- an increased amount of work (strength) can be done in the same period of time (speed).

Plyometrics can be used to improve a performer's power.

$$\text{Power} = \frac{\text{Work done}}{\text{Time}}$$

Power is measured in watts or joules/sec.

POWERbreathe: a piece of apparatus designed to improve the *strength* of respiratory muscles. The POWERbreathe uses a form of *resistance training* to develop the inspiratory muscles. It claims to improve endurance performance by up to 30% if used for 30 breaths, twice a day. It is therefore particularly useful to endurance athletes such as marathon runners and swimmers.

practice: allocated time that allows the performer to reinforce, develop and refine learning. Constructive use of the time is vital to maximise the individual's potential and several factors should be considered before deciding on the nature of the practice session, such as the size and structure of the group, the personalities and abilities of the performers within that group, the complexity of the task and the time and facilities available. Practice is classified in two ways:

- methods of practice – depending on how the skill can broken down into phases. (See also *part-method practice, progressive part-method practice, whole-method practice, whole-part-whole method practice*.)
- types of practice – the structure of the session in terms of active work and *recovery*. (See also *distributed practice, massed practice* and *variable practice*.)

The coach or teacher should be flexible in their use of these methods and types of practice to ensure the sessions are relevant, specific to the performer and maintain levels of *motivation*.

pre-competition meals: meals consumed ahead of competition. Pre-competition meals should be eaten at least 2 hours prior to the event and should consist mainly of *carbohydrates* that are easily digestible such as cereals, toast and juices in order to top up muscle *glycogen* and maintain blood glucose levels. For endurance-based activities such as a 10 km road run, the performer may wish to consider carbohydrates that release their energy more slowly (foods with a low *glycaemic index*) such as porridge oats or granary bread so that blood glucose levels are maintained throughout the duration of the event. Sugary foods that have a high glycaemic index should be avoided, however, as although they may give an immediate boost of energy, this can be counterproductive as greater levels of insulin will be released, ultimately leading to a dip in blood sugar levels.

prejudice: an opinion or attitude, especially an unfavourable one, based on inadequate facts, often displaying intolerance or dislike of people of a certain race, religion or *culture*. Where possible, such negative attitudes should be broken down, although this may be difficult, even when the prejudiced person is presented with contradictory evidence. As a result, **stereotypes** may be formed which, if acted upon, can lead to **discrimination**. Within a sporting context, this may limit the opportunities for individuals or groups. For example, women's sport may be viewed as less exciting when compared with men's and as a result may receive less **mass media** coverage and **sponsorship**.

prescribed leader gains their position of authority through being appointed to the **group** by an external source. This type of leader is in contrast to an **emergent leader**. For example, the manager or national **governing body** nominates the captain of a national football team.

prime mover: see **agonist**.

primitive cultures: non-industrial, tribal societies where the emphasis is on subsistence living with **ritual** and religious meanings attached to many aspects of life, including physical activities and sports. These would also have had a functional purpose to them such as defence or food hunting, which required speed and accuracy. The **cultures** of **native Americans**, **aborigines** and early Samoans would be such examples.

principle of moments: an equation used to explain how a **lever** system can remain balanced about a fulcrum. The moments of force must be equal. In other words:

Total clockwise moment = total anticlockwise moment

where

Clockwise moment = force × distance to fulcrum

Anticlockwise moment = force (of muscle) × distance of muscle insertion from the joint

therefore

FORMULA: force of resistance = force of muscle

principles of training: the rules or laws that underpin the effectiveness of a training regime. The main principles include **specificity**, **progressive overload**, **reversibility**, tedium, **warm-up**, **cool-down, periodisation** and the **FITT regime**. Essentially, for improvement to occur and for the training programme to be successful, the principles of training must be followed.

private provision: see **leisure provision**.

prize ring: originally this was a contest where almost anything was allowed, from **wrestling** to weaponry. Jack Broughton excluded weaponry and wrestling and established **pugilism** (bare-knuckle fighting) in its place. The supporters of the prize ring were called 'the fancy' and **gambling** was an inherent part of the activity. The prize ring was eventually driven underground due to government **legislation** banning the sport.

prizefighting: individuals were taught to defend themselves in gladiatorial schools in 'sword and buckle' contests. It was patronised by the wealthy and powerful, who wagered huge sums on the outcome of contests though would never have been combatants themselves.

The activity employed a virtually professional core of men fighting in regular circuits, mostly concentrated around London. Rules were fairly loosely enforced and death was not uncommon. When the sport was outlawed, contests were organised on private land away from magistrates. Notable figures were Jack Broughton, Daniel Mendoza and Tom Cribb.

proactive transfer: see *transfer of learning*.

problem-solving teaching style: refers to a teacher setting a problem, with the learner attempting to find a solution. It is an open-ended and creative approach, similar to the *discovery teaching style*, and contrasts with the **command style**. It is useful in developing the cognitive and performance elements of the performer, allowing them to explore various possibilities and take responsibilities for their actions depending on their own strengths and abilities. For example, a team of basketball players may be placed in a specific situation and set the task of devising set moves and exploring attacking options available to them. However, this method can be time consuming, and requires the performers to possess more experience, knowledge and skills. (See also **Mosston and Ashworth's spectrum of teaching styles**.)

process-orientated goals: goals that are specifically related to the development of the tactics or technique of the performer. For example, a sprinter may set the goals of developing their leg action or dip finish in order to improve their overall performance. These goals are closely linked to **performance goals** and their effective use should help to motivate the athlete.

processes: bony projections that aid in the smooth articulation of the skeleton. When flexing the arm at the elbow, the bony point that can be felt at the tip of the elbow is known as the olecranon process, which disappears into a depression on the humerus when the arm is straightened. Sometimes processes are also used in the attachment of muscles.

professional sport: a sporting activity that is engaged in for financial gain or as a means of livelihood. Training is synonymous with improving standards and specialising in an activity. The term 'professional' came into use in the 1850s but it did not only imply a monetary distinction. It also signified a **social class** distinction.

The Football Association (FA) and the Rugby Football Union (RFU) were both to feel the effects of professionalism in their games as commercialisation took root with large numbers of spectators willing to pay. In rugby this led to the north–south split in 1894 with the formation of the professional sport of **rugby league** and the amateur code of **rugby union football**, until 1996 when it too turned professional.

Cricket had always had a form of professionalism and had managed to create a system that maintained the social class divide while allowing both social classes the opportunities to play the game. The term 'gentlemen and players' was used, indicating the former being the **gentry**, while the latter came from the **working class**.

Rowing could not cope with competitions between the watermen, the lower-class rowers and the gentry. Eventually, the Amateur Rowing Association (ARA) brought in the **manual labour clause**, which excluded manual workers whether or not they were professional sportsmen. This resulted in the formation of the National Amateur Rowing Association (NARA) in 1890, which only excluded those who earned money through rowing.

profile of mood states (POMS) is based on the proposition that an individual with positive mental health will be more successful in a sporting situation. A profile is constructed of a performer's mood states before competition with levels of tension, depression, anger, vigour, fatigue and confusion being recorded. Those with good mental health will produce an 'iceberg profile', displaying more vigour but less tension, depression, fatigue and confusion when compared with unsuccessful athletes.

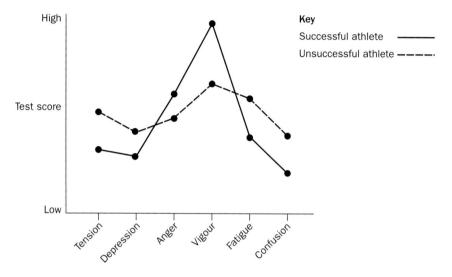

However, although this theory is widely accepted, many non-elite performers display an iceberg profile but not all elite athletes do so. For those who do, it may alter if training regimes are excessive causing a loss of vigour, with a corresponding increase in negative moods.

profiling: a term used in *disability sport* to describe the method of classifying sportsmen and women using the degree and nature of their disability. It uses a side view outline or representation of a body, which exhibits certain tested characteristics.

progressive muscular relaxation (PMR) is also known as progressive relaxation training (PRT) or Jacobsen's progressive relaxation. It involves the performer becoming aware of the alternating sensations of tension and *relaxation* of the muscles. Specific muscle groups are identified in succession, gradually reducing the tension throughout the body. Initially this may take time, but with practice athletes can focus and relax the whole body almost immediately. This is particularly useful prior to competition to facilitate sleep and during the event in periods of high *anxiety*. (See also *autogenic training* and *self-directed relaxation*.)

progressive overload: a principle of training based around two important concepts. The first, 'overload', suggests that in order to improve the body's strength or endurance, we must put it under some kind of stress. For example, to gain strength the muscles must be placed under great stress and loaded to a level greater than normal. The second concept, 'progression', suggests that as the body becomes stronger or better at coping with endurance-based activity, further increases in muscle loading or distances run must follow in order to stimulate further improvement.

progressive part-method practice is often referred to as chaining. It is a method of practice in which the performer learns one part of the skill before linking it to the next phase of the action. For example, a rugby team may have to learn a sequence of moves in order to complete a specific play. During training, the coach develops each move in isolation and gradually links them together, so they can be performed at speed with each player executing their own role. Similarly, this could apply to individual skills, such as a basketball lay-up shot. This method is useful for complex tasks and places less demand on the attention span of the performer, when compared with other forms of *practice*.

proletariat: one of *Karl Marx*'s major classes in *capitalist* societies. It refers generally to that group which does not own the means of production. It is generally accepted as meaning the *working class* (manual workers). Marx believed it was this group that threatened society by means of revolution.

pronation: a *movement pattern* characterised by the *medial rotation* of the forearm at the radio-ulnar joint so that the palm of the hand faces downwards. Pronation occurs in the horizontal or *transverse plane* about a longitudinal axis, for example when performing a top spin forehand in tennis. (See appendix, page 329.)

propaganda: the systematic distribution of information with the aim of persuading the views of a section of society. An example is the Nazi use of the Berlin *Olympic Games* in 1936.

proprietary colleges: *middle class,* privately owned schools set up to emulate their *gentry* counterparts; for example, Malvern College was based on Winchester College. (See also *philistine schools*.)

proprioceptive neuromuscular facilitation (PNF) is a stretching technique used to develop *flexibility* and mobility. Essentially, PNF seeks to inhibit the stretch reflex that occurs when a muscle is stretched to its limit, so that a greater stretch can occur. By isometrically contracting the muscle that is being stretched to its limit (see *isometric muscle contraction*), usually with the aid of a partner, the stretch reflex is diminished. (The stretch reflex is initiated by *muscle spindle apparatus* and *Golgi tendon organs*.) In the absence of the stretch reflex, the muscle can be stretched to a greater extent and, with continued practice of PNF, a new limit of muscle stretch can occur enabling a greater range of movement and therefore greater mobility that can be achieved before the stretch reflex is triggered. This is obviously of benefit to all athletes but particularly in activities where flexibility and strength are a necessity, such as gymnastics or activities involving jumping.

proprioceptors: see *sensory system*.

protein: energy-providing nutrient supplying up to 10% of the body's total energy requirements. It is made up of amino acid chains that provide the building blocks for tissue growth and *enzyme*, hormone and *haemoglobin* production, all of which are important for improvement in athletic performance. Typically, protein should comprise approximately 15% of the total calorie intake and good sources include red meats, fish, poultry, dairy products, beans and pulses. The benefits of protein supplementation remain unclear, as excess protein cannot be stored in the body. It is generally thought that sufficient protein can be gained from the athlete's diet. However, protein supplementation still occurs in activities such as weightlifting and bodybuilding.

Protestant work ethic: the belief of the Protestant religion associated with the Calvinists and Lutherans of the seventeenth century. The ethic emphasised that worldly work should be treated as a duty and as a means of earning salvation from God. Worldly success was seen as a sign that you were one of the 'chosen' to be saved, though reckless spending and enjoyment were not encouraged. Instead, a thrifty outlook towards life was valued. *Leisure* time and recreational activities therefore were given low status. This was to be a particular constraint for the *working class*, who had no private means for recreation and were subjected to the values of the moral *middle class*.

Protestants: see *Protestant work ethic*.

prowess: outstanding or superior skill.

proximal: a term of direction used to describe a structure or body part closer to the point of attachment of the trunk. For example, the proximal aspect of the femur would be the head of the femur which articulates about the hip. (See appendix, page 311.)

PRP: see *psychological refractory period*.

psychological refractory period (PRP) is the delay caused by an increase in information-processing time when the initial *stimulus* is closely followed by a second stimulus. This slows the *reaction time* of the performer, as the first piece of information needs to be cleared before the second can be processed (see *single-channel hypothesis*). This theory explains why 'dummy' or 'fake' moves can be successful. For example, a badminton player appears to be preparing to play a smash shot, but at the last moment executes a drop shot. The opponent prepares to receive the smash, but may not be able to alter their action to return the drop shot. The time delay is the psychological refractory period, as shown in the diagram below.

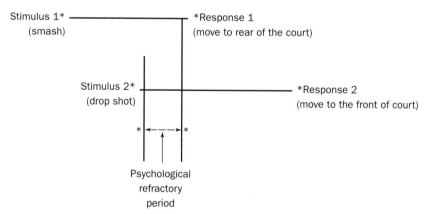

psychomotor ability: also known as perceptual motor ability, this is the capacity to process information, make decisions and execute a movement. *Reaction time*, limb *coordination*, dexterity, precision and aiming all depend on psychomotor abilities. They combine with *gross motor abilities* in varying degrees, depending on the nature of the task.

pub games: the pub was the focal point for the *working class* in the industrial towns. Pubs were often found on the corners of most streets and they were associated with sporting activities. Ex-boxers and professional footballers often became landlords and continued the old tradition of the *inns* by providing recreational activities, replacing *animal sports* and cockfighting with games such as billiards, darts and skittles. The pub was often used as a base for a football team who played in the rapidly expanding league system.

public provision: see *leisure provision*.

public schools: private, independent fee-paying schools. Public schools have a long tradition in Britain dating back to the original nine *barbarian* schools. The characteristics of these nineteenth century public schools include:
- being *elite* establishments for the *upper class*
- fee-paying
- owned by trustees
- spartan
- fagging system (prefects or sixth formers having control of younger boys, see *fag*)
- single-sex school
- non-local and rural
- boarding or residential.

The development of games occurred as the boys brought their local variations of activities, such as *mob* football (see *mob games*), to the school. These were played regularly in their free time, gradually developing unique school rules and an established competitive structure within a house system. Later, codified rules allowed inter-school fixtures to be played on a regular basis. The influence of public schools in spreading games in society was enormous because:
- old boys left schools and moved into positions of leadership
- universities codified rules
- employers spread games to workers
- officers spread games to troops throughout the Empire
- clergy spread games to parishes
- teachers spread games to schools
- diplomats spread games abroad.

In the *USA*, the term has a different meaning as it refers to schools within the maintained sector.

pugilism: the art, practice or profession of fighting with the fists. The term comes from the Latin word 'pugus' meaning 'bare fist' and is mainly used to refer to the time before *boxing* became an organised sport. Initially, *wrestling* was allowed before the *rules* were drawn up and more rigidly enforced. It was one of the first activities to have formal rules drawn up as early as 1743.

pulmonary artery: the *artery* that carries deoxygenated blood from the heart to the lungs, where the blood is subsequently oxygenated.

pulmonary circulation: the transport of blood between the heart and the lungs. The *pulmonary artery* carries blood from the right ventricle to the lungs, where it becomes oxygen-rich and unloads carbon dioxide. The pulmonary vein then transports the freshly oxygenated blood back to the heart and into the left *atrium*, from where it can be pumped around the body to the working muscles.

pulmonary diffusion: the exchange of gases between the lungs and the blood. (See also *gaseous exchange*.)

punishment: a form of *stimulus* that is used to weaken behaviour in order to reduce the likelihood of reoccurrence. For example, a player could be dropped from the team, penalised, booked, fined or substituted if they continually commit aggressive acts during a match. The continual use of punishment may cause emotional distress and resentment, so it may prove useful to use negative *reinforcement* as an alternative. It is important to understand the difference between punishment and negative reinforcement. The former is used to decrease the likelihood of the unwanted behaviour reoccurring, while the latter attempts to increase the chances of the desired action being repeated.

Puritans: the more extreme Protestants in the sixteenth and seventeenth centuries, who wished to purify the Church of England of most of its ceremony and other aspects which it associated with Catholicism. They were a growing body of influential townspeople with a strict, moral outlook to life, shunning the more pleasurable activities. Play was considered to be idleness and a sinful waste of time. By the early seventeenth century the argument between the pleasure-seeking cavaliers and the Puritans had escalated. It prompted King James I to write his *Book of Sports*.

purposeful leisure: a term used in *communist* governments which, as they operate an authoritarian system, require as much control over their population in *leisure* as in other areas of social life. This is *social control*, extolling the belief that rebellious tendencies can be curbed and political messages learned through the leisure situation. For example, activities that develop health and fitness were encouraged while those considered more anti-social, such as any that promoted *gambling*, were discouraged.

PWC$_{170}$ test: PWC stands for 'physical work capacity' and this sub-maximal test measures an individual's *aerobic capacity*. Subjects are required to perform three consecutive workloads on a cycle ergometer, while the heart rate is monitored. Initially, a workload is set that increases the subject's heart rate to between 100 and 115 beats per minute. The heart rate is measured each minute until the subject reaches *steady state*. The test is repeated for a second and third workload, which increases the heart rate to between 115 and 130, and 130 and 145 beats per minute respectively.

Each steady-state heart rate and respective workload are graphed and used to predict a workload that would elicit a heart rate response of 170 beats per minute. This can be predicted using the linear relationship between heart rate and exercise intensity. The score can then be compared to standard tables and a prediction made of *maximum oxygen uptake (VO$_2$ max)*.

pyruvic acid: the end product of *glycolysis*. The initial stages of energy production result in the breakdown of glucose to two molecules of pyruvic acid, which provides sufficient energy to resynthesise two moles of *ATP*. In the absence of oxygen, for example during very high intensity exercise such as a 400-metre run, pyruvic acid is converted into *lactic acid*. However, during *aerobic* activities such as jogging or cycling which are less intense, pyruvic acid is converted to *citric acid* from which a lot more energy can be produced via the *Krebs cycle* and *electron transfer chain* (36 moles of ATP).

qualitative: relating to the quality (rather than the quantity) of something. The **assessment** of sports like **gymnastics** is qualitative. This can involve opinions and judgements rather than relying on **quantitative** data. In other words, it is more **subjective** than **objective**. Many would argue that this makes it prone to more bias and is not an entirely just method of declaring a winner.

quantification: modern sports require finite measurements. Times and distances are recorded, and technology has enabled even finer measurements to be taken. The difference between **elite** performers in some events cannot be differentiated by the naked eye. These are **objective** forms of measurement and some believe sports measured in this way are considered true sports in comparison to those that require **subjective** opinions. The **USA** is a **culture** noted for its emphasis on quantification of all aspects of a sport.

quango: an acronym for 'quasi-autonomous national government organisation'. An example is **Sport England**. A large number of quangos exist outside government departments, with varying degrees of independence. They are not under the direct control of parliament but linked to the government in some way, either financial, or through policy accountability or statutory obligations. They share common characteristics, which include the tendencies:
- to be funded directly by the Treasury
- for the board in control to be elected by the appropriate government minister
- to perform promotional or developmental activities
- to have specialist expertise not found elsewhere in the government
- to remain slightly detached politically from sensitive issues such as racial and sexual equality, creating a 'buffer zone' for the government.

Quangos are often fragmented, lack coordination and contain increasing numbers of interested and sometimes competing parties.

quantitative: relating to the quantity (rather than the quality) of something, i.e. it is capable of being measured using numerical data. Many believe this is a fairer method of deciding sporting outcomes, as it is less prone to bias when compared with **qualitative** methods. Developments in technology have meant that an even finer measure of success can be achieved. For example, the time of a race can now be recorded accurately to one-hundredth of a second.

questionnaire: a series of questions whose purpose is to collect statistical information. Sports psychologists who wish to analyse **personality**, **attitude** and levels of **anxiety** often use them. Questionnaires are useful as athletes can complete them quickly in a variety of situations, questions can be specific to particular topics and responses can be confidential.

However, numerous problems, such as misinterpretation or lack of understanding of the questions, are inherent in this method of gathering information. Moreover, the respondents may not answer honestly, as they may wish to appear in a positive light or they may give the answers they think are required. Inappropriate questions could also be used, which may lead to biased results, and even the actual time of completion may influence the responses. Commonly used questionnaires include **Eysenck's personality inventory**, **Cattell's 16 personality factors questionnaire**, **sport competitive anxiety test** and **competitive state anxiety inventory (CSAI-2)** test.

quintain: a military activity where Roman soldiers would 'run at the quintain', which was usually a tree or post. They would be either on foot, horseback or in boats, and needed skill, accuracy of aim and a steady eye. It was an activity enjoyed by all **social classes** and continued into the seventeenth century, although by then it was used mainly ritualistically at festivals and wakes.

quoits: a game in which quoits – which are rings of iron, plastic or rope – are tossed at a stake in the ground in an attempt to encircle it. It has always been a popular rural and **pub game**.

Aiming for a grade A*?
Don't forget to log on to **www.philipallan.co.uk/a-zonline** for advice.

Q

race: a group of people sharing the same inherited physical characteristic. Various assumptions developed as a consequence of trying to divide population groups on this basis. Throughout history, theories of the physical and mental inferiority of some races have been used by others to justify their suppression. (See also *ethnic groups* and *racism*.)

racism: a set of ideas or beliefs based on the assumption that races have distinctive characteristics determined by hereditary factors, endowing some races with an intrinsic superiority. *Discrimination* often results and in sport this is evident in a variety of ways, for example in *stacking*, and in the difficulty players often have in reaching the administrative and managerial positions. Campaigns such as Let's Stamp Racism Out of Football, which began in 1993, have attempted to cut racial harassment out of football. It is supported by the Commission for Racial Equality (CRE) and Professional Footballers' Association (PFA).

rackets: a game similar to squash played in a large four-walled court by two or four players using rackets and a small hard ball. The game began in fairly humble circumstances in England and is mentioned in Charles Dickens's *The Pickwick Papers* as being played at Fleet Prison. Open courts existed in the backyards of taverns and *inns* and in many towns, while it was taken up by the *public schools* for its simple qualities and the possibilities of using architectural features within the school grounds. It was a game that suited the cult of *athleticism* containing *rules*, *etiquette* and *sportsmanship*.

radian: the unit of angular velocity. One radian is approximately equal to 57.3°. A knowledge of radians will enable a coach to calculate optimum rotational speed for a trampolinist, diver or gymnast when performing complex somersaults. One full rotation (360°) is equal to 2π radians.

radical ethic: one of the sport *ethics* in the *USA*, which expresses the view that the outcome of a sporting event or contest is important, but so too is the process. It is probably the closest to the British stance and is characterised by slogans such as Lifetime Sport, *Sport for All* and their *intra-mural sports*. The quest for *excellence* can be strived for and achieved, but it should not be at the expense of other values.

rags to riches: sport offers opportunities for individuals to experience upward *social mobility* through the accumulation of income or wealth through success in sport. As a consequence, an individual's social status is raised. This term has been synonymous with *professional sport* and the *working class* in particular. It requires an *open society* in which individuals can create their own success with little restrictions. Societies such as the *USA* embraced such opportunities from the nineteenth century, earlier than the UK, with its more closed *social class* system and dominant code of *amateurism*.

railways: the effect on sport of the development of the railways in the nineteenth century was immense as trains allowed:

- spectators and teams to travel to fixtures
- fixtures to became more regular and held further afield
- the rebirth of the *Olympic Games*
- ramblers, cyclists and mountaineers easier access to the countryside
- the sport of *angling* to develop, as a publication titled *The Rail and the Rod* revolutionised fishing, providing a guide to angling spots which could be reached within a 50 km radius of London
- factory owners to arrange special excursion trains for their employees to places like Blackpool.

RAS: see *reticular activating system*.

rational recreation: a term used to signify sporting activities that were characterised by:

- regular participation
- complex, written rules
- being highly structured in nature
- being spectator-based as well as participation-based
- the need to use refined skills rather than force
- being a middle- to upper-class development
- being regionally and nationally based
- the use of sophisticated equipment and facilities.

Rational recreation became prevalent following the *Industrial Revolution* when the middle classes wished to change the recreational habits of the *working class* from the more rowdy elements of *popular recreation*. They now required a more civilised population with orderly working habits and they wished to use sport to develop the moral qualities they admired. The movement was not only confined to sports: libraries, museums and parks also played their part.

rational sport: see *rational recreation*.

reaction force: a vertical force that occurs whenever two bodies are in contact with one another. Normal reaction acts perpendicular to the surfaces in contact. According to Newton's third law of motion, if weight is the only force acting on an object then the normal reaction force will be equal in magnitude but opposite in direction to the weight force:

FORMULA: Reaction force = weight force

Where the reaction force and weight force are equal, there will be no vertical movement of a performer or object up or down.

In many sporting activities, however, the reaction force may be greater than the weight force. This is because of the additional muscular force applied by a performer to a surface, so that:

FORMULA: Reaction force = weight force + internal muscular force

In this case, a performer will move vertically upwards, for instance when driving upwards to block in volleyball.

reaction time: the time between the onset of a *stimulus* and the initiation of that response. The speed at which the *information processing* system interprets the stimuli is a critical factor determining the chance of success. For example, when a water polo player thinks he or she has a goal scoring opportunity and decides to attempt a shot, the time taken to analyse the situation and start the shooting action is the reaction time. There are two forms of reaction time – *simple reaction time* or *choice reaction time* – and numerous factors affect the speed at which the process occurs, including age, *gender*, intensity of the stimulus, previous experience, *arousal* levels and the *stimulus–response compatibility*. The timing and number of stimuli can also affect the performance, causing a *psychological refractory period*. The time taken can be reduced through practice and *anticipation*. (See also *movement time* and *response time*.)

reactive strength: this is developed when an athlete performs a movement directly following an *eccentric muscle contraction*. For example, when a trampolinist drives from the trampoline bed directly after landing from a previous move.

real tennis: an ancient form of tennis, played in a four-walled indoor court with various openings, a sloping roofed corridor along three sides and a buttress on the fourth side. It is also called 'royal tennis', as the game was the sport of royalty and noblemen in France and England. The game originated in France and was made popular in England by the Tudors, but there were restrictive acts in the sixteenth century forbidding servants and labourers to play, enabling it to retain its privileged status. This game epitomised *rational recreation*.

recall schema: see *schema theory*.

receptors: see *sensory system*.

reciprocal inhibition: the process of one muscle contracting while its opposite relaxes. For example, the muscles in the upper arm work in an *antagonistic* manner to cause *flexion* and *extension* of the elbow. As the biceps brachii contract, the triceps brachii relax and they are in the process of reciprocal inhibition.

reciprocal teaching style: a teaching style in which a teacher sets a task that individuals have to complete in pairs, alternating roles as observer and performer. This allows them more responsibility, although the teacher retains overall control and monitors the progress, possibly offering assistance when appropriate. It helps to develop personal and social skills, evaluation and actual performance, as well as *self-confidence* and a greater understanding of the skill. For example, the teacher may give the group a *demonstration*, provide handouts to assist them and set the task of learning new dribbling techniques in pairs or small groups. However, it is difficult for the teacher to monitor all pairs or groups and fully assess their level of development and understanding. It can also be ineffective if the performers are unable to analyse and communicate, allowing poor and incorrect technique to develop. (See also *Mosston and Ashworth's spectrum of teaching styles*.)

recognition schema: see *schema theory*.

recombinant erythropoietin (Rh EPO) is a synthetic form of *erythropoietin* (EPO), which is a naturally occurring hormone in the body. Some athletes abuse this substance by injecting it into the body, aiming to boost *haemoglobin* content and therefore improve the oxygen carrying capacity of the blood. It has also been shown to improve the *maximum oxygen uptake (VO$_2$ max)* of a performer. The *International Olympic Committee* and all *governing bodies* outlaw this form of *blood doping*. Although it has proven benefits with respect to performance enhancement, there are some serious side effects. These include an increase in *blood viscosity* (thickness), an increased risk of blood clotting and heart failure. The use of Rh EPO also reduces the production of the body's natural erythropoietin which produces red blood cells.

recommended daily allowances (RDAs) are the levels of daily intake of essential nutrients considered to be necessary to meet the metabolic needs of individuals.

Recommended daily allowances

	Adults aged 19–50	Adults aged 50+	Boys aged 14–18	Girls aged 14–18
Calories	2000–2800	2200–2500	2200–2400	2000
Protein (g)	55	53	52	46
Fat (g) (25–35% of calories)	55–95	55–78	61–95	500–700
Saturated fat (g) (fewer than 10% of calories)	24–27	24–27	20	20
Cholesterol (mg)	Less than 300	Less than 300	Less than 300	Less than 300
Salt (g)	6	6	6	6
Sodium (mg)	1500–2300	1500–2300	1500–2300	1500–2300
Iron (mg)	14.8	9	11	15
Calcium (mg)	1300	1300	1300	1300
Fibre (g)	31–34	31–34	31–34	23
Vitamin A (μg)	600–700	600–700	600–700	600–700
Vitamin C (mg)	35–40	35–40	35–40	35–40
Folate (μg)	200	200	200	200

records: preserving knowledge or information about sporting facts or events. When information is collected methodically over a number of years, comparisons can be made and targets set to beat them: 'breaking a record' is the ultimate goal of many athletes. Common terms in sport are personal best, seasonal best and world record. The advancement in *technology* has enabled even more minute *quantitative* measurements.

recovery: the return of the body to its pre-exercise state. A key feature of the recovery process immediately following exercise is the Excess Post-exercise Oxygen Consumption (EPOC). This comprises two processes which use oxygen to aid recovery. The first is the fast component of EPOC, which resynthesises ATP and PC stores. The second phase is the slow component of EPOC, which helps to remove lactic acid. The recovery process also relates to the period between training sessions during which time adaptation can take place. Training can inflict some severe damage to the body: muscle tissue can tear, be poisoned by acidic substances such as *lactic acid* and have all its energy stores thoroughly depleted. During the recovery period, however, the muscle can take time to rebuild, oxygen delivery and toxin removal mechanisms improve and the energy stores fully replete themselves. However, in order not to suffer the same fate again through training, the body actually supercompensates and adapts to be able to cope with greater amounts of stress. If the body is stressed repeatedly through training and adequate recovery is not allowed, symptoms of **overtraining** can result and performance can actually deteriorate. It is essential that the coach and athlete build into the training programme sufficient recovery periods to enable adaptation to occur.

recreation: activities carried out during *leisure* time. Examples of activities would be reading, gardening, listening to music, *tourism* and participating in sporting activities. The word originates from the Latin word 'recreatio', which means 'to restore health'. Recreation has long been associated with *relaxation* and recuperation of the individual, particularly useful in restoring people's energies for work. Recreation can be viewed in different capacities:
- as an extension of the play experience
- as a personal experience, of value to the individual
- in terms of the nature of an activity, such as physical recreation or more sedentary activities such as reading
- as an institution having a structured framework
- as a process – part of personal development.

regatta: an organised series of races for *rowing* boats, yachts or other such craft. The earliest account of a regatta was on the River Thames in 1775 and later the famous Henley Regatta was established in 1839, purely as a means of boosting trade for the town. It soon became a traditional event, reflecting the Victorian love of combining sporting events with a grand social occasion and now has many prestigious school and club events, for example the Elizabeth Cup. The Henley Regatta reflected distinct social divisions between the classes, which are still maintained today.

reinforcement: the process used which increases the probability of behaviour reoccurring in the future. It is generally used in two forms:
- positive reinforcement, which involves the use of a *stimulus* to create feelings of satisfaction to encourage a repetition of the action, for example, praise from a coach or the feeling of completing a skill successfully
- negative reinforcement, which involves the withdrawal of an unpleasant stimulus when the desired response occurs, for example, the coach stops shouting at the team if their actions are correct.

In comparison, *punishment* is used to reduce the probability of the action being repeated.

relaxation: the reduction of muscle tension and levels of *stress* and *anxiety*. This can be achieved using either cognitive methods, which utilise thoughts to induce a calmer state, or somatic methods, which involve the control of muscle tension. Either can be used in training or competition, but care should be taken with some techniques if employed too close to an event as this may lead to under-arousal. (See also *stress management*.)

reliability: if the findings of a test can be repeated, it is said to be reliable. For example, when a performer completes a personality *questionnaire*, the data collected after analysis should reach the same conclusion on each occasion concerning their traits. Tests also require *validity* to be of true value.

religion: belief in a supernatural power considered to be divine or to have control over human destiny. Over the centuries, different religions have exerted considerable influence over the acceptance or non-acceptance of sporting activities. (See also *Church*, *evangelism*, *Methodists*, *Protestant work ethic*, *Puritans* and *sabbatarianism*.)

republic: a form of government in which the people or their elected representatives possess the supreme power. The head of state is an elected or nominated president, unlike a monarch who inherits the title. The *USA* is an example of a republic and there are many people in *Australia* who would like their country to become one.

residual volume: the volume of air that remains in the lungs following maximal *expiration*. Its approximate value is 1200 ml and changes are minimal during exercise. (See appendix, page 330.)

resistance arm: the distance between the fulcrum and the load in a *lever* system. The longer the resistance arm, the quicker the lever system can move. In sport, implements are often used such as rackets or bats to increase the length of the resistance arm, which will increase the outgoing *velocity* of an object such as a ball. However, the optimal length of an implement should be determined by the strength of the person handling it which is why, for example, junior tennis rackets have been designed to be shorter.

resistance training: a method of training that encompasses all types of exercising where resistance is applied to the body; for example, sand-dune running or running up hills (resistance of gravity), together with harness running or running in weighted belts. Perhaps the most common type of resistance training is weight training (see *strength training*).

respiratory exchange ratio (RER) also known as the respiratory quotient. It is a method of determining which energy-providing nutrient is predominantly in use during exercise, and therefore is a measure of how hard a performer is working. It is calculated by analysing oxygen consumption and carbon dioxide production, and is represented as follows:

$$FORMULA: \quad RER = \frac{\text{volume of } CO_2 \text{ expired per minute}}{\text{volume of } O_2 \text{ uptake per minute}}$$

The closer the value is to 1.0, the more likely the body is to be using *glycogen* as a fuel. The expected value for *fats* is 0.7, which indicates lower work rates. Intermediate figures suggest that a mixture of fuels is being utilised, which is the expected norm during endurance activities.

respiratory pump: a mechanism that aids in the return of blood to the heart via the veins. During exercise, breathing becomes deeper and causes pressure changes to occur in the thorax and the abdomen. Increases in pressure in the abdomen cause the large veins in that area to be compressed, which squeezes blood back to the heart rapidly. This, together with the *muscle pump*, forms part of the *venous return mechanism* and helps to increase and maintain adequate blood flow during exercise.

response programming stage: see *output*.

response selection stage: see *decision-making*.

response time: the time from the onset of the *stimulus* to the completion of the movement. The measurement includes the *reaction time* of the performer and the *movement time*. For example, when a water polo player attempts to score a goal, it would be the time taken to identify stimuli, assess the situation, make the decision and complete the shot. This can be expressed as:

FORMULA: Reaction time + movement time = response time

resultant force: see *net force*.

reticular activating system (RAS) is a cluster of brain cells located in the central part of the brain stem, which maintains levels of *arousal*. It acts as a filtering mechanism, either allowing information into the brain or inhibiting it. People who are *extroverts* tend to seek higher levels of arousal as their RAS lacks stimulation, while *introverts* already have a higher level of stimulation so they do not need as much excitement.

retro-active transfer: see *transfer of learning*.

reversibility: also known as detraining or regression, this is a principle of training that explains the deterioration in performance following the cessation of training or when a decrease in the intensity of training occurs. It appears that the physiological effects of training are lost once training ceases. The most noticeable deterioration occurs in *aerobic* efficiency, where a decrease in *maximum oxygen uptake (VO_2 max)* of up to 27% has been recorded. However, losses in muscle mass and therefore strength also occur, but at a much slower rate.

reward: any event that is pleasurable or satisfying to the individual receiving it. Rewards are often used as a form of *reinforcement* to shape behaviour and can be:
- tangible – e.g. cups, medals, certificates or money
- intangible – e.g. praise, personal bests, records or recognition.

Ringelmann effect: proposes that the performance of an individual may decrease as the group size increases. This is caused by a mixture of factors including low *motivation* and a lack of coordination within the group, leading to poor group *cohesion*. It could be categorised as a *faulty process*. For example, a footballer may perform better when playing five-a-side football than during a full game, because they feel lost within the team and their contribution in the latter may not be fully recognised, causing demotivation. (See also *social loafing*.)

risk is the possibility of incurring injury or loss or to expose oneself to *danger* or hazard. Outdoor and *adventurous activities* or outdoor pursuit activities pose situations of real and perceived risk.
- Real risk – risk from the *natural environment* such as a rockfall. Leaders need to be aware of the potential risks when planning routes, etc.
- Perceived risk – this is where the sense of adventure comes from and which leaders need to be aware of. However, if the perceived risk is too great for the ability level of the performer, feelings of *anxiety* could become too much.

There has been a considerable increase in traditional (e.g. canoeing, rock climbing) and 'new' (e.g. jet skiing, snow boarding) adventure sports. The reasons why people seem to be seeking greater risks can be explained by:
- increasingly sedentary lifestyles, which make some people seek a more active and exciting leisure time (the pursuit of vertigo)
- increased accessibility of these sports
- the development of new and exciting technology sports
- the appreciation of the natural environment, particularly as a release from urban pressures.

ritual: any established form of religious or other ceremonial type of behaviour, consisting of a series of actions performed in a prescribed order. Most sports and pastimes had such associations particularly because they occurred on **holy days** and pagan festivals such as **Shrove Tuesday** and **May Day**. Rituals can be a way of expressing social bonding and serve to affirm an individual's commitment to the group. For example, the Haka is performed by the **New Zealand** rugby team at all international fixtures and originated as a Maori war chant (see **Maori culture**).

role (social): the part played by a person in a particular social setting, influenced by the **expectation** of what is appropriate. Individuals may play various roles in their lives through their professional, family and other social relationships. Individuals learn their roles through **socialisation** and children often use their **play** activities to act out adult roles.

role (of the teacher/coach): the role of a physical education teacher is very different to that of a sports coach, even though they are both involved in teaching sporting activities. However, when a physical education teacher is involved with **extra-curricular sport** they are more likely to adopt the role of a sports coach. Below are the main differences between the two approaches.

Role of a physical education teacher	Role of a sports coach
Administration: comes under **Department for Children, Schools and Families**	Administration: comes government Department for Culture, Media and Sport
Compulsory: this is a **National Curriculum** subject	Voluntary: children have chosen to participate
Range of activities: the National Curriculum requires a variety of activities to be taught	Specialism: the sport coach tends to have specialised in their activity and may be to a higher standard
Ability level: mixed ability classes are the **norm** for physical education lessons	Ability level: performers will normally be taught according to their ability
Children's needs: physical, psychological and emotional needs are developed and nurtured and take precedence over performance levels	Performance: the coach is often measured by the progress of their performers and therefore there is a concentration on results
Values: values such as teamwork, **sportsmanship** and cooperation are encouraged	Values: values such as commitment, dedication to training and **competitiveness** are encouraged

role model: an individual whom a person admires in terms of skill, values or attitude. They are often termed **significant others** and can include parents, teachers, coaches, friends or heroes who can have considerable influence during the **socialisation** and learning processes. For example, a young sportsperson may look up to and wish to imitate a player from their favourite or national team.

Romantic movement: the late eighteenth-century movement in literature and the arts which laid an emphasis on subjectivity and the individual. The work of the Romantic poets such as Wordsworth and Coleridge focused on the beauty of the Lake District and so had a considerable influence on **recreation** in the countryside; their poems made the countryside attractive to town and city folk. Initially, the **middle class** began to use the countryside for activities such as rambling and cycling, and gradually the **working class** followed as their leisure time and affluence increased. These activities encouraged an appreciation of topography and local knowledge, and an *aesthetic* appreciation of natural beauty.

Rorschach inkblot test: a form of *personality test* consisting of ten bilaterally symmetrical inkblots. The individual describes what they observe in each and their responses are analysed to form personality characteristics.

rotation: a *movement pattern* that occurs in the horizontal or *transverse plane* about a longitudinal axis. Rotation of a joint occurs where the bone turns about its long axis within the joint and can produce *medial* movement (towards the centre of the body) or *lateral* movement (towards the outside of the body). When performing the butterfly stroke in swimming, for example, the humerus must rotate medially as the hands enter the water. In preparation of a forehand stroke in tennis, the humerus rotates laterally at the shoulder joint. (See appendix, pages 324–25.)

rotator: a muscle that causes *rotation*. For example, at the hip the gluteus medius and minimus rotate the hip medially, while the sartorius rotates the hip laterally. (See also *lateral* and *medial*.)

rotator cuff muscles: a group of four *rotator* muscles that allow movement of the shoulder. The rotator cuff group include the infraspinatus (*lateral rotation*), teres (minor lateral rotation), supraspinatus (*abduction*) and subscapularis (*medial* rotation).

rowing: the art of propelling a boat is practised as a sport in most countries. It began as a utilitarian activity when it provided power for war ships and transport in industrial towns. The River Thames provided one of the main highways in the *medieval era* in England; wealthy people had their own state barges and professional watermen plied for trade. By the eighteenth century there were over 40,000 watermen with frequent contests and wagering on the outcome was common. The standard of rowing increased in the nineteenth century as professionalism increased and rowing races attracted an enormous following and were widely reported in the press. Many rowers became coaches of amateur crews, but due to the powerful rise in *amateurism* and the power held by the middle-class administrators, professionalism soon died out.

The Amateur Rowing Association (ARA) was formed in 1882 but its strict *social class discrimination* meant the National Amateur Rowing Association (NARA) in 1890 soon followed, which based its amateur–professional rules strictly on monetary values rather than social class. (See also *manual labour clause*.)

rugby league: one of the two major codes of *rugby union football*. The league code is prominent in the UK and *Australia*, where the sport is played professionally. Rugby league takes its name from what was initially a breakaway faction of the English Rugby Football Union (RFU), known as the Northern Rugby Football Union when established in 1895, and since that time rugby league and rugby union have been very different sports.

Super League is a full-time professional rugby league club competition operating in the northern hemisphere. Super League (Europe) (SLE) began in March 1996 and saw the English season switch from winter to summer for the first time in over 100 years.

Rugby School: one of the nine *barbarian schools* in the nineteenth century. Under the headship of *Thomas Arnold*, the development of team games took place. It is the place that reputedly developed the game of *rugby union football* and became famous in Thomas Hughes's book *Tom Brown's Schooldays*.

rugby union football: a form of football played with an oval ball in which the handling and carrying of the ball is permitted. It is purported to have originated at *Rugby School* in the nineteenth century having developed from the *mob game*. William Webb Ellis is said to have picked up the ball and run with it and the game was accepted as it conformed to the cult of *athleticism* and *muscular Christianity*. The adoption of the game by the northern *working class* led to a struggle for the possession of the game. The Rugby Football Union (RFU) was founded in 1871 and became the custodian of the amateur game. However, *broken-time payments* and shamateurism (see *amateurism*) were to cause conflict within the *administration*, so in 1894–5 the northern clubs broke away and the Rugby Football League was formed, allowing professionalism to develop. In the twentieth century the distinction between amateurism and professionalism became increasingly blurred, and in 1996 all restrictions to payment were eliminated, allowing the game to become fully professional.

rules: a set of regulations or principles that govern behaviour. Rules for sporting activities used to be local in nature before they became codified, mostly in the nineteenth century, allowing fixtures to be played further afield. Nowadays, *international sport federations* decide on the rules for a sport and disciplinary action follows a breach of the rules decided by an official authorised to referee, umpire or judge the activity.

ruling class: the dominant group in society that controls the rest of society, either directly or indirectly. (See also *dominant culture*.)

rural sports: activities that originated in the countryside where the main economic activity was agriculture. They existed mainly before the *Industrial Revolution*, although rural activities did survive afterwards in many areas, probably because of their isolation and lack of the outside influences such as rapidly changing lifestyles in towns. The seasons were important, as were the festivals and fairs for shooting and all kinds of animal hunting. Rivers provided recreation such as fishing and skating in the winter months. The occasional *mob game* reflected the harsh lifestyle of the agricultural worker. (See also *blood sports*, *coursing*, *field sports* and *fox hunting*.)

S–R bond: see *stimulus–response bond*.

S–R theories of learning: see *associationist theories of learning*.

sabbatarianism: a religious sect whose members strictly observe Sunday as the sabbath. Sabbatarianism had the effect of restricting the *leisure* activities of the *working class* in the nineteenth century.

sacral vertebrae: a region of the vertebral column consisting of five bones fused together to form the sacrum. It is the sacrum which fuses to the pelvis to bear and distribute the weight of the upper body. (See appendix, page 316.)

saddle joint: see *synovial joint*.

saggital plane: also known as the median plane, this is an imaginary line that runs longitudinally through the body and limbs, dividing them into left and right halves. Movements such as *flexion* and *extension*, which occur at *synovial joints*, take place in this plane about the transverse axis. A knowledge of the planes of movement and *rotation* about axes is essential for the performer to know where their body is in relation to their environment. (See appendix, page 314.)

Samaranch, Juan Antonio: president of the International Olympic Committee between 1980 and 2001. Some of his achievements included:
- loosening of the eligibility code, rule 26, of the Olympic Charter – professionals were now admitted. One effect of this was to outweigh the unbalanced nature of the superiority of the state-sponsored amateurs (stamateurs). However, it also created the travesty of the stars of the National Basketball Association of the USA competing against Angola, Lithuania and Croatia in Barcelona 1992
- increasing the commercialisation and marketing of the *Olympic Games* so they could continue on a more secure financial basis
- broadening International Olympic Committee membership to include athletes, more members of the international federations and national Olympic committees, and women
- stabilising East–West, communist–capitalist relations in the run-up to the Seoul Games in 1988
- acceptance in 1992 of a team from the newly independent states from Russia
- drug programme improvements
- acceptance of South Africa back into the Olympic movement
- personal knowledge of most of the 172 national Olympic committees
- creation of an Olympic museum in Lausanne.

Samoa: a group of islands in the south Pacific, north-east of Fiji. It was an independent kingdom until the mid-nineteenth century when it was divided administratively into American Samoa (east) and German Samoa (west). The latter was mandated to **New Zealand** in 1919 and then gained full independence in 1962 as Western Samoa. Before the Samoan culture was exposed to outside influences, the economy depended on agriculture, each individual was only as important as the household group and most activities were cooperative until it came to contests between rival districts. Prizes were not given though success was highly valued. Games involving teamwork did not appear in Samoan life until contact with Britain, America, Germany and New Zealand. Cricket was adopted readily as it appeared to reflect their own values – there could be hundreds on each side and a game could last for ten to twelve days in order to let everyone have a bat. Rugby and baseball were also initially modified to make them more compatible to the Samoan way of life. (See also **primitive cultures**.)

SAQ (speed, agility and quickness): a type of training designed to improve the **speed**, **agility** and quickness of a performer. It involves a range of training activities including ladder drills, **resistance** drills and **plyometric** drills. Speed, agility and quickness have been singled out as three of the most important components of fitness required for a whole range of sporting activities, but especially for games players. These drills should therefore form a central role in the fitness training for such athletes.

sarcomere: the contractile unit of **skeletal muscle**, consisting of two proteins: **actin** and **myosin**. It is the interaction between these two proteins that cause the muscle to shorten (see **sliding filament theory**). When viewed under a microscope, the striped appearance of skeletal muscle is a result of the overlapping of actin and myosin.

During contraction, shortening of the sarcomere generates great forces, for example, the shortening of the triceps brachii can generate sufficient force to push the body up when performing a press-up.

A band   I band

Z line = boundary of each sarcomere
I band = actin only
A band = actin and myosin
H zone = myosin only

Z line   H zone   Z line

Sarcomere

S

sarcoplasm: the cytoplasm of a muscle cell. The sarcoplasm is a watery solution that contains **ATP** and other phophagens as well as the **enzymes** used in metabolic reactions and ATP resynthesis. The **alatic energy system** and **lactic acid energy system** take place in the sarcoplasm of the muscle cell.

saturated fat is **fat** found in meats and dairy products such as butter and cheese. Excessive consumption of saturated fat can raise cholesterol levels and increase the risk of obesity and heart disease.

Saturday half day was established in the nineteenth century. This was a dramatic change for the industrial **working class** as they now had increased **leisure** time and improved income, which led the way to the development of **association football** as a major **spectator sport**.

The Birmingham chocolate firm Cadbury was the first company to implement this for their workers.

SCAT: see *sport competition anxiety test*.

schema theory states that we store a generalised series of *movement patterns* that are modified to adapt to the current environment and situation. Therefore, when learning new skills or playing in a game, the performer will recall and alter stored motor programmes, such as jumping, catching, throwing, running and balancing to complete the task successfully. For example, a performer may modify the jumping schema to execute a high jump, gymnastic vault, basketball jump shot or volleyball block. The theory helps solve the problem of memory storage faced by the *closed loop theory*. The schema are initiated, evaluated and updated by two processes:

1 Recall schema – start the movement based on two sources of information:
   - Initial conditions or positional information, e.g. when completing a basketball shot, the position on court, the weight of the ball, location of defenders and the position of the player's own limbs are taken into account.
   - Response specifications or information about the task to be executed. The basketball player formulates a motor programme deciding on the speed, power and direction of the shot as well as the specific technique that needs to be used.

2 Recognition schema – control and evaluate the movement through:
   - Response outcome or the end result compared with the intended aim. Knowledge of where the ball hit the backboard or the ring and whether it successful is stored. This is vital for the development of strong schema.
   - Sensory consequences or the feeling during and after the movement. The player evaluates the feeling of the shot and the flight of the ball, and updates the memory stores for future performances.

In order to develop strong schema, practice must be varied to form a wide range of *parameters*. These need to be relevant to the game, challenging and progressive, with feedback provided to update the programmes for future reference.

scholarship: a grant awarded to a student to gain financial aid. This is important for American college students and ranges from partial grants to full scholarships. There is a question over the equality with which they are granted; for example, do women and African Americans receive their fair share?

school club links: the overall aim of school club links is to increase the proportion of children guided into clubs from the *School Sport Coordinator programme*. Primarily, seven major sports will be focused on (tennis, cricket, rugby union football, football, athletics, gymnastics and swimming). The reasons for their selection include:
- the capacity of the national *governing body*
- they are central to the *National Curriculum*
- their ability to help lead other sports
- they are popular with both sexes
- they involve multi-skills
- they are a mix of individual and team sports
- focus of government initiatives and investment.

(See also *Physical Education, School Sport and Club Links (PESSCL) strategy*.)

school sport coordinator programme: a partnership based around families of schools with a team made up of a partnership development manager (PDM), school sports coordinator and primary link teacher. Their role is to enhance opportunities for young people to experience different sports, access high-quality **coaching** and engage in competition. They are released two days a week. The partnership development manager (PDM) is usually located within a sports college and manages the development of the partnership and the links with other physical education and sport organisations. The overall aim of the partnership is to ensure children spend a minimum of 2 hours a week on high quality physical education and school sport.

secondary socialisation: see *socialisation*.

secularism: usually defined as the process in which religious thinking, practices and organisations lose their social significance. Weber argued that the development of scientific knowledge and rational thought would replace beliefs based on magic, superstition and the supernatural. On the other hand, Parsons claimed that religious institutions were becoming more highly specialised and were developing in different ways. Sport has been viewed as the 'new religion' evidenced by the **rituals** associated with sport events, the reverential treatment of sport stars, the use of symbols, etc. However, the ancient Olympics used to worship the God Zeus whereas the modern **Olympic Games** does not have this type of association.

segregation: to set or be set apart from the main group. Segregation can occur on the basis of **gender**, religious or racial groups, disability or because of **social class**. Competitive sport has commonly been separated into male and female divisions. Segregation in this case is not illegal as it is exempt from the **Sex Discrimination Act** under section 44. Segregation is not necessarily divisive and can enable individuals to realise their potential under more appropriate conditions. (See also **integration**.)

selective attention: a process that filters irrelevant information gathered by the **sensory system** and prioritises the **stimuli** that can affect that particular situation. For example, a badminton player will ignore the crowd, **advertising** boards and players on an adjacent court, and instead focus on their own and the opponent's position on court, actions that may indicate particular shots to be played, as well as the power and direction of the shuttlecock. This allows only the relevant information to pass into the **memory** system, allowing the execution of the shot to be faster.

The selective attention of a performer can be developed in a variety of ways, for instance, changing the intensity of the stimulus, increasing **motivation** levels and reaching optimal levels of **arousal** as well as directing **attention** to specific **cues**.

self-confidence: the positive attitude of an individual towards their ability to complete tasks. Performers with high levels of self-confidence tend to have higher levels of **motivation**. For example, an individual who is good at games generally will have the confidence in their ability when introduced to a new sport. However, this is not always the case, as self-confidence can be specific to certain situations (see **self-efficacy**).

self-directed relaxation: a *relaxation* technique in which the performer concentrates on specific muscle groups in order to relax each one in turn. Mastery of the technique takes time but, when developed, it enables the performer to relax particular areas of the body during competition as they see fit. For example, if an athlete sensed their upper body was developing tension hindering their performance, they could attempt to concentrate on that area. (See also **autogenic training** and **progressive relaxation technique**.)

self-efficacy: the degree of *self-confidence* experienced by the performer when placed in a specific situation. Those performers with high levels of self-efficacy in a particular activity will tend to choose to participate and display good levels of *motivation* and perseverance when compared with someone who has low self-efficacy and *expectations*. For example, a young basketball player may be happy to practise their shooting at home on their own, but may not be as confident of their skills when playing in a team situation.

Four factors influence an individual's level of self-efficacy:

- performance accomplishments – performers who have experienced success and enjoyment are more likely to develop high levels of confidence; for example, if the young basketballer scores several baskets during the game, they will have the confidence to continue to shoot
- vicarious experiences – performers who have watched others achieving the task will feel they are able to do so as well, especially if the model is of similar ability
- verbal persuasion – performers who receive encouragement about their *abilities* and actions, especially from significant others, will feel more confident about their actions or attempts
- emotional *arousal* – performers who are encouraged to perceive their physiological and psychological arousal before participation in a positive manner are more likely to develop high self-efficacy. For example, increased heart rate, respiratory rate and *cognitive anxiety* should be viewed positively in terms of being ready to compete, rather than as indicating being ill-prepared.

Therefore, in order to develop positive expectations, performers should experience early success, observe competent others of similar ability, set realistic goals, be verbally encouraged while developing effective *stress management* and *relaxation* techniques.

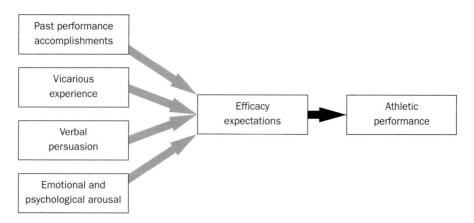

self-esteem: the value we place on ourselves as individuals based on an evaluation of our own *abilities* and performance when compared with others. This can contribute to our levels of *self-confidence* and *self-efficacy*, for example, a club-standard gymnast may feel they are competent compared with other pupils in a class at school and possess a high self-esteem both as a gymnast and sports performer. It is important that individuals are given positive encouragement to develop high levels of self-esteem, as this can affect their *attitude*, *motivation* and participation in numerous activities. (See also *esteem*.)

self-paced skills involve the performer initiating their actions based on their knowledge of the environmental conditions. They have control over when the movement has to be executed and control the rate at which the skill is performed. These types of skill are placed on the same **continuum** as **externally paced skills** and are often examples of **closed skills**. Examples include athletic throwing and jumping events, gymnastic moves and the serve during racket games.

self-serving bias: the tendency of performers to attribute their success to internal factors, such as effort and ability, and their failure to external influences, such as bad luck and task difficulty. This allows the individual to protect their **self-esteem** and maintain levels of **motivation** for future performances. However, if they can attribute failure to internal factors, taking responsibility for their actions, they may be more motivated to correct faults in the future. (See also **attribution theory**.)

self-talk involves the individual developing positive thoughts about their actions and performances. The aim is to eradicate any negative thoughts as they can be demotivating and increase **anxiety**. For example, a swimmer at the start of a race may alter thoughts such as 'Am I ready for this?' to 'My training has gone well and I'm prepared.' Similarly, a basketball team that are losing by four points near the end of a match may be told by their coach during a time-out 'We've got plenty of time left' rather than 'We've only got 2 minutes left to win the game.' This technique can be combined with **thought stopping**.

semantic differential scales: a **questionnaire** used to evaluate the **attitude** of an individual. The individual has to indicate their opinion, usually on a seven-point scale, with opposite words at either end of the scale. For example, to answer the question 'Do you feel exercise aids a healthy lifestyle?', the scale may range from 'beneficial' to 'harmful'. (See also **attitude tests**.)

semi-leisure: a concept developed by Dumazadier to refer to activities which are performed outside work but which may have a sense of obligation and compulsion attached to them. An example may be 'do-it-yourself' activities or playing for a club within a league structure each week. (See also **leisure**.)

sensory system: gathers information from the environment using various receptors, including sight, sound, touch and smell. This allows the performer to begin the **information processing** mechanism. There are three forms of receptors:

- proprioceptors – located on the nerves, muscle, **tendons**, joints and inner ear, which provide intrinsic information about the movement and **balance** of the body during the performance (see **sensory system**). This is commonly known as **kinaethesis**, allowing the performer to 'feel' the action; for example, the grip on a golf club, the force of a pass or the location of the body during a somersault
- **exteroceptors** – gather information from outside the body via the eyes, ears, nose and mouth. The most useful of these for a sportsperson are vision and audition, with the former being generally regarded as the most important form of receptor
- **introceptors** – pass information from within the body's internal organs such as the heart and lungs to the brain via the nervous system. This helps to regulate the various functions of the body and cater for the changing demands placed on it.

The information collected by the different receptors is analysed by the process of **perception** which is then passed on to the **decision-making** phase of the mechanism.

serial skills are composed of a number of **subroutines** that need to be completed in the correct sequence. These skills may have discrete elements that may be isolated in practice conditions. This type of skill is placed on the same **continuum** as **discrete skills**. Examples include athletic jumping actions, such as the high jump or triple jump, gymnastic routines, diving sequences and the basketball lay-up shot.

sesamoid bones: small bones situated within **tendons**, the function of which is to help in the smooth operation of two articulating bones. The largest sesamoid bone, the patella, enables a smooth action between the tibia and femur, prevents hyperextension occurring and protects the intricate network of ligaments behind it. Another exists in the knuckle of the thumb between the metacarpal and phalanx. Sesamoid literally means 'shaped like a sesame seed' as these bones are oval in shape.

Sex Discrimination Act: this Act of 1975 made sex **discrimination** unlawful in employment, training, education and the provision of goods, facilities and services. It stated that a female should be treated in the same way as a male in similar circumstances. However:
- competitive sport is excluded under section 44 of the Act. Separate competitions are allowed for men and women 'where the physical strength, stamina or physique puts a woman at a disadvantage to the average man'. Problems have occurred where female referees and physical education teachers have been denied promotion on the grounds of being a woman, and some successful appeals have been made
- private sports clubs can legally operate discriminatory policies under sections 19 and 34.

sexism: the belief that one sex is inferior to the other, and is most often directed towards women. It is sometimes based on the idea that women are not best suited to roles that carry prestige and influence. Traditionally, women have been denied the same legal, political, economic and social rights enjoyed by men. If sexism occurs, it can often be challenged by the **Sex Discrimination Act**. It is the more covert actions that occur due to sex stereotyping which are difficult to combat. For example, few women are in positions of power within the professional football structure.

shamateur: see **amateurism**.

Sharpey's fibres: a tough connective tissue that anchors the **tendon** or **ligament** to the **periosteum** of the bone. They are therefore central to the interaction of the skeleton and the muscular system in causing movement. In cases of severe stress being placed on these fibres, which is frequently experienced when the bones are still growing in length, damage can occur causing some discomfort when exercising. This is a medical condition known as Osgood Schlatter's disease.

shinty: a simple form of **hockey** originating in Scotland, played for centuries as part of the clan festivities. Rules were written down and an official association was formed in 1893 but it was not widely adopted in England because it was seen as a lower class activity, being violent and masculine, and was confined to a small geographical area. Hockey as a stick and ball game had already been started elsewhere.

shop window: the use by countries and governments of sport to portray a favourable image of its policies and politics. Success in sport can be seen to represent a successful and powerful country. The reality behind the show is often very different. The old societies of the Soviet Union and East Germany, and to some extent the modern society of China, can be seen as doing something similar.

short bones: bones found in the body, specifically designed for weight bearing, being compact in nature and often of equal width and length. The carpals of the wrist and tarsals of the ankle are examples of short bones and demonstrate great weight-bearing capacities when performing a handstand or withstanding the stresses of running and jumping.

short-term memory store: also known as working memory, this is a component of the *memory* process, which has a limited storage capacity for information gathered by the performer. The store of between five and nine pieces of information, which have been transferred through the *short-term sensory store* and reduced via *selective attention*, can be retained for up to approximately 30 seconds before being either forgotten or passed on to the *long-term memory store*. Due to this limited capacity, performers often use the technique of *chunking*. For example, a rugby player may use a set call or number to remember a pattern of moves, rather than each section individually. This allows other relevant information to enter the system, such as the changing positions and actions of the opposition.

short-term sensory store: a component of the *memory* process, with a huge capacity to receive information but which can only be retained for up to 1 second before it is lost. Information must be gathered constantly and updated via the *sensory system* and any *stimuli* that are relevant are passed on to the *short-term memory store* by the process of *selective attention*. For example, a rugby player will receive information concerning everything around them in the *display (psychology)*, including the position of players, the crowd, the referee, all sounds and weather conditions, but they will only process those stimuli that affect their performance at that particular moment.

Shrove Tuesday: the Tuesday before Ash Wednesday, therefore the last day of Shrovetide. Preparations were made for Lent and this was a time for feasting and fun. Recreations took place within a wide social pattern and activities included *mob* football (see *mob games*), wrestling, animal *baiting*, skittles and *bowls*.

shunting: also known as accommodation, this is the redistribution of blood that occurs in the body when exercising. The distribution of blood around the body changes significantly during exercise. At rest, only 15–20% of blood flow is directed towards *skeletal muscle*, the majority going to the liver and kidneys; however, during maximal exercise, blood is redirected to areas where it is required most. For example, a cyclist working maximally may have up to 80% of *cardiac output* directed to muscles of the legs ensuring that these working muscles gain sufficient oxygen and other nutrients. This increased blood flow to the muscle results from a restriction of blood flow to the kidneys, liver and stomach. Vasodilation and vasoconstruction of blood vessels facilitate the process of shunting.

significant other: someone who is held in high esteem by the individual. Such people can influence the actions of the performer either positively or negatively (see *social facilitation*) and they can considerably affect the *socialisation* process. Significant others may include family, members of one's peer group, teachers, coaches and *role models*.

simple reaction time: the *reaction time* taken to respond when presented with one *stimulus* and one possible response. For example, it is the time taken for a sprinter to start moving off the starting blocks when the gun has been fired. (See also *choice reaction time*.)

simple skills: actions that have basic *movement patterns* or those with little *decision-making* requirements and can be performed with minimum conscious control. Examples are running, swimming and cycling or more difficult skills that are well learned, such as passing and receiving a ball. They are easy to perform successfully in comparison to **complex skills**.

single-channel hypothesis: a theory which states that when processing *stimuli* from the *environment*, the brain can only deal with one piece of information at a time. Therefore, during a game a performer must clear the first stimulus received before reacting to the second and clear the 'bottleneck' that has been formed. For example, a defending basketball player may initially think that the attacker is going to pass the ball and so moves to intercept, but at the last moment the offensive player keeps the ball and plays it in another direction. The defender cannot clear the first information quickly enough to react to the actual movement of the ball. This creates the *psychological refractory period*.

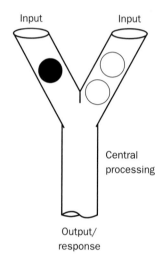

sinoatrial node (SA node) is a cluster of excitable cells within the heart which form the pacemaker. It is the sinoatrial node that generates the heart rate by emitting impulses, which are then conducted throughout the heart enabling blood to be pumped out and around the body. *Adrenaline* and *noradrenaline* are released prior to and during exercise by the *sympathetic nervous system*, causing an increase in the rate at which these impulses are emitted from the sinoatrial node and therefore an increase in heart rate. This ensures that adequate amounts of oxygenated blood can be transported to the working muscles and blood high in carbon dioxide can be transported to and expelled via the lungs, to ensure optimum performance during exercise. (See the diagram under *atrioventricular node*, page 28). The cardiac control centre situated in the medulla oblongata governs the actions of the sinoatrial node.

sit-and-reach test: a fitness test used to assess the *flexibility* of the hamstrings and lower back. The test can be easily administered and requires a sit-and-reach box. The subject sits on the floor with legs out straight, feet flat against the box and without bending the knees the subject reaches forward with arms outstretched and moves the cursor as far down the box as possible, holding the position for 2 seconds. The score is recorded and compared with standard tables.

skeletal muscle: a muscle of the body attached to a bone by a *tendon* and used primarily for movement. Skeletal muscle has several different properties which enable us to move and maintain posture:

- extensibility – the ability to lengthen, often while contracting
- *elasticity* – the ability to return to its normal resting length following lengthening
- *contractility* – the ability of the muscle to shorten when contracting.

Skeletal muscle is voluntary and is therefore under our own control and this has important implications in the sporting arena as it is the individual who decides when each of their muscles contract. (See appendix, pages 318–25.)

skeletal system: the bones and *ligaments* that form the skeleton. The term covers all aspects of the skeleton including structure of bone tissue, types of bones, types of joint, as well as the *movement patterns* which can occur at these joints. It is therefore central to our study of movement. Major functions of the skeleton include:

- protection of vital organs
- production of red blood cells
- storage of minerals
- movement.

(See appendix, pages 315–17.)

skill: the learned ability to bring about pre-determined results with maximum certainty, often with the minimum outlay of time, energy or both. Performers who are said to be skilled often display similar characteristics including consistency, efficiency, coordination, fluency, while completing a recognised technique allowing them to successfully achieve an end goal. Highly skilled performers are said to have reached the *autonomous phase of learning*. There are several types of skill, including:

- *cognitive skills* – those involving mental processes; for example, problem solving, planning tactics and strategies to outwit an opponent during a game of hockey
- *perceptual skills* – those involving the interpretation of information entering the body via the sensory system; for example, the position of players during the game and the possible options available to the performer
- *motor skills* – those involving the physical execution of the movement; for example, the passing of the ball or taking a shot at goal.

Skills are often classified using a *continuum*, with the most common being:

- *open skills – closed skills*
- *self-paced skills – externally paced skills*
- *gross skills – fine skills*
- *discrete skills – serial skills – continuous skills*.

skill-related fitness: those elements of fitness that involve the neuromuscular system and determine how successfully a performer can complete a specific task. The difference between the skill-related components (which include *agility*, *balance*, *coordination*, *reaction time* and *power*) and health-related components (such as *strength*, *speed*, endurance, *flexibility* and *body composition*) can best be explained using the example of a tennis player. The performer may have the necessary physical attributes such as speed, stamina and strength to play a match, but if they possess poor agility and coordination they will not be able to perform to a high level.

S

slice: a form of side spin applied to a projectile such as a golf ball, which causes a deviation of the ball to the right of its expected flight path as a result of the *Magnus effect*. The boundary layer on the left hand surface of the ball travels in the opposite direction to the air flow. This slows the flow of air on the left-hand surface, creating a zone of high pressure. The boundary layer on the right-hand surface travels in the same direction as the oncoming air flow, causing the air to travel more quickly than that on the right-hand surface and creating a zone of low pressure. The pressure differential (high pressure on the left-hand side of the ball, low pressure on the right-hand side of the ball) results in the ball moving towards the low pressure zone, causing it to swerve and deviate to the right of its expected flight path when struck without spin.

sliding filament theory: the sequence of events leading up to *skeletal muscle* contraction. It is a microscopic process explaining how muscles contract. When viewed under a microscope, the process of muscle contraction can be explained by the complex cooperation of two proteins: a thick filament called *myosin* and a thinner filament known as *actin*. The diagram opposite shows the structure of a muscle fibre when viewed under a microscope. During muscle contraction, the thin actin filaments slide inwards over the myosin filaments causing a shortening of each *sarcomere* along the entire length of the *myofibril*. This causes shortening of each muscle fibre and therefore the characteristic shortening of the entire muscle during muscle contraction.

The sequence of events of the sliding filament theory is described below. It is important to note that at rest the protein tropomyosin on the thin filament block access to the myosin-binding site.

- *Step 1 Preparing the binding site.* On receiving an *action potential* (the signal to contract), the sarcoplasmic reticulum (a specialist layer of cells that surround each myofibril) releases calcium ions (Ca^{2+}). The influx of calcium binds to a second protein on the actin filament called troponin, which pulls tropomyosin out of the way exposing the myosin binding sites on the actin filament.
- *Step 2 The power stroke.* The myosin filament extends a golf-club shaped 'cross-bridge', which attaches to the binding site of the thin actin filament. When it binds, the myosin head is in an energised state and pulls on the actin filament, pulling it inwards towards the centre of the sarcomere.
- *Step 3 The binding of ATP.* In order to re-energise the myosin head, ATP is required. Therefore, to expose the ATP-binding site the myosin filament uncouples from the actin filament, allowing ATP to bind on to it and causing the myosin head to return to its high-energy state.
- *Step 4 The ratchet mechanism.* Assuming sufficient calcium is available, step 2 can now be repeated. In fact, the power stroke pulling actin filaments past the myosin filaments will continue in a ratchet-like manner (which involves the sequential coupling and uncoupling of myosin and actin) until each sarcomere shortens and the H Zone disappears.
- *Step 5 The return of calcium ions back into the sarcoplasmic reticulum.* Once the action potential has diminished, all the calcium ions responsible for revealing the myosin-binding site on the actin filament will be returned into the sarcoplasmic reticulum. The shape of troponin will once again be changed, allowing tropomyosin to return to its protective position of covering the myosin cross bridge binding site. Tropomyosin will remain in this position as long as the muscle is relaxed.

Z Line = Marks the boundary of
one sarcomere
I Band = Actin only
A Band = Actin and myosin
H Zone = Mysosin only

Sliding filament theory

slow twitch muscle fibre are also known as type 1 muscle fibres. They are designed for endurance and are able to produce a large amount of energy using oxygen. They enable us to perform exercise over a long period of time and consequently there is likely to be a high percentage of slow twitch fibres in the legs of marathon runners and cyclists. Physiological characteristics include:

- high *aerobic capacity*
- high *capillary* density
- high *myoglobin* content
- high *mitochondria* density
- high resistance to fatigue
- low force of contraction
- high triglyceride store
- relatively small diameter

The fibres use *glycogen* and *fat* as fuels to produce contraction via the *aerobic energy system*. (See also *fast twitch muscle fibre*.)

smooth muscle: a type of muscle that lies internally within the body and contracts in response to nerve impulses sent via the *autonomic nervous system*. Smooth muscle is found within the muscular layer of the blood vessels, the intestines and the stomach.

The blood vessels also act in response to other factors such as hormones, temperature and oxygen and carbon dioxide levels in the blood, and are essential for the effective functioning of the body during exercise. For example, during exercise the carbon dioxide content within the working muscles increases, the chemo-sensitive areas of the blood vessels detect this and cause the blood vessel to dilate, enabling more blood to flow to the working muscle supplying oxygen and flushing away carbon dioxide. In this way the athlete can maintain optimal performance.

social classes: the divisions of a society defined on the basis of wealth, income, occupation and hereditary factors. Before the *Industrial Revolution*, Britain had a two-tier structure: *upper class* and lower class. With the development of society, increasing wealth through trade and education for all meant Britain became a three-tier social system: upper class, *middle class* and *working class*. Most people are found in the latter group. The upper class tends to occupy the highest positions of wealth and status. It is increasingly difficult to differentiate between the middle and working class, but generally the distinction is still based on the type of work done (manual or non-manual work).

social cohesion: the social interaction of group members and how well they trust, communicate with and support each other. The *cohesion* of a group can be improved if both social and *task cohesion* are good, although the group can be successful if only one of these elements is positive.

social construction of the body: the notion that the body might be of sociological interest has become popular since the 1980s. This can relate to the 'ideal' shape of women and men. There are four main perspectives of interpreting the body:
- medical model – the body is viewed as a machine that can break down and need repair. This is the dominant model for health and fitness
- social construct model – this belief holds the view that the way people view themselves and others is shaped by the sort of society in which they live and the sorts of ideas that are popular at any given moment. In a society like ours, a thin body shape is likely to offer high status and be sought after. Douglas's work (1966) showed that if women lived in societies where they were expected to do hard physical labour, larger body sizes for females are preferred and produced, as women seek to match up to these societal *expectations*
- feminism – gendered expectations exist for both males and females, although more negative connotations have become synonymous with the female body mainly due to natural bodily functions such as menstruation and shape. This can involve individuals having extreme responses to dieting and exercise
- phenomenological – this approach is interested in how self-image and identity are affected and how they shape notions of 'normal' body shape. Body shape can be changed by radical dieting, exercise programmes and cosmetic surgery. Individuals often express how different they feel as people when they undergo changes to their body shape that they consider being more acceptable. This approach concentrates on the perception of the individual rather than on the social or collective ideas about the body and body shape.

social control: the process whereby society seeks to ensure conformity to the dominant *values* and *norms* of that society. Formal and informal *socialisation* helps to ensure compliance. Sport has been used as a means of social control in many ways. (See also *athleticism* and *rational recreation*.)

social facilitation: the influence of the presence of others on performance, which may be positive or negative. The *arousal* level of the individual increases, which could improve the performance of an experienced player or inhibit that of a novice (see *drive theory* and social inhibition). The 'others' include:

- the *audience* – those watching either at the event or at home via the *mass media*
- *coactors* – those performing the same task but not in competition
- competitive coactors – those in direct competition with the performer
- social reinforcers – such as a coach.

For example, in front of a large crowd a skilled gymnast will perform well with increased arousal levels, whereas the performance of a novice may decrease and they may experience *evaluation apprehension*. To reduce the negative effects of social facilitation the coach should encourage the individual to use *mental practice*, train in front of a crowd, develop their *selective attention* and reduce the importance of the event.

social inequality: the uneven distribution of resources in society which is reflected in an unequal distribution of prestige and feelings of superiority and inferiority among individuals. Examples in sport would be women, disabled and ethnic *minority groups* having less access to facilities and funding.

social inhibition: the negative influence on performance caused by the presence of others during performance. This effect is the opposite of *social facilitation* and is caused when *arousal* levels increase (see *drive theory*). For example, when a young inexperienced player is being watched by a potential talent scout, they may become over-aroused and their performance decreases because the *skills* or *dominant habit* is not yet well learnt.

social learning theory proposes that people learn by observing others and then copying their actions. The repetition of an individual's behaviour is more likely to occur if *reinforcement* takes place, especially if it is received from a *significant other*. For example, if a young footballer observes a professional escaping a penalty or a booking after arguing with the referee they may feel this is acceptable behaviour. However, if the referee, disciplines the player and the child's parents agree that this decision was correct, the child will feel that this behaviour is unacceptable. Bandura suggested learning occurs in four phases:

1 attention – the amount of notice taken by an individual while watching a model

2 retention – the creation of a mental picture for future reference

3 motor reproduction – if physically possible, the imitation of the model's actions by the individual

4 motivation – the level of commitment to repeat the observed actions, which is often based on the reinforcement that is received and the importance of the task.

This form of learning is vital to the *socialisation* process within groups and society.

social loafing: the tendency of individuals to try to 'hide' when placed in a group situation and therefore not perform to their potential because they feel their contribution is not being observed, evaluated or valued. It is important to eliminate such tendencies in order to develop the *actual productivity* of the group and improve group *cohesion*. Various methods can be employed to eradicate this situation, including:

- giving the performer a position of responsibility
- highlighting their specific role within the group
- evaluation of performance, feedback and praise
- variation of practice to maintain motivation
- avoidance of situations in which social loafing may occur
- development of team cohesion and social support from the peer group
- use of video analysis
- development of fitness, so performers do not need to 'take a break'.

(See also *Ringelmann effect*.)

social mobility: movements up or down the *social class* 'ladder'. The type of society can determine the extent to which movement is possible. For example, a *closed society* such as the Indian caste system is rigid and allows little, if any, movement of individuals. A democratic or *open society* is likely to be more fluid. Sport has often been an avenue of social mobility because:

- the emphasis on physical skills and abilities means that few formal qualifications are required
- sport may allow progression through the education system; for example, with sport *scholarships*
- occupational *sponsorship* may lead to future jobs
- sport can encourage values such as leadership and teamwork skills, which may help in the wider world of employment.

(See also *stratification* and *upward social mobility*.)

social order: the patterned action or regularities that people display in their social lives. It is this that allows some predictability. This view tends to be conservative and stresses the need for *integration* and *cohesion* at the expense of conflict and change.

socialisation: the process whereby individuals learn the cultural *values* of their society. This is an ongoing process and individuals learn, via *social learning*, and they can expand, adapt or even reject the lessons learned. There are two types of socialisation:

- primary socialisation – where the family exert the greatest influence and which occurs in the early years
- secondary socialisation – where wider social agencies such as schools and the *mass media* operate.

Conflict can occur if the learning in each differs. (See also *significant others*.)

socialism: see *economic system*.

society: the totality of social relationships among organised groups of human beings and the distinctive cultural patterns and institutions they generate. A society will usually provide security, continuity and an identity for its members.

socioeconomic class: a broad collection of individuals who share similar occupational positions in the social hierarchy. They are wider than occupational groups but smaller than classes and hence form a sub-group within a *social class*. For example, skilled manual workers form a socioeconomic group distinct from unskilled manual workers.

sociological imagination: the ability to link the experiences of individuals to the social processes and structures of the wider world. It is the ability to examine the ways that individuals construct the social world and how the social world impinges on the lives of individuals.

sociological theories: see *functionalist theory, interactionism, Marxism* and *symbolic interactionism*.

sociology: the study of the development, organisation, functioning and classification of human society. It developed as a field of study in the eighteenth and nineteenth centuries following the dramatic social changes around the scientific and industrial revolutions. It is a search for understanding and insight into the world that we inhabit.

sociology of sport focuses on the relationship between sports and social relations, such as how sport interacts among other social institutions such as the family, politics and the *mass media*. Sport involves issues such as competition, *discrimination* and *socialisation*, all requiring a sociological analysis. Huge global events such as *World Games* raise questions about how and why they are conducted.

soda loading: the consumption of a solution of bicarbonate of soda an hour or so before an event or training to increase the amount of *bicarbonate ions* in the blood. Bicarbonate ions act as buffers to maintain the pH of the blood by attracting hydrogen ions from lactic acid therefore neutralising it. When soda loading, the pH of the blood increases, making it more alkaline. This enhances the *buffering* capacity of the blood improving its ability to neutralise the negative effects of *lactic acid*. In this way, soda loading helps to improve the athlete's tolerance to lactic acid, thereby delaying **onset of blood lactate accumulation** and enabling the performer to work harder for longer. Soda loading appears to be of benefit particularly to those activities that operate at near maximum intensities of between 1 and 7 minutes, including 400-metre runners, 1 km track cyclists and rowers. Although evidence suggests that performance may be improved through this practice, there are some side effects which include vomiting and diarrhoea.

somatic anxiety refers to the individual's physiological responses when placed in a situation where they perceive an inability to complete the task successfully. For example, before a race a swimmer may experience increases in heart rate, sweating, *blood pressure*, muscle tension and feelings of nausea. All of these could hinder performance initially, but these symptoms often reduce when the event has started.

somatotype: a method of classifying body shape. Three extreme body shapes have been identified:
- extreme endomorphs – characterised by a pear-shaped body, i.e. wide hips and narrow shoulders. They also tend to carry a lot of fat around their waist and limbs, for example a Sumo wrestler
- extreme mesomorphs – characterised by individuals with wide shoulders and narrow hips, rather like an inverted triangle, who tend to be much more muscular, for example a male gymnast
- extreme ectomorphs – characterised by individuals who are narrow at both the shoulders and the hips and tend to be very tall due to very long slender limbs; for example, a high jumper. Ectomorphs are generally very thin, possessing neither much fat nor muscle.

Although all extremes can be found, most people are made up of all three body shapes. For example, a basketball player might have ectomorph characteristics since they are very tall, but also possess some mesomorph qualities as they also tend to be very muscular.

spa town: a place or resort where a mineral spring is to be found. Spa towns originated in Roman times and the Tudors established 'taking the waters' in the fashionable inland spa resorts because the water was considered to have beneficial healing properties. During the

Georgian and **Victorian eras**, the tradition continued of visiting the spas, which offered rest and relaxation away from the growing industrial towns. Some of the notable spa towns are Bath, Buxton and Harrogate.

spatial anticipation involves a performer attempting to predict what the actions of their opponent will be and formulating a response in readiness. For example, a batsman watches the bowler's action in preparation for the type of delivery they may receive. (See also **temporal anticipation**.)

spatial summation: an increase in responsiveness of a nerve resulting from the additive effect of numerous **stimuli**. A certain level of intensity is needed before a muscle fibre responds by contracting. Spatial summation describes the progressive increase in size of the excitatory postsynaptic potential (EPSP) as a result of the arrival of a number of impulses at the synaptic cleft of individual muscle fibres.

On arrival at the **neuromuscular junction**, the transmitter substance **acetylcholine** is released which enables the impulse to cross the synaptic cleft and create electrical potentials in the muscle fibre (the potential to contract). However, if the EPSP is not of sufficient intensity the muscle fibre will not contract, so the additive effect of a number of stimuli arriving can be used to ensure that the excitatory threshold is reached and the muscle fibres contract.

specificity: a **principle of training** which suggests that any training undertaken should be relevant and appropriate to the sport for which the individual is training. For example, it would be highly inappropriate for a triathlete to concentrate solely on running as this is not relevant to the other two disciplines of swimming and cycling. The athlete would need to ensure that some training is undertaken in a swimming pool, some on a bicycle and some on the roads. In doing so the athlete will gain tremendous benefits by training all of the relevant muscles, types of fibre and **energy systems**, and of course improve technique.

spectator sport: a sport that attracts people as spectators rather than participants. The reorganisation of the population into large units during and following the **Industrial Revolution,** and the increased **leisure** time and income of the **working class**, created the ideal conditions and market for mass entertainment on a commercial basis. Spectator violence has been a traditional aspect of some sports, particularly football. The rise in popularity of the sport and creation of rivalry between towns led to an increase in the number of **hooligans** and a corresponding rise in hooliganism. The development of the **mass media**, particularly television, created a new type of sports fan; the 'armchair enthusiast'. This term suggests that the participant takes no active part and is viewed as having both beneficial and detrimental effects on the participants and the sport. On the one hand it can increase interest in the sport, but the lack of physical activity can have no physical benefits for the spectator.)

spectator violence: see **hooligans**.

speed: the maximum rate that a person can travel over a specific distance, and also how quickly a person can put body parts into action. A javelin thrower, for example, does not need to run at their maximum speed in their run-up but they do need to whip their arm through the centre line of their body as quickly as possible. Speed is classed as an ability that is largely genetically determined due to the physiological composition of the muscle, but it can still be improved through sprint **interval training** and **plyometrics**. **Biomechanics** and technique training are also essential in optimising the efficiency of the body's **lever** systems to improve speed of the body or body part.

sponsorship: the provision of funds or other forms of support to an individual or event for a commercial return. It is of mutual benefit to both parties. Sponsorship is now an intrinsic aspect of sports funding. Through the medium of television, business sponsors of sport can create the images they want, allowing identification with the sports and sportstars and introducing new **audiences** to their product.

The **Olympic Games** is one of the biggest global events in the world with sponsorship organised on a global basis. The Olympic Partner Programme works with selected partner companies, such Coca-Cola, Omega and Samsung, to provide crucial fundraising for the staging of the event.

Sponsorship has been a key factor in the redevelopment of many sports, providing capital for the sport and at the same time:
- securing an appropriate image for the sponsor, for example Gillette sponsors cricket, which creates an 'English' image for its product, while Coca-Cola sponsors the Olympics and school sport, conveying fun and liveliness
- achieving specific marketing objectives.

The disadvantages include:
- uneven development across some sports
- development of **elite** sport at the expense of **grass roots** sport
- male sport receives substantially more money than female sport.

sport: institutionalised competitive activities that involve vigorous physical exertion or the use of relatively complex physical skills by individuals whose participation is motivated by a combination of intrinsic and extrinsic factors.

Benefits of sport	Problems of sport
Acts as an emotional release	Can help to retain **discrimination**
Express individuality	Winning too important/financial **rewards**
Can help **socialisation**	Competition can be damaging
Individuals can achieve success	Spectatorism can outweigh participation
Can initiate social change	Dominated by **mass media** interest

sport competition anxiety test (SCAT) is also known as Illinois competition **questionnaire**. It is a self-report questionnaire used to measure the **competitive trait anxiety** of a performer when placed in a pre-competitive sporting environment. It is used in an attempt to predict the **anxiety** levels of the individual in a specific situation. As a result, the coach can develop appropriate **stress management** techniques to reduce high levels of anxiety. For example, if a sprinter knows they lose focus prior to the start of a race, techniques to improve concentration and **self-confidence** can be used. Further developments of this questionnaire produced the **competitive state anxiety inventory (CSAI-2)**, which measured both **cognitive anxiety** and **somatic anxiety**.

Sport Education in Physical Education Program (SEPEP) is a framework that schools in **Australia** can use according to their needs in order to deliver an effective physical education programme. Main features are:
- a loose curriculum framework that is adaptable and gives the teacher choice
- 100 minutes of physical education and 100 minutes of sport per week
- a government requirement

- development of skills and sport performance
- intra-schools sport involving games in lesson time and sport against other schools
- participation is the priority; *excellence* is a secondary consideration
- allows non-sporting roles for children in administration or officiating roles
- sports linkage scheme that links between school and club.

Sport England: the organisation responsible for leading the development of sport in England by influencing and serving the public, private and voluntary sectors. Its objectives are:
- start–get more people involved in sport
- stay–retain people once they have begun in sport
- succeed–allow individuals the potential for success

Sport England came into being following the government report *Sport: Raising the Game* in 1995. The *UK Sports Council* oversees matters that need to be dealt with at the UK level, including issues such as *doping* control and decisions regarding the site of the *UK Sports Institute*. Sport England is accountable to parliament through the Secretary of State for Culture, Media and Sport, who also appoints members of the Council of Sport England. There are ten regional offices across England which work with *local authorities*, sports *governing bodies*, plus regional and national organisations concerned with sport, recreation, education and the environment. The work of Sport England is jointly funded by grant in aid from the Exchequer, which pays for sport's infrastructure, and the National Lottery via the *Lottery fund*.

Its *Sportsmark* and Sportsmark Gold award schemes also commit Sport England to improving standards of school sport, promoting the ideal of the minimum time for *National Curriculum* physical education as 2 hours a week.

Sport for All: a national and international campaign initiated by the *Council of Europe* which aims to increase the participation in physical activities of large population groups. It first appeared in Britain in 1972, launched by the then Sports Council. The Council of Europe published the *European Charter on Sport for All* in 1976. Sport in this instance covers activities that come under the category of:
- *competition sport* and games
- outdoor and *adventurous activities*
- movement and *aesthetic* activities
- *conditioning activities*.

In the UK, the aim is to:
- increase the participation rate overall
- improve performance at all levels
- provide facilities and resources that can be utilised as a social service
- promote awareness of a healthy lifestyle
- improve the quality of life.

Today, two important campaigns are Football in the Community, which links professional football clubs with facilities open to the public, and Sport Action Zones, which places an emphasis on inner-city areas – this is popular with *local authorities*.

sport law: 'The application of legal principles to all levels of competition of amateur sport and professional sport and to physical activity.' Sport was traditionally considered to be a separate part of life to the law and they were rarely interlinked. However, the number of *deviant* acts within sport appears to have increased, or it may be that incidents have been more widely reported by the *mass media*. Therefore, the authorities have been forced to make sport as accountable as other social institutions. Sport law is becoming more common and covers aspects such as contracts and employment, negligence, safety and violence, forms of **discrimination** and child protection.

Sport Northern Ireland: as a lead facilitator in the development of sport, Sport Northern Ireland will work with partners to:

- increase and sustain committed participation, especially among young people
- raise the standards of sporting **excellence** and promote the good reputation and efficient administration of sport.

Sport Northern Ireland's aims will be achieved by developing the competencies of its staff who are dedicated to optimising the use of its resources.

Sport: Raising the Game: a 1995 publication that outlined the UK government's aims for sport in Britain. It supported the following initiatives to encourage participation and raise the standards of school sport:

- **Sportsmark** and Sportsmark Gold Awards/**Sports College status**
- schools were encouraged to make links with external clubs
- standards were recommended for the amount of opportunity for playing sport in physical education lessons and during **extra-curricular sport**
- Community Sports Initiative
- the training of teachers to run sports clubs and teams
- the **National Junior Sport Programme**.

The aim was to provide opportunities, from sport at primary schools through to Olympic levels, and it highlighted the benefits of competition and the lessons which could be learned for life.

sport space: the concept of sport space has emerged, whereby opportunities for other sports may have been limited by the domination of the **Big Four** in American culture.

Sports Aid: set up in 1976 to enable top amateur athletes at both junior and senior level to train with similar privileges enjoyed by state-sponsored athletes abroad. It is a self-financing organisation that draws its funds from commercial, industrial and private sponsors in addition to various fund-raising projects. Outstanding competitors usually receive the money according to their personal needs, cost of their preparation, training and competition, and are usually recommended by their **governing body**. Grants are also awarded through its charitable trust to talented athletes who are in education, on low income or disabled.

Sports Coach UK: the organisation responsible for the development of **coaching** in Britain based in Leeds. It was established in 1983 to provide a range of educational and advisory services for all coaches and to complement the award schemes of the individual **governing bodies**. Its role has been to:

- develop sports science courses and generic courses rather than sport-specific ones
- produce coaching literature, videos, fact sheets and databases
- establish a Network of National Coaching (NCC) in higher education institutions
- make links with **local authorities** and national **governing bodies**
- develop coaching qualifications such as the Diploma in Professional Studies, Coaching for Teachers and progressive coaching course levels.

Its main sources of funding are from the **UK Sport**, earned income and other grant aid donations.

In 2001 the National Coaching Foundation was rebranded as Sports Coach UK. Membership reached 12,000 and achieved recognition from Sporting Equals for their work to support the development of coaches from black and ethnic minority communities. The Sports Coach UK mission statement is aimed at guiding the development and implementation of a coaching system, recognised as a world leader, for all coaches at every level in the UK.

The central theme of the mission statement is to describe what a world-class coaching system looks like. It is likely to include:

- coach development linked firmly to player development
- continuous learning and inclusive practice based on a strong foundation of research, continuous professional development and ethical practice
- central coordination by an organisation empowered to do so but 'owned' by everybody
- simplicity and flexibility, not hierarchy and rigid bureaucracy
- use of a common framework of agreed national standards
- shared strategic approaches with common generic components
- effective management of coaches (paid and unpaid) and their development through registers/licences
- not allowing organisations and/or individuals to opt out of the system
- a focus at all levels on adding value to the experience of the individual player/performer and the individual coach as well as the player–coach interaction.

Sports College status: the Sports College initiative was launched in 1996 with the first schools viable in September 1997. The Department for Children, Schools and Families lays down the guidelines and the **Youth Sports Trust** offers development and guidance. It is part of a specialised schools programme, which includes centres for technology, the arts and modern languages – an attempt to allow schools with particular strengths to build on them and attract pupils with those interests. It was envisaged they would be centres for sport and physical education encompassing all sectors of the community. The objectives of the programme are to:

- extend the range of opportunities available to children which best meet their needs and interests
- raise the standard of teaching and learning for physical education and sport in schools
- develop characteristics which would identify the Colleges with their local communities and local schools
- be of benefit to local schools, within the 'family of schools network'
- attract local sponsors who should take an active role in the schools development
- show a 'vision' for each college in a document called a development plan.

Sports Council for Wales: the national organisation responsible for developing and promoting sport and active lifestyles. It is the main adviser on sporting matters to the Welsh Assembly and is responsible for distributing funds from the National Lottery to sport in Wales.

The Council fully subscribes to the Welsh Assembly's vision for a physically active and sporting nation, as outlined in its strategy document *Climbing Higher*. Its main focus is to increase the frequency of participation by persuading those who are currently sedentary to become more active and to encourage people, young and old, to develop a portfolio of activities through which to achieve healthy levels of activity.

The themes of the Council's work are:

- active young people.
- active communities – developing people and places.
- developing performance and **excellence**.

sports leaders awards: see *SportsLeadersUK*.

sports medicine: the application of medicine to sport, and includes the services of, but is not limited to, athletic trainers, physicians, physical therapists, coaches, athletic administrators, exercise physiologists and nutritionists. The sports medicine professionals are involved with preventing injuries and developing training schedules.

sports schools: schools that specialise in the development of young sport talent. Some British examples are Millfield, Kelly College, Reed's School and Lilleshall.

Advantages of sports schools	Disadvantages of sports schools
Quality *coaching* and education	Limits the pool of talent available
Accommodation and facilities	Exclusive
Medical science	Necessitates living away from home
Pooling of similar talent	High physical and psychological demand
Organised competition structure	*Burnout*
Links with professional clubs	

sportscotland: the national agency for sport in Scotland. Its mission is to encourage everyone in Scotland to discover and develop their own sporting experience. It aims to help to increase participation and improve performances in Scottish sport. The agency operates three national centres: Glenmore Lodge, Inverclyde and Cumbrae. It also acts as the parent company of the Scottish Institute of Sport (SIS).

SportsLeadersUK believes it needs to provide the opportunity and motivation for anyone to make a meaningful contribution to their local community. It aims to achieve this through the nationally recognised qualification of the Sports Leader Awards, whereby people can learn essential skills, such as working with and organising others, as well as motivational, communication and teamwork skills.

It is part of the £7 million *Step into Sport* initiative, which will see the British Sports Trust, the *Youth Sports Trust* and *Sport England* teaming up to help train a new generation of *volunteer* coaches, mainly aged 14–19.

- Junior Sports Leader Awards – for 14–16-year-olds and taught mainly in schools within the *National Curriculum* for physical education at *key stage* 4. The award develops a young person's skills in organising activities, planning, communicating and motivating.
- *Community Sports Leader Awards* – for those aged 16 years and over, this popular award is taught in schools, colleges, youth clubs, prisons, and sports and leisure centres nationwide.
- Higher Sports Leader Awards – builds on the skills gained through the Community Sports Leader Awards to equip people to lead specific community groups such as older people, people with disabilities and primary school children. The award includes units in event management, first aid, sports development and obtaining a *coaching* award.
- Basic Expedition Leader Awards – for those interested in the outdoors, this builds the ability to organise safe expeditions and overnight *camps*.

sportsmanship: qualities displayed by a person or team that are highly regarded in sports such as fairness, generosity, observance of the rules and good humour on losing. This was one of the defining qualities of the *gentleman amateur* and *athleticism*.

Sportsmark: a scheme introduced in the government report *Sport: Raising the Game* in 1995, which recognises and rewards schools that provide the best physical education and sports provision to their pupils and the local community. The additional gold award is presented to those offering exceptional provision. To obtain the award, various criteria have to be achieved. Recently the *Activemark* and Activemark Gold scheme have been introduced to include primary, middle and special schools. (See also *Active Sports Programme*.)

Sportsmatch: the government's '£1 for a £1' business *sponsorship* incentive scheme which was established in 1992. It provides funding for *grass roots* development of sport and funds of over £3.7 million a year in the UK to match funds from the private sector. It is administered by the *Institute of Sports Sponsorship* in cooperation with *Sport England* and provides an excellent opportunity for sports bodies and sponsors to double the value of their project investment or to mount extra activities or events, which must be competitive, challenging and physically skilful. The awards panel is particularly interested in developing projects for rural and inner cities that lack sporting resources.

stable personality: a person who is calm, even-tempered, lively, controlled and reliable with good leadership qualities. They display traits linked to their *autonomic nervous system*, which responds slowly and minimally to stressful situations, causing the individual to be even-tempered and stable. They possess the opposite traits to those with a *neurotic personality* and are placed at the other end of the *continuum*. These characteristics can be measured using the *Eysenck personality inventory* or *Cattell's 16 personality factors questionnaire*.

stacking: the disproportionate concentration of ethnic minorities in certain positions in a sports team, which tends to be based on the *stereotyped* view that they are best suited to roles that require physical skill rather than decision-making and communication qualities. In American football there has been a tendency to place ethnic players in running back and wide receiver positions rather than the pivotal position of quarterback. In baseball until fairly recently they have tended to be placed in outfield positions. (See also *centrality*.)

stages of learning: see *Fitts and Posner's stages of learning theory*.

stamateur: see *amateurism*.

Starling's law of the heart, also known as the Frank-Starling mechanism, suggests that *cardiac output* is dependent on venous return and the extensibility of cardiac muscle fibres. The more the cardiac muscle fibres are stretched during the diastolic (filling) stage of the *cardiac cycle*, the stronger the walls can contract and force blood into the circulatory system. The action is similar to filling a balloon with water: the more water that enters the balloon, the more the balloon stretches. Furthermore, during exercise the *elasticity* of cardiac fibres increases due to an increase in body temperature and the release of hormones such as *adrenaline* and *noradrenaline*, consequently causing *stroke volume* and therefore cardiac output to increase.

state: a term that encompasses all the major organisations which are agencies of the governing institutions in society. This includes, for example, the royal family, parliament and the civil service, the military, social security and education. State activity has increased during the twentieth century and this has meant an extension of state power. (See also *centralised*.)

state anxiety: also known as A state, this is a form of *anxiety* that occurs when the performer is placed in a particular situation that can vary from moment to moment. For example, an individual may become anxious immediately prior to the start of a race or match due to their perceived inability to cope with the situation. However, this may reduce when the event has started and increase again when faced with a new challenge, such as taking a penalty. Both *cognitive anxiety* and *somatic anxiety* may be experienced during this time.

state education: schools maintained by public spending, either through local education authorities or directly from central government as in the case of *grant-maintained schools*. State education began in Britain following the Forster Education Act 1870 (see *Education Acts*). (See also *state schools*.)

state schools: the purpose of the nineteenth-century state schools was to provide an education for the *working class*, who needed to acquire basic skills: the three Rs (reading, writing and arithmetic), and the fourth R of religious education. The working class were going to be the workers, obeying commands from their employers, therefore discipline and obedience were important values. State schools were small, cramped spaces with no recreational facilities. They were built in local areas, were day schools and catered for both sexes. Most age groups were taught together. These schools were also free of charge, in stark contrast to *public schools*. (See also *state education*.)

state sports confidence: also known as SC-state, this is the level of *self-confidence* experienced by an individual in a specific sporting situation. This is a key factor affecting the overall level of self-confidence. For example, a basketball player who practises free-throws regularly and has a high percentage success rate in matches will have a higher level of state sports confidence than a novice who has little previous experience in a pressured situation. (See also *self-efficacy* and *Vealey's model of sport confidence*.)

static flexibility a dimension of *flexibility* that refers to the range of movement at a joint which occurs without considering the speed of movement into position. Static flexibility relates to the maximum extent of muscle lengthening, for example when lengthening the hamstrings under control and holding the stretch. Good static flexibility is a necessary prerequisite for good *dynamic flexibility*. However, having good static flexibility does not in itself ensure good dynamic flexibility.

static strength: the development of force within a muscle in which the length of the muscle does not change and there is no visible movement at the joint. Activities such as gymnastics, judo and wrestling all demand high levels of static strength. Exercises such as isometric squats and the plank demonstrate static strength. Both exercises are outlined below.

Isometric squats

1   Place your back against a wall and lower yourself until your upper legs are parallel to the floor.
2   Shuffle your feet until your lower legs are parallel to the wall behind you. Your knees should be bent to 90°.
3   Hold your arms out in front of you and hold the position for 10–30 seconds. Repeat 2 or 3 times.

The plank

1   Start by lying face down on the ground. Place your elbows and forearms underneath your chest.
2   Prop yourself up to form a bridge using your toes and forearms.
3   Maintain a flat back and do not allow your hips to sag towards the ground.
4   Hold for 10–30 seconds or until you can no longer maintain a flat bridge. Repeat 2 or 3 times.

steady state: the plateau reached by the heart rate during sub-maximal, low-intensity exercise. If the heart rate is experiencing steady state, it is assumed that the oxygen demands made by the muscles are being met by the heart supplying sufficient quantities of blood. i.e. oxygen supply = oxygen demand. For example, a person jogging will be in steady state, whereas a sprinter during a 400-metre race will not.

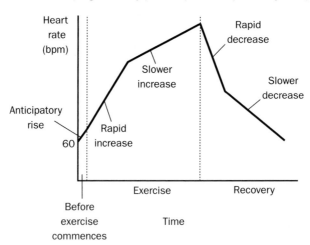

Steady state

Steiner's model of group productivity: see *group productivity*.

Step into Sport: sport relies on 1.5 million volunteer officials, coaches, administrators and managers. Step into Sport is aiming to build on this trend and extend the *grass roots* interest in this area into a more coordinated strategic approach by national *governing bodies*, county sports partnerships and clubs. It should ensure that clubs are ready to receive, develop and deploy a steady supply of volunteers.

Between 2002 and 2004, Step into Sport was delivered in almost 200 **School Sport Coordinator partnerships** across all 45 county sport partnership areas by a consortium of the **Youth Sports Trust** (via the Top Link Programme – see **National Junior Sports Programme**), the British Sports Trust (via **Sports Leader Awards**) and **Sport England**, each with their own responsibilities.

The aim is to provide a structured pathway to attract over 48,000 young people aged 14–19 into voluntary sports **coaching** over the next two years. The network of partnerships will be mainly focused around the government's Sport Action Zones.

stereotype: a standardised image or concept shared by all members of a social group. In other words, certain behaviour **traits** are associated with particular types of individuals or groups. This usually involves negative images relating to **gender** and race. Our **attitudes** can affect our behaviour towards these groups or individuals. This is significant when it comes to issues like the **expectations** of teachers regarding the sporting potential of boys and girls.

stimulants: drugs or similar substances that increase physiological activity. An example of a stimulant is **amphetamine**. Stimulants are one of the most widely used manufactured drugs, being used to improve endurance performance, increase mental and physical **alertness**, decrease **fatigue** and increase metabolism, but they can lead to increases in heart rate and **blood pressure**. The more an athlete uses stimulants, the less effect they have on the body, so the athlete needs to take more. (See also **doping** and **drug testing**.)

stimuli: (singular stimulus) any information that enters the body via the **sensory system**. Sports performers have to use the various stimuli presented to them from the **display (psychology)** during **information processing**, often ignoring irrelevant details and focusing their **attention** on useful **cues**. The effective interpretation of this data can reduce **reaction time**. For example, the performer will note the location of themselves, team mates and opponents, the speed and direction of any object being used, the position and decision of the referee, the reaction of the crowd, the weather conditions, instructions from the coach as well as any pain or discomfort they may be experiencing.

stimulus identification stage: see *input*.

stimulus–response bond: the relationship between a **stimulus** and the specific action that it initiates. These bonds form the basis of the **associationist theories of learning**. For example, when a badminton player sees their opponent at the rear of the court (stimulus), they may be conditioned to play their shot to the front (response).

stimulus–response compatibility: the degree to which the response to given **stimuli** appears 'natural'. If a performer is presented with a situation in which they have been before and know how to react, their **reaction time** will be reduced. For example, if a table tennis player receives a shot that is high enough off the table to play a smash return, and through experience they recognise that option is available, the chance of a successful return will be increased. Similarly, if an opponent always returns the ball to the same place when playing a backhand stroke, the performer can learn to recognise this and execute their own shot more quickly when it occurs.

stimulus–response theory of learning: see *associationist theories of learning*.

strategies: the plans and decision-making activities that are made in advance of sport performance. The type of strategy will depend on the nature of the sport being undertaken, for example:

- a *gymnastic activity* is about selecting or designing sequences that have varying levels of difficulty and also requires artistic interpretation
- an *invasion game* requires planning in advance as to how opponents are to be outmanoeuvred, but the strategy will need to be adapted depending on the opponents' play.

stratification: the division of society or any other group of people into layers based on biological, economic and social criteria, for example age, *gender*, race and *social class*. The *dominant culture* controls the more subordinate groups, which can include women, ethnic minorities and the disabled. Wealth, status and hereditary factors can be influential, with wealth and income being prominent in more modern societies. Those at the top have greater access to scarce resources compared with those at the bottom. Stratification in sport is inevitable when winning is highly valued. It is highlighted even more when monetary *rewards* are on offer. (See also *discrimination* and *social mobility*.)

streamlining: the reduction in *drag* and promotion of *laminar flow* as a body or other object passes through air or water. For example, cyclists have attempted to streamline through the design of cycling helmets, shape of the bicycle and adopting more streamlined positions while riding. Swimmers attempt to minimise drag by wearing shiny polyurethane swimsuits and swimming hats and shaving down (the removal of body hair), all of which allow the water to flow past the body more smoothly.

strength: the maximum force that can be developed within a muscle or group of muscles during a single maximal contraction. Strength is required in many activities but particularly in those that are *anaerobic* in nature and of high intensity such as weightlifting or gymnastics.

Several different types of strength have been identified, including:

- maximum strength – used in an all-out explosive event such as the shot putt
- *elastic strength* – evident in activities where a high speed of contraction is required such as in sprinting
- strength endurance – concerned with the avoidance of muscle *fatigue* and required in activities such as rowing and swimming.

Due to the diverse nature of strength, prescribing a training programme to encompass every athlete's requirements is obviously difficult. It is commonly agreed, however, that in resistance and weight training, to develop maximum strength the use of very high-resistance activities with relatively few repetitions is favoured, while strength endurance would involve the use of lighter resistance with a greater number of repetitions. Strength can be assessed by the use of dynamometers (the most common being the handgrip dynamometer) or by the one repetition maximum test (1RM). (See also *strength training*.)

strength training: a method of training used to develop *strength*. There are various ways to develop strength, such as *circuit training* or *plyometrics*, but the most common is weight training. The use of weights can be adapted to meet the needs of specific individuals. For example, the weightlifter wishing to develop maximum strength will use heavy weights (high intensity – 90% of 1RM) and perform a low number of repetitions (six). The sprinter wishing to develop **elastic strength** will use medium to heavy weights (75% of 1RM) with up to 12 repetitions. The rower wishing to develop strength endurance will use light to medium weights (50–60% of 1RM) but perform a high number of repetitions (20).

stress occurs as a result of the individual perceiving an imbalance between the demands of a task and their ability to meet them. Stress can have positive or negative effects on performance. Those who seek out stressful situations and benefit from them experience **eustress**, while performers who react negatively to stress experience **anxiety**. For example, one person might enjoy the feelings created by diving off a high-board, while another may become very anxious at the thought of such a task. The various factors which facilitate such a response are known as **stressors**. These cause the body to undergo a series of sensations known as the **general adaptation syndrome**. It is vital that individuals are able to control their stress levels, employing appropriate **stress management** techniques to achieve an optimum level of performance. (See also **type A personality** and **type B personality**.)

stress management: techniques employed to lower the levels of **anxiety** experienced by an individual in order to improve performance. For example, the heart rate of a diver may increase while preparing for their final dive of the competition and they may worry about executing the sequence incorrectly. If they can control their breathing and think positively about their performance, these symptoms of stress may decrease.

The techniques are generally subdivided into:
- somatic methods – aim is to decrease the physiological responses. They include **biofeedback**, breathing control or **centering** and **relaxation**
- cognitive methods – aim is to decrease the psychological worries. They include **goal setting**, **imagery**, **self-talk** and **positive thinking**.

stressors: demands that are placed on the performer that initiate **stress**. For example, the nature of the competition, any threat to personal safety, conflict, frustration, pressure, the audience, the unknown and climate may trigger such a response.

stroke volume: the volume of blood ejected from the left ventricle of the heart per beat. Normal stroke volume at rest is approximately 70 ml of blood, but this can increase two-fold during medium- to high-intensity exercise. This increase is largely explained by **Starling's law of the heart**, which suggests that the fibres of the heart muscle stretch during exercise, enabling the ventricles to fill with larger volumes of blood and causing the heart to contract with greater force. Resting stroke volume shows a significant increase following an endurance training programme, with highly trained athletes experiencing resting stroke volumes of up to 120 ml. This is largely explained by the enlargement (hypertrophy) of the heart that accompanies training, enabling the heart to fill with more blood due to a longer diastolic phase. Other factors affecting stroke volume include:
- age – stroke volume decreases with increasing age
- sex – females have a lower stroke volume due to their smaller hearts and lower **testosterone** levels.

structural functionalism: a form of **functionalist theory** associated with Talcott Parsons, which views social structures in a positive light, i.e. they exist for the good of society. However, it does not explain why structures such as criminal organisations exist.

Stuart era: the period after the death of Queen Elizabeth I, when King James VI of Scotland became James I of England. He issued the **Book of Sports** as a result of the growing influence of the **Puritans**. His son Charles I was executed but Charles II returned as monarch in 1660. This was known as the Restoration period, as it was to restore many of the previously banned activities such as the **Dover Games**. Charles II was in favour of many sports and his court enjoyed a lifestyle of ease, affluence and leisure, occupying themselves lavishly on sporting pursuits and enjoying a revival of the '**courtly** mould'.

subculture: a group in society which shares common values and attitudes that are based on social criteria (e.g. ethnicity) or on styles and trends (e.g. 'hell's angels'). These groups may well share some of the features of the **dominant culture** but may also be opposed to it in some manner. Examples within sport would include football **hooligans**, rugby clubs and surfers.

subjective: based on individual interpretation of behaviour, actions or events. Some testing methods, such as observation and interviewing, rely on the researcher's own interpretation of the results rather than interpreting them on the basis of **objective** data. For example, when observing a player during a hockey match who fails to receive a pass for several minutes, one person may feel they are being lazy or are **social loafing**, and not working to get the ball. However, another observer may conclude that simply play has not moved into that area of the field. The winners of some sporting activities are decided partly subjectively by a panel of judges, for example gymnastics, diving and skating.

subroutine: a phase of a **movement pattern** that must be executed at the appropriate time in the sequence if the skill is to be successful. A series of subroutines combine to form an **executive motor programme**. For example, the high jump could be split into the run-up, take-off, flight and landing.

summer camps: see **camps**.

super league: see **rugby league**.

superficial: structures or muscles of the body that lie closer to the surface of the body than others. For example, the soleus muscle in the calf lies above the tibialis posterior and is therefore classed as a superficial muscle.

superior: a structure above or closer to the head than another. For example, the superior vena cava lies above the inferior vena cava, entering the heart from above. (See appendix, page 311.)

supination: a **movement pattern** characterised by the **lateral rotation** of the forearm at the radio-ulnar so that the palm of the hand faces upwards. Supination occurs in the horizontal or **transverse plane** about a longitudinal axis and occurs, for example, during the recovery phase of a breaststroke arm 'pull' or at the forearm of the right arm during a 'flick' in hockey. (See appendix, page 329.)

Swedish gymnastics: **gymnastics** that originated from Sweden under the name of Per Henrik Ling. The British school boards of the nineteenth century tended to favour Swedish gymnastics as being suitable for **state schools** for a variety of reasons:

- its free-flowing, free-standing exercises were cheap to implement
- its method of instruction was based on discipline which was considered suitable for working-class children

- it drew on the knowledge of the human body available at that time
- its *therapeutic* effects were considered important for the *working class*, who were generally in poor health.

swimming: a method of propulsion through the water. It is highly valued as both *recreation* and as an opportunity for vigorous physical activity. The sport goes back to ancient Greece and Rome, being considered an important part of warriors' training. Swimming was introduced into the *Olympic Games* programme in Athens in 1896. It became popular in Britain with the building of public facilities under the Public Baths and Washhouse Act in 1840, the publicity of feats such as Captain Webb swimming the English Channel and the formation of the Amateur Swimming Association.

Syllabuses of Physical Training (1904, 1909, 1919, 1927, 1933) were outlined courses of exercises that were required by the *Board of Education* to be carried out in *state schools*. Due to concerns over the *model course*, the Board of Education established these syllabuses since they provided prescriptive outlines that teachers who were generally unqualified to teach *physical training* (PT) found easy to implement. They stressed the physical and educative effects of physical activities:

- the *therapeutic* effect – the correction of posture faults and exercises to improve the circulatory system
- the educational effect – the development of *alertness* and *decision-making* ability.

They were a *centralised* policy.

symbolic interactionism: a concept, developed by Weber, that assumes we live in a symbolic world in which symbols have shared meanings. An example would be language or sport. It assumes that human behaviour involves choices based on the meanings that individuals attach to events, and these are transmitted down through the generations. This theory relies heavily on the concept of the self, individuals interpreting the connections between themselves and their social world and hence calculating the effects of their actions.

In a sporting context, symbolic interaction looks at how people see the world of sport; how they see themselves in relation to sport and what choices they make regarding, for example, their level of sport participation. This theory is useful when looking at various social groups and how and why they operate, but it does not help when looking at issues such as inequality in sport.

sympathetic nervous system: one of the two subdivisions of the *autonomic nervous system* (the other being the *parasympathetic nervous system*), which is primarily in operation when energy is required. During exercise, its effects tend to oppose those of the parasympathetic nervous system, with the sympathetic fibres releasing *adrenaline* and *noradrenaline* which initiates the body's *fight or flight response*. This in turn produces many physiological effects designed to maximise performance. For example, both the rate and strength of contraction of the heart increase, blood vessels supplying *skeletal muscle*, cardiac muscle and the lungs all increase in size to ensure a greater volume of blood flow, the bronchioles dilate to ensure efficient exchange of oxygen and carbon dioxide and energy availability increases due to quicker conversion of *glycogen* to glucose. All these factors occur without us having to control them and are a natural response of the body.

synergist: a muscle also known as a neutraliser that contracts to enhance the efficiency of the *prime mover* by preventing any undesired movement. It forms part of the cooperation or *antagonistic* effect of the muscles which work together to ensure that coordinated movement can take place. For example, when performing a biceps curl, the deltoids are working as synergists since they work to prevent any undesired movement at the shoulder, and in doing so enable the biceps brachii to work as effectively as possible.

synovial fluid: a fluid rich in protein that is released from the synovial membrane of freely moveable *synovial joints*. It lubricates the ends of the bones, reducing friction as they move against each other (articulate) and nourishes the articular *cartilage* that covers the ends of bones. During exercise, more synovial fluid is released which is soaked up by the articular cartilage, causing it to swell and offer greater protection and ease of movement.

synovial joint: a joint that allows a wide range of movement and which is composed of two or more bones which exist in a joint capsule. The ends of these bones are covered in articular *cartilage* and are separated by a joint cavity filled with *synovial fluid*. Although all synovial joints are similar in structure and possess common features, variations do exist due to the shape of the articulating surfaces:

- *hinge joint* – the convex surface of one bone fits into the concave surface of another. Built for stability, movement only usually occurs in one plane and is limited to *flexion* and *extension*, for example the knee joint
- *pivot joint* – a rounded, peg-like structure of one bone that slots into a ring-shaped cavity of another to allow *rotation*, for example between the ends of the radius and ulna at the elbow, which enables *pronation* and *supination* of the forearm to occur and also at the neck
- *gliding joint* – the articulating surfaces in gliding joints are usually flat and often allow a small degree of movement in all directions, for example the bones of the carpals
- *saddle joint* – as the name suggests, one bone at this joint is shaped like a saddle while the other resembles a rider sitting in the saddle. This joint allows flexion, extension, *abduction* and *adduction* and only truly occurs where the carpal and metacarpal of the thumb meet
- *ellipsoid/condyloid joint* – an oval-shaped end of one bone fits into an elliptical depression of another bone allowing movements in two planes (flexion, extension, abduction and adduction). An example includes the wrist joint where the radius meets the carpals
- *ball and socket joint* – a rounded head of one bone fits into a cup-shaped cavity, enabling the widest range of movement. For example, the shoulder joint enables flexion, extension, abduction, adduction, *circumduction* and *rotation*.

systemic circulation: a component of the circulatory system that conducts oxygenated blood from the left ventricle to all the major organs of the body (excluding the lungs) and returns to the right *atrium* via the venae cavae. The distribution of blood throughout the systemic circulatory system alters significantly during exercise, so that more blood can supply the working muscles.

systole: the period of contraction of the heart during the ***cardiac cycle***. Atrial systole is the contraction of the ***atria*** forcing blood into the ventricles, whereas ventricular systole is the contraction of both ventricles causing blood to exit the heart and flow around the body and to the lungs via the aorta and pulmonary artery respectively. Training can result in an increase in the force at which the heart can contract, due to the thickening of the cardiac muscle (***myocardium***) and therefore the systolic capacity of the heart.

Do you need revision help and advice?

Go to pages 297–330 for a range of revision appendices that include plenty of exam advice and tips.

T-drill: a test of *agility*. The T-drill is a timed test that requires the performer to run forwards 10 metres, side-step to the left for 5 metres to touch a cone, side-step to the right 10 metres to touch a cone, side-step back to the left for 5 metres, and finally run backwards for 10 metres to the starting point. The T-drill can also be used as a training activity for sports such as badminton or netball, all of which require multi-directional movement.

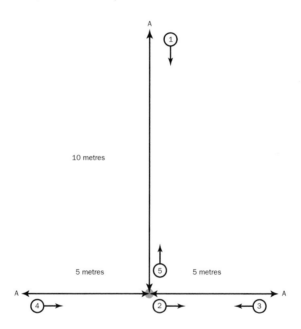

talent identification: a process of finding sporting talent, preferably at a young age, and developing programmes that can help to foster that talent in order to allow it to reach its potential. In addition to identification of skilled performance, testing could also be carried out to ascertain *attitudes*, *abilities* and *personalities*. *UK Sport* has programmes such as Pitch to Podium and Girls4Gold. An example of a systematic talent identification programme was the *East German model*.

Talented Athlete Scholarship Scheme (TASS) is a scheme that fast tracks young sporting talent, the potential medal winners of the future, and is specifically designed to cater for the special needs of athletes within the education system, aiming to reduce the *dropout* of athletes caused by academic and financial pressures. Organisations such as the *English*

Institute of Sport, Sport England, Sports Aid, UK Sport, University College Sport and the national **governing bodies** are all involved in this scheme.

tapering: the reduction of training load prior to competition. As part of the **periodisation** process, the performer reduces the duration (by about one-third) but maintains the intensity of their training in order to be at their peak of fitness. For example, a sprinter will complete fewer repetitions during training sessions and have longer **recovery** periods in order to specifically develop speed rather than endurance.

target game: a game that requires a high degree of accuracy when aiming at a target, which may be stationary or moving. Examples of such games are golf, darts and bowling.

target group: any group identified by **Sport England** as needing special attention in order to raise participation levels. Examples of such groups are women, **ethnic groups**, those aged over 50 and the disabled. These groups have certain factors in common – they are subordinate groups to the dominant group in society which can be classed as white, male, **middle class** and able bodied. Consequently, they share similar problems in participating in physical recreation and sport such as lack of access to specialist facilities, less provision in terms of clubs and less **mass media** coverage with the resulting fewer **role models** to inspire them.

task cohesion: the interaction of **group** members in order to work together effectively to achieve a common goal. Within a group, individuals may not have good **social cohesion**, but may combine their efforts positively to complete the task. For example, within a hockey team several players may not mix socially but they fulfil their roles and help each other to win matches.

task-orientated leader: see *contingency theory of leadership*.

task-oriented goal: see *performance goal*.

teaching: a *physical education* teacher is qualified to teach or instruct children in a range of physical activities. The main focus of the physical education teacher is on the needs and all-round development of the child, rather than aiming for sporting **excellence**. The UK has long had a tradition of keeping school physical education separate from sport **coaching** and hence the poor school–club links that exist as a result. (See also **role (of the teacher/coach)**.)

teaching styles: see *Mosston and Ashworth's spectrum of teaching styles*.

Team GB: the Great Britain and Northern Ireland Olympic Team. Every 2 years, the team represents Great Britain and Northern Ireland in the summer or winter **Olympic Games**. The team is selected by the **British Olympic Association** in conjunction with the national **governing bodies** from the best sportsmen and women to compete in 26 summer and 7 winter Olympic sports at the greatest sporting event in the world. The sportsmen and women who are selected to participate for Great Britain at the Olympic Games become members of Team GB.

There is only one Olympic team from Great Britain: Team GB. There is not an Olympic swimming team or Olympic rowing team. The individual sports join to become Team GB, the Great Britain Olympic team.

technology: the human body seems to be able to reach higher and higher levels of performance – what is helping athletes to improve so dramatically? Technology is undoubtedly the major influence, whether it is in the equipment and facilities or sports science that helps coaching and training methods. Athletic performance is now measured in minute detail, such as timing in the 100-metre sprint. Technology such as Hawk-Eye can help officials in their decisions.

Positive aspects of technology	Negative aspects of technology
Can help officials to make tough decisions	Can give developed countries an advantage
The referee can often choose when to use it	Conflict between governing bodies and manufacturers, e.g. illegal golf clubs
Gives officials confidence	
Can help fans realise the complexity of decisions	Competitions may be changed to accommodate new technology
In tennis, players can apply some choice in their use of technology	May take away human discretion
Can lead to higher, more exciting performances	Must be accurate and may only be useful for certain decisions
Records get broken	Useful in certain sports
Often encourages liaison between sports science, engineering and medicine	Money invested in sports that have a high mass media profile
Analysis of players and referees, e.g. ProZone	
Can assist coaches in their analysis of players or athletes; statistical data	

temporal anticipation: an attempt by a performer to predict when an action of their opponent will occur. For example, a batsman will try to anticipate when the bowler will release their delivery. (See also *spatial anticipation*.)

tendon: connective tissue responsible for attaching *skeletal muscle* to bone. The tendon attaches to the *periosteum* of the bone and transmits the 'muscular pull' to the bone, causing movement. Tendons are composed of collagen fibres, which are extremely strong and can therefore transmit huge forces to the bone, as can be seen in weightlifting. The capacity of a tendon to withstand stress can be improved through *strength training*.

tennis: see *lawn tennis* and *real tennis*.

terminal feedback: see *feedback*.

testosterone: a potent steroid hormone secreted by the testes that can be extracted or synthesised. It is a masculine hormone produced naturally in the body of both males and females. As it is a natural compound and is not easy to detect in *drug testing*. Side effects of using testosterone include the inability of the body to supply its own testosterone. (See also *doping*.)

tetanus: also known as tetanic contraction, this is a sustained muscle contraction when muscle cells are stimulated many times in quick succession to produce one smoothly sustained contraction. This type of contraction not only lasts longer but is several times stronger than a single *muscle twitch*. Performing a handstand in gymnastics, for example, requires the muscles of the shoulder and arm to work continuously for an extended period of time in order to maintain *balance*.

theory of reasoned action: see *Fishbein's attitude theory*.

therapeutic: a term relating to curative practices to maintain health. This was a popular term in the nineteenth century when linked to exercise and the poor health of the *working class*. It was used in *physical education* programmes from *Swedish gymnastics* to the present day *National Curriculum*.

thermoreceptors: a group of sensory cells in the body that detect changes in body temperature. Thermoreceptors form part of the cardiac, respiratory and vasomotor regulatory control centres, providing information relating to body temperature. As temperature rises during exercise, the body responds by increasing heart and respiratory rates while the vasomotor centre redistributes blood to the working muscles and the skin.

thermoregulation: the processes through which core body temperature is maintained. The aim of the thermoregulatory centre is to maintain core body temperature at around 37°C. At the heart of temperature regulation is the hypothalamus – the home of the thermoregulatory centre in the brain. The hypothalamus is sensitive to small temperature changes and reacts to changes in body temperature caused by both internal and environmental factors. The work of the hypothalamus is supported by a number of *thermoreceptors* located around the body which supply information to the hypothalamus, helping it to maintain a constant core temperature. The body disperses heat through a number of different processes:

- *conduction* – the process whereby heat is lost through physical contact between one object and another. The direction of heat flow is always from the warmer to the cooler object. For example, if an athlete sits on a cold metal chair heat will be transferred from their body to the chair
- *convection* – the process of losing heat through contact between the skin and moving air or water molecules. Standing in front of fan blowing out cold air to cool the body down is one example of convection
- *radiation* – a method of losing heat via infrared rays, where heat is transferred to the environment without physical contact with another object. We lose heat through radiation when our body temperature is warmer than the surrounding environment
- *evaporation* – the process by which the body loses heat through the conversion of liquid to a vapour. This is the form of heat loss with which we are perhaps most familiar, and is the major portion of heat loss during exercise as it involves the loss of body heat through sweating.

Thomas Arnold: see *Arnold, Thomas*.

thoracic vertebrae: the second region of the vertebral column containing 12 individual bones. Its function is to enable the 12 pairs of ribs to attach to the vertebral column so that the body's respiratory function can take place. The ribs pivot on the facet of the vertebrae enabling the rib cage to move upwards and outwards. In this way the lungs can inflate and *inspiration* can occur. (See appendix, page 316.)

Thorndike's laws of learning: three laws proposed by Thorndike which, if employed, were said to increase the likelihood of learning taking place during **operant conditioning**. The laws are:

- law of readiness – the performer has to be physically and mentally able to complete the task
- law of exercise – the performer must practice the task regularly in favourable conditions
- law of effect – the performer is more likely to repeat the task if their behaviour is followed by experiences of satisfaction (see **reinforcement** and **punishment**).

thought stopping: recognising and blocking worrying or negative thoughts about performance when they start to develop. As soon as this takes place, a **cue**, action or word is used to redirect **attention** to positive thoughts. For example, a basketball player who has missed several shots and is beginning to worry might click their fingers or say 'focus' to themselves. As a result, they concentrate on the action, technique or tactic for the next attempt, rather than think about the previous attempts. (See also **self-talk**.)

threshold: commonly used to identify the point at which one **energy system** becomes exhausted and another takes over. For example, the ATP–PC/**lactic acid** threshold will signify the point at which the lactic acid becomes the predominant system used in providing energy for resynthesis of **ATP**.

Thurston scale: a **questionnaire** used to evaluate the **attitude** of an individual. It is composed of a series of favourable and unfavourable statements about the **attitude object**. The individual simply agrees or disagrees with each statement and the average is calculated to produce a score, which can be compared with others. (See also **attitude tests**.)

tidal volume: the volume of air inspired or expired per breath. A normal resting volume is approximately 500 ml but this can increase during exercise by using the **inspiratory reserve volume** and **expiratory reserve volume**. Tidal volume can be calculated as follows:

FORMULA: $\text{Tidal volume} = \dfrac{\text{minute ventilation (volume of air inspired or expired in 1 minute)}}{\text{number of breaths taken per minute}}$

(See appendix, page 330.)

Title IX: federal **legislation** in the **USA**, under the education amendment of 1972, relating to the equality of opportunity for women in sport programmes. It made compulsory the equal treatment of men and women in education programmes that were in receipt of federal funding. The Department of Health, Education and Welfare released and enacted it in 1972. It stated that no **discrimination** should occur with respect to the programmes offered, the quality of teaching or the availability of facilities, medical services and travel allowances, and women could take a case as far as the supreme court.

tokenism: actions that are the result of pretending to give advantage to those groups in society who are often treated unfairly, in order to give the appearance of fairness.

Tom Brown's Schooldays: a book written by Thomas Hughes, published in 1860, based at Rugby School. It expanded the ideals of manliness within the **muscular Christianity** movement.

Top Club: see *National Junior Sport Programme*.

Top Play: see *National Junior Sport Programme*.

top spin: a type of spin applied to a projectile such as a tennis ball which causes a deviation of the ball downwards, shortening its expected flight path and thus its flight path to be, as a result of the *Magnus effect.* The boundary layer on the top surface of the ball travels in the opposite direction to the air flow. This slows the flow of air on the top surface creating a zone of high pressure. The boundary layer on the bottom surface travels in the same direction as the oncoming air flow, causing the air to travel more quickly than that on the top surface and creating a zone of low pressure. The pressure differential (high pressure on top of the ball; low pressure below the ball) results in the ball moving towards the low pressure zone, causing it to dip and deviate downwards from the expected flight path when the ball is struck without spin.

Top Sport: see *National Junior Sport Programme*.

torque: the turning effect of a body or object. It is dependent on the force and the length of the *lever* arm. The greater the lever arm or the larger the force, the greater the *rotation*. For example, a rower may increase torque by pulling harder or by lengthening the oar.

total lung capacity: the sum of *residual volume*, *expiratory reserve volume*, *tidal volume* and *inspiratory reserve volume* or, more simply, the volume in the lungs at the end of maximal *inspiration*. Because of the difficulty in measuring an individual's residual volume, it is difficult to give an objective figure to total lung capacity, but it averages around 6000 ml. Through endurance training, it may be possible to strengthen respiratory muscles and improve respiratory efficiency, and consequently increase total lung capacity. (See appendix, page 330.)

tourism: the commercial organisation of tourist travel from a place of residence to a holiday destination or place of interest. Generally, tourists stay long enough in a place to undertake some activities and use the local facilities. The most common motivations for tourism are rest and relaxation, visiting friends and relatives, business, attending festivals, exhibitions, conventions and sporting events. There are various sectors of the tourism industry, including:

- transport, for example air, rail, ferry
- accommodation and catering, for example hotels and restaurants
- tour operators and travel agents
- visitor attractions and events
- services, for example financial, guides, tourist information
- tourism organisations, for example tourist boards.

The increased demand for tourism has gone hand in hand with the growth of *leisure* time generally. There are definite links between leisure and tourism, and sport has been and continues to be an area of high-priority spending for many people. Activities such as cycling, walking and golf have helped to create new resorts, and events like the *Olympic Games* attract thousands of spending visitors. (See the diagram overleaf.)

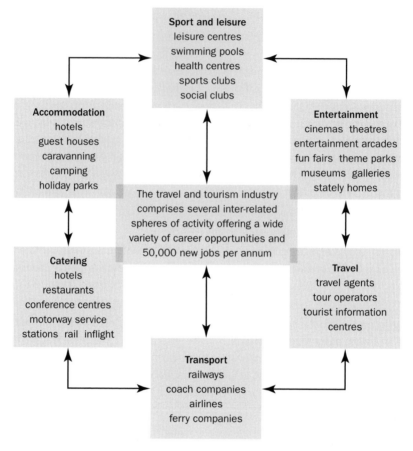

Tourism

trabeculae: the criss-cross matrix of bony plates which makes up *cancellous bone*. Training (particularly *strength training*) can cause an increase in the density of these bony plates thereby strengthening the bones.

trachea: an air passage forming part of the respiratory system extending from the larynx, directing air into the left and right primary bronchi. It is composed of 18 horseshoe-shaped rings of cartilage lined with a mucous membrane and ciliated cells which help to warm, moisten and filter the air ready for *gaseous exchange* in the lungs.

training unit: part of the *periodisation* process, a training unit is typically an individual training session. A number of training units will form a *micro cycle*.

training zone: the rate at which the heart should beat during training to be of benefit to the cardiovascular system. This is best determined using the *Karvonen principle*, but it can be calculated more simply as lying between 60 and 85% of *maximum heart rate*.

trait: an innate, enduring characteristic possessed by an individual that can be used to explain and predict their behaviour in different situations. Traits combine to form an individual's unique *personality*. For example, if a performer displays leadership qualities in one situation, they could do so in other situations. (See also *trait theory*.)

trait anxiety: also known as A trait, this is the general disposition of an individual to perceive situations as threatening. If a performer possesses this characteristic, they are more likely to become anxious in a wide variety of situations, experiencing a higher **state anxiety** than are those with low levels of trait anxiety. Such individuals may develop a high competitive state anxiety when placed in a challenging sporting environment. (See also **competitive trait anxiety**.)

trait sports confidence: also known as SC-trait, this is the stable characteristic of an individual's personality that is relevant to all sporting situations. The situation may be general or specific, for example a basketball player competing in a match or attempting a free-throw. Some performers may appear confident in all situations. (See also **Vealey's model of sport confidence**.)

trait theory: a theory that proposes that the personality of an individual is made up of a number of characteristics or **traits**, which determine their behaviour in particular situations. After completing a **personality test**, individuals are usually placed on two **continuums**:
- **extrovert – introvert**
- **stable personality – neurotic personality.**

It was suggested that because of these specific traits, participation and performance in particular activities could be predicted. For example, extroverts would be more likely to play team sports, while introverts would be drawn towards individual activities. However, this has never been proven conclusively and critics of the theory argue it is too simplistic, failing to take account of the effect of environmental situations and learning experiences. Individuals may have core traits, but behaviour is specific to a particular situation. For example, a professional footballer may appear extrovert on the field, but in private be more introverted and reserved.

transfer of learning: the effect that the leaning or performance of one skill has on the learning or performance of another skill. The coach can apply this knowledge in order to reduce learning time and maximise the effectiveness of training time with the performer. For example, a basketball player might be encouraged to use their skills of handling, movement and spatial awareness when introduced to the game of netball. However, the habit of performing certain skills may hinder their development, such as dribbling and shooting at the basket without the use of a backboard. Various forms of transfer exist, as outlined below:
- positive transfer – previously learned skills that aid the learning of new skills, such as the basketball player utilising their passing skills when playing netball. To be effective, practices should be relevant to those experienced in a game situation so that both skills and tactical decisions can be transferred. The performer should be aware of this form of transfer and possible links between skills should be encouraged
- negative transfer – previously learned skills that hinder the learning of new skills, such as the basketball player wishing to dribble the ball. Usually this is temporary and can be eliminated with careful construction of training practices, informing the performer of difficulties of which to be aware and allowing them the opportunity to reorganise their cognitive processes to adjust their **movement patterns**
- pro-active transfer – occurs when a skill currently being learned has an effect on a skill in the future. For example, the basketball player will learn the basic techniques of passing, footwork and dribbling before moving on to more advanced skills or implementing them in a game situation

- retro-active transfer – occurs when a skill currently being learned has an effect on one previously learnt. For example, the basketball player may develop new methods of dribbling the ball as they become more experienced and alter their initial technique, allowing them to execute more complex moves
- bilateral transfer – the transfer of learning from one limb to another, rather than task to task. The development of a skill with one limb will improve the performance of the opposite limb. There is no clear evidence as to why this occurs, but possibly the cognitive process of knowing how to complete the action and the creation of a generalised motor programme allows for adaptation. For example, games players are encouraged to practice their skills with both the left and right sides of their body, such as passing, dribbling and kicking, in order to improve their overall performance
- zero transfer – occurs when the learning of one skill has no influence on the development of another skill. For example, the skills of a basketball player would not affect the skills executed during a rock climb
- near transfer – occurs when the performer experiences practices which are similar to the 'real game'. For example, the basketball players may have to shoot from outside a zone defence or practice moves to execute when confronted with a 2 v 1 option, which they may have to face in a match
- far transfer – occurs when the performer experiences practices that develop general skills or tactics, which may be used later in more specific situations. For example, a coach may use a variety of small-sided games to develop the handling and movement skills of novices, which may be transferred later to a game of basketball or other ball game.

transitional economies: see *economic system*.

translatory mechanism: see *decision-making*.

transport revolution: the vast improvement made to the communication system in the nineteenth century. This included the expansion of the *railways*, canals and roads, which allowed people, ideas, services and goods to become mobile and spread around the country.

transverse abdominis: a major contributory muscle to *core stability*, the transverse abdominis is the deepest layer of abdominal muscles which act just like a corset or a weight-training belt. It stabilises the spine and helps compress the internal organs. In doing so, it stabilises the lower back and pelvis *before* movement of the arms and/or legs occurs. Good core stability allows the muscles that put the limbs of the body into action to generate greater forces by pulling against a more stable base, in this case the trunk.

transverse plane: also known as the horizontal axis/plane, this is an imaginary line running horizontally across the body, dividing it into superior (top) and inferior (bottom) sections. A person performing a tucked front somersault, for example, will rotate about the transverse axis. (See appendix, page 314.)

triadic model: see *attitude*.

trochanter: a very large protrusion found on the surface of a bone. The best examples include the greater and lesser trochanter found on the femur.

trust funds: the means for an amateur athlete to receive money from their sport. They are managed by *governing bodies* and accept money from subventions, *advertising* services or as participation money. They will be held until retirement from sport, but funds for athletic expenses can be withdrawn before retirement.

Tudor period: the era between 1485 and 1714. England changed rapidly during the time of the Tudors, and under the rule of King Henry VIII there was greater prosperity and more time for cultural pursuits like music, literature and the theatre. He was a great sports lover and created one of the liveliest courts in Europe. He participated in all-day hunts, wrestling and ordered his own *real tennis* court to be built at Hampton Court. Access to education, equipment and facilities allowed the *upper class* the privilege of exclusive recreational activities. Under Queen Elizabeth I, England prospered leading to the age of the Renaissance gentleman who was knowledgeable, took part in physical activities and was appreciative of art forms, while the mass of the population enjoyed their traditional pastimes of *mob games* and *animal sports*.

twenty-five metre hop test: from a flying start, the subject hops the 25-metre distance and the time is recorded. The test is performed first with the dominant leg followed by the non-dominant leg. The average time of the two attempts is calculated and compared to the table below.

% rank	Females	Males
91–100	3.13–3.75 secs	2.70–3.25 secs
81–90	3.76–4.50 secs	3.36–3.90 secs
71–80	4.51–5.70 secs	3.91–5.00 secs
61–70	5.71–6.90 secs	5.01–6.10 secs
51–60	6.91–8.15 secs	6.11–7.20 secs
41–50	8.16–8.90 secs	7.21–7.90 secs
31–40	8.91–9.45 secs	7.91–8.40 secs
21–30	9.46–10.05 secs	8.41–8.95 secs
11–20	10.06–10.34 secs	8.96–9.25 secs

Advantages of 25 m hop test	Disadvantages of 25 m hop test
Validity in testing the *elastic strength* of the legs is high	Timing is open to human error, although this can be rectified through the use of timing gates
Provides baseline data for self-comparison to judge improvement	

type A personality: a set of personality characteristics which, when present together, increase the risk of stress-related heart disease. Performers who may fall into this category are often competitive, self-critical, feel they are working against the clock, often multi-tasking and avoid delegation, preferring to complete the work themselves. Some type A performers are capable of achieving success and appear to be fully in control of situations. (See also *type B personality*.)

type B personality: a set of personality characteristics that may indicate a lower reaction to stressful structures. In comparison to *type A personality* performers, they are more relaxed, less competitive, delegate tasks easily, and are more tolerant and calmer when dealing with problem situations.

UK Sport: the organisation responsible for developing *elite* sport in the UK. Its main aim is to provide the best sportsmen and women with the support they need to compete and win at the highest level, with the express aim of achieving sporting *excellence* on the world stage. It takes the lead among the sports councils (England, Northern Ireland, Scotland and Wales) in all aspects of sport that require coordination or representation for the benefit of the UK as a whole. It has a range of objectives:

- to encourage and develop higher standards of sporting excellence in the UK
- to identify sporting policies that should have a UK-wide application such as sports science, *sports medicine*, drug control and *coaching*
- to identify areas of unnecessary duplication, overlap and waste in the way that sport is administered in the UK
- to develop and deliver appropriate grant programmes developed by the *governing bodies* with a UK or Great Britain remit in conjunction with the home country sports councils
- to coordinate policy for bringing major international sporting events to the UK
- to represent the UK internationally and increase the influence of the UK at an international level.

It delivers these objectives via four key directorates:

- Performance Development
- *UK Sports Institute*
- International Relations and Major Events
- Ethics and Anti-Doping.

UK Sport's World Class Events Programme reached new heights in 2008, with 17 major events supported throughout the year, including a record six World Championships. A total of £3.6 million of *National Lottery* funds were invested to bring events such as the UCI World Track Cycling Championships, the FINA World Swimming Championships and the World Cross Country Championships to the UK.

UK Sport runs the *World Class Performance Pathway*.

UK sport system: the sport system in the UK started from the *grass roots* level and the formation of *clubs*. Groups of clubs then developed *governing bodies* to administer their affairs. Therefore, there was initially no government involvement and the UK has managed to restrict the power of politicians compared with countries like the *USA* and *Australia*.

There has traditionally been little sport *legislation* and the ***Central Council of Physical Recreation***, ***Sport England*** and the ***British Olympic Association*** remain autonomous.

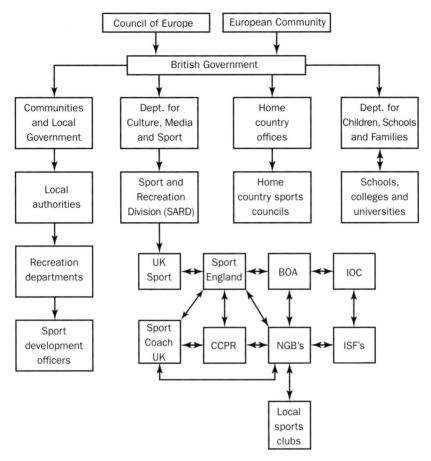

UK sport system

UK Sports Institute (UKSI) is a series of regional satellite centres coordinated by Central Services in London with the purpose of developing *elite* performers. The idea of an institute was raised by the government in its report ***Sport: Raising the Game*** of July 1995. The views of sports administrators, coaches and elite athletes were sought, with the concept being to focus on the needs of top-level performers and those with talent and commitment to succeed. As well as providing world-class training facilities, UKSI provides a support structure including coaching, sport science and medical expertise. The responsibilities of the UKSI are subdivided:

- ***UK Sport*** – coordinates central services, which administer the medical insurance scheme ***Athlete Career and Education Programme (ACE UK)***, Coach Development Programme and Web-based Access training
- home country sports councils (***Sports Council for Wales***, ***Sport Northern Ireland*** and ***sportscotland***) – coordinate regional satellite centres.

USA: the world's fourth largest country composed of 52 states based on a federal system, where the powers of government are divided between both national state and provincial governments. It is an *egalitarian*, *pluralistic* and *multicultural* society, where the dream of success is made possible whatever your social background. (See also *US sport system*.)

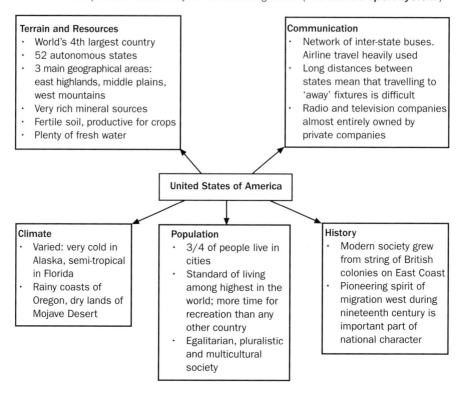

Terrain and Resources
- World's 4th largest country
- 52 autonomous states
- 3 main geographical areas: east highlands, middle plains, west mountains
- Very rich mineral sources
- Fertile soil, productive for crops
- Plenty of fresh water

Communication
- Network of inter-state buses. Airline travel heavily used
- Long distances between states mean that travelling to 'away' fixtures is difficult
- Radio and television companies almost entirely owned by private companies

United States of America

Climate
- Varied: very cold in Alaska, semi-tropical in Florida
- Rainy coasts of Oregon, dry lands of Mojave Desert

Population
- 3/4 of people live in cities
- Standard of living among highest in the world; more time for recreation than any other country
- Egalitarian, pluralistic and multicultural society

History
- Modern society grew from string of British colonies on East Coast
- Pioneering spirit of migration west during nineteenth century is important part of national character

US sport system: this system operates at four main levels:
- high school – interscholastic competition
- *collegiate* and university – the large institutions are controlled by the National Collegiate Athletic Association
- amateur – individual *governing bodies* control their sport, for example the Amateur Athletic Union
- professional – each *professional sport* has its own association, for example the National Basketball Association. Professional sport is the ambition of most sport performers, where they can earn lucrative lifestyles.

unbalanced forces: forces on a body that act in opposite directions but are unequal. This will result in a *net force* and the state of motion will be changed in the direction of the larger force. Unbalanced forces occur where a force acting in one direction is larger than that acting in the opposite direction. This causes an object or body to move or accelerate/decelerate in the direction of the greater force. For example, a high jumper is able to accelerate upwards because the *reaction force* is greater than the weight force:

FORMULA: Reaction force = weight force + applied muscular force

(See also *balanced forces*.)

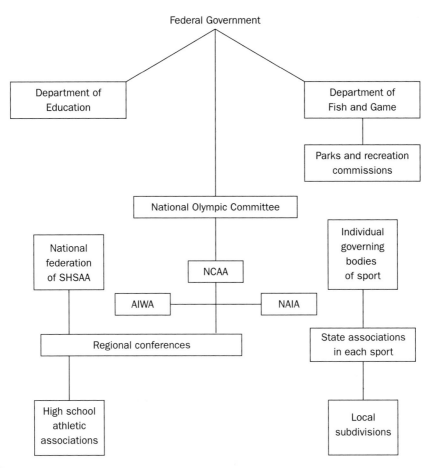

US sport system

unsaturated fat: a type of *fat* that should be included in everyone's diet. Unsaturated fats are sometimes referred to as 'good' fats as they perform some vital functions in the body. They can help reduce blood cholesterol levels and provide us with the essential *fatty acids* that the body needs to function properly. Unsaturated fats are divided into two groups:

- *polyunsaturated fat* – found in fatty fish like salmon, tuna and sardines, and in oils like corn oil, sunflower oil and soyabean oil
- *monounsaturated fat* – found in some nuts (e.g. peanuts, almonds, hazelnuts and pecans) as well as in certain oils like canola oil and olive oil.

Omega 3 fatty acids, which are a type of unsaturated fat found in oily fish, help to prevent heart disease. Therefore, it is a good idea to eat some foods that are rich in unsaturated fat as part of a healthy diet.

upper class: a term used to denote the dominant group in society. It traditionally concentrates on the aristocratic families who held power up until the first half of the twentieth century.

upward social mobility: the movement of an individual from a subordinate position in society to a higher or more powerful one. Education and sport are both avenues of *social mobility*.

urban areas are usually characterised by a high-density population living in towns or cities with people mainly occupied in manufacturing and service jobs. These areas grew considerably during the *Industrial Revolution*.

urban revolution: see *urbanisation*.

urbanisation: the process whereby the mass of a population changes its lifestyle from living in villages and rural areas to living in towns and cities. This was one of the greatest legacies of the *Industrial Revolution* in the nineteenth century. One impact was the loss of space and the consequent loss of the 'old ways of playing' such as *mob* football (see *mob games*).

validity: the ability of a test or measurement to produce accurate results that can be relied on. There are two forms of validity:

- internal validity – the ability of a test to produce the required data, with all possible variables kept to a minimum
- external validity – the ability to apply the data produced to a wider population. Often research conducted in laboratory conditions has lower external validity when compared with that completed in field experiments using a larger section of the population.

For example, the **sit-and-reach test** can be said to have both internal and external validity, as it measures the **flexibility** of the athlete's hips, which can then be graded in comparison with other performers.

values: the moral principles and beliefs of a person or social group. Within society the accepted values are often determined by the **dominant culture**. Examples include respect for property and honesty, while in a sporting environment the concept of **sportsmanship** is encouraged. Individuals or groups can accept or reject such values, consequently influencing the formation of their **attitude**.

variable practice: a type of practice in which the coach develops the skills of the performer using a mixture of **massed practice** and **distributed practice** methods. The choice of practice will vary depending on the nature of the group, task and situation. This will not only maximise learning but also maintain **motivation** and reduce **fatigue** when appropriate. For example, a coach may use massed practice for passing drills, but later use distributed practice to develop set moves performed at high intensity.

vasoconstriction: the narrowing of blood vessels, resulting in increased **blood pressure** and hence an increase in the speed at which the blood flows round the body. It is central to the process of blood **shunting** during exercise, where blood is diverted towards the working **skeletal muscles**.

vasodilation: the widening of blood vessels, resulting in decreased **blood pressure**. Vasodilation occurs after exercise, leading to a drop in blood pressure to its normal level. It is essential to the process of blood **shunting** during exercise to ensure that optimal volumes of blood and nutrients can reach the working muscles.

Vealey's model of sport confidence is 'the belief or degree of certainty individuals possess about their ability to be successful in sport'. The model suggests that each performer will approach particular situations from a different perspective due to several factors. Everyone has innate levels of confidence, known as **trait sports confidence** (SC-trait), which is applied to an objective sport situation. The situation may be general or specific, such as a basketball player competing in a match or attempting a free-throw.

The level of confidence is also influenced by the player's **competitiveness orientation**. This refers to how the individual perceives success and the type of goals used to judge their performance. The goals may be performance- or outcome-based depending on the nature of the task and consultation with the coach.

When trait sports confidence and competitive orientation combine, the result is the actual level of confidence or **self-efficacy** experienced by the performer. This is known as **state sports confidence** (SC-state). The level of confidence can then influence the behaviour and skill level displayed by the individual. Obviously, the more **self-confidence** the player has, the better their performance should be; the reverse is also true. After the match or event the player will judge their performance, giving subjective outcomes and providing **attributions** for their success or failure. This is turn will cause emotional responses of either satisfaction or disappointment, which will influence future behaviour patterns, resulting in either **approach behaviour** or **avoidance behaviour**.

Vealey's model of sport confidence

vector quantity: a biomechanical term referring to a quantity that has both size (magnitude) and direction. For example, the difference between **speed** and **velocity** is that speed can occur in any direction, whereas the velocity of a body must have a specified direction. Velocity is therefore a vector quantity.

vein: a blood vessel that conducts blood away from **skeletal muscle** and other tissues back to the heart.

velocity: the rate at which a body moves in a specified direction. It is measured in metres per second (m/s) and is calculated by:

FORMULA: $\text{Velocity} = \dfrac{\text{displacement}}{\text{time}}$

Velocity can occur in a straight line (linear velocity) or with *rotation* (*angular velocity*), and is a fundamental element of many sporting activities. These include the 100-metre sprinter whose aim is to cover the distance of 100 m in a straight line in the shortest possible time, and the trampolinist performing a triple back somersault who must ensure sufficient rotation and angular velocity to complete the task successfully. Velocity is a vector quantity.

venous return mechanism: the process by which the blood returns to the right side of the heart via the *veins*. At rest, the venous system (veins) contains up to 70% of the total volume of blood. This is important since it acts as a reservoir of blood for when it is needed, such as when exercising.

The body relies on its venous return mechanism in order to ensure an adequate supply of blood during exercise. This is because the more blood that returns to the heart, the more blood can be pumped out. Essentially, there are two 'pumps' involved in this process: the *muscle pump* and the *respiratory pump*. The muscle pump consists of the contracting *skeletal muscles* squeezing the veins and forcing the blood held within them towards the heart. Pocket valves within the veins ensure that blood flows only one way towards the heart, without any back flow. The respiratory pump relies on the changes in pressure that occur in the thoracic cavity during *inspiration* and *expiration*. This can cause compression of the veins, resulting in blood being 'sucked' into the heart. Other contributory factors to the venous return mechanism include gravity and smooth muscle.

verbal guidance: see *guidance*.

Veroff's stages of achievement motivation proposes that the *achievement motivation* of a performer develops in three distinct phases:

1   Autonomous competence stage – occurs during the first 5 years of a child's life when they master basic skills, only evaluating their actions against their own intrinsic goals, not those of other people. For example, the repeated throwing and catching of a ball to themselves until competent.
2   Social comparison stage – occurs from the age of 5 onwards, when individuals compare their actions and performance with those of others in their peer group. Some individuals will continually seek out competition to evaluate their skills, either in terms of end result or performance, and when content, progress to the final stage.
3   Integrated stage – occurs at any age, depending on the experiences and development of the individual. It is based on both internal and external standards. It allows the performer to alter their level of motivation depending on the requirements of different situations.

vicarious experiences: see *self-efficacy*.

Victorian era: the period of the reign of Queen Victoria from 1837 to 1901. Under her reign there was a period of dramatic social change that was reflected in the structure and organisation of games and sports. The social changes that occurred during this era include:

● social reformers campaigned for improvements in the physical and mental health of workers in society
● parliament passed many Acts such as the Ten Hour Act 1847 and the Municipal Reform Act 1835

- half day Saturday and early closing Wednesday began, increasing the *leisure* time of the *working class*
- *rational recreation* developed rapidly
- the working class became entitled to free education following the Forster Education Act 1870 (see *Education Acts*).

Victorian Institute of Sport (VIS) is a sporting establishment in the state of Victoria, *Australia* with the responsibility of promoting sporting *excellence*. It was established in 1990. Each state has its own institute, each of which is supported financially by the government and private sectors. Individual sports bodies can apply for admission and, if successful, the athletes will have access to advanced *coaching*, such as fitness, skill, tactical and psychological aspects of their chosen sport; competitive opportunities at national and international events; and career development in terms of personal skills, education and future employment prospects.

visual guidance: see *guidance*.

visualisation: see *imagery*.

VO$_2$ max: see *maximum oxygen uptake*.

vocational applies to skills needed for an occupation, trade or profession. This can mean sport as a means of employment; the link between work and *leisure*; the different *social classes*: the *upper class* as the landed gentry and the *middle class* as the white-collar workers; the *working class* with little recreation.

voluntary associations are those organisations that individuals choose to belong to and usually freely donate their home, skills and money towards the running of. An example would be a sports club. The *UK sports system* is based on this foundation.

voluntary provision: see *leisure provision*.

volunteers: people who work for no payment. Many sports events could not take place without the services of unpaid officials. Numerous schemes such as *sports leaders awards* and *Step into Sport* promote volunteering as a desirable skill, enhancing an individual's personal qualities as well as positively contributing to the community.

volunteers in sport are individuals who help others in sport through formal organisations such as *clubs* or *governing bodies*, while receiving no remuneration except expenses. There is universal acceptance of the important contribution and vital role volunteers make to the development of sport as coaches, administrators, managers and officials. The estimated number of volunteers is three times that of those working in paid employment in sports-related activity. For major sporting events such as the *Commonwealth Games*, it is not unusual for competitors to be outnumbered by volunteers.

WADA: see *World Anti-Doping Agency.*

wake: a watch or vigil held over the body of a dead person before burial and sometimes accompanied by festivity. Also, in England, a vigil kept in commemoration of the dedication of a parish church. The latter type of wake consisted of an all-night service of prayer and meditation in the church. These services, officially termed 'vigiliae' by the **Church**, appear to have existed from the earliest days of Anglo-Saxon Christianity. Each parish kept the day following its vigil as a holiday. Activities such as animal **baiting**, dog fighting and cock fighting were common.

Wakes soon degenerated into fairs; people from neighbouring parishes journeyed over to join in the merrymaking, and the revelry and drunkenness became controversial. As the days usually chosen for church dedications were Sundays or Saints' days, the abuse seemed all the more scandalous. In industrial England, wakes became an annual holiday in various towns in northern England, when the local factories would close down. Community holidays to places such as Blackpool became the norm and later holiday camps such as Butlins helped to foster a similar community spirit.

warm-up: a period of light activity and stretching exercises undertaken prior to the commencement of any exercise. Not only does a warm-up ensure that the body is ready for exercise, it also prevents injury and muscle soreness. Where possible, warm-ups should be specific to the activity that follows and prepare the appropriate muscles and the **energy systems**. A warm-up consists of three stages:

1   a period of light continuous activity, such as jogging, which raises heart rate and body temperature and prepares the body for stage 2
2   stretching activities can follow now that the muscles are warm. Stretches should aim to take the muscles through their full range and each should be held for a minimum of 15 seconds. It may be necessary to replicate movements from the activity that follows to ensure that the muscles are fully prepared. For example, a long jumper may perform some bounding exercises
3   skill-related practices should form the basis of the third stage, which works the neuromuscular mechanisms. For example, shooting baskets in basketball, practising turns in swimming or serving in tennis.

wars: see *Boer War*, *World War I* and *World War II*.

Washhouse Act: *legislation* under the Public Baths and Washhouses Act 1846, which was to increase the provision of public baths. The main aim was to clean up the **working class**. Large towns would have separate baths for the different **social classes**, which were called 'penny baths' because there was a fixed limit on charges for the second-class facilities. Swimming, water polo and diving were developed as a result of these social changes.

W

WASP: a term that originated with reference to White Americans of Anglo-Saxon descent, who were Protestant in religious affiliation ('White Anglo-Saxon Protestant'). It is generally used to describe those who formed a powerful elite. For our purposes the term reflects that segment of the *USA* population that founded the nation and has largely negative connotations today. Less than 25% of the US population is technically WASP. Nevertheless, they continue to have disproportionate influence over American institutions. They would be the group with the greatest access to opportunities, provision and *esteem*.

water: as the body's major component, water is an essential ingredient for successful exercise performance. It is the main constituent of the blood, providing the means of transport in the body for all that is required to produce energy such as oxygen, nutrients, hormones and *enzymes*. Similarly, water makes the disposal of harmful waste products and toxins resulting from exercise possible. Water is also fundamental in the maintenance and regulation of the core temperature of the body, particularly important when exercising in warm environments.

water–electrolyte balance: considered a nutritional *ergogenic aid*, the consumption of water and a range of sports drinks is chiefly designed to replace fluids and *electrolytes* lost by sweating and boost blood glucose levels. Ahead of competition, performers will need to consider their fluid intake in order to prevent *dehydration*. Losing the equivalent of 2% of your body weight as sweat can impair performance by up to 10–20%. If you do not replace the lost *water*, core body temperature will rise which brings with it a number of performance inhibitors. The blood becomes thicker or more viscous (*hyperviscosity*), which slows down the flow to the working muscles. To try and compensate, the heart beats faster, putting the body under greater stress. This increase in heart rate is referred to as cardiovascular drift. The loss of electrolytes through sweating can cause *fatigue* and cramps, so it is essential that performers remain hydrated. As a general rule it is recommended that approximately 15 minutes before training or competition performers should drink 400–500 ml of fluid, whereas during exercise 150–200 ml should be drunk every 15–20 minutes.

Isotonic sports drinks are designed to replace electrolytes lost through sweating. The main electrolytes include sodium, potassium and chlorine, which help to maintain the correct rate of exchange of nutrients and waste products in to and out of the muscle cells so that effective muscle contraction can take place. Hypertonic (high levels of *carbohydrate* content) and hypotonic (lower levels of carbohydrate content) sports drinks, on the other hand, can provide a well-needed boost to blood glucose levels for the performer exercising for over an hour or so.

Advantages (perceived benefits)	Disadvantages (associated health risks)
Fluid replacement prevents dehydration	Drinking too much fluid can dilute levels of blood sodium and induce fatigue – a condition known as hyponatremia
Isotonic sports drinks maintain levels of electrolytes in the body, which allows the muscle cells to function properly	
Hypotonic and hypertonic sports drinks can help to maintain blood glucose levels during endurance activity	

wave summation: a method of increasing the force of contraction of a muscle that results when *stimuli* (nerve impulses) arrive in rapid succession. On receipt of a nerve impulse, a muscle fibre will go through a period of contraction followed by a period of relaxation. This is known as a **muscle twitch**. If a second impulse arrives at the muscle fibre before it has had time to relax, the muscle responds with a stronger contraction since the effect of the second stimulus is added to that of the first. This is known as wave summation and is illustrated in the diagram below. In order to overcome great forces such as in weightlifting, the brain must constantly fire impulses to the muscle to ensure that the contraction is strong enough to overcome the resistance.

A = Muscle twitch
B = Wave summation
C = Tetanus
S = Stimulus

weight force: the force that a given mass feels due to gravity. As weight always acts downwards from the **centre of mass**, it has a direction as well as a magnitude. Weight is therefore a vector quantity. Mass, on the other hand, only has size (no direction) and so is a scalar quantity. Weight is a force and as such is measured in **newtons** (N).

weight training: see *strength training*.

Weiner's model of attribution: see *attribution theory*.

Western European sport: sport that has developed in Western Europe, where it is run by both governmental and non-governmental organisations. It is a result of private and public interest and activity.

White Australia policy: an Anglo-Celtic creation to keep *Australia* free of immigration from the East; it was not until the 1950s that large numbers of people from Europe and Asia were accepted. This policy also limited the amount of friction between different religious sects and was mainly restricted to the Protestant–Catholic divide.

whole-method practice: a practice method in which the performer attempts to complete the entire movement after observing a **demonstration** or being given verbal instructions. This form of **practice** has the advantage of helping the individual to experience and develop the feel or **kinaesthetic** awareness of the whole action, allowing them to begin to understand the relationship between the different phases. It can be used when learning to catch and throw a ball, swing a golf club or throw a javelin. It is advisable to use this method when the performer is motivated, experienced and possesses high levels of attention, or with skills that are simple, discrete, ballistic in nature and comprised of easily interlinked **subroutines**.

whole-part-whole method practice: a combination of the *whole-method practice* and *part-method practice*. This format utilises the benefits of each, allowing the performer to gain experience and understanding of the complete skill before refining specific

w

subroutines. For example, a long jumper may be taught the basic technique and after several attempts complete drills to develop the take-off and flight phases.

whole sport plan (WSP) is a national *governing body* plan for the whole of a sport from *grass roots* right through to *elite* level, which identifies how it will achieve its vision and how it will contribute to *Sport England*'s *Framework for Sport in England*. Whole sport plans will identify the help and resources national governing bodies need, for example via partners such as county sports partnerships and programmes (e.g. the *Physical Education, School Sport and Club Links (PESSCL) strategy*). They will give the population the opportunity to measure how the governing bodies are delivering their sports.

wilderness areas: tracts of land that are uninhabited, uncultivated and isolated. Countries like the *USA* and *Australia* all have such geographical features, whereas the UK, which is relatively small and densely populated, does not. This type of land provides access for outdoor pursuit activities in extreme conditions. Within Britain the nearest equivalent would be *National Parks*.

William Clarke XI was a professional player who was the first person to organise a national professional touring side in 1847, realising the possibility of making money and running parallel to the gentry teams like Marylebone Cricket Club. County gentlemen's clubs raised sides to play the England XI and huge crowds turned out to see cricket of the highest standard for the day. This was one of the major influencing factors in making cricket popular across the country.

win ethic: see *Lombardian ethic*.

Wingate cycle test: a fitness test designed to measure *anaerobic* capacity. This test involves the subject pedalling as fast as possible on a cycle ergometer for 30 seconds (against a resistance adjusted for body weight – usually 75 g/kg body weight). The number of revolutions pedalled by the subject per 5 seconds of the test are counted. The test is able to determine:

- mean power – the average work output over the 30-second test period
- peak power – the highest power output in a 5-second period
- fatigue index – the difference between peak power and the lowest output of 5 seconds divided by peak power.

The Wingate cycle test is of use to the exercise physiologist or coach, since it can assess an athlete's maximum capacity over a 30-second period. If, for example, an athlete fatigues rapidly after 15 seconds the coach may need to adjust the training programme to accommodate more endurance-based work. More recently, the Wingate cycle test has been developed to assess the anaerobic capacity of the arms, which is obviously of benefit to performers such as swimmers and rowers.

women in sport: an issue that focuses on the role of women in sport. Traditionally, women have participated in sport to a lesser extent than men, even though they comprise approximately half the population. This has occurred in most *cultures* and is an issue that extends far beyond the world of sport and into society generally. The major basis for sexual *discrimination* in sport have been biological differences (women are deemed less well suitable physically and physiologically to certain sports than men); sexual *stereotyping* and the domestic role of women which has left them less *leisure* time in which to pursue their sporting interests. Efforts to counter the problems include:

- Equal Pay Act 1970
- *Sex Discrimination Act* 1975
- *Title IX*
- *Brighton Declaration on Women and Sport*.

Women's Sport Foundation (WSF) is a voluntary organisation promoting the interests of women and girls in sport and recreation. There is a network of regional groups and a wide range of activities and events are organised. Their regular publication is *Women in Sport* magazine.

work done: the product of the force applied to an object and the distance through which the body moves in the direction of the force:

FORMULA: Work done = force (N) × distance (m)

work–life balance is the relative importance of work and personal life to a particular individual. An imbalance (where work commitments and career ambition prevail over family or *leisure* commitments) can lead to *stress*, which is a contributory factor to chronic illnesses such as cardiovascular disease.

work-to-relief ratio: a method of expressing the length of the rest or *recovery* period during an *interval training* session. A work-to-relief ratio of 1:3, for example, means that the resting interval is three times longer than the work period.

working class: the position in the social structure occupied mainly by manual labourers. This is changing as machinery takes over the need for physical labour. Traditionally, this class within society has been linked with *low culture*.

working memory: see *short-term memory store*.

World Anti-Doping Agency (WADA) is the World Conference on Doping in Sport held in Lausanne on 2–4 February 1999, which produced the Lausanne Declaration on Doping in Sport. This document provided for the creation of an independent international anti-doping agency to be fully operational for the *Olympic Games* to be held in 2000 in Sydney, *Australia*. WADA was set up as a foundation under the initiative of the *International Olympic Committee* with the support and participation of intergovernmental organisations, governments, public authorities and other public and private bodies fighting against *doping* in sport. The agency consists of equal representatives from the Olympic movement and public authorities. WADA works towards a vision of the world that values and fosters doping-free sport. One of its most important achievements to date has been the drafting, acceptance and implementation of a harmonised set of anti-doping rules, the World Anti-Doping Code, which were revised 2009.

World Class Performance Pathway: to ensure that the UK's most talented athletes have every chance of realising their potential, UK Sport has created the World Class Performance Pathway. This covers all summer Olympic and Paralympic sports, together with the high-performing winter Olympic sports, and operates at three levels:

1 World Class Talent – designed to support the identification and confirmation of athletes who have the potential to progress through the World Class Performance Pathway with the help of targeted investment

293

2   World Class Development – comprising of athletes whose performances have suggested that they have realistic medal-winning capabilities for 2012 and newly funded sports that are demonstrating the ability to be competitive by 2012

3   World Class Podium – supporting athletes with realistic medal-winning capabilities at the next *Olympic Games*/*Paralympic Games* (i.e. a maximum of 4 years away from the podium).

World Games: founded in 1981, the International World Games Association (IWGA) is a non-governmental international organisation. Made up of international sports federations, the IWGA administers a multi-disciplinary sports event, the World Games, which is held every 4 years in the years following the *Olympic Games*. Competitions are held at the highest level in a multitude of diverse, popular and spectacular sports. The world's best athletes in these 32 sports unite in their common search for *excellence* during the World Games.

World War I (1914–18) is also known as the Great War. This conflict was fought mainly in Europe and the Middle East, in which the Allies (France, Russia, Britain, Italy and the USA after 1915) defeated the Central Powers (Germany, Austria, Hungary and Turkey). Millions were to die in static trench warfare. *Nationalism* came to the fore and public school men were enthused with idealism about the coming conflict as if it were a football match. The football match between Britain and German soldiers at Christmas 1914 set the tone for the role of sport during the entire war. Football grounds were used extensively for recruiting, although eventually the *Football League* bowed to moral pressure to stop fixtures for the duration of the conflict. Following the war there were hopes of a more equal society, but this was not immediately realised.

World War II (1939–45) is the war in which Britain and France declared war on Germany as a result of the German invasion of Poland. After this war there was an extensive rebuilding programme and new sports facilities were more sophisticated than ever before. The *therapeutic* effect of recreational activities was once again highlighted. Commando training during the war had developed the use of obstacle training and the first apparatus began to appear in schools. The *movement approach* was adopted in *physical education* lessons in schools, with the Butler Education Act 1944 (see *Education Acts*) reforming education in Britain.

wrestling: an individual *combat* activity; strength, skill and stamina combine to make it one of the most basic sports. Its origins are ancient and are illustrated in wall paintings in ancient Greece, Egypt and China. In Britain it was popular from the village green to the royal court.

Nations developed their own styles of wrestling and Britain was no exception. Notable ones were:

- Cumberland and Westmoreland – commence chest to chest, 'take hold' round the body. Competitors were allowed to use all legitimate means to throw
- Devon and Cornwall – bouts controlled by three judges called 'sticklers'. The wrestlers wore jackets and had to hold collar and sleeve.

This activity took place at fairs, as part of *prizefighting* and in music halls. Later developments included safety considerations, with the introduction of weight categories, rules, training, preparation and referees.

Yerkes and Dobson's theory: see *inverted U theory*.

YMCA: a non-sectarian, non-political Christian lay movement that was established in London in 1844. Its aims were to develop high standards of Christian character through group activities and improve the spiritual, social, recreational and physical life of young people. The games of basketball and volleyball developed directly through this organisation in the USA in the nineteenth century. They were designed to enable young and middle-aged men to enjoy using indoor facilities. Later, a similar association was established specifically for women, the YWCA.

youth movements are organisations providing *leisure* activities for young people, often associated with a church. During the nineteenth century the invention of adolescence as an age-defined social cohort segregated the young from adult status and created a social problem whose solution became the provision of adult-supervised leisure pursuits. The *middle class* were to use the combination of *evangelical* Christianity, *public school* manliness, militarism and imperialism to instil their values in the middle class. The gradual loss of control by the established *Church* led to the middle class organising the leisure of adolescents. Youth movements were seen as a way to curb juvenile restlessness. Examples of such movements were the *Boys' Brigade*, the Church Lads' Brigade, the Scout movement and the Girl Guides.

Youth movements helped to:
- smooth the way for upper-working class and lower-middle class into the urban industrial order of British society
- instil religious, moral and militaristic values
- provide an opportunity for the working class to experience something of the elite public school education and values
- provide a mass leisure outlet for working class adolescents controlled by middle-class adults
- provide opportunities for outdoor activity
- promote acceptance by young people of social order.

Youth Sports Trust (YST) is a registered charity set up in 1994 to improve sporting provision for young people in the UK. Its mission is to develop and implement a linked series of quality sports programmes, known under the umbrella term as the *National Junior Sports Programme*. The Trust also works alongside the Department for Children, Schools and Families to support maintained secondary schools that are applying for specialist sports college status.

Zajonc's theory: see *social facilitation*.

zero transfer: see *transfer of learning*.

zig-zag test: a fitness test designed to measure *agility*. Similar to the *Illinois agility run test*, it requires the athlete to run a course in the shortest possible time. A rectangle measuring 3 m by 4.8 m is marked out by four cones, with one cone placed in the centre of the rectangle. The subject starts at cone 1, runs to the centre cone, then on to cones 2 and 3, back to the centre cone, and finally to cone 4 and back to cone 1. The time taken in completing the course are compared with standard tables. Some coaches prefer this test to the Illinois agility run test as the total distance covered is shorter and therefore *fatigue* does not become an issue.

zone of optimal functioning: the unique level of *arousal* for an athlete, which allows them to perform with maximum concentration and effort. Within a team, each player may have a different optimal arousal level and must work in conjunction with the coach to find how to reach and maintain this zone to function effectively in the match. Rather than occurring at the mid-point of the arousal *continuum* and at a specific point, there is an optimal band-width or area in which the performer achieves their maximum *attention* capacity.

When 'in the zone', the athlete often experiences the feeling of the movement being effortless and without conscious control, and has the ability to select the correct *cues* and make decisions quickly and effectively. In addition, they remain focused on the task without being distracted by other players or the *audience*. (See also *inverted U theory*.)

Physical education revision lists

Using A–Z Online

In addition to the revision lists given below, you can use the A–Z Online website to access revision lists specific to your examination board and the particular exam you are taking. Log on to **www.philipallan.co.uk/a-zonline** and create an account using the unique code provided on the inside front cover of this book. Once you have logged on, you can print out lists of terms together with their definitions, which will help you to focus your revision.

On the pages that follow, we have listed revision terms for the AS and A-level examinations for the three main awarding bodies:

- AQA, see pages 298–300
- OCR, see pages 301–304
- Edexcel, see pages 305–306.

This is to help you use this handbook as effectively as possible. On the website we have set out revision lists for other examination bodies which may provide the physical education exams at your school or college, including:

- Council for the Curriculum, Examinations and Assessment (Northern Ireland) (CCEA)
- Welsh Joint Education Committee (WJEC)
- Cambridge International Examinations (CIE)
- Scottish Higher
- International Baccalaureate (IB).

AQA revision lists

AQA PHED 1

Skill acquisition

Abilities
Anticipation
Associationist theories of learning
Classification of skills
Closed loop control
Cognitive theories of learning
Feedback
Guidance
Hick's law
Information processing
Input
Insight learning
Inverted U theory
Learning
Memory
Mental practice
Motivation

Motor programme
Movement time
Observational learning
Open loop control
Operant conditioning
Practice
Psychological refractory period
Punishment
Reaction time
Reinforcement
Response time
Schema theory
Single-channel hypothesis
Skill
Social learning theory
Teaching styles
Transfer of learning

Opportunities for participation

Adventurous activities
Best Value
Discrimination
Equal opportunity
Inclusiveness
Leisure
Military drill
Movement approach
National Curriculum
Outdoor pursuits
Physical Education
Physical Education, School Sport and Club
    Links (PESSCL) strategy
Play
Prejudice

Private provision
Public provision
Public schools
Rational recreation
Recreation
Sport
Sport England
Sports schools
State schools
Stereotype
Target group
Voluntary provision
Whole sport plan
Youth Sports Trust

Physiological aspects

Aerobic capacity
Agility
Agonist
Antagonist
Arterio-venous oxygen difference
Balance
Blood pressure
Body composition
Body mass index
Bohr effect
Bradycardia
Carbohydrate
Cardiac cycle
Cardiac hypertrophy
Cardiac output
Cardiovascular drift
Concentric muscle contraction
Coordination
Eccentric muscle contraction
Energy balance
Fat

Fitness
Flexibility
Haemoglobin
Health
Isometric muscle contraction
Levers
Mechanical advantage
Mechanical disadvantage
Muscular endurance
Myoglobin
Obesity
Partial pressure
Power
Protein
Reaction time
Speed
Starling's law of the heart
Strength
Stroke volume
Venous return mechanism

AQA PHED 3

Psychological aspects that optimise performance

Achievement motivation
Aggression
Anxiety
Assertive behaviour
Attitude
Attribution retraining
Attribution theory
Baron's distraction conflict theory
Catastrophe theory
Channelled aggression
Chelladurai's multi-dimensional model of
  leadership
Cognitive dissonance theory
Cue utilisation theory
Drive theory
Evaluation apprehension
Fiedler's contingency model of leadership
Goal setting
Group
Group dynamics

Group productivity
Interactionist theory
Inverted U theory
Leadership
Learned helplessness
Peak flow experience
Personality
Persuasive communication
Profile of mood states
Ringelmann effect
Self-efficacy
Self-serving bias
Social facilitation
Social inhibition
Social loafing
State sports confidence
Stress management
Trait sports confidence
Zone of optimal functioning

Evaluating contemporary influences

Amateurism

British Olympic Association

Commercialism

Continuum

Contract to compete

Deviancy

Drug testing

English Institute of Sport

Gamesmanship

Industrial Revolution

Legislation

National governing bodies

National Lottery

Olympism

Professional sport

Rational recreation

Sponsorship

Sports Aid

Sports Coach UK

Sportsmanship

Talent identification

Technology

UK Sport

World Class Performance Pathway

World Games

Physiological aspects

Acceleration

Adenosine triphosphate

Aerobic energy system

Alactic energy system

Altitude training

Anabolic steroids

Angular momentum

Angular motion

Beta blockers

Caffeine

Creatine monohydrate supplementation

Electron transport chain

Erythropoietin

Excess post-exercise oxygen consumption

Fast twitch muscle fibre

Fatigue

Glycogen loading

Glycolysis

Human growth hormone

Hyperbaric chambers

Ice baths

Impulse

Krebs cycle

Lactic acid energy system

Maximum oxygen uptake (VO_2 max)

Mitochondria

Moment of inertia

Momentum

Motor unit

Newton's laws of motion

Onset of blood lactate accumulation

Oxygen deficit

Oxygen tent

Periodisation

Plyometrics

Proprioceptive neuromuscular facilitation

Respiratory exchange ratio

Sliding filament theory

Slow twitch muscle fibre

Soda Loading

Spatial summation

Thermoregulation

Vector quantity

Velocity

OCR revision lists

H154 Module G451

Acquiring movement skills (Section B)

Abilities

Anticipation

Arousal

Associationist theories of learning

Bandura's model of observational learning

Catastrophe theory

Classification of skills

Closed loop control

Cognitive theories of learning

Drive reduction theory

Drive theory

Guidance

Hick's law

Information processing

Insight learning

Inverted U theory

Memory

Mental practice

Motivation

Motor programme

Movement time

Observational learning

Open loop control

Operant conditioning

Practice

Psychological refractory period

Punishment

Reaction time

Reinforcement

Response time

Schema theory

Single-channel hypothesis

Skill

Social learning theory

Thorndike's laws of learning

Transfer of learning

Socio-cultural studies relating to participation in physical activity (Section C)

American Dream

American football

Australia

Aussie rules football

Culture and sport

Discrimination

Drug abuse

Equal opportunity

Esteem

Ethnic sports

Mass media

Mass participation

National Curriculum

National Institute of Sport

Olympic Games

Outdoor education

Outdoor recreation

Participation pyramid

Physical education

Physical recreation

Play

Private provision

Public provision

Public schools

Recreation

Shop window

Sport

Sport England

Sports schools

Target group

UK Sport

UK Sports Institute

USA

Voluntary provision

Anatomy and physiology

Agonist
Altitude training
Angular motion
Antagonist
Arteriosclerosis
Asthma
Atherosclerosis
Atrioventricular node
Blood pressure
Carbon monoxide
Cardiac cycle
Cardiac output
Cardiovascular diseases
Centre of mass
Concentric muscle contraction
Cool-down
Core stability
Eccentric muscle contraction
Fast twitch muscle fibre
Fixator
Gaseous exchange

General motion
Hypertrophy
Isometric muscle contraction
Linear motion
Movement analysis
Multifidus muscle
Muscle pump
Newton's laws of motion
Osteoarthritis
Osteoporosis
Oxyhaemoglobin
Partial pressure
Rotator cuff muscles
Shunting
Slow twitch muscle fibre
Stroke volume
Transverse abdominis
Vasoconstriction
Vasodilation
Venous return mechanism
Warm-up

H554 Module G453

Option A1 Historical studies

Amateurism
Athleticism
Athletics
Clarendon Commission
Cricket
Football
Industrial Revolution
Lawn tennis
Middle class
Model course
Moving and Growing

National Curriculum
Planning the Programme
Popular recreations
Professional sport
Public schools
Rational recreation
Swimming
Syllabuses of Physical Training
Tennis
Urbanisation

H554 Module G453
Option A2 Comparative studies

American sports
Australia
Australian Institute of Sport
Australian sports system
Little League
Summer camps

Title IX
UK sport system
USA
USA sport system
WASP

H554 Module G453
Option B1 Sports psychology

Achievement motivation
Aggression
Anxiety
Anxiety management techniques
Assertive behaviour
Attentional styles
Attitude
Attribution retraining
Attribution theory
Channelled aggression
Chelladurai's multi-dimensional model
  of leadership
Cognitive dissonance theory
Cue utilisation theory
Emergent leader
Evaluation apprehension
Goal setting

Group
Group dynamics
Group productivity
Interactionist theory
Leadership
Learned helplessness
Peak flow experience
Personality
Prescribed leader
Ringelmann effect
Self-efficacy
Social facilitation
Social inhibition
Social loafing
Trait theory
Zone of optimal functioning

Option B2 Biomechanics

Acceleration
Air resistance
Angle of attack
Angular acceleration
Angular analogues of Newton's laws
Angular displacement
Angular momentum
Angular motion
Angular velocity
Back spin
Balance
Balanced forces
Bernoulli effect

Centre of mass
Displacement
Drag
Eccentric force
Effort arm
Free body diagrams
Friction
Impulse
Inertia
Lift force
Line of gravity
Linear motion
Magnus effect

Mechanical advantage
Mechanical disadvantage
Moment arm
Moment of force
Moment of inertia
Momentum
Net force
Newton's laws of motion
Parallelogram of forces
Reaction force

Resistance arm
Speed
Streamlining
Top spin
Torque
Transverse axis
Unbalanced forces
Velocity
Weight force

Option B3 Exercise and sport physiology

Active stretching
Adenosine triphosphate
Aerobic capacity
Aerobic energy system
Alactacid debt
Alactic energy system
Altitude training
Anabolic steroids
Basal metabolic rate
Bioelectric impedance
Blood doping
Body composition
Body mass index
Caffeine
Circuit training
Continuous training
Cooling aids
Creatine monohydrate supplementation
Creatine phosphate
Direct gas analysis
Dynamic flexibility
Dynamic strength
Dynamic stretching
Endothermic reactions
Energy
Energy balance
Energy continuum
Energy systems
Ergogenic aid
Erythropoietin
Excess post-exercise oxygen consumption
Exothermic reactions
Fartlek training

Flexibility
Goniometer
Human growth hormone
Hydrostatic weighing
Interval training
Karvonen principle
Lactacid debt
Lactic acid energy system
Macro cycle
Maximum oxygen uptake (VO_2 max)
Measurement of fitness
Meso cycle
Metabolic equivalent values
Micro cycle
Multi-stage fitness test
Obesity
Onset of blood lactate accumulation
Oxygen deficit
Periodisation
Physical activity readiness questionnaire
Plyometrics
Proprioceptive neuromuscular facilitation
PWC_{170} test
Recombinant erythropoietin
Recovery
Sit-and-reach test
Static flexibility
Static strength
Strength
Strength training
Threshold
Training unit

Edexcel revision lists

8PE01

Unit 1 Participation in sport and recreation

Advanced Apprenticeship in Sporting
   Excellence
Aerobic capacity
Agility
Americanisation of sports
Balance
Basal metabolic rate
Body composition
Cardiovascular diseases
Commercialism
Continuous training
Coordination
Drug abuse
Energy balance
Fitness
FITT regime
Flexibility
Gamesmanship
Globalisation
Interval training
Lifetime sports
Long-Term Athlete Development
Measurement of fitness
Nutrition pyramid
Obesity
Osteoporosis

Olympic Games
Participation pyramid
Physical activity readiness questionnaire
Plyometrics
Power
Proprioceptive neuromuscular facilitation
Public schools
Rational sport
Reaction time
Recovery
Sponsorship
Sport England
Sport for All
Sportsmanship
SAQ
Speed
Strength
Strength training
Stress
Talent identification
Talented Athlete Scholarship Scheme
Target groups
UK Sport
World Anti-Doping Agency
World Class Performance Pathway
Youth Sports Trust

9PE01

Unit 3 Preparation for optimum sports performance

Achievement motivation

Alactacid debt

Anabolic steroids

Anxiety

Attribution theory

Cardiovascular drift

Centres of excellence

Circuit training

Cohesion

Continuous training

Cool-down

Cooling aids

Core stability

Creatine monohydrate supplementation

Delayed onset of muscle soreness

English Institute of Sport

Ergogenic aid

Evaluation apprehension

Excess post-exercise oxygen consumption

Fartlek training

Fatigue

Goal setting

Glycogen loading

Home advantage

Human growth hormone

Ice baths

Interval training

Lactacid debt

Plyometrics

Proprioceptive neuromuscular facilitation

National Lottery

Recombinant erythropoietin

Recovery

SAQ

Social facilitation

Stress management

Strength training

Technology

Thermoregulation

Warm-up

Water

Water–electrolyte balance

Advice on revision

The following pages offer advice on revising for AS and A-level in physical education. On pages 307–310 you will find some general guidance, including hints on how to revise and definitions of examiners' terms. You can find revision lists given by the three main awarding bodies on pages 298–306.

For your revision you will be required to bring together different aspects of the course and relate this knowledge to practical situations. The examiners will test this by creating questions that demand an integrated solution. Each examining board will have its own unique style of questioning and you should become familiar with your awarding body's particular requirements before you devise your revision programme. The following revision methods will need to be adapted accordingly and should be used after your normal revision has taken place.

When answering questions, you need to plan quickly what is involved in different parts of the topic. As an example, shown below is a spider diagram that outlines the possible factors to discuss when looking at the development of excellence. The arrows show the broad relationships that can be further expanded as required.

Having completed the spider diagram, it is useful to develop each 'leg' a stage further, in order to extend your thoughts using a planning hierarchy, as shown in the diagram overleaf. The final stage of the process involves looking at how the different elements relate to each other. This is represented by the dotted arrows.

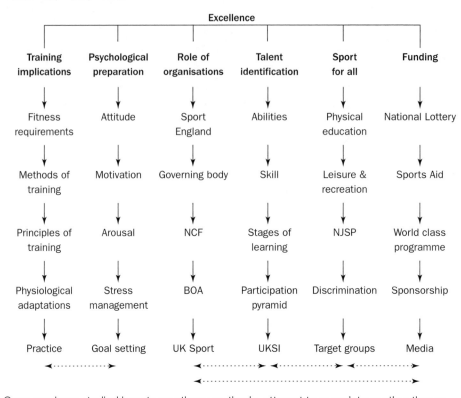

Once you have studied how to use these methods, attempt to complete another theme from the suggestions below. It may be advisable to complete one theme per day leading up to the examination:

- the value of developing 'sport for all' policies
- the effects of the media on individuals and their sport
- the effects of commercialisation on performers, spectators and sport
- the use of world games for political purposes
- the implications of doping for performers, spectators and sport
- the value of developing talent identification programmes for the athlete, sport and country
- the value of developing assessment structures within sport
- discrimination within sport in different cultures and countries
- the functions of play, leisure, physical education and sport within a society
- the benefits of developing technology to optimise performance
- the analysis of activity categories using the following terms: structural, strategic, technical, physical and psychological.

Don't forget to make use of your *A–Z Sport and Physical Education Handbook* in your revision. Carry out the exercises without help initially, but if you encounter difficulties try looking up the key words and look for cross-references in the handbook to add greater detail.

Examiners' terms

To maximise your examination performance, it is vital for you to understand the nature of the question and its requirements. This will help you to structure your answers and not waste valuable time on questions that only require short answers. Study the terms below so that you are familiar with their meanings and attempt to locate them in the question before constructing your answer.

What are the advantages … ?

This requires a description of why one situation or factor is better than another. Often this requires evaluation, justification and explanation.

Calculate

This requires a mathematical calculation, including relevant workings and correct units.

What are the characteristics … ?

List the common features that identify a term, process, situation or structure. Such questions usually need short answers, but do not repeat yourself with similar terms.

Compare

You need to make a comparison between two or more terms, ideas or situations. Discuss both items equally and do not emphasise one at the expense of the other.

Define/What is meant by … ?

This requires a statement outlining the meaning of the term. Usually a formal definition is not needed, only key words to demonstrate a clear understanding.

Describe

Here quantitative or qualitative information should be used to demonstrate an understanding of the topic and any relationships that may exist.

Describe how you …

The onus is placed on you as the student, drawing on experiences within school, college or other relevant situations to explain an understanding of the specific topic.

Discuss

This requires the presentation of a reasoned argument, outlining points both for and against, supported by relevant knowledge and summarised with a justified conclusion.

Draw

A fully labelled diagram is required.

Explain

Provide reasons and justifications, not a simple description. When interpreting graphs or tables of figures, it is not sufficient to outline the shape or comment on the numbers; the causes and reasons for changes or patterns must be provided.

Give the evidence for … using examples from …

To support the theory, idea or viewpoint, and to demonstrate a clear understanding of it, relevant practical examples must be given.

Identify and explain

Show that you can recognise an idea or viewpoint and explain it, or apply your understanding to solve a problem. Make links between causes and effects, problems and solutions.

List

Short answers are required, normally covering one or two key points. There is no need for elaborate descriptions or explanations of what each means.

Name

Short answers are needed (usually technical terms), covering one or two key points.

Outline

Give a brief summary of the major points. Note the mark allocation so that answers can be structured accordingly. Use examples if relevant to your explanation.

Plot a graph

This requires an accurately drawn graph with coordinates joined correctly. Remember to label the axes, use correct units and include a title.

Sketch a graph

You need to draw a freehand curve to interpret the data. Remember to label the axes, use the correct units and include a title.

State

Short answers are required, normally covering one or two key points. There is no need for elaborate descriptions or explanations. Use of bullet points is often sufficient.

Suggest

Draw on your general understanding of the subject rather than what you have been taught directly. There may be many correct answers rather than a definitive response.

Terms of direction and planes of the body

Directional terms for humans

Terms	Etymology*	Definition
Left		Toward the left side
Right		Toward the right side
Superior	L, higher	A structure higher than another (usually synonymous with cephalic)
Inferior	L, lower	A structure lower than another (usually synonymous with caudal)
Cephalic	G, *kephale,* head	Closer to the head than another structure (usually synonymous with superior)
Caudal	L, *cauda*, a tail	Closer to the tail than another structure (usually synonymous with inferior)
Proximal	L, *proximus*, nearest	Closer than another structure to the point of attachment to the trunk
Distal	L, *di-* plus *sto*, to stand apart or to be distant	Farther than another structure from the point of attachment to the trunk
Medial	L, *medialis*, middle	Toward the middle or the midline of the body
Lateral	L, *latus*, side	Away from the middle or midline of the body
Anterior	L, before	The front of the body (synonymous with ventral)
Posterior	L, *posterus*, following	The back of the body (synonymous with dorsal)
Ventral	L, *venter* or *ventr-*, belly	Toward the belly (synonymous with anterior)
Dorsal	L, *dorsum*, back	Toward the back (synonymous with posterior)
Superficial	L, *superficialis*	Toward or on the surface (not shown in figure A1.1, pages 312 and 313)
Deep	OE, *deop*, deep	Away from the surface, internal (not shown in figure A1.1, pages 312 and 313)

* Origin and meaning of the word: G, Greek; L, Latin; OE, Old English

Source: Seely, Stephens, Tate, *Anatomy and Physiology* 3rd ed., Mosby, 1995

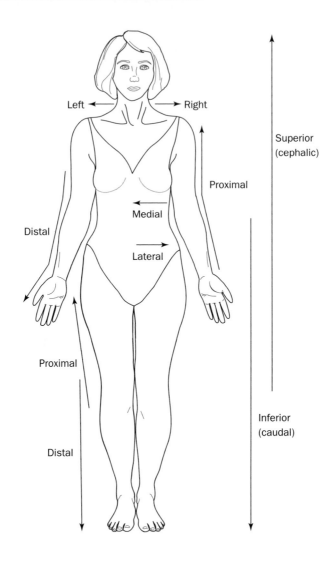

Figure A1.1 Directional terms for humans (continued on page 313)

Figure A1.1 (continued)

Figure A1.2 Three planes of motion

1 = *Median plane/saggital plane*

2 = *Frontal plane/coronal plane*

3 = *Horizontal plane/transverse plane*

Source: Aaberg, *Muscle Mechanics Human Kinetics*, 1998

The skeleton

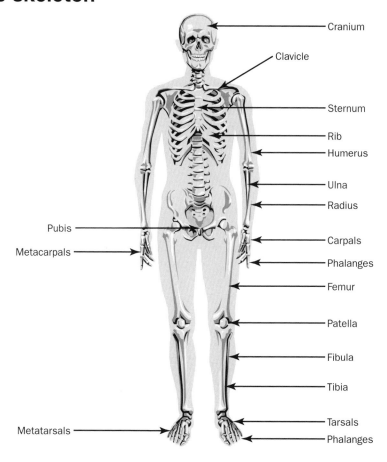

Figure A2.1 The skeleton: anterior view

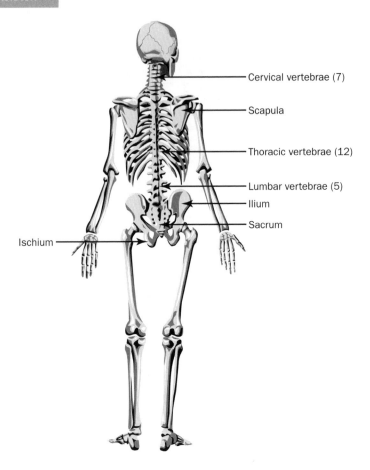

Cervical vertebrae (7)

Scapula

Thoracic vertebrae (12)

Lumbar vertebrae (5)

Ilium

Sacrum

Ischium

Figure A2.2 The skeleton: posterior view

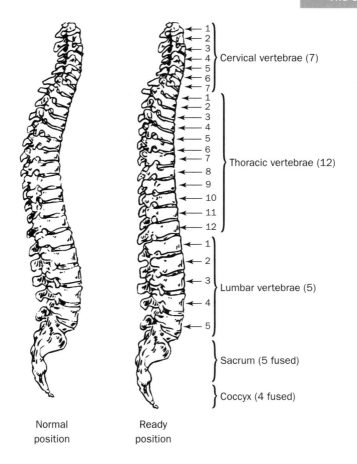

Cervical vertebrae (7)

Thoracic vertebrae (12)

Lumbar vertebrae (5)

Sacrum (5 fused)

Coccyx (4 fused)

Normal position   Ready position

Figure A2.3 Spine positions

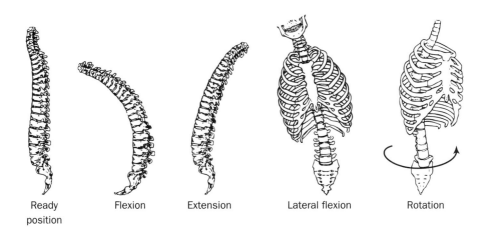

Ready position   Flexion   Extension   Lateral flexion   Rotation

Figure A2.4 Spine positions during exercise

Muscles of the body

Sternocleidomastoid

Trapezius (upper)

Anterior deltoid

Clavicular pectoralis major

Medial deltoid

Sternal pectoralis major

Biceps brachii

Serratus anterior

Rectus abdominis

Internal oblique (underlying)

Brachioradialis

Palmaris longus

External oblique

Flexors

Extensors

Tensor fasciae latae

Sartorius

Pectineus

Adductor longus

Rectus femoris

Vastus lateralis

Gracilis

Vastus medialis

Gastrocnemius

Peroneus longus

Tibialis anterior

Extensors

Soleus

Figure A3.1a The muscles: anterior view

Source: Aaberg, *Muscle Mechanics Human Kinetics*, 1998.

Levator scapulae
(underlying)

Rhomboids
(underlying)

Posterior deltoid

Trapezius
(middle)

Teres major

Triceps brachii
(lateral head)

Trapezius (lower)
Latissimus dorsi

Triceps brachii
(long head)

Erector spinae

Gluteus medius

Pectineus

Gluteus maximus

Gracilis

Semitendinosus

Biceps femoris
Semimembranosus

Popliteus

Gastrocnemius

Gastrocnemius

Soleus

Figure A3.1b The muscles: posterior view

Table A1 Movement analysis of major joints

Joint	Action	Plane	Muscles used	
Hip	Flexion	Median	Psoas	
			Iliacus	
			Rectus femoris	
	Extension	Median	Gluteus maximus	
			Biceps femoris	
			Semimembranosus	
			Semitendinosus	
			Gluteus medius (posterior)	Extension ⟵⟶ Flexion
	Abduction	Frontal	Gluteus medius	
			Gluteus minimus	
			Tensor fasciae latae	
	Adduction	Frontal	Adductor magnus	
			Adductor brevis	
			Adductor longus	
			Pectineus	
			Gracilis	Abduction ⟵⟶ Adduction
	Medial rotation	Horizonal	Gluteus medius	
			Gluteus minimus	
			Tensor fasciae latae	
	Lateral rotation	Horizontal	Gluteus maximus	
			Adductors	Lateral ⟵⟶ Medial

Knee	Flexion	Median	Semitendinosus	
			Semimembranosus	
			Biceps femoris	
			Popliteus	
			Gastrocnemius	
	Extension	Median	Rectus femoris	
			Vastus medialis	
			Vastus intermedius	
			Vastus lateralis	
			Tensor fasciae latae	
	Medial rotation (when flexed)	Horizontal	Sartorius	
			Semitendinosus	
	Lateral rotation (when flexed)	Horizontal	Tensor fasciae latae	
			Biceps femoris	
Ankle	Dorsiflexion	Median	Tibialis anterior	
			Extensor digitorum longus	
			Peroneus tertius	
	Plantar flexion	Median	Gastrocnemius	
			Soleus	
			Peroneus longus	
			Peroneus brevis	
			Tibialis posterior	
			Flexor digitorum longus	
	Inversion	Frontal	Tibialis anterior	
			Tibialis posterior	
			Gastrocnemius	
			Soleus	
	Eversion	Frontal	Peroneus longus	
			Peroneus brevis	

Shoulder	Flexion	Median	Anterior deltoid
			Pectoralis major
			Coracobrachialis
	Extension	Median	Posterior deltoid
			Latissimus dorsi
			Teres major

	Adduction	Frontal	Latissimus dorsi
			Pectoralis major
			Teres major
			Teres minor
	Abduction	Frontal	Medial deltoid
			Supraspinatus

	Horizontal adduction	Horizontal	Pectoralis major
			Anterior deltoid
	Horizontal abduction	Horizontal	Posterior deltoid
			Trapezius
			Rhomboids
			Latissimus dorsi

	Medial rotation	Horizontal	Subscapularis
	Lateral rotation	Horizontal	Infraspinatus
			Teres minor

Elbow	Flexion	Median	Biceps brachii
			Brachialis
			Brachioradialis
	Extension	Median	Triceps

Flexion

Extension

	Pronation	Horizontal	Pronator teres
			Pronator quadratus
			Brachioradialis
	Supination	Horizontal	Biceps brachii
			Supinator

Supination   Pronation

Wrist	Flexion	Median	Wrist flexors
	Extension	Median	Wrist extensors

Extension   Flexion

Movement of the trunk	Flexion	Median	Rectus abdominis
			Internal obliques
			External obliques
	Extension	Median	Erector spinae
			Iliocostalis
			Spinalis

Extension   Flexion

	Lateral flexion	Frontal	Internal oblique Rectus abdominis Erector spinae Quadratus laborum	 Lateral flexion
	Rotation	Horizontal	External obliques Rectus abdominis Erector spinae	
Movement of the scapulae	Elevation	Frontal	Levator sapulae Trapezius Rhomboids	
	Depression	Frontal	Trapezius (lower) Pectoralis minor Serratus anterior (lower)	

Protraction   Frontal   Serratus anterior

Retraction   Frontal   Rhomboids

Trapezius

Upward   Frontal   Trapezius (upper)
rotation   Serratus anterior

Downward   Frontal   Rhomboids
rotation   Levator scapulae

Movement analysis

Figure A4.1 Flexion and extension of the arm

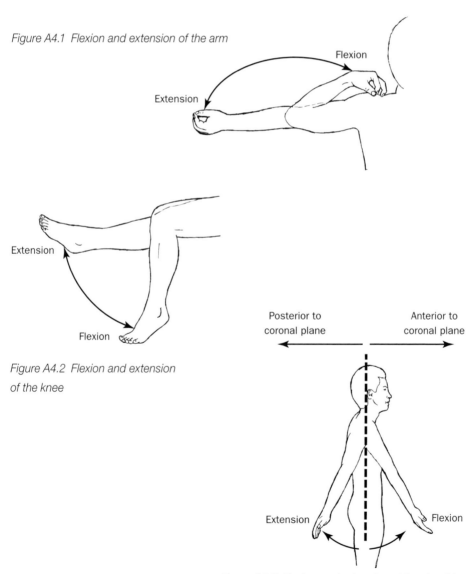

Flexion

Extension

Extension

Flexion

Figure A4.2 Flexion and extension
of the knee

Posterior to
coronal plane

Anterior to
coronal plane

Extension

Flexion

Figure A4.3 Flexion and extension of the shoulder

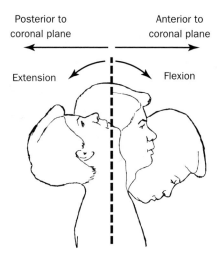

Posterior to
coronal plane

Anterior to
coronal plane

Extension

Flexion

Figure A4.4 Flexion of the neck

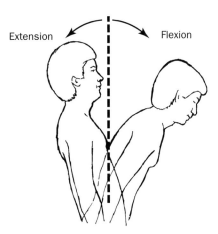

Extension

Flexion

Figure A4.5 Flexion and extension of the trunk

Dorsiflexion

Plantar flexion

Figure A4.6 Plantar flexion and dorsiflexion of the ankle

Figure A4.7 Abduction and adduction of the upper limb

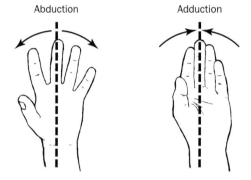

Figure A4.8 Abduction and adduction of the fingers

Figure A4.9 Medial and lateral rotation of the humerus

Pronation

Supination

Figure A4.10 Pronation and supination

Circumduction

Figure A4.11 Circumduction of the shoulder

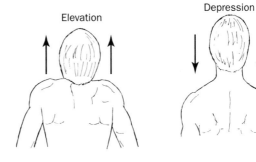

Elevation

Depression

Figure A4.12 Elevation and depression of the shoulder

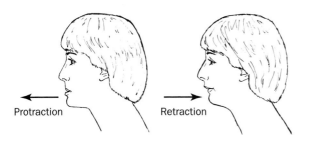

Protraction

Retraction

Figure A4.13 Protraction and retraction of the jaw

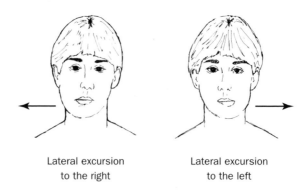

Lateral excursion to the right	Lateral excursion to the left

Figure A4.14 Lateral excursion of the jaw

Opposition	Reposition

Figure A4.15 Opposition and reposition of the thumb

Eversion   Inversion

Figure A4.16 Eversion and inversion of the ankle

Lung volumes

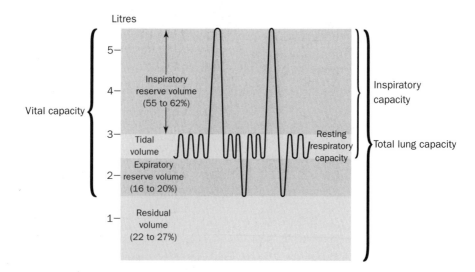

330